DUTY, HONOR, PRIVILEGE

To Toni—

A GREAT FRIEND—
FUN TO BE AROUND!
THANKS A MILLION!
STEVE

Stephen L. Harris

Duty, Honor, Privilege

NEW YORK'S
SILK STOCKING REGIMENT
and the BREAKING
of the HINDENBURG LINE

Stephen L. Harris

BRASSEY'S, INC.
WASHINGTON, D.C.

LIBRARY OF CONGRESS CATALOGING-IN-PUBLICATION DATA

Harris, Stephen L.
    Duty, honor, privilege : New York's Silk Stocking Regiment
and the breaking of the Hindenburg Line / Stephen L. Harris.
        p. cm.
    Includes bibliographical references and index.
    ISBN 1-57488-201-5
    1. World War, 1914–1918—Regimental histories—
United States.   2. World War, 1914–1918—Western Front.
3. United States. Army. Infantry Regiment, 107th—History.
I. Title.
D570.33 107th .H37 2001
940.4′1273—dc21

                                            00-066732

        ISBN 1-57488-201-5 (alk. paper)

Printed in the United States of America on acid-free paper that meets
the American National Standards Institute Z39-48 Standard.

Brassey's, Inc.
22841 Quicksilver Drive
Dulles, Virginia 20166

First Edition

10 9 8 7 6 5 4 3 2 1

Maps by Molly O'Halloran.

To Sue, best friend always

To the memory of William Craig,
author, historian, mentor

Contents

Maps

Preface

My story of the 107th New York Infantry began with my great-uncle Raeburn Van Buren, the magazine illustrator and creator of the comic strip "Abbie an' Slats." His tales about his Bohemian days in Manhattan before World War I and later about the war itself thrilled me as a young boy. After he died in 1987, I read for the first time his letters home to his mother (my great-grandmother) in Kansas City and knew that here was a story. I began reading about the old Seventh Regiment, known affectionately or derisively as New York's "silk stocking soldiers." During the war, the Seventh merged with the First and Twelfth Infantries from upstate New York, known as the "appleknockers," to form the 107th Infantry. The more I read the more I realized that the horrible slaughter these New Yorkers suffered in World War I has long since been forgotten. I felt it was time to remind all Americans of the great sacrifice these boys made to "make the world safe for democracy." And I wanted to tell the story through their own words and actions.

Among the best sources for letters and comments from the soldiers themselves is *The Seventh Regiment Gazette,* a literate and spirited monthly founded in 1886. The Twenty-seventh Division magazine, *The Gas Attack,* also known as *The Rio Grande Rattler,* is another wonderful source of soldierly insight. Among its narratives were the hilarious "Dere Mable" letters by Edward Streeter. Many of the quotations are from articles and letters culled from these two publications as well as from a number of now-defunct local newspapers I found at historical societies, local libraries, or in tattered family scrapbooks. In many cases, newspaper clippings did not include dates. Where there are dates I include them in my notes, otherwise the undated articles were published either in 1918 or 1919. Dozens of families of the soldiers who had fought with the 107th Infantry Regiment shared letters, diaries, and, as just mentioned, old scrapbooks. In many instances, these families chatted with me about their fathers, grandfathers, uncles, or cousins. It is here that I want to acknowledge their help, and trust that I treated their kin fairly and honestly.

Bruce C. Adamson, grandson of Sgt. George Ely II

Virginia Cairns, daughter of Pfc. Arnold C. "Dutch" Wilbur

Delores D. Capuani, niece of Cpl. George Delahay

Barbara Cunningham, granddaughter of Capt. Rowland Tompkins

August Engler, son of Pvt. August Engler

John W. Fetherolf, son of Pvt. George Fetherolf

Samuel J. Foley III, son of Cpl. Samuel J. Foley

Frank W. Garvin II, son of Pvt. Frank W. Garvin

Phil Haselton, grandnephew of Cpl. Morgan S. Baldwin

Brigid Hayes, niece of Cpl. Bernard T. Hunt

Joan Hellquist, grandniece of Lt. Oscar Hellquist

Robert V. Kissam Sr., grandson of Pvt. Adrian Kissam Jr.

John Latham, son of Sgt. John Latham

Jean Green, cousin of Sgt. John Latham

Hunter Leaf, son of Pvt. Hunter Leaf

Meta Lytle, niece-in-law of Pvt. Scott Harrison Lytle

James W. Marlor, nephew of Pfc. Vanderbilt Ward

Shirley Mills Hudson and Marian Mills Boswell, daughters of
    Cpl. Harold Strycker Mills

Ellsworth Mills, nephew of Cpls. Harold Strycker Mills and
    Van Strycker Mills

Jeffrey Nicoll, grandson of Capt. Fancher Nicoll

Pat Egan Procak, daughter of Capt. Raphael Egan

William Roosa, son of Pfc. Clinton S. Roosa

Jeannine Schoeffer, grandniece of Lt. Philip Rhinelander and
    Pvt. T. J. Oakley Rhinelander

John B. Rhinelander, cousin of both Rhinelanders

Frances M. Smith, niece of Pfc. Angelo Mustico

Roger Niedlander, grandson of Lt. Ralph Polk Buell

Ruth V. Ross, niece of Capt. Perley Gray

Mrs. William Trafford, daughter-in-law of André Chéronnet-
Champollion

Alexander T. M. Van Rensselaer, son of Pfc. Alexander T. M. Van
Rensselaer

Dorothy Werley, daughter of 1st Sgt. Dill H. Werley

Reginald White, grandnephew of Albert "Bert" Lobdell

William F. White, son of Pfc. William F. White

Nancy Hawley Wilsea, niece of Pvt. Bronson Hawley

And, of course, my own reminiscences and collection of letters written by my great-uncle Pfc. Raeburn Van Buren, art editor of *The Gas Attack*.

Because I use the words of so many soldiers, I believe it unwieldy to keep repeating the sources for those quotes. Instead, when I first introduce an individual soldier, I reference where I obtained his quotation. Subsequent quotes are generally from the same source. Where they are not, I cite that source. Also, I have kept their grammar and spelling intact.

Three soldiers published books about their war experiences, and only on occasion do I use footnotes for them. Maj. Gen. John F. O'Ryan wrote one of the best divisional histories by an American commander in the war and his two-volume memoir, *The Story of the 27th Division*, is cited frequently in my book. O'Ryan was also interviewed as part of the Oral History Collection of Columbia University. Kenneth Gow's letters were collected by his family in *Letters of a Soldier*. Claude Leland's account of the war appeared in *From Shell Hole to Chateau*. He also left numerous letters that are held at the New York Public Library. In addition, the 107th Infantry published several histories, each containing numerous first-person accounts of the war. These are *History of the 107th Infantry, U.S.A.*, edited by Gerald Jacobson, the regimental supply sergeant; *The Story of a Machine Gun Company*, compiled by Walter Andrews; *History of Company "E," 107th Infantry*, edited by Nicholas H. Krayer; *The First Hundred Years: Records and Reminiscences of a Century of Company I*, edited by George P. Nichols; and *Company L, 107th Infantry, 54th Infantry Brigade*, by Sgt. Harry T. Mitchell. All are well-written accounts of the regiment's war experiences. Except for Mitchell's book, the chapters in these histories were often written by different soldiers—creating diverse experiences and points of view. I have decided not to use footnotes for either Mitchell's book or the *Gazette,* unless necessary, and I hope the reader will understand where the quotes originated. In most cases, I mention the source within the text.

Two other histories I used are *History of the Seventh Regiment, 1889–1922* by DeWitt Clinton Falls, one of the old Seventh's illustrious officers, and *A Handbook of Company K* by Sgt. Richard Greene Holbrook. I also counted on *Seventy-first New York in the World War,* compiled by Robert Stewart Sutcliffe; *Squadron A: A History of Its First Fifty Years,* compiled by a panel of men headed by Herbert Barry; *Squadron A in the Great War, 1917–1918,* by Stanton Whitney, who briefly served with the 107th Machine Gun Company; *Between the Big Parades,* by Franklin W. Ward, who commanded the 106th Infantry; *Newburgh in the World War,* edited by Edward P. Dunphey; and a special section of the New York *Evening Post,* dated 25 March 1919, which chronicled the exploits of the Twenty-seventh Division through the eyes of the men who fought overseas. I gained the Australian perspective from *The Australian Victories in France* by Sir John Monash and *The Official History of Australia in the War, 1914–1918* by C. E. W. Bean.

What I discovered when stringing together hundreds of quotes was a narrative so compelling that after nearly a century of silence, the voices of these silk stocking soldiers from New York City and its suburbs and the appleknockers from upstate are still very much alive. Their voices carried me along on an exciting roller-coaster ride and made writing this book a joy.

Before starting work on this story, I discussed the idea with the historian William Craig. He thought it worthy and encouraged me to write it. Bill died before I finished my book. Kenneth H. Powers, the historian of the Sixty-ninth Regiment, took over Bill's place as mentor. He helped me see this project through. He introduced me to Dr. Douglas V. Johnson II, associate research professor at the U.S. Army War College's Strategic Studies Institute at Carlisle Barracks, Pennsylvania, and coauthor of *Soissons 1918;* and Eric Miller, an ex-soldier who, as he told me, "walked in the footpaths of history along the western front, remembering 1914–1918." They both went over my manuscript. Their counsel and insights are immeasurable.

Early on and in the very last stages, Kenyon FitzGerald, president of The Seventh Regiment Fund and one of the most knowledgeable persons about military history in general and New York military history in particular, opened up for me the doors of the great armory on Park Avenue. His thoughts about my book were indispensable in shaping its final draft. Inside the armory, I counted on Paul Haydon, its curator, for additional help.

Three other military historians who came to my aid were Peter J. Linder, among the foremost experts on World War I casualties; John J. Slonaker, chief, History Reference Branch, U.S. Army Military History Institute; and Michael Aikey, librarian and archivist for the New York State Military Museum and Veterans Research Center in Latham, New York.

In Westport, where I lived before moving to Vermont, William Abbott was the first to truly get me started on this project. At the Westport Public Library, Claire Quigley obtained rare and out-of-print books and manuscripts. She made my research appear almost effortless. In Vermont, Mike Knapp at Middlebury College loaned me books from his personal library. The deeper I got into my research, the longer grew the list of people willing to lend a hand. Elaine Massena at the Westchester County Historical Society and archivist for the City of White Plains volunteered to dig into files that had not been looked at in years. Bruce Adamson allowed me use of George Ely II's diary, included in his, Adamson's book, *The Life and Times of George W. Ely.*

The following organizations were also helpful: New-York Historical Society; New York Public Library; the historical societies of Newport, Vermont (Barbara J. Malloy), Oneida County, New York (Donald Wisnoski), Ossining, New York (Roberta Amiro), Queens, New York (John Driscoll), Stamford, Conn., Summit, New Jersey (Arthur J. Cotterell); Bryant Public Library, Roslyn, New York (Myrna Sloam); Cornwall, New York, Public Library (Vivian Milcazrski); Malone, New York, Mead Library (Deborah A. Trickey); Montclair, New Jersey, Public Library (Elizabeth Shepard); Richard Free Library, Newport, New Hampshire (Andrea Thorpe); Ogdensburg, New York, Public Library (Sandra M. Putney); Poughkeepsie, New York, Library's Local History Department; Saranac Lake, New York, Free Library (Shirley Morgan); Stamford, Connecticut, Ferguson Public Library; Historian Leslie P. Connell of the Town of Newburgh; and Kathleen F. Cockey of Cornwall. Also, American Legion William A. Leonard Post 422, Flushing, New York (Joseph Miceli); American Legion Post 353 Cornwall, New York (Adj. Frank O'Donnell); Harrison P. Lindaberry, historian, Summit, New Jersey, Calvary Episcopal Church.

The following college and university libraries: Columbia University's Archives and Columbiania Collection and Butler Library, Cornell University's Carl A. Kroch Library's Rare and Manuscript Collection, Dartmouth College Rauner Special Collections Library, Fairfield University, Harvard University (Bill Seybold), Princeton University's Seeley G. Mudd Manuscript Library, Rutgers University Library (Janet Reimer), Seton Hall University (Alan Delozier), Trinity College, Williams College Archives and Special Collections, and Yale University Library's Manuscripts and Archives.

And I owe a special thanks to my sister Lynn Worth and her son, David. After all, they knew our great-uncle and warmly recounted his stories, helped with the research, and read my manuscript.

Acknowledgments

Several publishers and institutions have generously granted permission to use extended quotations from copyrighted works.

The Official History of Australia in the War, 1914–1918, Vol. VI, by C. E. W. Bean. Copyright 1942 by the University of Queensland Press. Rights reverted to the Australian War Memorial. Reprinted by permission of the Australian War Memorial.

The Private Papers of Douglas Haig, edited by Robert Blake. Copyright 1952 by Eyre and Spottiswoode. Reprinted by permission of The Random House Group Ltd.

A Doughboy with the Fighting 69th, by Albert M. and A. Churchill Ettinger. Copyright 1992 by White Mane Publishing Co., Inc. Reprinted by permission of the publisher.

From Shell Hole to Chateau with Company I, by Claude G. Leland. Copyright 1950 by the New York Seventh Regiment. Reprinted by permission of The Seventh Regiment Fund and The New York Public Library, Manuscripts and Archives Division, Claude G. Leland Papers, Astor, Lenox, and Tilden Foundations.

The Vanderbilt Feud, by Cornelius Vanderbilt Jr. Copyright 1957 by Hutchinson. Reprinted by permission of The Random House Group Ltd.

Permission has also been granted by the Cornwall Press to publish excerpts from selected letters and articles that appeared in the Cornwall Press, 1917–1918. Also, the New York State Division of Military and Naval

Affairs (New York State Military Museum) has granted permission to reprint material from the diary of Sgt. Maj. Albert Breunig, the "Company K Scrapbook," and selected documents.

A Big Game
Can Be Played But Once

I n the early morning of 25 September 1918, three packed troop trains, bristling with 2,257 doughboys of the 107th Infantry Regiment of the Twenty-seventh Division, armed to the teeth and itching for their first major scrap against the Hun, crept southeastward across France toward a rendezvous with death. They were a spirited bunch, these young Americans. Society boys many of them; silk stocking soldiers from uptown Manhattan or the wealthier suburbs of New York. Some farm boys and small-town merchants' sons were thrown in, too; "appleknockers" people had nicknamed them, mostly from around Newburgh, or from the towns that sprawled along the Mohawk River or were scattered as far north as the St. Lawrence River. Their destination: the invincible Hindenburg Line. Feared by the Allied forces, it was the place where the Imperial German Army vowed to make its last stand.

For three days the entire division had been on the move. Known as the Empire Division because its soldiers hailed from every corner of New York State, it was en route first to Tincourt and then by foot to the small villages of Haut Allaines, Bois de Buire, and Ronssoy, all within rifle shot of the Hindenburg Line. Here it was ordered to relieve two weary divisions of the British Fourth Army, the Eighteenth and Seventy-fourth. Both divisions were now staggering out of the line. The Germans had proven obstinate. After a hard week of fighting, they had repulsed every assault designed to bring British, American, and Australian troops up to the very edge of their dreaded bulwark for the coming battle to decide the war. A veteran officer of the Eighteenth stated that his men, many of them youngsters, had fought hand-to-hand "against machine-gun fire that was more murderous than at any period of the war."[1]

As it later turned out, the failure of the two British divisions to make any headway against the entrenched enemy would cost the approaching New Yorkers dearly.

The trains carrying the 107th Infantry inched along at a snail's pace of five miles an hour. Each locomotive pulled a string of forty boxcars. Crowded inside the first train were 15 officers and 743 men of the First Battalion, commanded by thirty-six-year-old Capt. Clinton Earle Fisk, a lawyer back in New York and son of the former commander of the regiment, Col. Willard Fisk. The soldiers were bundled in heavy overcoats, equipped with gas masks, bayonets, British Lee-Enfield .303 caliber rifles, and 100 rounds of ammunition. They carried rations for one day. On board with them were an additional 138,200 rifle rounds. Also, there were 54,966 rounds for their Lewis machine guns that were being lugged to the front by a convoy of thirty trucks, 10,316 rounds for sidearms, 492 hand grenades, and 204 rifle grenades. On the second train, trailing the first by more than three hours, huddled 14 officers and 728 men of the Second Battalion, similarly outfitted, and commanded by thirty-eight-year-old Capt. Rowland Tompkins, in his civilian days a prominent engineer and graduate of Cooper Union. Their ammunition consisted of 133,960 rifle rounds, 74,653 machine-gun rounds, 12,525 .45 caliber rounds, 806 hand grenades, and 239 rifle grenades. Less than an hour behind that train, the third creaked along, bearing 15 officers and 742 men of the Third Battalion, led by thirty-one-year-old Capt. Raphael Egan, a promising young attorney from Newburgh, whose older brother was in league with Tammany Hall. His battalion was loaded with 141,448 rifle rounds, 74,448 machine-gun rounds, 12,800 for the pistol, 806 hand grenades, and 268 rifle grenades.[2]

The trains swayed and groaned and clacked over tracks that meandered through land scarred by four years of the worst warfare ever known at that time. It was the old Somme battlefield, where in the spring the Germans had pushed the British toward the sea in a last-ditch effort to end the war before the Americans arrived, and where the British commander in chief, Field Marshal Sir Douglas Haig, called on his armies to fight to the last man. "With our backs to the wall and believing in the justice of our cause, each one of us must fight on to the end," he urged.[3] It was here, as if by an act of providence, that the exhausted German army outran its line of supplies and then, like a wolf with its tail between its legs, slunk back to the safety of the Hindenburg Line.

The men of the 107th stared from their trains at this landscape of death and destruction as if they were on some alien planet. One New Yorker described the place "pitted like microscopic pictures of the moon."[4]

In fact, it was in the eerie light of the moon that most of the regiment first saw the beginning of the battleground that within the next few days would be the last place on earth many of them would ever see. Second Lt. Kenneth Gow wrote home to his parents in Summit, New Jersey, "Once beautiful cities are just heaps of brick and debris, not a living thing to be seen, even the trees all shot off, leaving nothing but stumps, which look like ghosts in the moonlight. The graveyards are turned upside down by terrific shell fire. The ground is covered with all the signs of a great battle—smashed guns of every calibre, wrecked tanks, dead horses and here and there a dead Boche overlooked by the burying parties."[5] To 2d Lt. Claude Leland, the superintendent of libraries for the New York City Board of Education, the town of Peronne, a few miles south of Haut Allaines, "looked to us as though a great wind storm had swept through, smashing all the buildings but leaving the streets strangely clean and tidy."[6]

Since 8 August, a date the British would mark as the start of the Hundred Days' Campaign, considered the greatest action in English military history, the German army had fled to the Hindenburg Line. But even in retreat, the army continued to lay waste to a countryside that had already been fought over many times. Maj. Gen. Sir Frederick Maurice of the British Fourth Army, to which the Twenty-seventh Division had only recently been attached, recalled how the "trees were cut down, not even the orchards being spared, the villages were set on fire, the towns were gutted, explosives being used for the more solid buildings which fire could not damage sufficiently, the wells were fouled, every road and railway bridge was destroyed, the railway embankments were blown in, the rails were torn up, and mines were exploded under every cross-roads, making craters which effectively barred wheeled traffic. As a last refinement a series of devilishly cunning booby traps was devised, consisting of wires connected to German helmets, pianos, door-handles, the steps of dug-outs or of houses, which when touched exploded charges and cost us the lives of many of our men."[7]

The war correspondent George Clarke Musgrave, a former member of the old Seventh and who earlier in his career had covered the Boer War, drove over the battered land. What he saw compelled him to dash off *Four Flags under France,* a book rushed into publication by the retired commander of the regiment, Daniel Appleton, and then excerpted and advertised for sale in the regiment's magazine. Musgrave's book, filled with unsubstantiated charges, stirred up much of the anger the 107th felt toward the Germans. "History affords few examples of such methodical spoliation and no record to approach the filthy grossness which tainted the work," he asserted. "Hamlets and small houses everywhere were burned. Catalogs of every article of value checked and the wholesale looting was systematized." He told how the German officers "supervised the seizure of important art treasures and antiques for Germany, including Latour pastels of St. Quentin. Then the rest was divided, and demolition patrols started. All wells were unprintably defiled, roads and bridges were mined and fuel stacked in large buildings. Some stained glass was removed from the churches; the rest was pulverized. Altars were torn down, sacred vessels looted, and walls dynamited. Cottages were pulled down by horses while their owners wept."

His lurid details painted the Hun as a ghoulish beast: "All women from sixteen to thirty-five were carried off, ostensibly to labor, but the world will gasp with horror when the full story is written. Hundreds of young girls had been debauched by officers, and these pitiful victims were then the unwritten law of property of the soldiers. Special houses of ill-fame, legally controlled, were filled by the victims of vicious orgies. In many outlying strongholds girls were kept caged—white slaves maintained for the garrison."[8]

*   *   *

Four years of warfare had changed France's once serene, rolling farmland. As Australian Lt. Gen. John Monash noted, "For months the opposing artilleries had pounded the country to pieces, effaced every sign of civilization, and churned up the ground in all directions over a belt some three miles wide. Heaps of broken bricks marked the sites of once prosperous villages. Broken telegraph poles, charred tree trunks, twisted rails, a chaos of mangled machinery, were the only remains of what had been gardens, orchards, railways and factories."[9]

In the silvery moonlight, the passing New Yorkers saw salvage corps hunting through the wreckage, saving whatever material could still be used in the coming fight. Bombs, shells, rifles, and machine guns with belts of live ammunition were piled everywhere. Now and then, among the heaps, a dead German was left to rot.

Maj. Tristram Tupper, an aide to the commander of the Twenty-seventh, Maj. Gen. John F. O'Ryan, saw it as the most desolate area the division had yet passed through since landing in France almost six months earlier. Tupper, whose brother-in-law Col. George C. Marshall was busy making a name for himself elsewhere on the western front, described fields "furrowed with deserted trenches and ploughed with shells, and the only crops that grew were briar-like rusty barbed wire and broken pieces of the machinery of war."[10]

The librarian, Leland, was as much struck by this spectacle as was Tupper. "Nothing, I think, gives one such a staggering sense of the utter folly of war and the wastage of it as the sight of the battlefields. The waste of material is more impressive at times than the sight of the dead and wounded. You expect to see death in all its form, but you are shocked at the wanton destruction of thousands and thousands of dollars of property, of munitions, of food and clothing, of everything into the making of which have gone the labor and ingenuity of the so-called human race."

But another sight caught the librarian's sensitive eye, interjecting a touch of intimate humanity amid the carnage.

"Up on the hill south of Longavesne," Leland wrote, "was a German cemetery, quite a large one. There had evidently been a field hospital nearby, for all the graves were well cared for and the crosses well made and painted. Faded flowers in tin cans and jars still bore witness to some soldier's grief for a fallen pal."

A few miles to the east, beyond the cemetery at Longavesne, beyond the smashed towns of Tincourt, Allaines, Haut Allaines, Bois de Buire, Peronne, and Ronssoy awaited a wholly different sight, a wholly different circumstance. Here was the place where Sir Douglas Haig, the leader of all British forces on the western front that now included two divisions from the United States, the Thirtieth as well as the Twenty-seventh, staked his legacy. Here was where the chief of the general staff of the German Imperial Army, Field Marshal Paul von Hindenburg, meant to fight to the last man.[11]

And here the war must finally end. If not, it would certainly drag on through another winter of despair; even though every month hundreds of thousands of American doughboys were pouring into France.

For here stood the famous Hindenburg Line.

This feared obstacle, according to a British officer of the Eighteenth Division, whose boys had just been stopped cold on its outer barricades, was the "vastest and most powerfully organized defensive line the world has ever seen, constructed at leisure and strengthened by every resource which the science of military engineering had at its disposal."[12]

The Hindenburg Line was not the name the Germans gave it. The British dubbed it that in mock honor of the German field marshal.

More lofty in their designation, the Germans called it *Siegfriedstellung;* the Siegfried Line. In fact, the system that made up the so-called Hindenburg Line was a series of defensive strongholds, with each stronghold named after a hero in Teutonic folklore. Together, they zigzagged for almost the entire length of the western front. From the coast at Ostend south to the Saint Mihiel salient, they cut through the land like a monstrous open zipper. In the center stood the strongest sector of all, the Siegfried Line.

In 1916 Hindenburg and Gen. Erich Ludendorff ordered the construction of rear defensive lines. These lines were designed in such a way that they would shorten the area to be defended. The Hindenburg Line, for example, shrank the front line by twenty-five miles. Troops could thereupon be released and used in reserve. In the case of the Hindenburg Line, thirteen divisions were freed up for reserve duty. Ludendorff realized that the best way to fight the Allies was to go on the defensive. Let the Allies attack. The Imperial German Army would stop them dead in their tracks and then mount a savage counterattack.

To build the Hindenburg Line, the Germans used a huge army of workers divided into 141 labor companies. Some twelve thousand Germans and three thousand Belgians were brought in, along with fifty thousand prisoners of war, nearly all of them Russians. Reporting on this, the journalist Musgrave pointed out that to the Hun "age, sex and law of war didn't exist—military prisoners and civilians were impressed by the thousands and lashed as a great human plow to excavate deep defenses on a new line to modify the front. And on the thousand square miles before it—devastation."[13]

The genius behind the design of the Hindenburg Line was Col. Fritz von Lossberg, chief of staff of the German First Army. After careful thought on the art of trench warfare, Lossberg called for the repositioning of the frontline trenches. Instead of siting them on a forward slope where they were more vulnerable to artillery bombardment and assault by infantrymen, he had them redug on a reverse slope. Here the trenches would be more protected. He also pulled the artillery observation posts out of the front line, moving them well behind that part of the battlefield the artillery would hit first. In addition, he recommended that an outpost line be carved from the earth. Once across this outpost line, British troops would then face the first of two main trench lines about twenty-five hundred yards apart. Between these two lines, British troops would be caught in a battle zone where their own artillery could not see them and would therefore be unable to fire accurately, while the German artillery would put down a thunderous shellacking of its own on the bewildered enemy. Along the entire front, he planned for a series of fortified redoubts, manned by crack machine-gun squads, many of the gunners encased in body armor. Behind the main trench, he added yet more lines of trenches, where reserve troops would bide their time, waiting to be ordered into battle, mostly as counterattackers. Everywhere there were concrete machine-gun emplacements, or pillboxes, strategically situated to give the shooters excellent fields of fire. Mining timber lined the pillboxes for added strength. Steps from these machine-gun nests burrowed deep into the ground as much as twenty and thirty feet where sheltered rooms provided protection from the rain of artillery shells. Underground passages catacombed the entire battle zone.

Maurice Swetland, a former Seventh Regiment man now with the Twenty-seventh Division, recalled: "Toward the British and American lines, the hills were honey-combed with 'pillboxes' [machine-gun forts, he also called them] cleverly nestled into the slopes and surrounded by huge concrete emplacements, well sheltered and carefully covered and camouflaged."[14]

Then there was the barbed wire. A nasty product of the American wild west, the wire Lossberg relied on to maul the British attackers sported razor-sharp one-inch barbs. Entanglements of rusted wire covered the ground thick and tight as briar patches. Rolling and twisting in angry belts, oftentimes in loops ten-feet high, the wire created a cunning maze that herded soldiers down deadly paths and into the sight of itchy-fingered machine gunners.

The Australian general who would oversee the attack on the very center of the Hindenburg Line, John Monash, declared that it was the barbed wire that formed the groundwork of the defense. He wrote that the trenches, which had been perfected with dugouts, concrete machine-gun and mortar emplacements and underground shelters, "were protected by belt after belt of wire entanglements, in a fashion which no one understood better, or achieved more thoroughly than the Germans."[15]

But once past this lethal obstacle, the Americans faced a more forbidding barricade before they reached the main defensive line: the cavernous St. Quentin Canal Tunnel.

Built by Napoleon early in the nineteenth century, the St. Quentin Canal Tunnel was six thousand feet long. It was part of an ambitious canal system that connected two rivers—the Somme in the south and the Scheldt in the north, cutting through the softly undulating region's high country. Outside the village of Bellicourt, northwest of St. Quentin, the canal went underground. After traveling beneath Bellicourt, it ran past another village, Bony, and then reemerged at a place called The Knob. Col. Joseph Hyde Pratt, commanding officer of the 105th Field Engineers of the U.S. Thirtieth Division, which fought side-by-side with the Twenty-seventh, later measured the inside of the tunnel. Its roof was between 37 and 195 feet below the surface of the ground. The pounding of artillery hardly shook the interior, a vaulted arch twenty-six feet high and twenty-six feet wide. Passageways connected the tunnel to Bellicourt and to hidden machine-gun emplacements in front of the Hindenburg Line. Pratt counted 155 concrete emplacements. But what really astonished the engineer was that the tunnel was "an underground city capable of housing a division in comfort and yet in direct contact with the front-line defenses."[16]

Twenty-six barges were anchored inside the tunnel, serving as billets for the German troops as well as depots for stores and munitions. Monash recollected that "tier upon tier of comfortable quarters for the troops had been tunneled out. Here support and reserve troops could live in safety and defy our heaviest bombardments. They could be secretly hurried to the front trenches whenever danger threatened."[17]

Major General O'Ryan of the Twenty-seventh agreed. "No bombardment, no matter how severe, could affect reserve troops stationed or billeted within the tunnel. The entrances of the tunnel were blocked off by heavily reinforced concrete walls, defended by machine guns."

Electrically conducted exploding mines and booby traps were also planted throughout the tunnel. The worst of these mines and traps were at the northern entrance, the sector assigned to the Twenty-seventh.

O'Ryan's aide, Major Tupper, found the tunnel an "ingenious stronghold," where it was possible for the enemy to feed fresh forces unexpectedly into any part of the battlefield. This meant, he said, that Germans could pop up from their hidden burrows after the Americans had passed over, and then mow them down from behind.[18]

Meanwhile, as the 107th Infantry rattled on amid the growing roar of distant artillery, its anxious men had no way of knowing that in this very sector of the Hindenburg Line the British Eighteenth and Seventy-fourth Divisions were just then being pummeled by the Germans. Following this brutal encounter, it was obvious to General Maurice that in the "third week of September, the German resistance was far from broken. If the enemy's infantry had lost much of the dash and initiative which distinguished it in 1916, and the subordinate leaders had not the skills of their predecessors who had fallen in battle, his artillery, though weakening, was still powerful and well directed, and his machine-guns were manned by picked men of high courage, and had, from long experience, become more formidable than ever."[19]

The goal of the Brits, fighting with the Aussies and Canadians, had been to straighten the whole length of an assault line along the outer defenses of the Hindenburg Line so that on 29 September, from St. Quentin north to near Armentieres, a sixty-seven-mile stretch, fifty-two infantry divisions and three cavalry divisions under Field Marshal Haig would "go over the top." The assault, or start line, needed to be straight so the artillery could lay down a creeping barrage behind which the infantrymen would then charge the main trenches and tunnel stronghold. Everywhere in the preliminary battle the Allies had been successful, except at the northern end of the tunnel. In this sector the assault line had not been moved forward. Instead, for almost a mile it remained a gaping two thousand yards short of the Allies' objective. Any troops attacking here, where six German divisions lay in wait, would now do so without much artillery support. Such a dash toward the entrenched enemy would most certainly turn out to be every bit as daring, foolhardy, and just as bloody as when, fifty-five years earlier, Gen. George Pickett's men charged the center of the Union Army at Gettysburg. For the New Yorkers of 1918, a suicide mission if ever there was one.

At about three in the morning of September 25th, the last of the 107th's troop trains finally rolled into Tincourt. The men from Captain Egan's Third Battalion clamored down from the boxcars, their joints stiff from the twelve-hour, seventy-eight-mile trip. They formed up and marched for another three hours to Allaines, Haut Allaines, and Longavesne before joining the other two battalions and the headquarters company and support units. Shelter tents were then pitched on a rolling plain chewed up by abandoned trenches and shell holes around which freshly planted white crosses marked where the British and Australians had fallen in combat only days before. Scattered just beyond the makeshift campground were the unburied corpses of hundreds of Germans.

One New Yorker never forgot his first night sleeping on that ground. "I remember my blankets were laid on a nice flat spot, the only one I could find, on a section of German trench which had been filled in for twenty feet. In the morning, at my side, I saw a sign, 'Two mules buried here,' and down near the bottom of this fill stuck out a German boot, and it was filled."

"There must be piles of unburied bodies," Sgt. George Ely II of K

Company jotted down in his diary.[20] A cousin of Commodore Vanderbilt, Ely was the grandson of the secretary of the New York Stock Exchange, who himself had been in the old Seventh.

The entire regiment was together again, sleeping where it could, while all around them the other regiments of the Twenty-seventh also tossed and turned, and awaited orders. For the first time since arriving in France, the silk stocking soldiers and their comrades from upstate New York sensed something momentous was about to happen. Sergeant Ely noted, "The stage is being set for a big party. Just what part we are going to have we don't know." Although the Americans weren't part of General Pershing's great army encamped further down on the western front—but were rather seemingly lost inside the belly of the huge British Fourth Army—they knew that the task ahead of them would change the course of the war.

When the order came at last, the suicide mission to punch a hole into the Hindenburg Line so the Australians could then pour through it to rout the Germans, Lieutenant Gow of the Machine Gun Company penned a letter home that caught how the entire 107th felt at that moment. "I am writing in the field with guns going all around me. We are about to take part in the biggest thing of the war, and our company has been honored above all other companies in being awarded the danger post. The all-American cry is: 'Over the top!' You will have read of it long before this gets to you, if we succeed. If we don't, you will read of it through the casualty lists. Our division has had a rare honor laid upon it, because we are the best, and we are going in to sacrifice it all if necessary. A big game can be played but once."

And now it was time for the untested doughboys, many of them the sons of New York society, to join in this big, deadly game that had already been raging across France for four horrible years.

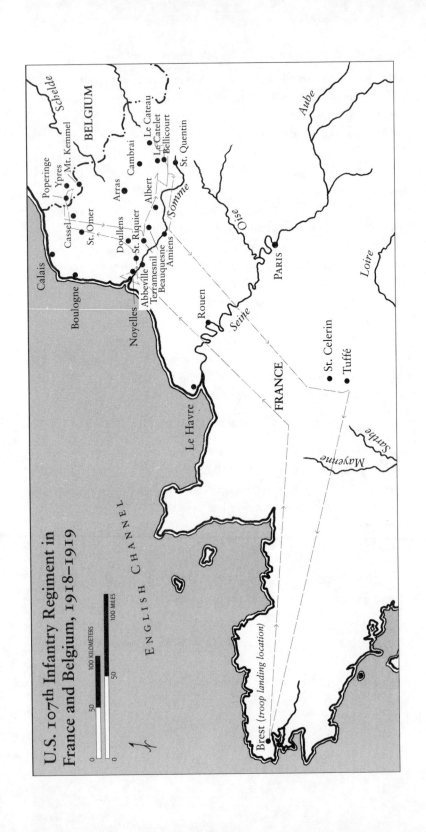

U.S. 107th Infantry Regiment in France and Belgium, 1918–1919

ENGLISH CHANNEL

BELGIUM

Schelde

FRANCE

Aube

Loire

Oise

Somme

Seine

Sarthe

Mayenne

100 KILOMETERS

100 MILES

50

50

0

0

Calais

Boulogne

Novelles

Abbeville

Terramesnil

Beauquesne

Amiens

Rouen

Le Havre

Brest (troop landing location)

PARIS

St. Celerin

Tuffé

Poperinge

Ypres

Mt. Kemmel

Cassel

St. Omer

Doullens

St. Riquier

Albert

Arras

Cambrai

Le Cateau

Le Catelet

Bellicourt

St. Quentin

CHAPTER 1

True Soldiers
Every Man of Them

I f ever there was a Holy War, it is this war!" thundered Teddy Roosevelt at Harvard University in that long, hot patriotic summer of 1917.[1]

In this holy war to crush the Hun and make the world safe for democracy, men from every walk of American life dreamt of being the first crusaders to reach besieged France and Belgium. Gallant knights, they saw themselves, fighting at last under the red, white, and blue banner of their own country. Before the United States entered the war, thousands of men had enlisted in the armies of France, Great Britain, or Canada or had dashed off to Europe as ambulance drivers. Even Teddy Roosevelt, within weeks after the declaration of war, sought to raise a volunteer division, another band of heroic Rough Riders like those he had led up San Juan Hill in 1898. John L. Sullivan, the ancient heavyweight boxing champion, offered his fists of iron to Roosevelt's cause.

Those who dared call for caution in these fervent times or showed any sympathy toward the Germans felt the wrath of an aroused people. Elihu Root, secretary of war and of state during Roosevelt's administration, and in 1912 recipient of the Nobel Peace Prize, speaking at the Union League Club in New York, warned that "there are men walking about the streets of this city tonight who ought to be taken out at sunrise tomorrow and shot for treason."[2]

In Europe, Gen. Black Jack Pershing, with a stubbornness that bordered on insubordination, took on the high command of the Allies—generals, presidents, and prime ministers alike. Turning a deaf ear to their pleas for fresh bodies as trench fodder, the ex-Indian fighter and pursuer of Pancho Villa set out forging an American army all his own.

There wasn't a division or a regiment in the United States that didn't want to be part of Pershing's fledgling military force.

In New York City alone, where a dozen National Guard regiments were headquartered, the battle for the honor of being selected into the newly created Forty-second Rainbow Division was intense. Slotted to be among the first fighting forces to head for the western front, the Rainbow Division was to be comprised of guardsmen from around the country. In all, twenty-six states and the District of Columbia.

Inside their elegant armory on Park Avenue, the well-heeled officers and men of the Seventh Infantry Regiment, the first unit in the United States to carry the name "National Guard," recognized by their stylish "Greyjackets," and led by a luxuriantly mustachioed, sixty-one-year-old lawyer and brother-in-law of the famed actress Minnie Maddern Fiske, Col. Willard Clinton Fisk, waited and watched and worried.

The rumor mill was working overtime. Would the Greyjackets of the Seventh get the nod over the Sixty-ninth Regiment?, wondered these sons of New York society. A frustrated officer from I Company fretted that "there were new rumors every day about the future of the Regiment. It was to be broken up. It was to be recruited up and officered by regulars. It was to be—the Lord knows what."[3]

Pvt. Eugene J. O'Brien showed his impatience with the War Department in the September 1917 issue of *The Seventh Regiment Gazette.* "The old saying that 'We're here because we're here' most befittingly applies to our situation. Nobody knows how, when, or where we are going, and no one seems to care particularly where, as long as it is somewhere and soon."

The Sanitary Detachment's Don Emery, in civilian life a commercial artist from Newport, Vermont, where his father was mayor, piped in: "Well, our chances of seeing early service abroad seem about as far off as they did the last time we sent our notes, and while all of us are glad enough to spend as much time at home as possible, still, hanging around New York on thirty dollars a month with no free rides on the trolley lines and elevated railways is no joke, to say the least. And to think we used to figure close to make that much last us a week, and still keep out of debt."

Sgt. Frederick C. Gudebrod Jr. agreed. "We are still in New York and we are becoming more . . . broke each day. One cannot live the fast life of a great city on army pay, yet we attempt to. It is easy to tell pay day is approaching. The mess line gets longer, the cigarette stubs shorter, and the seven-and-a-half crowd play a penny limit."

Like all the other regiments, the men of the Seventh felt they deserved to be chosen for the Rainbow Division. But always in time of national peril, it seemed the War Department or the State of New York snubbed them. In its long history, going back to 1806 when it was first organized as a New York militia of four infantry companies of the Third Artillery, the Seventh never felt a shot fired against it in anger. Except, of course, by mobs of working-class New Yorkers in the scores of riots and strikes that shook the city in the nineteenth century; from the Astor Place Riot in 1849 to the violent draft riots of 1863 to as late as the Croton Dam Strike in 1900.

The fact that as a unit the Seventh never fought in wartime might be used against it. Or the fact that its men were blue bloods, and perhaps a bit too wealthy for their own good, looked down upon as dilettantes in uniform. Hardly the stuff of heroes.

Silk Stocking Soldiers, the newspapers dubbed them, in honor of their Upper East Side address.

Symbolic of their wealth was the armory that fronted Park Avenue. Built in 1880 for $2.5 million and privately paid for without a penny pinched from city, state, or federal coffers, the uptown citadel covered an entire block between East Sixty-sixth and East Sixty-seventh streets, which it leased from the city for one dollar a year. The armory stood four stories high. The watchtower that once rose majestically above it had been lopped off during renovations in 1912. Still, it was tall enough to take in the ever increasing upward thrust of the Manhattan skyline. A block away glistened the greensward of Central Park, where on weekends the dandies of the Seventh played soldier. The rear of the armory abutting Lexington Avenue housed a massive drill hall that measured two hun-

Funding for the Seventh Regiment Armory on Park Avenue between East Sixty-sixth and East Sixty-seventh Streets, built in the 1870s, included substantial donations from New York City's wealthiest merchants. This is how the armory appeared circa 1904. The Seventh Regiment Fund

dred feet by three hundred feet, bigger than the playing area of Brooklyn's Ebbets Field. Designed by the Delaware Bridge Company to look like the inside of the railroad shed at Cornelius Vanderbilt's original Grand Central Depot with its massive iron-truss system, it easily handled a regimental muster of two thousand men. A gallery overlooked the drill hall so dignitaries, wives, and sweethearts comfortably viewed New York's captains of industry, as if in a Broadway theater—its leading merchants, lawyers, bankers, and stockbrokers; newspaper and magazine editors, reporters and illustrators; and actors, artists, poets, and musicians in full military regalia. Greyjackets on parade. However, the most impressive feature of the Seventh Regiment Armory was its interior. Here the likes of Louis Comfort Tiffany and Associated Artists, Stanford White, the Herter Brothers, Leon Marcotte, Alexander Roux, Pottier and Stymes, and other eminent artisans of the Gilded Age virtually had free reign in the design and furnishings of the regimental headquarters and company rooms, reception parlor, library, mess hall, and gymnasium. Each outclassed the other in elegance and grandeur. The spirited competition was too obvious, and in the end the splendid stronghold that safeguarded the fashionable East Side rather showed off the money and artistic virtuosity of its owners than their military might.

Silk stocking soldiers indeed.

Still burning in the memory of old Seventh veterans was the treatment they had received during the Spanish-American War. Ready and willing to fight, their commander back then, Col. Daniel Appleton, offered the regiment to the state and the nation—as long as it was kept intact and fought as a single unit. New York governor Frank Black hemmed and hawed about calling out Appleton's boys. Infuriated, Appleton, president of D. Appleton & Co., publishers of Charles Darwin and Edith Wharton, and a personal friend of Chauncey Depew, the influential Republican stalwart and the Vanderbilts' right-hand man when it came to running their railroads, went over Governor Black's head—directly to President William McKinley. Using Depew as a courier, he begged McKinley to call out the Greyjackets. When the president discovered that the Seventh was cooling its heels in its Park Avenue armory, he said, "This is very pathetic. We want the Regiment and must have it!"[4]

Feeling slighted by Appleton's presidential end-around, Governor Black stonewalled the Seventh. His adjutant general for the State of New York, Gen. C. Whitney Tillinghast II, remarked to the press that if the regiment stayed in the armory, it was going to have a long wait, because no order for mobilization would be forthcoming.[5]

The Seventh was never called up, and the reason why was never publicly stated. Therefore in the 1899 Memorial Day parade, ignorant bystanders hissed the Greyjackets as they marched down Fifth Avenue. At Forty-seventh Street a knot of curbstone hecklers yelled, "Cowards! Cowards!" Miss Helen Gould, daughter of the old robber baron, Jay Gould, and one of the richest women in the country whose money was then helping veterans of the Spanish-American War, along with a party of friends, took their cue from the hecklers and, with an air of righteous indignation, booed the Seventh as it passed by her stately mansion.[6]

Appleton later declared that the hissing was "simply an indication of the feeling on the part of a certain class of people who dislike the Seventh."[7]

The silver-tongued Depew got in the last word. He said in a speech to the Greyjackets in their armory, eerie in its premonition of the events to come: "Governor Black and General Tillinghast will long be forgotten while the Seventh Regiment will continue to live with a future of brilliant deeds that will add more to the glorious record of this distinguished Regiment."[8]

Nonetheless, in subsequent Memorial Day parades, white feathers, a fitting symbol of cowardice, were floated in front of the proud regiment of the seething soldiers of the Seventh. Thus it came as no surprise that when at last the makeup of the Rainbow Division was done, the War Department snubbed the Seventh again. Instead, the honor of representing New York went to the Sixty-ninth.

The Sixty-ninth was no regiment of blue bloods. Nicknamed the "Fighting Sixty-ninth," it was Irish to the core, and had the backing of Tammany Hall. There's no doubt that some sorely disappointed officers of the rival Seventh were sure they spotted the political cunning of Tammany's shrewd sachems behind the selection of the Sixty-ninth—even though at the time it was in need of soldiers from New York City's other National Guard units to bring it up to the newly established numerical strength required of a regiment by the War Department of 3,600 men.

Indeed, one of the Seventh's top officers, Maj. Robert Mazet, former New York State deputy attorney general, had earned the acrimony of Tammany Hall. When he was an assemblyman in 1899, he had led a legislative probe into city corruption. The Republican-packed Mazet Committee, as it was called, hammered away at "Boss" Richard Croker in what proved to be the beginning of the end of the powerful Tammany politician. But that was eighteen years ago, and Tammany now had a new boss, Charles Murphy; and his personal attorney, Arthur J. Baldwin, had allowed his son, Morgan Smiley Baldwin, to enlist in the Seventh. Even the sons of Greenwich Village chieftain Charles Culkin, Charlie and Tom, joined up. And so did the youngest boy of John Ahearn, boss of the Fourth Assembly District. In contrast, the late "Battery Dan" Finn, for many years a colorful Tammany leader in the First Assembly District, probably turned over in his grave when his son, Philip Schuyler Finn, mulling over which organization he wanted to fight with, selected the silk stocking regiment.

Meanwhile, adding insult to injury, the Seventh, along with four other city regiments, the Twelfth, Fourteenth, Twenty-third, and Seventy-first, were required to help the Sixty-ninth meet its quota of able-bodied men so it could be quickly trained and sent overseas. This meant sending 1,750 of their own soldiers to the Sixty-ninth despite the fact that the Irish regiment already had a waiting list of five thousand men.

That made Regimental Order No. 27, dated 16 August 1917, almost too much to bear. Written and signed dutifully by Colonel Fisk, it read in part:

> In compliance with instructions from the Commanding Officer, Eastern Department, received through Headquarters, 6th Division, by letters of August 11th and August 13th, 1917, the soldiers set out in the list below, are hereby transferred to the Sixty-ninth Regiment.[9]

The list carried the names of 350 stunned enlisted men. Sergeants of every stripe, corporals, privates, privates first class; buglers, cooks, mechanics, and wagoners. Whether or not they wanted to go from the Seventh to the Sixty-ninth made no difference. Regimental supply sergeant Gerald F. Jacobson, destined to stay with the Seventh and write its history after the war, said that those men sent to the Sixty-ninth "seemed to be among the best men we had."[10]

Maj. Gen. John F. O'Ryan, commanding the Twenty-seventh Division and a former member of G Company of the Seventh, called the order a great shock to all the regiments concerned. "To take a man away from his own regiment and place him in another is like taking a child away from its own home and placing it in the home of some other family."

At first, Fisk, who had enlisted as a Greyjacket in 1874 when he was only seventeen and whose son, Clinton, his law partner, was now a captain in D Company, had two choices when it came time to select who in his regiment would go. The Seventh had always been particular in the men it recruited. It was almost as difficult to get into the Seventh to play soldier as it was to get into the upper echelons of Manhattan society. Beginning in the early 1800s, members of the Seventh bore such prominent

Col. Willard Fisk, commanding officer of the
Seventh Regiment until June 1918.
The Seventh Regiment Fund

New York names as Vanderbilt, Van Rensselaer, Roosevelt, Schermer-horn, Belmont, Gracie, Fish, Hamilton, Harriman, Rhinelander, and Tiffany. But when Congress declared war on Germany on 6 April 1917 and then three months later federalized the National Guard, the regiment's rejection of undesirables slackened. Soon there were a number of new enlistees who failed to measure up to the social standards of the Seventh. Fisk could easily pack them off to the Sixty-ninth, keeping the best for himself.

Who would know? Or care?

The other choice was to play it straight. And there was a compelling reason why Fisk wanted to play it straight.

Despite the jealousy that the Sixty-ninth would soon sail for France as part of the Rainbow Division, a deep friendship existed between the Irish regiment and the Seventh. That friendship went back to the Civil War. Because the Seventh as a unit saw no action during the war, a number of its members temporarily transferred out so they could get into battle. Actually, the Seventh supplied more officers to the Union Army than any other organization, including the United States Military Academy. One of them, Robert Gould Shaw, led the Fifty-fourth Massachusetts, the all-black regiment that won glory on the beaches of South Carolina. Another, Maj. Theodore Winthrop, lawyer, novelist, and descendent of Massachusetts governor Jonathan Winthrop, was believed to be the first Union officer killed in battle in the Civil War. Many of these society men swelled the ranks of New York's other regiments. They took part in nearly all the bloody battles of the Civil War, and six of them earned the Medal of Honor. (In fact, even before the war, a Greyjacket had won the country's initial Medal of Honor. The heroic deed of Irish-born Dr. Bernard Irwin took place in mid-February, 1861, against Cochise at Apache Pass in the Arizona Territory. Although not the first medal awarded—that took place in 1863 after Congress established the honor to encourage Union soldiers to reenlist—it was the earliest action in history for which the medal was given.) Therefore, the men from the Seventh had truly proven worthy comrades-in-arms, and Fisk was not about to slander that hard-fought reputation by sloughing off *any* ne'er-do-well who had slipped into the Seventh at the expense of the Sixty-ninth, as he knew other regiments in the city would surely do.

As it turned out, he was right. After the war, Martin Green of the New York *Evening World* recalled, "Other regiments of the New York National Guard, summoned to the aid of the Sixty-ninth, were not so ardent as the Seventh. In the high commands of these regiments there was displayed a degree of selfishness more or less excusable under the circumstances."[11] In some cases, these regiments simply paid the subway fare from their armory to the Sixty-ninth's armory of the guardsmen they felt were deadwood. Father Francis Duffy, the famed chaplain of the Sixty-ninth, felt that a "couple of our sister organizations have flipped from the bottom of the pack in some instances and worked off on us some of their least desirables." The commander of the Sixty-ninth, Lt. Col. Latham Reed, called for an investigation into the manner in which the transfers were selected. He was sure that many of the soldiers were unfit physically and mentally for active service. The Sixty-ninth struck the undesirables from its ranks with what Duffy called "thirty-five distinct damnations" that the regiment's surgeons uncovered during the physicals, so that any man who failed to pass muster was "returned to civilian life to take his chances in the draft."[12]

But Fisk would have none of it. Green wrote, "Col. Fisk, a grand old warrior, one of the best regimental commanders in this country or in France . . . said in effect, as he complied with the orders of the War Department: 'By God, this is the country's war and if the Sixty-ninth is going over ahead of the Seventh, I want the Seventh's representation in the Sixty-ninth to be the best blankety-blank representation in the whole Mick outfit.' "[13]

The selective system that determined the lot of the men was devised by 1st Lt. Leo F. Knust of E Company. A native of Germany, Knust looked and acted the Prussian officer, a blond, hard-nosed disciplinarian. His plan was methodical. Taken in alphabetical order, every fifth man would go, twenty-seven from each company. Those who wanted to volunteer had the right to do so. Maj. Dewitt Clinton Falls, who in 1902 represented the United States and the regiment as military attaché at the coronation of King Edward VII, thought the plan unfair. "It was particularly hard on the non-commissioned officers, as all transfers were to be made privates and they were accordingly reduced to the ranks. With the slow promotion in the Seventh many of these men had had long service and were of excellent officer material for the future. This order raised a storm of protest."[14]

First Sgt. Earle D. Grimm, an advertising genius and avowed yachtsman serving in Knust's E Company, reported that the numerical system "hit old and new alike and while those detailed were naturally more than reluctant about leaving their comrades and friends in the regiment, the knowledge that they would be among the first to go see active service, cheered them up."

Mess Sgt. Robert J. Bell Jr. noted, "Every man shook in his boots, for notwithstanding the fact that the old 'Fighting 69th' is as fine an outfit as any man could wish for, the thought of parting from pals, to go with strangers, was by no means a pleasant outlook."

Billy Leonard, city editor of the Flushing *Daily Times,* and a newly enlisted private in I Company, wrote in *The Seventh Regiment Gazette,* "It cannot be said that the order drafting our men into another regiment was received with great joy, but the men upon whom the choice of fortune fell accepted the situation with fine spirit and, in many instances, other men volunteered to take the places of those reluctant to go, inspired by the prospect of early service in France."

One of the happiest volunteers was Albert "Red" Ettinger of L Company, son of the New York City superintendent of schools. Red never wanted to be in the Seventh, what he called the "Kid Glove 7th." He especially thought the men there too highfalutin. When the National Guard was called out for service on the Mexican border in 1916, Red, then only sixteen years old, tried to enlist in the Sixty-ninth. But word got back to his father that he was in the armory at Twenty-sixth Street and Lexington Avenue, playing hooky from school so he could join up. The elder Ettinger raced over to the armory to put a stop to such foolishness. He then had his son promise that if he truly wanted to be a soldier he must graduate from school before he enlisted. And the regiment had to be the Seventh in fitting with the position the family enjoyed in the hierarchy of city politics, not the Sixty-ninth. Red honored his father's request. He enlisted in the Seventh two days after the declaration of war. But the moment his company commander, Capt. Fancher Nicoll, asked if there were any volunteers willing to transfer over to the Sixty-ninth, he eagerly stepped forward.[15]

Another transfer was the literary critic for the *New York Times* and famous as the poet of "Trees," Alfred Joyce Kilmer.

Joyce wanted to leave for another reason.

Episcopalian by birth, he was named after the Rev. Alfred Joyce, parish rector of Christ Church of New Brunswick, New Jersey, where he was christened in 1886. But in his heart Joyce believed himself a Roman Catholic Irishman. He later converted to Catholicism when in his midtwenties—much to the great disappointment of his mother, an ardent Anglophile and quite proud of her connection to the Church of England, which she traced back to the 1600s. Her seemingly blasphemous son even went so far as to state that he was half-Irish. When it was pointed out that he was no more Irish than the English king, he shrugged it off. In a letter to his wife he wrote, "As to the matter of my own blood . . . I did indeed tell a good friend of mine . . . that I was 'half Irish.' But I have never been a mathematician."[16]

It was ironic then that Joyce and one of his close literary friends, Louis H. Wetmore, enlisted in G Company of the Seventh Regiment. The Irish regiment would have been more in fitting with Kilmer's mindset. On the evening of 5 August, however, almost four months after he and Wetmore committed themselves to the silk stocking regiment, Joyce met Father Francis Duffy for the first time. The chaplain of the Sixty-ninth took an immediate liking to Joyce. He found there was nothing "long-haired" about the poet. Rather he was "a sturdy fellow, manly, humorous, interesting." Father Duffy asked him why, if he was so enamored with the Irish, had he not enlisted in the Sixty-ninth?

"I went to the Armory twice, but failed to find a recruiting officer," Joyce said, a little shamed-faced, according to the chaplain.

Father Duffy replied that if the Sixty-ninth could not have him the next best place was the Seventh. Joyce then surprised the chaplain by stating that he wanted to transfer. With his connections to the Seventh Regiment, Father Duffy agreed to take care of the paperwork. Writing in his diary later that night, Father Duffy thought about their fortuitous meeting. "I shall be glad to have him with us personally for the pleasure of his companionship, and also for the sake of the regiment to have a poet and historian who will confer upon us the gift of immortality."[17]

Now that Fisk had signed the transfer order, his next move was to see that his boys bound for the Sixty-ninth marched out of the Seventh Regiment Armory for the last time in a blaze of glory. He wanted this moment in the sun for them because he felt a foreboding of change coming over his regiment.

Change that was certain to be bad.

It wasn't only that the Sixty-ninth got called to the Rainbow Division and not the Seventh. Or the unpopular transfer of these 350 men.

It was the little things.

The Sixty-ninth had just been redesignated the 165th Regiment, wiping out its illustrious name. The same could happen to the Seventh, a new number handed down by some bureaucratic bean counter in Washington who had no clue of the grand history and traditions of his regiment. In fact, the division in which the Seventh was assigned kept having its numerical designation changed. First it was the Sixth New York Division.

Then the Twenty-seventh. Then back to being called the Sixth. Rumors were now that it would most likely end up as the Twenty-seventh.

Or maybe the Seventh would be disbanded. It was about to happen to the Seventy-first Regiment.

Or it may never get the call to battle, as had happened in previous wars. Another snub from the War Department or else the state. Fisk still remembered the Memorial Day parades at the turn of the century. The boos. The hisses. The white feathers. Therefore, he couldn't blame the Greyjackets who had already bailed out of the regiment for just those reasons. A lot of them took off as early as 1914, the moment war erupted in Europe.

One of the first to go was André Chéronnet-Champollion, the type of silk stocking soldier the War Department had in mind when it turned its back on the Seventh. Darkly handsome, with a black mustache, extremely tall at six-six, half French, half American, André enlisted in the French army within weeks after the German invasion because, as he wrote to a former Harvard classmate, "[I]f I stayed away from this war I should suffer in my self-respect (as perhaps I should), and that my French friends would regard me with contempt."[18] While in the Seventh, the Paris-born André, a naturalized U.S. citizen, never took to the spit and polish ways of the military, although his uncle Hailet Borrowe had served with Roosevelt's Rough Riders. He preferred the free and easy sporting life of Paris, New York, and the vast, wooded family estate in Newport, New Hampshire, that his own wealth afforded him. His paternal great-grandfather was the Egyptologist Jean François Champollion, the Frenchman who had deciphered the Rosetta Stone. His maternal grandfather was American capitalist Austin Corbin, who built the Long Island Railroad and then set out developing Coney Island. His wife, Adelaide, was the youngest daughter of John Jay Knox, comptroller of the U.S. currency.

Resigning from the Seventh, where he loved its gala social gatherings inside the plush regimental armory more than the dull drilling in Central Park's Sheep Meadow, he found army life in France rough; sleeping on straw, mingling with poor, uneducated French boys. No wonder in late December, he wrote, "fancy being obliged to live an indefinite length of time with the aristocracy of the Bowery of Third Avenue, to be bossed by streetcar conductors or cab drivers, with your personal liberty absolutely gone, no more family, no more friends, no more distractions. Only filthy and distasteful duties fit only for human brutes, without the end ever being in sight." His aunt, a countess, pulled a few strings with the French government. André was permitted to rent a room in town, far from the squalor of the cantonments. Later, Adelaide joined him. His superiors granted him special favors. He was grateful. "You are perpetually thrown in with men who, if they do not positively drive you to drink by their idiotic coarseness, at least bore you stiff."

Still, with special favors, the foremost, of course, permission to bunk in with his wife, he lost interest in the "accursed struggle." After almost six months behind the lines, he longed for home. "Call me a coward or a quitter, if you like, but the most glorious vision will be New York harbor and Fifth Avenue with the faces of my American friends, and to cap the climax, my return to my home and the park in New Hampshire!"

On 28 February 1915 he at last arrived at the front, near Verdun. The French and German trenches were separated by thirty-five yards of hostile no-man's-land. Bullets crackled overhead. Because of his height, André discovered that he had to keep "stooping down so as not to get my head knocked off by the enemy's snipers." Constant bending over was a nuisance. "Being taller than the average French soldier, I was continually admonished to stoop down and not show the top of my head. This enforced stooping position often resulted in a backache.[19]

On 23 March he forgot to stoop. A German sniper shot him in the forehead. André was the second American killed in combat in the Great War, and the first from the Seventh Regiment to die.

More Greyjackets were also in France.

William H. Harton of A Company enlisted in the Fifth Canadian Mounted Rifles. Promoted to sergeant, he took part in the Battle of Ypres. His platoon came under heavy bombardment. He was in his dugout when a shell landed, killing six men and burying him up to his waist in mud. He suffered two compound fractures to his left leg. After being freed from the mud and stretched out on the slimy duckboard that lined the bottom of his trench, he was injected with morphine and left there. Another shell exploded next to him. A fragment tore deep into his right thigh, bringing bits and pieces of raincoat and breeches in with it. A doctor sawed off his left leg above the knee. A priest then performed last rites. Yet Harton survived. After his ordeal, he wrote to his friends back at the Seventh Regiment Armory, "I thank God I saw my duty and went without being fetched like so many Englishmen had done in England."

Haskell Clark Billings, I Company alumnus, also went north to fight with the Canadians. After enlisting on 7 January 1916, he was quickly promoted to captain in the Princess Patricia's Canadian Light Infantry and shipped to France as an instructor in the fine art of the bayonet.

F Company's Billy Tailer, wealthy enough to enlist the help of a former regimental colleague, August Belmont, to get him out of the Seventh and into the Lafayette Escadrille, was a pilot in France. A Company's Donald Page stayed on the ground in France as an ambulance driver.

By the time America entered the war, Maj. Francis Griswold Landon, recently of I Company, felt too old to seek a place in some established military organization where the top brass had been entrenched for years. Instead, the fifty-eight-year-old former state assemblyman from Duchess County, whose motto was, "You do your best, and then do a little better," decided to create his own regiment. He then planned to place it at the disposal of Col. Teddy Roosevelt, who, on a grander scale, was hoping to raise a division of volunteers. Landon had known the Roosevelts since the early 1880s, when he and Teddy's younger brother, Elliott, enlisted in the Seventh. Another connection to Teddy was Francis's brother, Henry, a West Point graduate and famed Indian fighter. Like Teddy, Henry had fought in the Spanish-American War and then served as military governor of Bayamo, Cuba. When Roosevelt was president, he had appointed Francis to the staff of the U.S. embassy in Berlin and later sent him to the embassy in Vienna.

On 19 April 1917 Landon fired off a letter to the adjutant general of the army, offering his services for the "Colonelcy of a Volunteer Regiment." He pointed out that he had already organized a "skeleton" staff that consisted of three majors, fifteen captains, fourteen lieutenants, and one chaplain. "This infantry unit will volunteer for the war, and is ready for active service at once," he wrote, "and I have the honor and satisfaction of herewith tendering to you their services."[20]

*Maj. Francis Landon and the other officers of the Seventh
offered themselves to former President Teddy Roosevelt's short-lived
all-volunteer division.* The Seventh Regiment Fund

Among the Greyjacket volunteers were Wade Hampton Hayes, a stockbroker and former Sunday editor of the New York *Tribune;* Byrd Wenman, former track star at Columbia University whose grandfather had helped found the New York Cotton Exchange; Arthur W. Little, a publishing executive who within a few weeks would be assigned to the Fifteenth Regiment that during the war earned the nickname "Harlem Hellfighters"; Ralph Polk Buell, a lawyer and veteran of the Spanish-American War; Claude G. Leland, the superintendent of libraries for the New York Board of Education; and young attorney Lyman C. Butler, whose father was president of the prestigious Lawyers' Club. Unfortunately for Butler, he later fell off the subway platform at Grand Central Station and was crushed by an express train.

Two days after his letter to the adjutant general, Landon contacted Colonel Roosevelt. The regiment was his, he told his old friend. His letter arrived about a week after a hastily organized upstate regiment from Orange County, calling itself the "Orange Blossoms" and made up mostly of men from the First New York Infantry that would later merge with the Seventh to form the 107th, had let the former president know it was also ready to serve in his volunteer division. With two New York regiments now at his beck and call, Roosevelt invited Landon to his home on Oyster Bay. On 25 April Landon, with a party of thirteen, including Hayes and Little, spent two hours with Roosevelt.[21] At the time there seemed to be a groundswell rising across the country in favor of Roosevelt's idea of a volunteer division. Newspapers predicted that within a week of recruiting, more than two hundred and fifty thousand men would volunteer. One of the first volunteers was Hailet Borrowe, the old Rough Rider and uncle of the recently slain André Chéronnet-Champollion. Former heavyweight champion John L. Sullivan wanted in. And so did two other boxing champions, Charles "Kid" McCoy and "Battling" Nelson.

In the meantime, Landon dreamt that Roosevelt's division would be formed, and his regiment would be a part of it. But on 22 June Roosevelt dashed that dream in a letter to Landon. Stating that President Woodrow Wilson was not about to allow him to a raise his division, he was releasing Landon and his men from their commitment to serve with him. He told Landon that he believed that if he could have had his own division, it would have equaled the record of his Rough Riders a "hundredfold."

"I regret from the standpoint of the country that your services were not utilized," Roosevelt added. "But the country has every reason to be proud of the zeal, patriotism and businesslike efficiency with which you came forward."[22] A similar letter was sent north to Newburgh, dashing also the dreams of the "Orange Blossoms."

As the war went on, Landon never got his regiment nor his colonelcy, and never got overseas. Instead, he served in an obscure office, shuffling papers.

Meanwhile, as the summer wore on, requests for transfers within the ranks of the Seventh washed across the desk of Colonel Fisk like an endless tidal wave. Working hard to keep the regiment together, he worried at the number of men who sought out military units that were sure bets to head overseas soon while his own cooled its heels—just as if it was 1898 all over again.

The *Gazette* kept publishing lists of those commissioned "graduates," as the editor labeled them, who had gone elsewhere. The list was impressive. Like in the Civil War, it was obvious that the Seventh was supplying more officers to the U.S. military than probably any other organization. Eventually, more than one thousand ex-Greyjackets served somewhere as officers. K Company alone provided over one hundred and twenty-five men—August Belmont, Wilmerding Biddle, Herbert Parsons, Schuyler and William Scheiffelin, Arthur Schermerhorn, John Suydam, and John Wickersham, to name a few of the more wealthy to leave the regiment. Cpl. Robert Patterson also left. In World War II, he served the nation as under secretary of war. Capt. Samuel T. Hubbard, president of the New York Cotton Exchange, was the intelligence officer on General Pershing's staff who on the eve of the Second Battle of the Marne warned that German troops were massing for a major attack. The French scoffed at Hubbard because he was an American. When the Germans did attack, it turned out to be one of the worst debacles of the war for the Allies. Other family names famous in New York history included A Company's Frank Totten, B Company's James and Philip Schuyler, G Company's George Delafield and Burgoyne Hamilton, and H Company's Ulysses S. Grant IV and George F. Pelham Jr.

As far as the 350 transfers to the Sixty-ninth were concerned, there was nothing for Colonel Fisk to do but turn them over to the Irish regiment.

The day and time for the transfer was 16 August at two-thirty in the afternoon. Those headed to their new outfit assembled for the last time in the armory's great drill shed on Park Avenue. Looking nervously at their comrades who would stay behind, they donned full field packs and shouldered their rifles. When Fisk gave the order to march out of the armory, the men bound for the Sixth-ninth took up the rear and followed the men staying with the Seventh down the steps and onto Park Avenue. Then the regimental band, led by bandmaster George Colyer, swinging his silver-topped baton with martial precision, ushered the entire contingent, over two thousand soldiers, southward. The line of march followed Fifth Avenue to Twenty-sixth Street.

At Twenty-sixth Street the men remaining with the Seventh suddenly parted, forming a line on both sides of the street. Rifles were brought up to present-arms. Fisk, his predecessor, Brig. Gen. Dan Appleton, and all his officers stood at attention, saluting the transfers as they passed by. At that moment, the Sixty-ninth Infantry band swung into view, playing its regimental tune, "Garry Owen." A reporter noted that the men were visibly affected. "The heavy packs and muskets which they carried seemed nothing as they straightened with pride and looked quickly with flushed and happy faces at Col. Fisk and his officers. It made the heartaches of separation seem worthwhile."[23] Among those men flushed with pride were Pfc. James G. duB. Tiffany of A Company; Privates Michael J. Shea and Michael Jr. of C Company; D Company's Private Philip Schuyler Finn, the son of the late "Battery Dan" Finn of Tammany Hall fame; and K Company's Pfc. Vanderbilt Ward, great-grandson of Commodore Vanderbilt.

The crowd by now had grown thick. The roar turned deafening as the two New York regiments merged on the city streets. Nearby, on the steps of the Sixty-ninth Regiment Armory on Lexington Avenue, Lieutenant Colonel Reed waited to greet the transfers. Inside, the armory was packed to the rafters. Men from the Sixty-ninth sat precariously on girders, overflowed the galleries above, and lined the walls of their drill hall four and five men deep. The moment the transfers marched through the front door, the greeting they received threatened to tear the roof of the armory.

Recalled Private O'Brien of B Company, "The meeting of the bands was the signal for vehement outburst at the doors of and within the armory. Bugle calls, band music and commands all were drowned in the friendly pandemonium which made the Seventh's men feel that long friendship between two regiments was cemented into a union which will carry the best traditions of two organizations into the trenches 'over there.'"

Red Ettinger, the volunteer from L Company, remembered that "wonderful day." "As we entered, those Irishers . . . gave us a rousing roar of welcome. Men were up in the balcony and hanging from the rafters, and they cheered and cheered, because we were the first troops from the other regiments in New York to make the transfer."[24]

Father Duffy recorded his thoughts on that momentous day. "Our

2,000 lined the walls and many perched themselves on the iron beams overhead. They cheered and cheered till the blare of the bands was unheard in the joyous din—till hearts beat so full and fast that they seemed too big for the ribs that confined them, till tears of emotion came, and something mystical was born in every breast—the soul of a Regiment. Heaven be good to the enemy when these cheering lads go forward together into battle."[25]

Watching the last of his fellow men from M Company disappear into the huge fortress, Sgt. John L. MacDonnell, a lawyer from Norwalk, Connecticut, felt a deep sorrow mingled with joy and tears. He knew that wherever they went their actions and deeds would reflect honor upon their mother company. "True soldiers every man of them. Ah, but more, they were our brothers."

First Sergeant Grimm of E Company also felt it was hard to see such good men go. "While we smiled as much as possible, it did not relieve the sorrow we felt in our hearts. We know that they will be a credit to their old company, and trust that they'll not forget us, and here's hoping we will all meet again in Paris."

CHAPTER 2

The Regiment ...
Has Always Done Its Duty,
and It Always Will

At precisely seven A.M. on Monday, 5 June, two months before the Seventh transferred its men over to the Fighting Sixty-ninth, bells and whistles rang out in New York harbor and city church bells tolled, signaling the start of National Registration Day. From Manhattan's Battery Park to San Francisco Bay, men between the ages of twenty-one and thirty were ordered to register for the draft. Three weeks earlier Congress had passed the draft act. "It is not an army that we must shape and train for war, it is a nation," President Woodrow Wilson stated (*New York Times*, June 6, 1917). In New York, the first day of the workweek felt more like a carnival than another day of drudgery. On almost every block were places of registration, with booths setup in shoeshine shops and barbershops, schools and armories. Men brought their families with them as if on a picnic, as they stood in line to register.

In churches and schools and public parks, orators whipped citizens into patriotic fervor. The evangelist Billy Sunday told a throng of four thousand that the "reason there is not peace on earth and goodwill toward men is that if hell were turned upside down you would find 'Made in Germany' stamped on the bottom of it" (*New York Times*, June 6, 1917).

The able-bodied men in the crowd who had already registered for the draft were then asked to stand. An estimated one thousand rose to their feet. A lusty cheer went up from those remaining in their seats.

Not all festivities were for purely patriotic reasons. Some ten thousand followers of the sport of kings took the day off to play the horses at Belmont Park. The steel girders holding up the stands of the Polo Grounds, designed for fifty-six thousand people, felt the weight of eighty thousand fans packed in like sardines to watch the Yankees take on Ty Cobb and his Detroit Tigers in a doubleheader. At the time, it was the largest crowd to ever watch an American League game in New York. The cantankerous Cobb feasted on the circus atmosphere of the crowd. In the second game he slammed two triples and a double and beat out a pair of bunts for singles.[1]

On the darker side, the National Guard and police were mobilized to put down any expected trouble from anarchists or socialists. A contingent of Seventh men was ordered to stay in the armory, just in case. The *Gazette* recorded in its July number that "our enemies . . . whispered in our ears just what we might expect to get mixed in upon that day." As it turned out, there was very little trouble throughout the city. Two Italians from the Bronx were arrested while trying to be the first to register for the draft by forcing their way to the head of the line. A Columbia University student, opposed to conscription because, as he put it, he was a moral and physical coward, refused to sign up. At midnight, police dutifully arrested him.[2]

All across the country, an estimated ten million men registered for the draft. In New York, nearly six hundred thousand enrolled.

At the Seventh Regiment Armory on Park Avenue the atmosphere was more subdued on Registration Day, in keeping with the quiet reserve of silk stocking soldiers. Still, there was a festiveness that went on inside the great drill hall.

Using Registration Day to recruit, the Greyjackets wanted to bolster their ranks by more than four hundred men. But they had to be the right men. In notices circulated within the armory, old-time veterans and ex-members of the regiment were called upon to go out and find unmarried men between the ages of eighteen and twenty-five. "You know the kind of men to propose," the notice warned. Another circular read: "It is desired that a special effort be made at this time to secure the required number from young men of spirit, character, social position and physical development, and concerted action to this end is urged."[3]

K Company, manned by millionaires, camped out at the university clubs and even traveled to Harvard, Princeton, and Yale, and the more prestigious preparatory schools, among them St. Mark's and St. Paul's, to find the right men. Rye, New York, resident, Vanderbilt Ward, the great-grandson of Commodore Vanderbilt and cousin to both the Cornelius Vanderbilts, father and son, who would serve in the Twenty-seventh Division, did his share of recruiting at his alma maters, St. Paul's and Yale.

In the meantime, the armory opened its foot-thick, oaken door at ten A.M. on Monday to let in prospective recruits. They were interviewed, examined by regimental doctors, and, if they fit the bill, invited to enlist. Many of the prospects carried slips of paper, addressed to the recruiting officer and signed by veterans of the Seventh that recommended them as "desirable recruits." In the afternoon, "ladies of the families of veterans" arrived, giving the armory a homey feeling. They served light refreshments to the young men in the third-floor mess hall. Afterward, in the drill hall, a two-hour concert by the regimental band was held. When the concert ended, the band played on so everyone could then dance.

"Ain't it a grand and glorious feelin' to go 'round that drill floor with a fair one on your arm," Pfc. Edward G. Bradford, a budding young stockbroker and direct descendant of the governor of Plymouth Colony, William Bradford, later wrote in the *Gazette*, "and the band playing a snappy one-step!"

At the end of the day, two hundred recruits signed on.

Among new enlistees that spring and summer were Arthur Briggs Church, John Howell Westcott Jr., and Ulysses S. Grant IV. Church and Westcott, like Bradford, traced their families back to Plymouth Rock. Westcott, on his mother's side, was descended from John and Priscilla Alden. Grant, of course, was the grandson of the president and Civil War general. His fellow Greyjackets called him "Useless." Another recruit was William A. Leonard, city editor of the Flushing *Daily Times*, who'd been endorsed by the librarian Claude Leland, I Company sergeant. Billy, however, didn't own the pedigree of a Church, a Westcott, or a

Grant. His father, who died in 1912, had been deputy sheriff and jailer of Queens County.

Twenty-six years old, Billy was blessed with big round eyes that blazed with a quick wit and self-deprecating humor and that mesmerized just about anyone who looked into his handsome face. A friend said that he was one of those people who radiate that something that just couldn't help being felt.

Unlike Westcott, still a student at Princeton, or Grant, a stockbroker for Pierpont Morgan and a Harvard graduate, Leonard had gotten only as far as St. Michael's parochial grammar school. As far as he was concerned, that was the end of his formal education. At fourteen, he needed to earn a few dollars so he could help put food on the family table, where at meal time his ailing father, his mother, three brothers, and five sisters crowded around. So in 1903 Billy walked into the offices of the *Daily Times*

The most popular soldier in the regiment was Flushing native
Billy Leonard.   The Seventh Regiment Fund

and asked the owner for a job. He said he'd do anything—sweep floors, deliver newspapers. Anything!

"He didn't have much in the way of schooling," offered a fellow newspaperman in a sketch about Leonard that appeared in the Flushing *Daily Times.* "But he had a keen, adaptable brain and in the days when other boys were playing and frittering away their time, Leonard was seeing and working and learning, and before he attained his majority, he had earned the reputation of being one of the most promising young newspaper men in the Queens county field."

When he wasn't at the editorial offices of the *Daily Times,* he held court at Mattie Roberts's Little Brown Shop in Flushing. His circle of friends included the humorist Ellis Parker Butler, whose book *Pigs Is Pigs* was a roaring success for more than three decades; Queens Magistrate John Kochendorfer, a former New York City alderman; and Sergeant Leland.

Leonard's friendship with Leland, who was eight years his senior, extended beyond the Little Brown Shop to their love of books and writing and their love of the water, which they shared as members of the Bayside Yacht Club. Because America was at war, Leland wore his uniform on many occasions. The sight of the librarian dressed in khaki, coupled with his tales of the Mexican border, where in 1916 the Seventh stood ready in McAllen, Texas, while Pershing's forces chased Pancho Villa and his army of bandits, stoked Leonard's patriotic fire. He loved listening to Leland, a born storyteller. And through the telling of those stories, Leonard learned that behind his friend's bookish bearing lurked the heart of a true soldier.

Hearing that former president Teddy Roosevelt was a raising a volunteer division, Billy wrote the colonel. The idea of another outfit of Rough Riders thrilled the romantic newspaper editor. He wanted in. But his letters to Roosevelt went unanswered. It wasn't long before he found out why. President Wilson opposed Roosevelt's idea and by the middle of May, the groundswell for the all-volunteer division that had rolled through Congress ebbed in favor of the draft. Then on 18 May Wilson signed the national draft act, killing Roosevelt's bid for military glory. With its death went Leonard's chance to be a modern-day Rough Rider.

As Registration Day neared, Billy lunched with his companions at the

Little Brown Shop. His big, boyish eyes flashed. "Fellas," he said, "I'm going to enlist! I can't stand it any longer! We've got to get in there and give the Kaiser and his whole crowd the beating of their lives!"[4]

It wasn't long after that Billy headed for Manhattan. The train ride from Flushing to Pennsylvania Station took eighteen minutes. The trip uptown to Sixty-sixth Street and Park Avenue took longer. Heedless of the light, sporadic rain that spattered the sidewalk, and the noisy Monday traffic made noisier and more frenetic by the crowded registration booths and recruiting stations that lined his route and tempted him like sirens, Billy felt the flush of excitement. The army was out in full force, and so were the marines and navy. Officers from the Twelfth and Fourteenth National Guard Regiments and the Second Artillery staked out Fifth Avenue, counting on shaming the men of New York to avoid the draft altogether and sign up in one of their outfits.

Billy's heart was set on the Seventh, although he knew that the Silk Stocking Regiment had a snobby habit of selecting its own. In fact, to ensure they got into the Seventh, some potential soldiers paid for the privilege. But on this day it had opened the doors of its swanky Park Avenue armory to almost any man privileged or daring enough to step through the imposing portal and into a realm of rare regimental wealth and privilege. Billy mounted the thick stone steps leading into the armory that his friend Ellis Parker Butler warned was nothing more than a "stuffy place." Taking a deep breath, the jailer's son entered the cavernous stronghold, perhaps wondering, in spite of his friendship with Sergeant Leland, if an uneducated newspaperman like himself, growing up on the other side of the East River, away from the glitter of Manhattan, could ever fit in with the moneyed flock of blue bloods from the Seventh. Inside, the armory gave off an aura of hushed richness that to Billy seemed alien to his perception of a military fortress. The paneled walls held many portraits of notable men of the Seventh, a miniature Metropolitan Museum of Art. Ahead of him two sets of stairs swept down from the floors above, each hugging the outer walls before turning inward, where they merged together. Here the stairs became wide enough to allow eight men to march abreast as they descended from their company rooms on the second floor. Beyond the stairs was the impressive drill shed. Echoing voices from inside drew Leonard to the massive enclosure. Tables were set up. And behind each table sat uniformed officers. Standing in front were civilians, talking earnestly with the officers, signing papers, and looking nervous.

Walking up to one of the officers, Billy said that he wanted to enlist in I Company, that he knew its sergeant, Claude Leland. The officer nodded and directed him to a table where the officer there would take care of him. Leonard went over to the table. The officer, wearing captain's bars, introduced himself in a Virginia drawl as Wade Hampton Hayes, the former Sunday editor of the New York *Tribune*. Although Hayes had recently left his editorial post to be an investment banker, Leonard, as city editor of the Flushing *Times*, felt a sudden kinship with the ex-newspaperman. He signed on as a private.

Leaving the armory, Leonard undoubtedly paused briefly just inside the door. Outside, the rain had stopped. The skies had cleared. As his heart beat faster, he believed he had done the right thing. He then marched down the steps, his eyes wide with expectation, and headed into the newly minted summer sun that lit New York's Upper East Side with its own brand of gold. He was no longer a free man, but a soldier now owing his allegiance to others and to his country's flag. There was no doubt that, as he later confessed to Butler, "I am prepared to give all—if it is required of me."[5]

Raeburn Van Buren, a distant relative of the eighth president of the United States, was just beginning to make it in the big city and, therefore, was a reluctant recruit. Like Leonard, Van was a newspaperman—an ex-newspaperman, actually—who didn't string words together but was a sketch artist. He'd come from Missouri in 1913, after a four-year apprenticeship on the *Kansas City Star*, to be a magazine illustrator.

A bashful redhead with a face full of freckles, Van Buren hid from his mother, a Christian Science practitioner, the fact that he smoked and knocked back an occasional highball. He owned a wonderful sense of humor that would serve him well during the war. His gag drawings appeared regularly in the humor magazines of the day. He was also a leading contributor to *Photoplay*. Yet he hadn't cracked the big time, and that meant seeing his work in the pages of the *Saturday Evening Post* or *Collier's*, even though he knew the managing editor of *Collier's*, Charles Phelps Cushing, former reporter at the *Kansas City Star*. For months, even before

Illustrator Raeburn Van Buren was persuaded to join the Seventh by the managing editor of Collier's, *Charles Phelps Cushing.* Author's Collection

America had declared war on Germany, Cushing kept urging Van to enlist in the National Guard. But the redhead wasn't ready. He could feel his big breakthrough coming. And besides the life of a Bohemian was too exciting to give up just yet.

"This city is full of artists and they seem to be able to understand each other better than any other clan," he once explained in a letter to his girlfriend back in Kansas City, a dark-haired beauty named Fern Ringo. "I have drifted into this bunch and have found most of them very broad minded. Out of this mess I have selected a few for friends and so far have found them to be just the kind of people I have wanted to associate with all my life. We have dinners together, take short trips together, work together, dance together and get along fine. Some of these people are singers, some musicians and some are ink and paint twisters like myself."[6]

Van's closest friends in this "clan" were the artist Thomas Hart Benton, the actor William Powell, and Ralph Barton, later famous as one of the leading caricaturists of the Jazz Age. The four of them, all Missourians, shared a studio in a rundown apartment building at West Sixty-fifth Street and Broadway called the Lincoln Square Arcade. Rats scurried loudly in the rafters overhead. The building itself teemed with "old ladies and their pet parrots." The starving artists shared food, models, and their Missouri background. It seemed that Benton's grandfather, the famous Missouri senator with the same name, killed one of Barton's relatives in a duel. In their high school days in Kansas City, Barton had stolen away Powell's girlfriend.

Living above Van in another decrepit apartment was Neysa McMein, struggling as hard as the men to make it as an artist. Although Van loved Fern Ringo, his hometown girl, he was swept away by this free spirit from Quincy, Illinois. Her biographer described her as a "tall, lithe beauty," who at the time was gaining "something of a reputation as a siren in New York's more sophisticated and bohemian circles." She had a "softness in her manner and calmness in her person which many men found very reassuring."[7]

Van couldn't help himself. In letters to Fern, he constantly talked about McMein. "Miss McMein, an artist with a studio on the second floor, was kind enough to pose for me this evening," he wrote in one letter. In another, "McMein is having trouble making good pictures." Whenever she wanted Van, Neysa would stamp her foot on the floor, and he would answer by scaling the fire escape to her apartment. She introduced him to her crowd, which included the critic of the *Times*, Alexander Woollcott, and the columnist Franklin Pierce Adams.[8]

But then the day came when McMein's trouble in making good pictures ended. She hit it big, becoming the almost exclusive illustrator of covers for *McCall's* magazine. She also worked for the *Saturday Evening Post*. With a steady income, she soon moved out of the Lincoln Square Arcade to the more posh Shropshire apartments. It was time, too, for the others to seek fortunes elsewhere. Barton took off for Paris. Powell traveled with a short-lived stock company, always borrowing money from Van as he headed out the door and never repaying him when he returned. Then he ran off and married one of his traveling costars and never returned. Benton found the Lincoln Square Arcade too expensive and took up quarters in an even cheaper place closer to Broadway. Van suddenly was alone with those old ladies and their parrots.

Still the Bohemian life beckoned. He visited Neysa often at her new

The free-spirited Neysa McMein.   Author's Collection

studio apartment, which was gaining a reputation as a salon. Here she ruled, wearing a paint-smeared smock. There were also the transplanted men of the *Star* to hang out with at Jensen's chop house—Lauren Stout, another illustrator; the poet Charles Edson, who one day would write a paean to Kansas City that is recited to this day; and, of course, Charles Phelps Cushing.

The managing editor of *Collier's* was unrelenting in his efforts to get Van and Stout to enlist. Finally the two illustrators gave in. Armed with letters of recommendation from Cushing, they marched over to Park Avenue and joined E Company.

"I suppose you have heard the big news about my enlisting," Van scratched out in a letter to his grandparents. "Yes, the thing is done and I am now a proud soldier in the 7th Regiment, N.Y. I am happy now and satisfied that I have done the best and only thing for a real man to do. I have on my uniform and have had it on for about four days. It feels good and the thrill I get out of it is the thrill that comes once in a lifetime."

Maj. Robert Mazet tried to bust Tammany Hall at the turn of the century when he was a New York assemblyman and a young commander of the Seventh's L Company. He almost succeeded. His powerful Mazet Committee dealt a blow to Squire Richard Croker, Tammany's two-fisted boss, from which he never recovered. Dethroned in 1902, Croker was replaced by Charles Francis Murphy. However, before he skipped town he got in one last lick. He waged a down and dirty street brawl to oust the Republican from his assembly seat in Manhattan's Nineteenth District. His tactics paid off. Mazet was knocked out of the state legislature, where he had done the most damage to Tammany Hall. Feeling vindicated, Croker called the election a revolt against "Mazetism." Satisfied, he sailed off in self-exile to Ireland.

Now, as the Seventh's ranks began to swell in the spring and summer of 1917, Mazet had to put up with the sons of the very same Tammany sachems he had battled tooth and nail a generation earlier.

The first of the sons to enlist was Morgan Smiley Baldwin, whose father, Arthur, was private counsel to Boss Murphy. Morgan wanted to follow in the footsteps of his father and uncle, two of the most effective corporate lawyers in the country. But the war got in the way. In fact, when he finished his studies at Columbia Law School in 1917, instead of sitting for the bar examination, he joined C Company as a private. Arthur approved, as did Uncle Leonard and the New York State appellate division. In a special session, the appellate division waived its entrance requirements for Morgan and admitted him into the legal world as a full-fledged attorney. It was a gesture that in all likelihood was done because of who his father was.

Another son of a Tammany Hall sachem was Philip Schuyler Finn. His father, a native of Limerick, Ireland, was "Battery Dan" Finn, the colorful and adored leader of the First Assembly District. He was a Civil War veteran and saloonkeeper. As city magistrate, appointed to the post in 1905 by Boss Murphy's handpicked mayor, George McClellan Jr., "Battery Dan" always reached out to the poor people of his district in a way that created good copy for the city's newshounds. He died in 1910. At his wake at the Finn home on Broome Street, rich and poor alike passed by his coffin by the hundreds. Perhaps the most touching moment came when five Italian boys, all bootblacks, placed a small wreath at the foot of the open coffin.[9] The boys then knelt and prayed before they were led away weeping. "Battery Dan," it is most certain, would have wanted his son Philip to enlist in the Fighting Sixty-ninth, the Irish regiment. Not the Silk Stocking Seventh. But Philip picked the uptown regiment—as far from his roots at the southern tip of Manhattan as the moon. Yet even in death, the old magistrate must have had some influence left with Tammany Hall. When it came time to pick men from the Seventh who were to transfer to the Sixty-ninth, among the chosen was young Philip Finn.

Although there's no record, Major Mazet, representing the Republican wing of the Seventh, probably wondered in dismay at the changes wrought within the regiment by the Great War. Was there no justice? Now this old foe of Tammany Hall had to break bread with the sons and the associates of his sworn political enemies.

If ever a family held the "social position" the Seventh sought, it was the Rhinelanders. One of the richest clans in the country, the Rhinelanders were connected by blood or marriage to almost every moneyed family in New York City and environs. Only the Astors owned more Manhattan real estate. Edith Wharton, a Rhinelander, wrote about the exclusive circles in which her kin moved in her short stories and novels such as *The*

House of Mirth and *The Age of Innocence*. In 1895, when the famed social secretary of Manhattan's elite "four hundred" (the number of people who
could fit comfortably into Mrs. William Astor's ballroom), died, the bon
vivants of Fifth Avenue gossiped about who would—or should—take
Ward McAllister's place. At the top of the list was Maj. T. J. Oakley
Rhinelander of the Seventh. "Is there another who can reign as censor of
the social prestige," asked the *Morning Journal* upon the death of McAllister? After it "sounded society's opinion," the newspaper came up with
two possibilities: Oakley and his dashing cousin Lispenard Stewart.[10]

Oakley Rhinelander and brother Philip, seven years his junior and
also a major in the Seventh, had been connected to the regiment since before they enlisted in K Company in the early 1880s. Their father, William,
a real-estate tycoon, had answered the call for help that the Seventh sent
to wealthy merchants of New York to donate money for the construction
of a new palatial uptown armory when it was decided that the regiment
had to move out of its cramped quarters at the Tompkins Square Market
Armory. William's family history in New York dated to the mid-1600s
and boasted as kin Benjamin Franklin; Alexander Hamilton; two mayors
of New York; a mayor of Bristol, England; and the eminent jurist Thomas
Jackson Oakley. The Rhinelanders held leases on Trinity Church, owned
huge swathes of property along the waterfront, and were among the first
settlers of Washington Square. In fact, the Rhinelanders financed the
building of the Washington Square arch, designed by Stanford White. In
the 1870s William Rhinelander joined city leaders John Jacob Astor, William Henry Vanderbilt, department store king Alexander T. Stewart,
and others, in giving generously to the building of the Seventh Regiment Armory.[11]

A few years after the new armory opened on 17 November 1879,
Oakley (named for his grandfather, Thomas Jackson Oakley) and Philip
enlisted in K Company. It was the right place for them. Counted as members of this elite unit at the time were Archibald Gracie (Gracie Mansion); Alexander S. Webb Jr., married to Eliza Vanderbilt, daughter of
William Henry Vanderbilt; the financier Edward H. Harriman (father
of W. Averell Harriman) and his cousin J. W. Harriman; Elliott Roosevelt; Philip, Robert, and William Livingston; Maunsell, Stephen, and
Cortland Schuyler Van Rensselaer; and the Frothinghams, Schermerhorns, Schieffelins, and Wainwrights.

After the death of their father in 1908, Oakley took over the Rhine-lander Real Estate Company by default. That right ought to have been passed down to the eldest son, William. But he committed a grievous sin when, in 1884, he ran off with the family's comely chambermaid, Maggie McGinnis. For that, he was disinherited by his father and, worse, his name stricken from family records. Thus son number two headed the family business, with Philip second in command. By this time, a new gen-eration of Rhinelander boys was waiting in the gilded wings to enter the world of real estate and don the Greyjackets of the dandy Seventh. They were Philip II, the only son of Oakley, and Philip Kip and T. J. Oakley, sons of Philip.

In 1916, when the Seventh was mobilized for duty along the Rio Grande to keep Pancho Villa's Mexican mob from raiding Texas, K Company was home to four Rhinelanders. A fifth Rhinelander, however, did not join the elite company. Philip Newbold Rhinelander, son of Thomas Newbold Rhinelander and Edith Wharton's favorite cousin, went overseas the summer of 1916 as an ambulance driver. Later, when the United States entered the war, he stayed in France as a pilot. In Sep-tember 1918 he was killed in aerial combat over enemy lines. By the time the youngest Rhinelanders enlisted in the Seventh, the aging Oakley had retired. His brother Philip stayed on—joined by Philip II, Philip Kip, and T. J. Oakley, who, like his uncle, was now called Oakley. Although he was in his fifties, the elder Philip needed to keep busy because remaining in the Seventh was the best remedy to combat the grief he felt by the sud-den loss of his wife. The year before, in a rented cottage in Tuxedo, New York, Adelaide Kip Rhinelander, mother of Philip Kip and T. J. Oakley, burned to death when a dressing lamp exploded while she was combing her hair. Blazing liquid fuel showered her gown, engulfing her in flames. Another tragedy would hit the elder Philip in 1918, but that's getting ahead of the story.

In the interim, all three boys went to Texas. Before shipping out, Philip II hastily married Miss Le Brun Parsons in a private ceremony in early May at her family home at 126 East Seventy-third Street. A large wedding had been planned for June and invitations sent out. In the hurry-up ceremony, there was no best man or maid of honor. Only the parents of the couple and Uncle Philip witnessed their vows. At about this time, Oakley, a freshman at Harvard, Class of 1920, decided it was his place to

*Pfc. Alexander Van Rensselaer (front) is seen here with his fellow
"Border Rats" while stationed along the Rio Grande in 1916.
The others are unknown.*   Van Rensselaer family

be on the Mexican border with his newly wedded cousin and older brother. The seventeen-year-old dropped out of the university. He never went back.

The crisis along the Mexican border, coming amidst the growing mood to wage war on Germany, or at least to prepare for it, led in 1915 and 1916 to a surge in enlistments for the Seventh. Among this new band of New Yorkers, dubbed "Border Rats," were brothers Alexander and Arthur

RIGHT: *First Lt. Kenneth Gow,*
the spiritual leader of the "Jersey Gunners."
The Seventh Regiment Fund

BELOW: *Billy Tailer transferred out of*
the Seventh to become a flyer in the famous
Lafayette Escadrille. Bryant Library
History Collection (Roslyn, N.Y.)

Van Rensselaer, Kenneth Gow, William Hallet Tailer, and Scott Harrison Lytle.

The Van Rensselaers didn't have the kind of wealth that set the Rhinelanders apart from even their own fellow soldiers in K Company. But they had the name. And they had the lineage. The land on which Albany, the state capital, was built had once belonged to their family. Rensselaer County was named after them. The Van Rensselaer's came from a long line of soldiers, and it was a badge of honor for them to carry on that tradition. There were generals and majors, veterans of the French and Indian War, the Revolutionary War, and the Civil War. Gen. Steven Van Rensselaer III was the brother-in-law of Alexander Hamilton and the son-in-law of Philip Livingston, a signer of the Declaration of Independence. Van Rensselaers had served in the Seventh Regiment since before the Civil War. Alexander and Arthur's father, Maunsell Van Rensselaer II, enlisted in K Company in 1881. Three years later, cousin Cortland Schuyler Van Rensselaer joined him.[12]

Of course, the brothers had to carry on the family's military tradition. To do anything else was out of the question. They enlisted as privates in K Company. When he signed on, Alex was on the editorial staff of the *New York Sun*. Arthur, three years older and a Harvard graduate, was a mining engineer.

Kenneth Gow hailed from Summit, New Jersey, a beautiful turn-of-the-century health resort and silk-manufacturing town on the Passaic River, where many wealthy New Yorkers resided in the summer months.

Gow's family, not as illustrious as the Rhinelanders or the Van Rensselaers, had emigrated from Scotland. When he volunteered on 16 May 1916, at age twenty-five, Kenneth, who was in constant need of glasses to see his way about, was salesman for the William G. Hewitt Press in Brooklyn. A choirboy in the Calvary Episcopal Church, he was one of many residents from Summit who eventually enlisted in the Seventh. The church's rector, Rev. Walker Gwynne, remembered Gow as "a little singing boy, always reverent, always happy, always straightforward and manly." He said that "as boy and man [Kenneth] loved to sing God's praises. Long after his boyhood days, year after year, he would come back to sing in his old place and in the service which he loved, and always there was the same warm smile of greeting and the same strong hand-clasp that was ever genuine and true."[13]

William Tailer, however, was more like the Rhinelanders and Van Rensselaers. Handsome, blond, with a cherubic face, descended from an old New York family, he first enlisted in F Company. By the time the regiment departed for the Mexican border, he had transferred to the Machine Gun Company. His father, Henry Pennington Tailer, was a wealthy stockbroker and owned a large slice of land bordering Hempstead harbor in the town of Roslyn, Long Island, New York. The house where they lived was once described as Roslyn's "show home."[14] William worked in his father's brokerage firm.

Gow, much taken by Tailer's background, wrote to his family from Texas about his new friend with whom he shared a tent. "You ask me who the fellow is in the picture with me. His name is W. H. Tailer, of a prominent N.Y. family. He is a descendant of the first governor-general, or whatever he was called, of the territory which now comprises the New England states, whose name was the same as his (William Tailer) appointed by the King of England."

Scott Harrison Lytle, as his middle name suggests, was related to President Benjamin Harrison. His step-grandfather was Harrison's brother. A Princeton man, Scott buried himself in the Seventh Regiment, trying to put behind a tragedy that left him mired in dark depression. The summer Scott graduated from Princeton, in 1911, his mother, Mary Elizabeth Arnold Lytle, thinking she was biting into a piece of candy, accidentally ate a tablet of rat poison. It was Scott who had left the poison out on the kitchen counter. When his father, Dr. Richard Ridgeley Lytle, a diagnostician of contagious diseases for the New York Board of Health, returned home that night he found his wife near death. Efforts to save her failed. The loss of his mother overwhelmed Scott. For almost a year, the dazed son, certain her death was his fault, dragged himself through the motions of his job as a clerk for the Western Union Telegraph Company. With each passing day, he sank into deeper fits of depression.[15] On 8 March 1912, in his own apartment at 319 West Ninety-ninth Street, perhaps to atone, he poisoned himself. Only a chance visit by his sister, Sophie, engaged to marry the Rev. Roscoe Conkling Hatch, later the Episcopal chaplain for the Fighting Sixty-ninth, saved Scott's life. She found him "lying on the bed in a paroxysm," reported the *New York Sun*. Frantically, she summoned the nearest doctor. It took the physician an hour, but he finally revived Scott enough to walk him to a waiting ambulance. "The young man was taken to the hospital," wrote the reporter for the *Sun*, "a prisoner charged with attempted suicide."[16]

Enlistment in the Seventh and then the trip to the Mexican border as a private with H Company seemed to be the right antidote. At least his brother Ridgeley, an Episcopal minister, thought so. For one thing, the life of a soldier took his mind off his own troubles. And now in the hot, swirling sand of southeast Texas, there was Pancho Villa to worry about.

Serving near the cowtown of McAllen, sprawled across the Rio Grande from Reynosa, Mexico, turned out to be an exercise in futility for the Seventh and the other regiments, including the Sixty-ninth, that made up the Sixth New York Division. The soldiers marched a lot, rode horses, and practiced their rifle marksmanship, firing bullets across the river at cactus plants and sagebrush. Saloons were off limits. It was a hot, thirsty, weary time waiting for Pancho Villa and his band of cutthroats to show their ugly faces. As it turned out, the only punitive action for the Seventh was killing rattlesnakes and scorpions. So plentiful were the snakes that the division named its new magazine *The Rio Grande Rattler.*

Pvt. Alex Van Rensselaer remembered the weather. "This is the land of opposites, extremes, impossibilities, and Mexicans. Here the grass is brown instead of green, and man wears an overcoat when the thermometer registers 60 degrees. You can't go swimming because the sun will blister your back. When it is dry the roads are hard as rocks, dry as fire, and dusty as pepper, but the touch of a drop of water is like the touch of a magician's wand and the hot, dusty rock-hard road turns into a mire of cement."

To his "Mama, and Pop and family," the bespectacled Gow provided assurances not to worry about his health. "We have some of the most prominent doctors and surgeons in New York down with us, besides a very efficient hospital corps, with three dentists. The men who have been bothered the most are the ones who have been drinking pop and the rest of the slop that is sold just outside the picket lines and in town."

The corps of prominent New York doctors and surgeons that Gow described proved worthless to some of the soldiers. Three died. One of them, H Company's 1st Sgt. George H. Chichester, in private life an architect, was struck down by disease. Maj. Dewitt Clinton Falls, whose long career had ushered him into the halls of power both in the United States and Great Britain, was stricken with an illness the physicians failed to treat properly so that upon the regiment's return he was forced to transfer to the reserve list. Pvt. Arthur Van Rensselaer's sickness was more severe; his treatment unforgivable. To the New York *Post* he bitterly related what had happened.

"After a long march in blazing heat I was completely paralyzed with the exception of my arms and shoulders. This happened in September at McAllen and I was sent back to the base Hospital in San Antonio. There the doctors told me that my only hope was to get a discharge from the service and go back East to be treated by specialists. I was held for a month until strong enough to stand the journey and then was shipped to New York.

"There I was a helpless cripple, left without any Government support whatsoever to fish for my self."[17]

Arthur never recovered. He remained paralyzed all his life. But his fertile mind refused to give in. Six years after his illness he invented the electric wheelchair, a three-wheeler that was referred to as an auto for the legless. Although Arthur's ailment was bad enough—he couldn't get out of bed for two years—brother Alex was in for it, too. He was turning deaf. Now that one of the Van Rensselaers was suddenly unable to carry on their family's noble military tradition, Alex feared he'd make it two. And with the United States soon to be engulfed in the Great War, he wasn't about to give in—even if his hearing was shot. No one was going to call him a slacker.

After the five-month-long ineffectual expedition to the Mexican border and soon after the urgent and excited atmosphere of National Registration Day, the days and weeks that followed in the spring and summer of 1917 seemed to drag on, even as more and more eager recruits poured into the Seventh Regiment Armory. Like Alex Van Rensselaer, none of them wanted to be labeled slackers. It was a good lot, and Col. Willard

Fisk felt satisfied. Training turned serious. Veterans and recruits alike drilled daily in Central Park's Sheep Meadow. They marched into the upper reaches of Manhattan and Harlem, fully uniformed, armed, and loaded down with field packs. Each day their treks grew longer. Their bodies hardened.

Pfc. John S. Slattery of L Company noted, "At nine every morning we hustle over to the park and proceed to trample down any fresh blades of grass that may have had the courage to raise their tender shoots to the morning sun. A group of animals which we had relieved on the detail huddle in the corner of the field and make sheep's eyes at us."

Pvt. Eugene J. O'Brien of B Company, a city newspaperman, was willing to wager a month's salary that every man in his company "can draw a correct map of Central Park with his eyes shut."

To Pvt. Red Ettinger, before his transfer to the Sixty-ninth, drilling at Central Park was a picnic. "We took every opportunity to wave at the pretty girls sitting on the park benches—we had regular cheering sections—and during the lunch hour, we'd make dates for the evening."[18]

Pvt. Billy Leonard, the Flushing journalist, reported, "To the daily grind of drill and setting-up exercises an interesting feature was added. ... A. B. Shore, who is an expert in bayonet work, instructed the company in the bayonet drill, and the men are rapidly becoming proficient in this supremely important branch of modern infantry work."

Drills also meant guard duty. Every night the armory was cordoned off. All the military rituals of performing this task were adhered to in the strictest sense, although any curious civilian pedestrian might have thought otherwise. "Every night," explained I Company Sergeant Edward Harrah, "one man is detailed to simulate a mule wandering from the picket line, an essential step in the process of hardening, while some one else represents the sentry of another outfit and exchanges adverse comments with the neighboring post. The instruction has been practical as well as theoretical."

Even the Seventh's most famous soldier pulled guard duty. "Dear Brat," Joyce Kilmer wrote to his mother, a term of endearment that she loved, "For the last twenty-four hours I've been on guard duty—two hours on and four hours off. By the way, I'm supposed, you know, to have become much thinner since I joined the army. Well, I got weighed yesterday and the scales showed 178 pounds—only two pounds less than I weighed last winter! So either I've not lost fat or I've gained muscle."[19]

The troops were ordered to stay overnight in the armory, unless they lived close enough so that they could go home. Joyce always went home to Larchmont. He had good reason. His daughter Rose was dying of infantile paralysis. Joyce, meanwhile, continued his role as literary critic for the *Times* and found time to lunch at least once a week with his adoring mother. Raeburn Van Buren spent nights at his Lincoln Arcade apartment, eventually subletting it to a friend for the duration of the war. In the meantime, a regular barracks was set up on the roof at the armory. If the boys couldn't spend the night in their company rooms on the second floor, they bunked beneath the summer stars, while in the streets below the hustle and bustle of the city sang them to sleep.

"An odd lot of soldiers—odd because they thoroughly enjoyed the experience," regimental supply Sergeant Gerald Jacobson said of the roof dwellers.

With the Seventh readying itself for war, weddings were hurried up. One of the most celebrated took place at St. Thomas's Church on Fifth Avenue, when Lt. Philip Kip Rhinelander wed Miss Helen Alexander, daughter of attorney Henry Alexander. Philip's cousin, the Rev. Philip Mercer Rhinelander, the Episcopal bishop of Pennsylvania, and the Rev. Howard C. Robbins, the dean of the Cathedral of St. John the Divine, performed the ceremony. Walton Oakley, another cousin just back from the Plattsburgh Officer's School, served as best man. Ushers were cousins Philip Rhinelander and Lathrop Weld, whose father was president of the New York Cotton Exchange.

Finally, on 9 September, almost a month after 350 of its men had been sent over to the Sixty-ninth, the Seventh received its marching orders. Since war had been declared back in April, five months had groaned by. The orders called for the Seventh to depart New York City in two days for training at Camp Wadsworth in Spartanburg, South Carolina. Leaves were canceled. There were no more nights at home. The men were confined to the armory. Families were not allowed in, unless by special pass—and then they could only visit with their loved ones in the confines of the first-floor Veterans Room.

By this time, Joyce Kilmer had already said his good-byes to his family and to the regiment. His transfer to the Sixty-ninth, promised by Father Francis Duffy, had come through at last. As soon as Kilmer joined the ranks of the Irish regiment at Camp Mills in Mineola, New York, the poet confessed in a letter to a friend that what he liked best were the "wild Irish—boys eighteen and twenty who left Ireland a few years ago, some of them to escape threatened conscription, and traveled about the country in gangs, generally working on the railroads. They have delightful songs that have never been written down, but sung in vagabond camps and country jails." The day the Sixty-ninth pulled out of Camp Mills, Joyce's wife, Aline, and mother, Annie, were there to see him off.

The friction between the two women over his affections was extraordinary. In a tribute to her son, Annie chronicled that "fateful day" when she saw him for the last time. "His wife was there that day also, and as he bid us good-bye I kissed him and said to his wife, 'Aline, you may kiss him last.' I felt it was her right, although only God knew how hard it was for me to do it!" Later, she wrote, "He kissed me as had been his custom for many years, first on the mouth and then on the left cheek—always that cheek! Then I got in the car. He kissed Aline, and she got in beside me; as we were taking her to the 42nd Street Station. He stood at the window of the car. I can see him so plainly as I write! His dear brown eyes looked so steadily in mine—then his wife—but last, at me, thank God!"

That look Annie never forgot. It sent a "cold chill" through her.[20]

A year later, on 1 August, Kilmer was killed in battle. Assigned to the intelligence section as a sergeant, he had been on a scouting patrol and had crept alone into no-man's-land. Sgt. Maj. Lemist Esler found his body. "I suddenly caught sight of Kilmer lying on his stomach on a bit of sloping ground, his eyes just peering over the top of what appeared to be a natural trench. Several of us ran toward him, thinking he was alive and merely lying there with his attention fixed on the enemy.

"We called him, but received no answer. Then I ran up and turned him on his back, only to find that he was dead with a bullet through his brain."[21]

On the morning of 11 September, departure day, Fisk and his bustling staff couldn't help but notice during their last minute preparations a glorious work of art hanging inside the armory. Painted by the illustrator and political cartoonist Thomas Nast, an old Seventh man, it captured a great moment in the history of the regiment—the bittersweet farewell when, during the Civil War, the Seventh marched off to save the nation's capital from threatening Confederate forces. Every colorful inch of Nast's canvas was alive with proud New Yorkers cheering their departing men as row after row they tramp down Broadway. Flags fly from every building. Daring men stand on the rooftops of marble-columned porticoes, doffing their stovepipe hats. Impassioned women lean from packed windows, waving handkerchiefs. Adventuresome boys shinny up street lamps for better views. One civilian runs among the soldiers to embrace a friend. Never was there such excitement—and patriotism—shown the Seventh than at that moment, and Nast had preserved it for all time.

Worrying Fisk, and certainly all the veterans who remembered the hisses and boos and white feathers showered upon them in parades at the turn of the century, was how New Yorkers would treat the Seventh this time when it marched off to war. Would it be hoping too much for a send-off that might match the one depicted in Nast's painting? Fisk certainly would settle for half that—at least for the honor of his son, Clinton, and all the deserving men of his regiment.

Departure was set for one-fifty in the afternoon. At that time, the regiment was to assemble on the floor of the great drill room and then march downtown to the Twenty-third Street ferry dock, cross the Hudson River, and train southward to Camp Wadsworth. Since dawn, the armory had been packed with eighteen hundred Greyjackets plus their family and friends. Fisk had thrown open the doors for them for one last farewell. Sergeant John L. MacDonnell recalled the thronged armory. "From the early hours of our departure the crowds kept up an incessant stream. They soared in on the drill floor and up in the galleries; jammed the corridors and the company rooms, in fact, left no conceivable space that would afford the opportunity for a last fond embrace." Among the crowd were members of the Seventh's Veterans Association—retired soldiers. The night before, retired Brig. Gen. Daniel Appleton, who clearly never forgot the ill treatment his boys had suffered in '99 and '00 under his watch, had placed notices in the city's newspapers that ordered all veterans to report to the armory to give their dear regiment a rousing send-off. The notices were repeated in the morning papers. More than five hundred old-timers poured into the armory, dressed in civilian clothes and sporting arm-bands that identified them as veterans.

Appleton had persuaded former veteran Samuel W. Fairchild, president of the Union League Club, to erect a reviewing stand in front of the club at Thirty-ninth Street and Fifth Avenue. Then he had gotten Mayor Mitchel to agree to review the parade. On the reviewing stand with the mayor were Brig. Gen. John H. Foote, commander of the Second Brigade of the New York National Guard; Gen. Rush C. Hawkins, retired, who during the Civil War led the famous Hawkins' Zouaves; financier Cornelius Bliss; Joseph H. Emery, president of Lord & Taylor; August Belmont, K Company veteran who had been a major serving in the U.S. Air Service; and Col. William G. Kip, another veteran of the Seventh.

MacDonnell was struck by Appleton's presence in the armory. "His tall, graceful figure, his firm step, and his marked gait were all indicative of his soldierly spirit and in harmony with the seriousness of the occasion."

Sgt. Thomas J. Byrne Jr. thought the boys set a splendid soldierly example themselves, at least those in F Company. In the *Gazette* he wrote, "The day of the farewell parade found us all dolled up in our newest shining shoes and smiling faces, ready to show our veterans and the public the results of the hard work our new captain and his lieutenants had done with us during the time of waiting."

Meanwhile, outside the armory, the sidewalks quickly overflowed so that Park Avenue was massed with people who couldn't push their way through the thick, oaken doors and into the drill room. The sidewalks all along the route of the parade were filling up—from Park Avenue down to Fifty-seventh Street, west to Fifth Avenue, south past the Union League Club to Twenty-third Street, and west to the Hudson River. At the ferry slip, lashed to her mooring, waited the *Cincinnati,* the huge Pennsylvania Railroad double-decker ferry that was ready to transport the Seventh across the river. In Jersey City, three special trains of sixty-five cars each were also poised to carry the soldiers southward, their great engines snorting steam since early morning.

At precisely one-fifty in the afternoon, the blare of a bugle broke over the din of the crowd. Bugler Harry Jackson of E Company was calling the

Seventh to war. The sound of his bugle resonated off the upstairs walls of the twelve company rooms. Its notes soared out open windows, alerting the crowd below on Park Avenue that New York's silk stocking soldiers were now ready to leave.

Inside the armory, loving hands held tight for the last time. Tears were shed. Lingering kisses were pressed against lips and cheeks that, in too many cases, would never be touched again. Then the regiment filed into the drill room for its final orders of departure. Although there is no record of it, Fisk, before joining his men, most likely cast one last look at Nast's famous painting. Would his farewell parade be as exciting and memorable as when his Civil War predecessor, Col. Marshall Lefferts, led the regiment down Broadway and off to Washington on 19 April 1861?

As his men assembled in the drill room in their summer khaki uniforms, bedrolls slung at a diagonal over their left shoulders and their wide-brimmed campaign hats pulled tight over their heads, the gallery above them bulged with anxious families and friends, who only a moment ago had touched them for perhaps the last time. Many in the crowd waved flags and colorful banners and pennants. On the floor, captains barked their companies to order. Soldiers rattled to attention as an eerie hush settled throughout the drill room; only a cough or two broke the silence. Then the regiment closed together tightly, elbows touching elbows—a custom dating back to Civil War times so that each man felt the presence of every man in the ranks and knew that all his comrades-in-arms were there by his side. And standing at attention, on all four legs, was the pup, Greyjacket, the regimental mascot.

Then the Seventh Regiment Band, which in the months to come would play the dual role of burial party, struck up "Over There!" Next it played "Auld Lang Syne." When the music was over, captains gave the command, "Forward!"

Led by Fisk, Lt. Col. Robert McLean, Maj. Robert Mazet, and Maj. James Schuyler, followed by Maj. Nicholas Engel, Chaplain William McCord, Adj. Douglas Despard, and three battalion adjutants, eighteen hundred men stepped toward the exit, their faces grim with the task ahead. From the gallery, a mother shrieked, breaking the silence. Her shriek was followed by another. In a heartbeat, everyone in the gallery

*Leaving the armory on 11 September 1917, the Seventh
marches off to war.*   National Archives

rose to their feet. They cheered and shouted, "Good-Bye!" and "Good
Luck!" They stamped their feet. And a sea of white handkerchiefs waved
as in Nast's painting.

"Col. Fisk led us out of that deafening roar," remembered Wagoner
Robert J. Bell Jr. of the Service Company.

Outside the armory, the honorary escort of four hundred veterans under Appleton's command awaited in the unseasonably cold afternoon
sun. A reporter for the *New York Times* wrote that there "never was a leader
prouder of his men than this tall, erect, gray-haired soldier, with two stars
on his shoulders." Both sides of Park Avenue and then Fifth Avenue overflowed with onlookers, thousands of them pushing and shoving to get a
better look at their heroes until they spilled out onto the street. Because
spectator and soldier alike knew each other well, the parade took on a
"personal element in the farewell," according to one city newspaper. The
regimental historian noted that "in many places along the line of march
the strong police lines were unable to keep the wildly enthusiastic spectators in check." At Sixty-fourth Street, more members of the Veterans Association, led by Samuel Fairchild of the Union League Club, joined the

parade. Constantly, men and women broke through the crowd, darted onto Fifth Avenue to clasp the arm of a friend or lover now in uniform or slap him on the shoulder. Names were called out.

"Sgt. [Phillip] Harnischfeger was a popular boy along the line," C Company Sergeant Thomas Kerr recalled. "All his friends were there and called him all sorts of cognomens, but he was a good soldier and kept his eyes straight to the front."

Fisk couldn't help but smile now and then, nodding his head when people called out his name. "It seemed as if at least twenty years rolled from the shoulders of every veteran in the ranks and the hundreds watching and cheering from the sidewalks and windows," noted the *Times*. F Company's Sergeant Byrne felt that at last "it would surely seem that the Seventh has come into its own again—in the hearts of all New York, whether East Side or Fifth Avenue—from the greeting given us." As the parade neared Twenty-third Street, the Service Company got the warmest welcome, because, according to Wagoner Bell, "that is the neighborhood from which most of our boys come, and all the fathers, sisters, brothers and friends were on hand to wave, cheer and cry as the boys marched away."

Turning west onto Twenty-third Street, Appleton and his troops of veterans formed a line of honor. Looming at the end of the street almost like a warship, the *Cincinnati* rocked in the gray waters of the Hudson. As the Seventh neared the ferry, the police band, joined by the regimental band, broke into "Auld Lang Syne." Then row upon row, the Seventh boarded the *Cincinnati*. Amid final farewells, the great crowd surged frantically toward the soldiers. Families broke through police lines. As the New Yorkers swarmed about their boys, "thousands of women—mothers, wives, sweethearts and sisters—eluded the blue uniforms by seeking protection at the hands of the khaki-clad boys, and in that way slipped through the gates leading to the ferry boat."[22]

On board, the wives of Colonel Williard and Captain Clinton Fisk, Ida and Margery, joined their husbands. Because both Fisks lived in Jersey City, the women would cross the Hudson with them. Captain Fisk, square jawed, clean shaven, held his three-year-old son, Clinton Jr., in his arms. Reporters pressed against the regimental first family. In the commotion, the youngest Fisk began to cry. One look at the tears of his grandson, and the colonel smiled. "He is the only male representative of the Fisk family staying at home," he said. "But he'll be enlisting in the Seventh in about sixteen or seventeen years."[23]

With a blast of its great horn, the *Cincinnati* pulled away from its mooring. "Every boat in the river blew a whistle," said MacDonnell.

Somehow families and friends were finding ways to cross the river, too. And when the *Cincinnati* finally docked on the western banks of the Hudson, ten thousand people were there, waiting to continue their farewells. Hundreds tried sneaking aboard the three trains.

"The Regiment's departure from Jersey City was accompanied by an impressive bevy of beautiful girls," recollected Sgt. Paul Gadebusch, a machine gunner from Summit, Princeton graduate, and heir to the presidency of F. Schumacher & Company of New York. "And many members want to return just to say good bye to them all over again."

Sgt. Walter Davenport, an ex-newspaperman, summed up the whole scene in *The Gas Attack*, the division magazine. "We quit our several jobs, went down to the armory and enlisted. The Colonel spoke the word and we were off down Main street with the band out in front. The mayor called us heroes. The clergyman prayed for us publicly and the population, generally, got together and showered us with ten thousand things that added to our naturally curtailed creature comforts. And, to be brief about it, a fairly good time was had by all if the home newspaper was to be taken seriously." He added that the newspapers reported that the Seventh marched off to Camp Wadsworth "like veterans—grim, stern, self-reliant, determined."

Meanwhile, back on the New York side, Appleton, who had missed the Spanish-American War because of a political mix-up and then had to endure years of humiliation, felt vindicated at last.

Turning to a reporter from the *New York Sun*, he said, "We don't call ourselves the 'Gallant Seventh' or the 'Fighting Seventh.' We're just the Seventh. The regiment is 106 years old. It has always done its duty, and it always will. It is ready to a man. Watch em!"[24]

CHAPTER 3

The First and the Seventh
and Nothing In-Between

Among the first to survey Camp Wadsworth, Spartanburg, South Carolina, before the arrival of the Twenty-seventh Division were its youthful commander, Maj. Gen. John F. O'Ryan, and the tall, gaunt, goateed, chain-smoking colonel of the Twenty-second New York Engineers, Cornelius Vanderbilt. They were aghast at what they saw in mid-August. The camp was far from ready for the more than forty thousand soldiers soon to be en route to the sunny south.

At forty-two, O'Ryan was the youngest divisional commander in the United States Army. He was also one of the most powerful military figures in New York State. During the war, General John Pershing, a graduate of and former instructor at the U.S. Military Academy, counted mostly on West Point graduates to head the divisions in his American Expeditionary Force. There were eleven such commanders. O'Ryan was not one of those graduates. He earned his degree from New York University Law School and, of course, was an alumnus of the Seventh New York Regiment. Still, his conduct in France would earn the respect of his superior officer and give him a certain cachet among his military peers. Nevertheless, after touring Camp Wadsworth in the summer of 1917, he kept his mouth shut publicly about what he believed was the War Department's lack of preparedness. Camp Wadsworth was a case in point. "Very much could be written in criticism of the construction of Camp Wadsworth," he stated after the war, conceding only that the pencil-pushing bureaucrats in the War Department were "handicapped by the necessity of relying upon . . . new and untried officers" of which many were "timid or incompetent."

To get Camp Wadsworth at least partially ready for the onslaught of soldiers soon to arrive, O'Ryan turned to his friend Neily Vanderbilt, one year his senior, and ordered the millionaire yachtsman to get the job done.

To the general populace, the name Vanderbilt conjured up untold wealth and life on easy street. How could the great-grandson of Commodore Vanderbilt, a man who dwelt in luxury in one of the stately mansions adorning Fifth Avenue and who loved to race yachts, be entrusted with turning hundreds of square miles of mostly forested, hilly land into a crackerjack training ground for their boys?

In fact, the rich colonel, who had been appointed a second lieutenant in the Twelfth Regiment in 1901, was just the man for the job.

Besides his love for yachts, Vanderbilt had two other passions. One was the military life, because it kept him away from his wife's annoying social parties, which had begun at the turn of the century when she wanted to put Mrs. Astor and her elite "Four Hundred" in their place. His other was that he delighted in building things. He held an engineering degree. His work on his father's railroad resulted in several key inventions, including patents for thirty devices to make locomotives run more efficiently. He allied himself with August Belmont to help start the Interborough Rapid Transit Company (IRT) to bring the first subway to New York City. It ran from City Hall to Grand Central Station, over to Times Square, and then north to the Bronx. It was the fastest subway in the world at the time. On his yachts he kept a wood lathe.

Vanderbilt's marriage to Grace Wilson in 1898 did not sit well with his father, also named Cornelius. Although Neily was heir apparent to the vast family fortune as a result of the death of his older brother, William, he was basically cut out of the will. When his father died, he was given a $1 million trust fund and $500,000. Each of his siblings received

$7,500,000, except his younger brother Alfred Gwynne, who walked off with the bulk of the estate, $42,575,000.

The will, according to Neily's son, was dated the day his father and Grace married. However, Alfred promised to share part of the estate with his brother. A few days after the reading of the will, Chauncey Depew, the family lawyer, announced that Alfred, out of the goodness of his heart, was giving $6 million to Neily. Neily, it was reported, snorted, "Out of the goodness of his heart!"[1] He'd been promised $10 million! From then on, the strain between the two brothers was unbearable—until 7 May 1915, when a German U-boat sank the *Lusitania.* Alfred, along with 127 other Americans on board, went down with the ship.

In 1916, when the Twenty-seventh Division, then known as the Sixth, went to the Border under O'Ryan's command, Vanderbilt was promoted colonel of the Twenty-second Engineers. The promotion was tempered by the fact that his son, Neil, showed up in Texas, begging to be a soldier. He was too young. But even so, O'Ryan gave him a job as Neily's chauffeur. "Father was angry," Neil wrote, adding that he believed his father thought he was down there on orders from Grace to keep an eye on him.

A year later, at Camp Wadsworth, the father would again be hounded by the son, only this time Neil was a private in the Seventh Regiment. Grace had nothing to do with it and had tried to discourage him from enlisting. Ex-President Roosevelt told her she was wrong. Neil's place was indeed in the army, and near his father's side. And as before, O'Ryan gave him the cushy job of chauffeur. Instead of driving his father, he drove the divisional judge advocate, Lt. Col. J. Leslie Kincaid, former state assemblyman from Syracuse.

In 1917, when Colonel Vanderbilt first set foot there, Spartanburg was the fastest growing city in South Carolina. According to a report in the *Seventh Regiment Gazette,* the thriving city "sprawled irregularly up and down a group of red-clay hills." It was filled with fine hotels. It had two colleges, one that would certainly catch the fancy of every red-blooded soldier. Converse College for Women. The male readers of the *Gazette* probably howled in delight when the report described the women's college as "well endowed and finely equipped." Perhaps that's why the writer added that the "social standards of Spartanburg are not only high, but its moral tone is also strong and sane. It is a city of fine churches, and of an unusually large proportionate church membership. All the leading denominations have attractive houses of worship, and by their friendly co-operation contribute to furnishing a sound moral basis to the life of the community."

Spartanburg was linked to New York and Washington, and all points north, by the Southern Railway, the route that would soon carry the more than two thousand men of the Seventh Regiment southward.

The eastern edge of Camp Wadsworth was three miles from Spartanburg. It was connected to the city by an unpaved and oftentimes washed-out rut that slithered through the hills and woods and was called Snake Road. Turning this road into a highway that could handle the traffic of a fully manned division plus other military units was Vanderbilt's first task. Along the camp's northern border there was another route to and from the city—an "interurban electric line," according to the *Gazette*. This train did not concern Vanderbilt or his band of engineers—an oversight that within a few months would prove disastrous.

Camp Wadsworth was a forest of trees that needed to be cleared, a job that was to be left for the most part to the soldiers themselves. Thousands of tents had to be erected, latrines dug, and mess halls built. (The proximity of the latrines and mess halls later horrified young Private Vanderbilt, who discovered that on occasion the "nighttime pissoir" was "scoured out . . . for use as a soup or stew pot."[2]) No wooden barracks or permanent latrines were planned, because the division was not expected to stay in South Carolina for the winter, but instead be shipped to France for more intensive training.

Another task assigned to Colonel Vanderbilt, and his most challenging, was to re-create the western front so that O'Ryan's men could get a taste of life in the trenches. Assisting the colonel in designing and laying out this trench system so it'd be as realistic as possible were Captain Veyssiere of the French army and Capt. George D. Snyder of D Company, Twenty-second Engineers. Before the war, Snyder, a prominent engineer, had worked on the construction of one of the first tunnels to successfully burrow beneath the Hudson River. The trenches that he, Veyssiere, and Vanderbilt dreamed up covered a linear front of seven hundred yards, but in actual distance twisted and meandered for eight miles. A battalion of men could easily get lost in this maze—but only if they were unfamiliar with the layout of Manhattan, which was unlikely for the boys from Gotham.

Cleverly, Vanderbilt's engineers patterned their trench system after the grid system that marked the streets of New York City. Neatly lettered signposts told the troops in an instant where they were within the maze. The two main arteries through the trenches were dubbed "Broadway" and "Fifth Avenue." Among the other names were "Columbus Avenue," "Forty-second Street," "Thirty-fourth Street," and "Battery Place." The reserve trenches were called "the Bronx" and "Wall Street." O'Ryan explained that the layout and names "will make unnecessary the use of a map and will enable any soldier who might be dropped in any part of the trench system to tell upon reaching the first sign his approximate position in the system as a whole and how he may get to any other point in the system."[3]

Twenty-five miles from Camp Wadsworth, at a place called "Glassy Rock," the engineers built an all-purpose firing range. Here the troops learned to fire rifles, automatic arms, machine guns, one-pound cannon, and Stokes mortars. Yet, there were no one-pounders in camp and teaching was theoretical. Stokes mortars didn't arrive until shortly before the division headed for France. Instead, makeshift mortars were fashioned from stovepipes. Milk cans were used as bombs.

O'Ryan was right. Not only was the War Department unprepared to wage a war, it even lacked the wherewithal to train its country's soldiers.

Meanwhile, the construction company of Fisk & Carter was hired to assist the engineers in building the camp. Nearly four thousand men were employed. The weekly payroll averaged sixty thousand dollars. O'Ryan calculated that twenty million pieces of lumber and six thousand kegs of nails were used. There was 1,559,577 feet of electric wiring, eighteen miles of road built, and twenty-seven thousand dollars spent just on showers and faucets. When the camp was finally completed at the end of December—more than three months after the troops arrived—the total bill to the War Department was $2,223,223.59![4]

In mid-September, a month after the first sound of hammers and saws rang throughout Camp Wadsworth and road-working crews started to straighten out Snake Road, trains carrying the men of the Seventh Regiment rolled southward, through New Jersey, Delaware, and on to Washington, D.C. Although the Seventh was a little late in coming—other regiments of the Twenty-seventh had already been in South Carolina for more than a week—they were finally on their way.

On board one of the trains, L Company's Pfc. Albert "Bert" Lobdell Jr. dashed off a note to his father, "You should have heard all the noise in the Jersey towns when we past [*sic*] by. Every factory whistle blew and people cheering by the hundreds, and at railroad terminals the engines all opened up."

Bert, twenty-four, was from Salem Center, New York, where since 1850 a Lobdell had served as postmaster. His great-great-grandfather had fought in the Revolutionary War for the Fourth Westchester County Regiment, commanded by Col. Thaddeus Crane. Bert enlisted in the Seventh because his older brother Whit had been a Greyjacket from 1901 to 1907. He perhaps also enlisted here because General O'Ryan lived in Salem Center and was well known by the Lobdell family. On the ride down, Bert reported that for breakfast "we had coffee, bread and butter and shredded wheat and milk on a paper plate. Can you imagine shredded

Pfc. Bert Lobdell could trace his military heritage back to the Revolutionary War.   Reginald White

wheat and milk on a paper plate! The paper soaked up all the milk and we had no sugar but I'm not hungry and the trip is quite a lark."[5]

K Company private Jim Nelly made sure he didn't starve aboard the train. R. Cade Wilson Jr. recounted one of Nelly's meals for the *Gazette*, "a whole roast chicken, nine pieces of corn bread, five cups of coffee, two jars of jam and three boxes of crackers, all in a single sitting." After that meal, K Company nicknamed him "Tape." Food was plentiful the entire trip because at every railroad station and crossing, people came out to greet the soldiers and sell them food. Writing to his mother, Sergeant Gow told her that in Salisbury he bought an apple pie. "Everyone seems to know the Seventh by reputation and charge us accordingly."

When they finally arrived in Spartanburg, the boys "found [it] to be a bustling little city, well paved and with real honest to goodness trolley cars operating." Gow thought the city "old-fashioned."

On 13 September, a fleet of thirty army trucks met the regiment at the Spartanburg train station and transported all its training gear three miles over precarious Snake Road to Camp Wadsworth. The soldiers marched. When they got there, Sergeant John L. MacDonnell said they bivouacked "in the prettiest grove in the Reservation, and the boys immediately set to the task of clearing a site on which to pitch their tents." He then chided Pvt. John Darcy of M Company because he "doesn't like guard duty as well in the woods of South Carolina as he did when stationed at the rear door of the armory. He used to get an occasional smile on the Lexington Avenue post as the cars went by, but of course it was his duty to 'observe everything within sight.' And if my memory serves me right, John was some observer."

That first night, Pvt. Eugene J. O'Brien of B Company found the "air is chilly . . . and it is quite necessary to use two blankets to be comfortable." He added, "There is much work to be done, for the camp was evidently a forest a short time ago."

In the first week, the G Company scribe reported, "We have developed many fine axe-men from the fellows who never swung anything heavier than a Waterman self-filler," referring to the popular fountain pen. He also wrote, "For making camp give me McAllen. There were no stumps there."

The soldiers quickly found a rhythm to camp life all its own—a rhythm peculiar to the dandies of the Seventh Regiment. The wife of I

Company bugler Lyle Ray, for example, sent him a Victrola and records. "Needless to say," Billy Leonard said, "they are greatly appreciated. We have music with every meal." Not to be outdone, Sgt. William Bible of E Company "in some mysterious way," said Sergeant Earle D. Grimm, "unearthed a piano and now we have music with our meals in addition to flies."

"Everything is fine and dandy—McAllen was a bad dream compared to our present camp," Sgt. Thomas Kerr, C Company, noted in the *Gazette.*

Kerr also noted that several boys in his company were to be envied because their wives and sweethearts had already moved down to Spartanburg. "Lucky boy that can have his wife so near. How about it Reeves [Cpl. Alfred A. Reeves Jr.]? Some girl, believe me, and I can pick out a fine girl every time. Great smile." Kerr was jealous of Pfc. Charles Scerbo, too, who was about to be married "His future happiness is now staying at Spartanburg. Understand that it will be some wedding and that representatives of the royal family of Italy are to be there. Charles says she is a fine woman, of course."

Joseph Walsh said in the *Gazette* that he was "following the example of many other would-be saviours of their country from the heel of Prussian despotism" and "took unto himself a bride: Miss Margery Middletown Aman of Philadelphia, so consented to share our lot through thick and thin. Mrs. Walsh is now one of the rapidly growing colony of war brides who are flocking to Spartanburg in very increasing numbers."

Another of the boys to take a bride was H Company Pvt. Ulysses S. Grant IV, who married Miss Matilda Bartikofsky of New York City in a secret ceremony in Spartanburg. Grant did not let anyone know about the marriage until four months after he tied the knot and just before he was commissioned a second lieutenant and sent to Washington, D.C. He even kept the news from his own family for almost the entire four months.

Kenneth Gow sent word back to his sister in Summit, New Jersey, that Lt. Edward Willis, nephew of the town's mayor, Ruford Franklin, had just announced his engagement. "She is a fine girl. He has it bad; would sit with me, and still does for that matter, and talk about her. I was the only one outside of his family that knew it until he announced it to the Summit men last night."

For Lieutenant Willis, known among his friends as Jun, there were a lot of Summit boys in camp who needed to be told of his engagement. Nearly all of them were members of the Calvary Church and had sung in the choir. Along with Gow, the others were Sgt. Oscar Hellquist, a graduate of Cornell; Cpl. Alan Eggers, another Cornell man who had dropped out to enlist in the Seventh; Sgt. Paul Gadebusch, a Princeton man; Pvt. William Drabble, a Dartmouth track and field star whose brother Phillip was a corporal in the division's 105th Machine Gun Company; Cpl. Thomas O'Shea, private secretary to his grandfather George Weed, president of the Morgan Iron Works and a charter member of the Society of Naval Architects and Marine Engineers; and Pvt. John Mallay, a centerfielder for the Seton Hall College High School baseball team. He left the Catholic high school at the end of his junior year to enlist in the Seventh. Although he was not from Summit, Sgt. John C. Latham, a gardener who had recently emigrated from England, worked in the New Jersey town. It was there that he had enlisted in the Machine Gun Company. In the Battle of the Hindenburg Line, this tight-knit congregation would gain fame at an astonishingly high cost as the "Jersey Gunners." In a foreboding farewell speech to these "Jersey Gunners" in 1917, and to other Summit soldiers when they left for France, Mayor Franklin said, "Boys, you may not all come home as generals, but we know you will give a good account of yourselves as soldiers and be a credit to Summit and to your families."[6]

Meanwhile, Mechanic Harley Vernon de Vol of I Company was in such a hurry to get hitched that he talked the divisional chaplain, Maj. William E. McCord, into conducting the ceremonies in his, the chaplain's, tent. A Seventh man since 1890, McCord couldn't resist. His wife was matron of honor. Even Col. Willard Fisk got into the act, giving away the bride. The best man was Sgt. Washington Irving Clayton, quite a lady's man in his own right and one of the more popular noncommissioned officers in camp. After the exchange of vows, the happy couple strode to a waiting car to take them on a five-day honeymoon while the men in his company formed an arch of crossed rifles.

For those boys less fortunate when it came to women, their main worry before serious training got under way was to get themselves adjusted to living in tents with the boys. Usually, there were eight soldiers to a tent.

On the first night, Bert Lobdell informed his father back in Salem Center that the "boys here say it's as cold as Iceland nights, but we each have two woolen blankets, a poncho and a shelter half and I have my big gray sweater. I expect to be plenty warm enough." In a letter to his mother he said, "We've heard from the fellows that have been here is [*sic*] that it's so cold we'll need ten blankets and a stove to keep warm. All we need is a carpet on the floor and a piano and we could think we were living on 5th Avenue."

Billy Leonard apparently received a pair of pajamas for warmth from his good friend in Flushing, the humorist Ellis Parker Butler.

"Dear Ellis," he wrote back, "Ain't it tough when you're hungry and a package comes from home and you open it and you and the gang standing wide-mouthed and expectant and find it's pajamas. Now ain't that *tough?*" Butler replied: "It is tough as you say when you're expecting a chocolate cake from home and open the package that come from home and find it's pajamas. But it would be a durn sight worser if you were expecting pajamas and had to go to bed in a chocolate cake."

Lobdell asked his father that when he sent "goodies of any character" that he "don't be stingy because they have to be divided amongst my tent-mates, which number six." He mentioned that a corporal in his squad had gotten a tin box full of Brownies. Bert had never in his life seen such a treat. "Do you know what they are?" he queried his sister Nea. "It's almost fudge, but not quite as rich. They're very good."

The nights were getting colder, and one of the camp wags was right when he had bragged that it would be as "cold as Iceland nights." The whole East Coast was soon to face one of the bitterest winters in memory.

"The frost is on the tent pole and the pumpkin is on the shock or whatever it is, and doggone it, here we are in South Carolina," lamented Sergeant Grimm. "South Carolina with its balmy southern skies of which we read and dreamt, but we never read nor did we ever dream about the very wet rain and muddy mud and cold damp winds that are also common occurrences when the sun is negligent."

Cpl. Edward Streeter, who after the war wrote *Father of the Bride*, poked fun at the cold and other camp hardships in letters addressed to a fictitious gal back home, "Dere Mable." In one of his letters, published in *The Gas Attack*, he pointed out that it was "gettin awful cold. No wonder this is a healthy place. All the germs is froze. I guess there idea of the hardenin process is to freeze a fello stiff."[7]

Gow let his father know, too, that the "nights are very cold. I had to buy a mattress and also I bought a pillow."

One frigid night, Gow "heard some darkies singing . . . the first time I have ever heard this far-famed Southern darky singing. It is the weirdest thing I ever heard. Their melodies are very primitive and seem to revert to what might have been African dirges. We asked them to sing 'My Old Kentucky Home,' 'Suwanee River,' 'Old Black Joe,' or some other darky song and (will you believe me?) they never heard of any of them."

On another night, "a beautiful still night," while alone in his tent, he heard "the men singing all over the camp. It makes one feel very melancholy. The band is in the next street to us, and they are practising very softly. As I write, [they are now playing] 'Carry Me Back To Ole Virginny.' A bugle can be heard for miles tonight."

In another tent, Pvt. Raeburn Van Buren, the magazine artist, was also taken in by the music. "My Dear Little Mother, Tonight our tent door is wide open and our stove is the coldest thing in the tent. I can see the stars from where I am sitting and they look good. Everybody is singing and those tents sporting Victrolas are working them every minute. I am very, very happy and feel fine in every way."

Within a few weeks at Camp Wadsworth, the first of several orders hit the Seventh Regiment hard. It called for the reorganization of the Twenty-seventh Division. Four New York regiments were kept within the division, the Second, Third, Twenty-third, and, of course, the Seventh infantries. Other New York regiments, such as the First and Seventy-first, were dismantled. Men from those regiments were then transferred to other regiments. And worse, what happened to the Sixty-ninth Infantry one month earlier, happened again. Numerical designations were changed. Basically, the Second Infantry, after picking up over thirteen hundred men from the Seventy-first, became the 105th, the Third became the 106th, the Twenty-third the 108th, and the Seventh, the proud Seventh, was now the 107th.

Looking back on the renumbering, O'Ryan, formerly of the Seventh, wondered how the War Department could do such a thing. "In the case of our own state, the 7th Infantry, with a continuous existence of over one hundred years and with a fine record of accomplishment, particularly in the development of officer material, lost the prestige of its name and became known as the 107th Infantry."

Capt. Henry Maslin, a native of Ireland's County Galway and Seventy-first Infantry veteran who had been wounded in the charge up San Juan Hill in 1898, recalled the breakup. "Heartaches must be borne, old associations and friendships severed, and as the 71st men, it was up to each individual officer and man to 'play the game.' I was assigned to command Company D, 105th Infantry, and with the exception of ten men of Company F, who had asked me to take them with me, every man in the new company was a stranger to me."[8]

Trying to keep up a good front concerning the numerical change, Sergeant Kerr of C Company wrote in the *Gazette*, "What could be better? That old seven stays with us and our parents and friends will have a much easier time following us through whatever may happen."

A Company's Ben Franklin shrugged. "From the 7th to the 107th—a rose by any name is just as sweet."

But not only had the War Department fiddled with tradition, it had begun to bleed the old Seventh dry of its men. It took them singly or in clumps. Twenty-four enlisted men were sent to the First New Hampshire Infantry because they spoke French. One of the transfers was Louis Wetmore, who had joined the Seventh with his friend Joyce Kilmer. In fact, the First New Hampshire received 275 Twenty-seventh Division men. One of the lucky soldiers who spoke French, but was not transferred, was Pvt. John Howell Westcott Jr., who before the declaration of war had been an ambulance driver in France. And one by one boys were yanked off to officer's training school. Each issue of the *Gazette* kept a running list of those commissioned officers under the heading, "Graduates of the Seventh." By war's end it was an impressive list. The April 1919 issue ran the names of 1,099 officers.

In his memoirs, O'Ryan pointed out that the War Department wanted "officers and men who possessed special capacity or experience in particular fields of activity." More than five thousand officers came from his division. "Fortunately the earlier shortages were immediately made up by drawing upon other New York units at the camp, but the 'raids' were so heavy and continuous that soon this source of supply was depleted."

Such was not the case for Alex Van Rensselaer. His hearing was getting worse, and he knew that at any moment he faced being cut away from the army like a diseased limb, the last thing in the world he wanted. With his brother Arthur still bed bound, Alex knew that somehow he had to carry on the family's military tradition. Almost from the moment he arrived at Camp Wadsworth he campaigned to stay in the armed services. He had friends in high places write letters of recommendation. One of them sent a missive to Col. Hiram Bingham of the Signal Corps, stating that Alexander was a "brimful of unquestioned patriotism. I have known his father since my boyhood, we served together in the same company of the Seventh Regiment, N.Y.N.G. I believe the Government would make no mistake in affording Mr. Van Rensselaer an opportunity of becoming an officer, otherwise this letter would not have been written." In time, his hearing forced him out of the 107th. He was given an honorable discharge. He immediately left for Washington to lobby to get back into the service. "Because of my excellent physical condition I cannot reconcile myself to the thought of staying in this country when there is so much work to be done on the other side; work that I am capable of doing in spite of my deafness."[9] Eventually Van Rensselaer was given a second chance. He was taken back into the army and sent to Boston, where, as a sergeant, he worked for the U.S. Army General Hospital No. 10 and, because he was a former reporter, edited the hospital's newspaper, *Whizz Bang*.

The old Seventh, now the 107th Infantry, was rocked again on 1 October. Divisional General Orders No. 9, complying with the same orders issued by the War Department that dismantled the Seventy-first Infantry, called on the First Infantry Regiment to send sixteen hundred enlisted men to the 107th. The orders also detailed the Twelfth Infantry Regiment to transfer 320 men to the 107th.

The soldiers from the First and Twelfth were mostly upstate boys, farmers a lot of them. Both regiments were the first National Guard units in the country called into service—a full three months before the United States declared war on Germany. Governor Whitman feared for the water supply of New York City. He believed that at any moment German agents might blow up the aqueducts that carried five hundred million gallons of water daily from the Catskills into New York's five boroughs. On 5 January two companies of the First Infantry from the Newburgh area and other companies further upstate were ordered to protect the reservoir system and the aqueducts that ran for more than one hundred miles from Gilboa and Lackawack and other small towns to the Croton Aqueduct and then on into the city. When the First Infantry marched out of Newburgh, a blizzard pounded the Catskills. Snow piled up waist high. The wind howled through the streets of Newburgh, and a shivering crowd silently watched the men depart.[10] One of those frozen Newburghers had all the credentials to be a blue-blooded silk stocking soldier. Pvt. Adrian Kissam Jr., a young sporting man who did not need to work, was related closely to both the Vanderbilts and Roosevelts and cousin to another Vanderbilt descendant, Sgt. George Ely II of K Company of the Seventh Regiment.[11]

"The physical suffering on this aqueduct duty," wrote Edward Dunphy, managing editor of the Newburgh *Daily News,* "was greater than that to which they were subjected in France."[12] Second Lt. Arthur Brundage, later an officer in the 107th Infantry, recalled the send-off. "The men who were on that trip will remember the day they landed at the state reservation as long as they live. The snow was up to their waists, and it was biting cold. There were many cases of frostbite. It was necessary to hike up the long mountainous road, and the march was not unlike a sample of Napoleon's journey over the Alps. The men will still have memories of their night in the barn with the state mules in Peekskill; men in one end and the frightened animals in the other. Rumor had it that some of the men slept between the mules to keep warm."[13]

Now at Camp Wadsworth, almost ten months later, the First and Twelfth Infantries were assigned to companies in the old Seventh that corresponded with the companies they had been in while members of their old regiments. "This arrangement," noted Sgt. Jack H. Tingle in the *Gazette,* "kept the men from certain communities together and they, too, were able to retain their identity, for their company letter [was to] be the same."

The First Infantry drew on cities and towns not just from the Newburgh area, but from places as far way as Albany and Utica, as well as Ogdensburg on the St. Lawrence River, to fill its ranks. Dunphy stated, "Early in October the regiment was plunged into gloom by the announcement that it was to be broken up. This decision was the result of

Capt. Raphael Egan returned to the Seventh Regiment
in 1917 to command the Third Battalion.
The Seventh Regiment Fund

another which practically doubled the size of the old companies. Many of the non-commissioned staff were transferred and the regiment was merged with the famous Seventh of New York."[14]

One of the new officers from Newburgh was an old Seventh man, Capt. Raphael A. Egan. Tall, barrel-chested, extraordinarily handsome, every inch of him the ideal soldier, Egan first joined the National Guard on 13 December 1909, when he signed on to serve in D Company of the Seventh. In those days, he was a young attorney fresh out of New York Law School. His older brother, Jim, urged him to leave Newburgh and their family's dairy business and settle in the big city. There was opportunity everywhere, as long as you were hooked in with Tammany Hall. Raphael practiced law in New York for several years, only to return to Newburgh after a real-estate deal, based on a tip from a Tammany Hall politico, turned sour. Back in Newburgh, Raphael opened a law office and transferred over to the First Infantry, where he was commissioned a second lieutenant on 26 January 1912.[15] With his First Infantry now part of the old Seventh, Captain Egan was put in charge of I Company, replacing Capt. Wade Hampton Hayes, newly assigned to regimental headquarters. Egan's job, according to one I Company man, was "fusing the 'dudes' and the 'appleknockers'—a job requiring real skill, tact and all the qualities of leadership."[16]

"You certainly must feel honored," wrote his mother. "I hope you will keep up the good name and be a good boy and attend to all your religious duties strictly, for you know, my dear, that it is the one important thing in your life."[17]

I Company's 1st Sgt. Charles H. Floyd remembered the day when the entire regiment "went out on the drill ground and had a farewell parade and review, the last parade under our old name. Then we prepared to give the new men a rousing welcome. When they arrived, they marched by a cheering throng of 7th men and that night we gave them a special dinner. They were a splendid body of men from the large towns of up-State New York and from the country districts, but it was a long time before the different groups were entirely amalgamated and training was delayed in consequence."[18]

On 15 October Bert Lobdell explained the change to his mother. "Tomorrow we get 130 men from the First Regiment. It's going to mess things up here for a while, but suppose we'll get settled down again soon." Five days later fifteen men from the Twelfth were assigned to L Company. "There are now nine men living in each tent," Bert told his mother. "They look and seem like nice fellows and do not appear as tough as some people think the 12th Regiment are." Then on 24 October, Bert informed his father that he had been switched from the fourth squad to the fourteenth squad. "Guess I was born under an unlucky star in some respects. I have the consolation of two Seventh men in my squad—the rest are First and Twelfth Regiment men and although they're quite amiable they're different. This morning I was so darned disgusted I went to town and can imagine how anyone feels when they go out and get soused for spite. Swell chance of it in Spartanburg if I was a toper!"

E Company's Van Buren was almost as upset as Lobdell. To his mother back in Kansas City, he explained that "one of the biggest drawbacks to the army is the men you are forced to mingle with. You would be surprised to know how low men get mentally and how dirty some of them

Underage Pvt. August Engler hoodwinked his German-speaking mother so that she unwittingly signed his enlistment papers.   August Engler Jr.

are. I have tried to overlook such things, but never until I entered the army did I know that it was possible for a man to go through twenty-six years of life and not be able to write his own name. There are four of them in this company, or rather were until they were kicked out. The conversation, in general, is so crude I stare with amazement at the fellows."

Private O'Brien wrote in the *Gazette* that B Company had gotten its "full quota of 250 men, the majority from the 1st N.Y. Infantry of Utica. For the benefit of those who do not know about Utica, we wish to say that it should be capitalized on the map, for according to the men we received from that city—well, it's worthy of all that can be said of it and we are sure that together with the nineteen men from the 12th N.Y. Infantry, B Company will continue, true to its name." Utica also sent a large number of boys to the Machine Gun Company. Among them was Pvt. August Engler, a youngster from the German neighborhood of Utica that crowded the banks of the Mohawk River. In 1915, after working in the Savage Arms Corporation that manufactured Lewis machine guns, Engler desperately wanted to enlist. But he was underage. So he tricked his German-born mother, who could not read English, into signing his enlistment application by assuring her that the papers in front of her were for membership into the Boy Scouts of America.[19]

Billy Leonard discovered that most of the boys from the First Regiment who were sent to I Company came from Middletown. "They have talked so much about Middletown that it has kindled in us a desire to see the place. They tell us that Middletown is one of the principal stations on the Erie Railroad, and after the war is over we're going to walk to Middletown or travel there on the Erie, some week-end." One of the Middletown boys was Pvt. George Fetherolf, who had enlisted while he was still in high school. Fetherolf lived with his aunt Mollie and a blind uncle, Archibald Holmes, because when he was seven, he lost both his parents. His mother had died and his father abandoned him for California. Fetherolf's uncle owned the popular Holmes Music Company. He sold pianos manufactured under his own name, Victrolas, Grafonolas, Victor and Columbia records, and "talking machine needles."[20]

Sergeant Tingle stated that D Company was "one of the last companies to receive a consignment of men from the First New York Infantry. These boys all hail from Ogdensburg, N.Y., and if this town is to be judged by its representatives who are now in our midst it is ill named a 'burg,' for they are certainly a 'Fine Body of Men' and a credit to their home town. We know they will uphold the traditions of the old Fourth

Pvt. George Fetherolf was still in high school when he signed on with the First Infantry in Middletown, N.Y. John W. Fetherolf

*K Company's Cpl. Harold Strycker Mills and his wife, Josephine Schaus Mills,
who served in the U.S. Navy.* Marian Mills Boswell and Shirley Mills Hudson

Company." One of the transfers was Michael Valente, an Italian immigrant whose heroic deeds in front of the St. Quentin Canal on 29 September 1918 would take the U.S. government eleven years to honor.

A transfer from the Twelfth Infantry, Pvt. Walter J. Silick wasn't about to be cowed by the rich boys in his new company. He strolled into his tent sporting silk socks, an unlit cigar clamped between his teeth. Quietly he pulled out a roll of one-dollar bills, lit them with a match, and then lit his cigar with the burning money. From then on, the upstater was called "Silk Stocking Silick."

Not all the new members of the 107th were transfers. K Company welcomed from Manhattan a pair of draftees who fit the mold of the old Seventh: Harold Strycker Mills and his younger brother Van Strycker Mills, grandsons of a well-known artist, John Harrison Mills. The boys carried the same middle name in honor of their mother's old Dutch heritage. Before enlisting, Hal had been an agricultural researcher out in eastern Long Island. There he met and married a young woman from Southampton, Josephine Schaus, who later joined the U.S. Navy. Van was twenty-one, with blue eyes and blond hair, and was a crack shot with a rifle. Their grandfather had come to New York City in 1886 to establish the first business in the country that packed and shipped fine art so that towns and cities could put on exhibits and shows that they otherwise could not afford to do. By 1917 their father had taken over the business.[21]

The 107th was now abustle with men, well over thirty-five hundred strong, with two hundred and fifty soldiers in each of the twelve line companies. There were also a headquarters, machine-gun and supply company, and the sanitary detachment. A captain, senior first lieutenant, first sergeant, mess sergeant, supply sergeant, one corporal, four mechanics, four cooks, two buglers, and four privates were assigned to each company. The companies themselves were divided into four platoons, each commanded by a lieutenant. Each platoon was then broken down into four sections, consisting of bombers and rifle grenadiers, riflemen, and a small detachment of machine gunners. Also assigned to the companies were five wagons, twelve mules, and two bicycles.

Colonel Fisk knew that his bulging regiment, perhaps the *most* New York of all the regiments in the division, sensed that he and his staff had to make the transfers, especially from the First, feel that they had found a home among the silk stocking soldiers. Addressing the men from both the torn up First and renumbered old Seventh, he told them that neither regiment had lost its original name. "We are still the First and Seventh," the Colonel said, "but with *Nothing* in between!"[22]

"A very pretty thought," Albert H. Sawtell of the Machine Gun Company recalled for the *Gazette*. "And we believe the old First feels just as much at home now as they did in their old 'hang out,' in fact more so, for several of the old First men in my tent feel so much at home that they don't know the difference between my cigarettes and theirs when it comes to taking them."

Sergeant MacDonnell likened the merger to "marrying a girl from your own home town. Our home town extends to the limits of the State so we are proud to be wedded to our quota—the boys of New York. We are all here for the same cause and under the same flag. We'll bear hardships and joys on equal shoulders, and we assure the folks back home in the grand old Empire State that in the ranks of Company M, the 107th United States Infantry, peace and harmony will always reign supreme."

CHAPTER 4

The Most Marvelous, Miraculous and Impressive Thing I Ever Witnessed

In the midst of the reorganizational turmoil that rocked the Twenty-seventh Division, General John F. O'Ryan was ordered to France. He sailed from Hoboken aboard the transport ship *Antilles*, with chief of staff Col. H. H. Bandholz, 1st Lt. Charles Franchot, and Sgt. Maj. Albert Breunig from Brooklyn, whose father and maternal grandfather had been born in Germany. The *Antilles* docked in St. Nazaire, on the coast of France, on 7 October. O'Ryan and his entourage were taken to Paris, where they joined five other divisional commanders and their staffs and began an extensive tour of the front lines. Their first stop was in Amiens. Here they met with Gen. Sir Hubert Gough of the British Fifth Army, engaged in the Battle of Passchendaele. Next they were assigned to the British Twenty-ninth Division and then the British Thirty-first Division, with the sobriquet "They Win or Die Who Wear the Rose of Lancaster."

Hiking through a trench one thousand yards from the front, they were buzzed by a German airplane that quickly vanished over the horizon. Less than five minutes later, the scream of a howitzer shell froze them in their tracks. They crouched against the muddy walls of the trench. The shell landed nearby, showering them in a rain of dirt. Seconds later another shell came whistling toward them. It exploded with such sudden force that the concussion knocked Lieutenant Franchot off his feet. O'Ryan and his staff ran for their lives as more shells rained down on the spot where they had just been. By the time they reached the front line, exhausted and panting, the Germans had opened up with a *minenwerfer*, or small mortar, bombardment. The Americans scurried like frightened rabbits into the safety of an underground shelter.

A few days later, they were sent to the French front, assigned to the French Thirty-eighth Division, which at the moment was embroiled in the Battle of Chemin des Dames. Here in an old factory building, they witnessed the interrogation of prisoners. O'Ryan's impression was that the Germans were confident that back in the United States German-Americans would refuse to fight against their Fatherland. Instead, they would disrupt American life. Talking with a German major, "very intelligent and apparently well-educated," O'Ryan asked, in English, if he'd like to meet a German-American? The major jumped at the chance. Sgt. Maj. Breunig, who had no idea what was going on, was summoned. The Boche major looked at him, surprised to see he was indeed in the American army. Breunig told the officer that his father and his mother's father were both natives of Germany.

"Then why are you in the American army?" the major asked.

"I am here to fight the Germans," Breunig answered.

Turning to O'Ryan, the major muttered, "My God, I cannot understand it!"

Soon afterward, O'Ryan and his staff returned home. His impression was that the war was likely to continue. Also, that training had to be intensified, and that the best place was at Camp Wadsworth and not France.

While O'Ryan was away, a new regiment of New Yorkers showed up in South Carolina. The appearance of the Fifteenth New York Infantry, later the 369th, which by war's end would see more action than any other U.S. regiment and thereby merit the nickname "The Harlem Hellfighters," roiled the waters of racial bigotry in Spartanburg—a city earlier lauded by the Seventh for its "strong and sane" high moral tone. But that moral tone didn't keep the city fathers from stating that they didn't want a "colored" regiment anywhere near them, particularly uppity New York City blacks.[1] And especially when their arrival came on the heels of a violent race riot in Houston, Texas, where, during the last week of August, African American soldiers of the Twenty-fourth Infantry rampaged through the streets armed with service rifles and ammunition. Seventeen people were killed.[2] The government moved swiftly in its punishment of the mutineers, even though the blacks felt justified in their action because of the raw treatment given them by the white population of Houston. Before the year was out, thirteen blacks were hanged for the crime, forty-one sentenced to life imprisonment, and only five acquitted. More blacks would hang later.

Spartanburg mayor J. F. Floyd protested to the War Department, fearing that colored men from New York would demand to be treated differently than southern colored men. "With their northern ideas about race equality," he predicted, "they will probably expect to be treated like white men. I can say right here that they will not be treated as anything except Negroes. We shall treat them exactly as we treat our resident Negroes. This thing is like waving a red flag in the face of a bull." He warned of certain trouble.

As the Fifteenth Infantry headed toward South Carolina, the soldiers of the Twenty-seventh Division prepared a warm welcome for their New York City brethren. The old Seventh Regiment was anxious for its arrival. Nine officers of the Fifteenth, white, of course, were former members of the Seventh. They numbered one major, six captains, and two first lieutenants. The major was Arthur W. Little, who had been with Major Francis Griswold Landon when he visited ex-President Teddy Roosevelt at Oyster Bay in the hope of raising a volunteer regiment for the hero of San Juan Hill.

Some of the members of the old Seventh had another reason for wanting to welcome the Fifteenth with open arms—its renowned forty-four-member regimental band. Led by Lt. Jim Reese Europe, the first black to direct an orchestra at Carnegie Hall and musical director for dancers Vernon and Irene Castle, the band had played throughout New York and was a favorite among the fashionable class of Manhattan.

The day after the Fifteenth settled in to life at Camp Wadsworth, its commander, Col. William Hayward, a powerful New York attorney and husband of one of the wealthiest women in the country, assembled every soldier in his regiment, officers and men, white and black. After scaling a bathhouse, he told them to gather round so they could hear him plainly. The first thing he did was to remind them all of the mutiny and bloodshed in Texas. He explained that the citizens of Spartanburg did not understand the ways of northern blacks. As Major Little later recalled, Hayward then said they had the "opportunity to compel the South to recognize the differences which the people of the North already appreciated, simply by accepting the Spartanburg situation as an opening for the educated colored man to prove his moral worth as a citizen, by refusing to meet the white citizens of Spartanburg upon the undignified plane of prejudice and brutality which had been so fundamentally advertised, by Mayor Floyd, as the standard of the community."

He warned them that they faced certain physical abuse.

"See to it," Hayward said, "that if violence occurs, if blows are struck, that all of the violence and all of the blows are on one side, and that side is not our side. If wrong by disorder is to occur, make sure and doubly sure, that none of the wrong is on our side." Then, his voice booming out over his men from his bathhouse perch, he asked, not ordered, every one of them to promise to refrain from any violence by raising their right hand. Noted Little, "A sea of hands shot up over that sea of heads—and the meeting was dismissed."

But trouble started right away. In town, whites heckled the African Americans almost every chance they got and tried to force their hand in fights. One of the members of the band, the drum major Noble Sissle, a noted composer, was assaulted in a hotel lobby. Small stores that were thrown up around the camp to sell candy, soda, and tobacco to the soldiers refused to serve blacks.

According to Little, however, white soldiers of the Twenty-seventh Division who bought from these stores inquired if "any of those colored soldiers were going to be served here?" When they were told no, they said, "Then, you might as well put up your shutters. These colored soldiers are all right. They're fighting with us for our country. They're our buddies. And we won't buy from the men who treat them unfairly."

In another incident, in downtown Spartanburg, two men pushed a black soldier off the sidewalk and into the gutter. When he got to his feet a crowd had gathered. One of the bullies tried to pick a fight with him. The soldier said he couldn't oblige, that he had promised his colonel that he wouldn't strike back. He'd have to take his "licken" like a man. As the crowd pushed forward, a voice stopped them in their tracks.

"Well, I didn't promise my Colonel to keep my hands off you bullies!" The speaker was, as Little described him, "a clean cut youngster, in Seventh Regiment uniform."

Next to him was another Seventh man. "Nor did I!" he shouted.

The two white soldiers then knocked the "town toughs into the gutter from which their victim had just arisen."

At any moment, Spartanburg had the potential to erupt into real violence. Colonel Hayward knew this. He immediately went to Washington to see if he couldn't get his regiment sent over to France right away, where, ironically, it would be out of harm's way. Hayward got his wish, and in December, while thirteen blacks in Texas were strung up for mutiny, the Fifteenth sailed for Europe.[3]

Among the whites, life went on as usual in Spartanburg. Churches opened their doors to the soldiers. Home-cooked meals were offered. I Company Sergeant Washington Irving Clayton, an Episcopalian, joined the choir of the Church of the Advent. At city hotels, there was dancing, and pretty girls from Converse College twirled around the ballroom of the fancy Hotel Cleveland with the officers of the Twenty-seventh.

Cpl. Leslie Rowland of L Company, a writer who before the war had an apartment on Broadway, longed to meet one of those southern belles. He even wanted to meet the beauties from Manhattan. "Every time I mussed around the lobby of Spartanburg's most fashionable hostelry feminine fantasies of every description greeted my eyes," he wrote in the pages of the *Gazette*. "Some of the rarest class who affixed the beloved letters, 'N.Y.,' to their names on the register, sauntered to and fro across the mud-besmirched tile floor. Others who brag they were never north of the Mason and Dixon line, added gobs of color to make the bewitching picture. What a joy to hold down the plush furniture, ostensibly to devour the contents of the dailies, when the fairest of the fair parade before you."

While Rowland ogled the girls, his Broadway colleagues, professional actors, musicians, composers, and other writers within the division, treated their host city to a Broadway-bound show, *You Know Me, Al* The musical farce was produced by the soldiers themselves, including coauthor Cpl. W. Anson Hallahan of the 107th's M Company. *You Know Me, Al* actually ran on Broadway in April for ten days to sold-out audiences.

Hundreds of soldiers took advantage of church suppers. It beat the meals back at the camp.

"Dear Mom," wrote Pvt. Bert Lobdell, "Last night I went to town. We went down early, right after retreat, and had dinner at the Episcopalian church. It was delicious. Cost me 85 cts. They run a little tea room there for soldiers and charge just enough to pay expenses." In another letter, he told of going to Spartanburg on a Saturday night. "There was a new order went into effect that day, that Saturday night anybody could go to town without passes. Well the roads were full of soldiers walking the five miles. You'd ought to have seen the town. It was worse than an anthill. Khaki all over. There was hardly a civilian to be seen."

The walk to town along Snake Road was tedious. Soldiers grabbed rides whenever possible. Another route to town was the so-called interurban electric line that ran along the camp's northern border. On the 17th, the train, packed with three hundred soldiers, was struck from behind by a work train. Men went flying everywhere. The last car was a "tangled shell." Two men on the work train, one of them a black, were killed. Cpl. Arthur Wright of the Third Heavy Artillery also died. Scores of others were injured, many seriously.

"About half the fellows in [H] Company prepared to go to town to a dance at the Cleveland Hotel," reported Pfc. Edward G. Bradford. "Nearly forty took the late train in, which was unfortunately run into by a workmen's train. The accident was pretty bad. Everybody was well shaken up and some more or less bruised, but out of all who were seriously injured there was only one from this Company. Harry D. Triantafillu, who ordinarily calls his home White Plains, was taken to the Steedley Hospital in Spartanburg for two days with a fractured shoulder and arm."

Pvt. Harry H. Williams of C Company "hurt his hip quite badly, but is expected to be back in a few days," detailed Sergeant Thomas Kerr. "Consider him very lucky. There were a bunch of our men on the same train, but they managed to escape without getting hurt."

Two uninjured men from the 107th raced from the tangled trains to camp, calling out for Maj. Edmund Fowler, commander of the Sanitary Detachment. Within five minutes, Fowler, the son of the health commissioner of New York City and one of the top ear specialists in the country, had his men on the run back to the wreck, lugging litters. One of Fowler's men, Don Emery, marveled at the way the major "took supreme command of the entire situation and with the able help of Lts. [Dr. Perley] Gray, [Dr. Albert Newell] Benedict, [Dr. Henry] Bancel and [Dr. William] Coogan went about the work of rescuing as coolly as though he were performing an operation for adenoids."

The wreck didn't slow up training. When O'Ryan returned to camp in late November, after his month stint on the battlefields of France, training took on a more urgent pace. Even the cold and snow that hounded the division through the winter months couldn't stop the task of getting the men ready for their long-awaited trip overseas.

"We have been gassed. We have hurled bombs that flew back at us so rapidly that we received the impression that we had thrown them backward," lamented Sgt. Walter Davenport of M Company. "We have vibrated at the safe end of Chauchat automatic rifles. We have speared Dummy Huns on a bayonet run that would discourage the Ringling Brothers."

"Dere Mable," penned Ed Streeter in *The Gas Attack*, "We're doin bayonet drill now. We have one place where we hit the Hun in the nose an rip all the decorashuns offen his uniform all in one stroke. Than theres another where you give him a shave an a round hair cut an end up knocking his hat over his eyes."

Sergeant Grimm agreed with both Davenport and Streeter. "The early part of February was spent squads easting and westing, bombing, bayoneting and in doing all those peaceful little stunts in vogue for soldiers this year."

Alienists appeared at camp to check the soldiers for their "mentality and nervous durability," according to O'Ryan. "Every man was examined by officers expert in nervous diseases and all peculiarities were carefully noted. All those who seemed likely to break down under nervous strain of battle were checked for transfer." Almost two hundred men from the 107th were either discharged or transferred for various mental or health reasons.

* * *

Thirty-one-year-old Cpl. Arthur Briggs Church, a New York City lawyer and Harvard man, found camp life good for his health. "Am feeling fine—better than for years. I weigh 138 and am hard as nails—nothing the matter with me that I can see, and I stand the hard game better than I ever dreamed I would. The other fellows, a good many of them, are falling by the wayside, but so far I have kept up and am getting better all the time."[4]

Although Church felt himself to be in the pink of health, the first signs of the flu that would later kill more Americans than the war itself worked its deadly way into camp. Sgt. Floyd Neely recorded that Pfc. Charles W. Rowe died from pneumonia, the first man from I Company to give his life for his country. "He was a general favorite in the company and his loss was a terrible blow. The company attended his funeral at the church in Spartanburg, and Bugler Potter blew 'Taps' over his coffin. Charley's name stands first on our long Roll of Honor."[5]

C Company's Stanley Lahm also died from pneumonia. "Stanley was one of the best," Sergeant Kerr wrote in the *Gazette*. "And to him is due all the credit and glory of one who died in battle. He died for his country and gave it his all." Like Rowe, his funeral service was held at a church in Spartanburg

Bert Lobdell caught pneumonia, too, waiting outside as the regiment passed in review for the governor of New York.

"The day Gov. Whitman reviewed us was such a raw, cold, damp day and we had to stand around so long that I got chilled through and through and Friday afternoon went to bed," he informed his mother. Twenty-year-old Cpl. Clarence Osterhoudt of Headquarters Company described that review to a friend back in his hometown of Cornwall-on-Hudson. "Well, we started past the reviewing stand at 8:30 in the morning and at 4:30 in the afternoon the parade was still on and he did not see us all yet, and no man passed him twice." Lobdell, after being examined by a doctor in his tent, was wrapped in blankets, put on a stretcher and carried to the head of the company street. There he was placed inside a truck and driven to the camp hospital. "My bones ached so and had been for so long that I didn't care what they did to me." A brass bed, soft mattresses, white sheets, and pillowcases and the "cutest, little red-headed Red Cross Nurse you ever saw" perked up the Salem Center soldier. Lobdell feigned fear of the little pills he had to take "just to hear her talk."

Lobdell's stay in the camp hospital dragged on for days and then several weeks. On 13 November he "had a high fever but no pain in the head except when I coughed. It felt then as if it would split." He let his mother know that the wards were "all full all the time, mostly with colds and grippe. Influenza they put it down as on the records." He was discharged on the night of the 16th.

Sgt. Harry Mitchell noted Lobdell's return "after a siege in the base hospital." He especially commented on the nurses there, stating that "Bert says he received the best care. Her hair was golden red and many of Bert's visitors inclined to linger."

It's likely the same nurse who tended Lobdell also tended Billy Leonard of I Company during his stay at the base hospital, also for pneumonia. In a letter to a friend in Flushing, the smitten corporal described her. "There's a nurse with the most wonderful hair I've ever seen—a rich bronze, masses of it, curled around a dainty head. Can't be more than 20 and she's slim and graceful and dimples when she smiles. She just took my temperature and pulse. Her hands are very cool. When she finished I said: 'What's the . . . reading Nurse?' That's when she smiled. I'll have to think of other things to make her smile. And get her address. This war can't last forever."[6]

Another ailment that swept through camp was homesickness. L Company's Pvt. John Donnelly, a Newburgh native whose father had come to the United States from Ireland when he was five, wrote to his sister Sarah, "This is the first Thanksgiving I have been away from home. I wish I were there [Newburgh]. How is little Helen [another sister] getting along? I miss her. I suppose she is getting bigger all the time. Tell her I send her some kisses."[7] Donnelly was considered the quietest man in L Company, perhaps because he longed for home. Sergeant Mitchell remembered him as the "most conscientious man among us, and couldn't even be drawn into the friendly arguments that many of us indulged in."

As November passed and winter settled in, all the soldiers could talk about was the horrible weather.

Pvt. Raeburn Van Buren wrote to his mother that "while I was on my post the water in my canteen on my hip froze. I had on three heavy suits of underwear and an extra undershirt—two sweaters and a flannel shirt, two pairs of socks—heavy trench shoes and an overcoat and helmet. I only got cold in the toes and fingers and got rid of this just as soon as I had a chance to exercise. Forty-six men in our company of 225 men answered the sick call this morning, 20 men passed out in the trenches."

Van Buren's company sergeant, Earle Grimm, explained that there are "two kinds of water, now, frozen and dirty."

F Company's Sgt. James L. Richmond told of how "a wonderful thing is the Sibley stove. Nothing, but a big, black megaphone with a bit of a door in the side, a cup-shaped cut-out at the bottom for draft and two or three lengths of stove pipe at the top; yet you can have a good fire in two minutes."

In another letter to "Dere Mable," Edward Streeter described that "A Sibley stove, Mable, is a piece of stove pipe built like the leg of a sailurs trowsers." He also told her that "a fello tried to take a shower the other day. Before he could get out it froze round him like that fello in the bible who turned into a pillar of salt. They had to break the whole thing offen the pipe with him inside it an stand it in front of the stove. When it melted he finished his shower and said he felt fine."

Sergeant Grimm said that the company street "resembles Pittsburgh on a busy day, as though our endeavor to keep the heat 'in-tents,' we secured Sibley stoves, the pipes of which project through the tops of tents, and belch forth all kinds of smoke, not to mention sparks, cinders and soot."

One way to stay warm was to pull kitchen police duty. As Billy Leonard described his five-day experience on K.P., he peeled at least eighteen thousand potatoes, he claimed, and when he finished, he peeled eighteen thousand onions. "Peeling onions is worse than peeling potatoes. They get into your eyes. They got into my eyes so I didn't see two ladies approach. It wasn't until they were quite close that I recognized them. I had met them in Spartanburg and invited them to call me in camp. And what a time they picked! Fortunately they didn't recognize me at all. They asked me was I in and I told them I wasn't. I told them I had been put on special duty for five days, and they asked me to tell myself they had called. I promised them I would." Surprised that he wasn't recognized, Billy stole back to his tent to look at himself in the mirror. "I am not a vain man.

But in those far-away days of peace and plenty I had a face that was not unpleasing. That face was now streaked with mud and grease. My hair was matted thickly as the coat of a wire-haired terrier. My O. D. breeches were caked with a smelly mixture of everything I'd handled."

Leonard's humor endeared him to the troops of the 107th. *Gazette* editor, Private Eugene O'Brien, said of Billy in the May issue, "If you ever want to meet one of the most delightful personalities in seven counties, just amble down Company I street and intermittently yell, 'Billy Leonard.' You'll amble all the way to [the] end of the street, for he's hidden away in the last tent, but you will feel the cheerfulness of his smile many tents before the last. . . . He usually makes us laugh and laugh heartily; but often he touches a different key, and then we know there are such depths to him and his writings that he'll show up big on the final sheets."

Meanwhile, Van Buren, the artist as skinny as a pencil, was constantly freezing no matter how many layers of clothing he threw on. Yet he always found time to draw for *The Gas Attack* or the *Gazette*. For *The Gas Attack*, he illustrated the cover of the 13 April 1918 issue, a realistic portrait of men at war. For the *Gazette*, he submitted several cartoons. In the April number, he had the centerfold, a picture of a soldier sunk deep in a soft bed. The only part of him visible is his nose and a cigarette and puffs of smoke rings rising toward the ceiling. A beautiful, dark-haired girl is carrying a tray of steaming food into the plush bedroom where the soldier is enjoying himself. The caption below read: "And then the bugle blew."

In telling his mother about the magazines, he said, "I've been making a picture now and then for them because they found out I was here in camp and have pestered the life out of me. One magazine, called 'The Gas Attack,' wants me to be their art editor. It is a 'thank you' job, but will get me out of drill about two afternoons a week and I will have a nice little office to work in over in the Y. M.C. A. building." Later, he wrote, "I believe [camp life] is helping my artistic eye. Since I have been here I have made quite a few sketches and they have showed marks of real art. I seem to be able to see better."

When the magazines came out, they were sent to the editorial offices of the newspapers in New York because the magazines' editors and reporters and other artists were ex-newspapermen from the city. Reading one of the issues was the famous *Tribune* columnist Franklin Pierce Adams. Spotting Van Buren's signature on a number of the illustrations, F.P.A. wrote to him. They had become friends at the cluttered apartment of the free-spirited Neysa McMein. Van Buren immediately let his mother know. "I had a letter from F.P.A., now Captain Adams, which tickled me very much because he is such a big man in his line of work."

Both publications, particularly the *Gazette,* were among the best magazines put out by soldiers anywhere in the country. Their strength was in the humor, from Ed Streeter's letters to "Dere Mable" to the inside jokes of the company scribes to the gag drawings by the staff of talented cartoonists and illustrators. Among the 107th Infantry writers were future editors of the *Saturday Evening Post, Collier's, Scientific American,* and *Yachting.* On the art staff with Van Buren was his close friend Lauren Stout; also, the set designer of "You Know Me, Al," Pfc. C. C. Beall, whose portrait of President Franklin Roosevelt, "Double Vision," hung in the White House for many years; George Breck, who because he was in Streeter's company illustrated "Dere Mable"; and Harold Kunkle from Brooklyn, another promising artist, tall, handsome, and raw-boned. Adding a poetic touch was H Company's Charles Divine, dubbed the "Poet Laureate of the Twenty-seven Division." A Binghamton native, with jet black hair, who had studied at the Sorbonne, Divine joined the staff of the *New York Sun* in 1910 when he was twenty-one and moved into a small apartment at Washington Place in Greenwich Village. "The Village," said a fellow staffer on the *Sun,* "which spoils utterly so many talents, could not spoil Divine. He saw its poetry and the real wistfulness that underlines the freakish surface. If you don't believe that, read . . . *At The Lavender Lantern.* It is simple and honest and charming a bit of verse as ever came from a poet turned soldier."[8] The poem appeared in *City Ways and Company Streets,* published in 1918, two months after the 107th reached France.

I wonder who is haunting the little snug cafe,
That place, half restaurant and home, since we have gone away;
The candled dimness, smoke and talk, and tables brown and bare—
But no one thinks of tablecloths when love and laughter's there.

I wonder if it's crowded still, three steps below the street,
Half hidden from the passing town, where even poets eat;
I wonder if the girls still laugh, the girls whose art was play;
I wonder who the fellows are that try to make them gay.

Some said it was Bohemia, this little haunt we knew,
Where hearts were high and fortunes low, and onions in the stew.
I wonder if it's still the same, after dinner ease—
Bohemia is in the heart, and the hearts are overseas.

Oh, great were all the problems that we settled here, with wine,
And fates of many nations were disposed of, after nine,
But France has braved a fate that brought us swarming to her shore—
I wonder who is sitting at the table near the door.

I wonder who is haunting the little snug cafe,
That place, half restaurant and home, since we have gone away;
I wonder if they miss me, I don't suppose they do,
As long as there is art and girls and onions in the stew.

The first of the year, 1918, brought sad news to the men of F Company and the Machine Gun Company. One of their own was killed in France. Twenty-three-year-old Lt. William Hallet Tailer of the famed Lafayette Escadrille's *Groupe de Cigones* (storks), who had shared a tent with Gow on the Mexican border, was shot down near Verdun. A friend of Billy's said he was "endowed with one of the rarest natures, a cheerful spirituality which looked only on the bright side of life." According to one account, Tailer was killed in a "terrific air duel while trying to avenge the death of his friend, Peter Benney of Pittsburgh. Although outnumbered, 'Bill' Taylor, as he was called, put up a splendid fight but was finally over-powered. Friends who witnessed the unequal battle saw Taylor's machine plunge to the ground."[9] Tailer was the first soldier from Roslyn, New York, to be killed in the Great War.

"It was quite a shock to me," Gow, now a first sergeant, wrote home, "when I first heard the news last night. Billy Tailer was one of the finest men I ever met, and died in a way we would expect of him. He is the first of our old company to pass on. It brings home with a smash the fact that we have men at the front. Billy's father died only last month, and it is harder therefore for his mother and sister. The Captain and I are writing them. It just seems a crime that a man who has everything to live for should suddenly be snuffed out like a burning candle."

While Gow lamented the death of his friend, he also wondered if he might not be up for a commission. "I am convinced that the 27th Division is going to be the best one to go to France, and I want the position that will give me the power to play my part of assisting and shaping its destinies."

Two friends from Summit kept Gow's spirits up. The first was Sgt. Paul Gadebusch, his tentmate. "Helmuth is here writing beside me," he informed his "Pop." "He is the best company in the world, and my right-hand man in the company, always there when I want him." The other was Lt. Edward Willis. "Jun has arrived back in camp with his bride. She is a wonderful girl and has started to run things already, including me."

On 14 January, Gow nervously polished his ever-present glasses and then appeared before O'Ryan and "received a grilling." Two weeks later he got his commission. "Dear Mama, I appeared at retreat tonight with my shoulder-bars, collar insignia and black-and-gold hat cord. I cannot begin to express in words the satisfaction that I feel in being commissioned in my own regiment in the old Seventh way. The Colonel and all of our old officers enlisted as privates."

Cpl. Albert Sawtell was happy for Gow. "Every man in the Company has a proud feeling when he comes to attention and salutes him. We are glad to have as one of our officers, a man who has run the first sergeant's job so well, and, has kept the good will of every man."

The new lieutenant was put in charge of the transport, where he could continue to take care of his beloved horses and mules. Gow called his men together and said to them, "You fellows can swear all you want to at the mules; I know they are exasperating at times; but if I catch one of you calling another an obscene name, into the guardhouse you go!" Wagoner Thomas C. Janson said the "respect for the man made us quit, as we thought if Gow said so it must be right." Soon after, the transport was called "Gow's Sunday School."[10]

Gow wasn't the only Summit resident to win a commission. Twenty-three-year-old Oscar Hellquist, who had enlisted in the Seventh on 17 May and was a member of F Company, received his gold bars after attending officer's training at Camp Stuart. He was then reassigned back to the 107th Infantry. Delicately handsome, with blond hair and gray eyes, he had an expression of quiet strength that later on, in the face of battle, his boys found reassuring. He was bright enough to graduate from Summit High School at sixteen and enroll in Cornell's civil engineering course. He and Gow sang together in the choir of the Calvary Church in Summit.

Another new lieutenant was Sergeant Grimm, the advertising genius, who eventually became a battalion intelligence officer. Combining his advertising skills with a deadly sense of humor, he would soon be tormenting the Germans in the frontline trenches of Flanders.

After Hellquist, Gow, and Grimm earned their lieutenant's bars, forty-two-year-old 1st Lt. Harry Woodford Hayward was named captain of E Company. A law partner with Marshall McLean, whose grandfather, as associate justice of the U.S. Supreme Court, wrote the dissenting opinion in the Dred Scott Case, Hayward had been a veteran of the old Seventh since 1903. During the previous winter, he had gone to Europe to study the war. Now, with his new orders in hand, he walked into the tent of Capt. John Augustus Barnard, who was busy signing papers. Both were former K Company men, where Hayward had been Barnard's first sergeant while the regiment was on the Mexican border. Several things about Hayward, a confirmed bachelor, that struck Barnard, were that he was not afraid of any man, that he spoke his mind freely, and that he was modest to a fault. Hayward had been born in the Maine wilderness in 1875, where his father, a Canadian, was in the lumber business. He loved

*The daring Lt. Oscar Hellquist
of Summit, N.J.* Joan Hellquist

Capt. Harry Hayward, a lawyer, loved his Maine woods more than Manhattan. The Seventh Regiment Fund

the woods and every year spent his vacation hunting and fishing. Once inside Barnard's tent, Hayward showed his friend the orders.

"Thank heaven it has come at last," said Barnard, who back in New York was a stockbroker.

"But think of the responsibility," Hayward said.

"Never mind, Harry," Barnard replied, thinking not of the men now under Hayward's new command but of filling out reams of paperwork. "As soon as we get to France there will be no more of that," he assured him.

Looking at Barnard's cluttered desk, Hayward said, "Great heavens, that is not bothering me."

Barnard's eyes swept across the mounds of paperwork and then he saw what Hayward meant. "That remark," he recalled years later, "showed that he, after some fifteen years of National Guard training, thoroughly realized the responsibility that went with the Captaincy in the Infantry and gave to such a man the power over 250 enlisted men."[11] Hayward's utmost regard for the responsibility just bestowed upon him would serve E Company well in the coming year. After the war, Sgt. Nicholas Krayer remembered him as a "strict disciplinarian, one who insisted on military precision in every movement . . . [a]nd it was not long before the company was recognized as the most precise and best drilled unit in the regiment."[12]

Another new officer was Sgt. Thomas Kerr, who was made a second lieutenant. Unlike Hellquist, Gow, Grimm, and Hayward, however, he did not stay with the 107th. Instead, the War Department packed him over to the 108th Infantry. At least he was still in the Twenty-seventh Division. In fact, fifteen men from the 107th were commissioned and sent to the 108th. Four others headed for the 106th and three more saw service with the 105th, including former Sgt. Walter Davenport, the ex-newspaperman.

As O'Ryan recollected, it was indeed true that the War Department was bleeding the old Seventh Regiment dry.

Before they were commissioned officers and sent off to other regiments, Kerr, Davenport, and the rest first had to experience life in the trenches that had been cleverly designed by Vanderbilt and his engineers.

When it was the 107th's time to go into the trenches for its seventy-two-hour stint, it was mid-February. The weather had worsened—a bone-aching cold that worried O'Ryan. On a number of occasions, the general postponed the trip to the trenches. At one time, rumors reached New York City that several men had frozen to death. Anxious parents wrote to the division commander, letting him know their sons were "not any too strong constitutionally and might succumb under the rigors of the trench training."

Finally, when the 107th went in, the weather changed, turning warmer, and the skies cleared. Cpl. Clarence Osterhoudt of Headquarters Company marveled at the trench system. "We have seen miles of practice trenches," he penned to a friend, Walter, in Cornwall, "and they are the greatest things I ever saw. We have underground tunnels, bomb proofs, machine gun pits, underground kitchens and hospitals. They are places for practice gas attacks and all the comforts or discomforts of modern warfare." Osterhoudt, who had been a railroad clerk in Cornwall when he enlisted in the Seventh, found trench life thrilling. "The other day we had some defensive hand grenades; the real ones. They kill everything above ground within a hundred-yard radius. We stand in a trench, throw them as far as possible and duck out of range. If you put your head above the trench where it went off, you would look like a sieve."[13]

For L Company, the first forty-eight hours in the trenches were a lark in such a magnificent environment. Then on the third day the rains came.

"Picture: A long strip of trench ending with a flight of steps leading to the ground level; sidewalls are dripping wet, and the floor is a squashy strip of bog flooded with two and a half feet of water, the color of split-pea soup," wrote Sgt. Mitchell. "We shall always remember those three days and three nights. They were at once a test and an experience. They proved that the months in camp have hardened us; that we can stand much exposure without worrying about pneumonia and the like; that we can be human ground moles for an extended period without losing spirit."

In the same company as Mitchell, Private Lobdell let his parents know that they should have seen the "water rush down through the entrance of the dugout. We were actually washed out." The company was ordered to evacuate the dugout, and by the time the last man out made it to safety, the water was waist deep. "Never saw it rain so hard in my life and everything was soaken wet and red mud. Even our guns were caked with mud from muzzle to butt."

Don Emery of the Sanitary Detachment said the thunderstorm that struck was a "beautiful, genuine, uncamouflaged thunder storm such as 'haint been known in these yere parts nigh onto forty year.'" Emery and most of his comrades thought their situation funny. But he added that Pfc. Francis Callahan, drenched to the skin, failed to see the humor. "Standing against a wall with a stream of muddy water trickling down one's spinal column with one's feet in six inches of water while one attempted to sleep did not tend to harden one, he contended."

"We were wet to the hide," recalled Mitchell.

E Company's Cpl. Howard L. Boggs stated, "We have simulated going 'over the top' so frequently lately that we are sure it will be a matter of habit before we go over with fire in our eyes. They even had us practice walking through trenches with water up to our waists and [1st Sgt. Frank B.] Scherer swears the water was out there on purpose."

The good news about the thunderstorm was that it was the first harbinger of spring. That meant a twenty-five-mile trip to Glassy Rock for small arms training and to the artillery range nearby where the regiment would taste for the first time the rumble and roar of real bombs. And it also meant that at last training had to be drawing to an end; that orders to sail for France were sure to be sent soon to division headquarters.

Of all the experiences the soldiers shared at camp none compared to the thrill of actual artillery fire. On 10 April the troops marched to Glassy Rock in the foothills of the Blue Ridge Mountains, twelve miles from Campobello, South Carolina. Regimental Supply Sgt. Gerald Jacobson saw the place as "vast, romantic, silent, majestic." The artillery fire was "terrific," according to Jacobson. "A real barrage was put down by the 27th Division artillery, and under the curtain of fire the regiment moved forward, as some months later it moved forward in actual battle, in wave formation."

"When we reached the range and learned that the four-point-sevens which would chuck the shells over us would be posted a mile and [a] half behind us, there was nary a man Mike among us who didn't feel a tiny bit apprehensive," said Mitchell. "And when we slung our packs and trudged out to the scene of the racket we imagined all manner of dismal things that could happen."

G Company Sgt. Frederick Gudebrod Jr. remembered how the "shells whistled 20 feet over our heads, and burst not a 100 yards in front of us. We were told to duck our heads. We did."

As the men got ready to advance, they crouched as close to the ground as possible and stared in a "hypnotized gaze" at the "thundering pyrotechnics 50 yards in front of them." The barrage kept up for three minutes and then the "steel curtain began creeping away from us," Mitchell reported. "Down the line some officer bellowed out a command. We thrilled. Across the torn field started our first attacking wave."

"Some action alright," K Company's Pfc. Raymond Van Rensselaer Schuyler hollered to Bugler Walter Flack as they followed the barrage. "Listen to those things whistle!"

Mitchell described the tumult as "screaming, whining, banging. Boom! boom! wheee-e-e-e! bang!"

One of the coolest boys under fire was D Company's Pvt. Joe

"Cuckoo" Mastine from Ogdensburg. Sgt. John McCormick remarked that right after the barrage Mastine displayed a hunk of shrapnel that "he claims to have caught by a quick grab as it sailed past just over his head." A small man, not quite five-and-a-half feet tall, with hazel eyes and a demeanor that a hometown buddy described as "meek," Mastine would show his coolness again six months later—only this time in real combat.

Pvt. George Fetherolf of I Company, the transfer from Middletown, described to his Aunt Mollie what a "great sight" it was "to see a whole regiment deployed in skirmish line with fixed bayonets slowly creeping along behind a curtain of bursting shrapnel shell from a battery of artillery three miles behind them." He told her that "the shrapnel shell are little lead balls about 3/8 of an inch in diameter. Each shell contains 250 of these and it is timed to explode about five feet above the ground throwing the lead in all directions. I picked a few of them up and will send them home to be added to my souveneres."

After it was over, Lt. Kenneth Gow couldn't wait to write to his parents. "My experience today has been the most thrilling thing of my life." He told them of the shrieking overhead, how "d——d close" the shells landed. He described the attack that followed behind the creeping barrage. "It was the most marvelous, miraculous and impressive thing I ever witnessed. The deadly accuracy of the artillery was wonderful. The guns were four miles away from us, and had to fire over two mountain ranges at a target they could not see. A slight mistake would have meant death to dozens of us."

When the men of the regiment marched back to camp, adrenaline flowed like intoxicating wine through their veins.

"The hike home from the range is likely to linger long in the memories of those who made it," Billy Leonard said. "Twenty-six miles between sunrise and sunset carrying full packs!"

L Company led the way, and Mitchell couldn't stop from boasting. "We loped along at a pace that made the Companies in the rear say unkind things about us, for they surely didn't have the lively step to keep up."

Sergeant McCormick pointed out, however, that "not a man caved in on the long hike back. Some of the boys made the last few miles chiefly on nerve—and blisters."

Mitchell then admitted that "after we lopped off the first 20 miles or so we felt as if we were toting Jumbo, Barnum's baby elephant, on our backs."

After the march, Van Buren wrote that the regiment was a "very tired but happy bunch." He added, "Imagine marching along a mountain road very rough from recent rains for twenty-six miles with fifty pounds on your back and with only five ten-minute rests and you can realize just what we had finished when we pulled back the flaps of our tents and gave our cots the glad once-over. So now our soft cot looks like the Astor to us tonight."

Pvt. John Donnelly, the quiet man from L Company, wrote his sister in Newburgh, "We have had about all of our training and are ready for the Trenches and the Germans."

On 15 April, while the silk stocking soldiers were still at Glassy Rock experiencing the "thrill of their lives," official orders came down from the War Department. Finally, during the first week of May, New York's Twenty-seventh Division was headed for the western front.

Second Lt. Oscar Hellquist, assigned to D Company of the First Battalion, quickly penned a note to his mother in Summit, hoping to reassure her that in the end all would be fine. "Don't worry. We're all coming back and I hope real soon."

CHAPTER 5

I Can Only Say
Good-bye — Good Luck —
God Bless You

Maybe it was the cold, gray winter they'd just endured in South Carolina. Maybe it was the last two weeks they'd spent lolling aboard two gray transports, the USS *Antigone* and the USS *Susquehanna*, with not much to do except stare at the vast gray north Atlantic. Maybe it was the simple fact that in their entire lives the only sailboats they'd most likely ever seen had been rigged in white. Or more likely it was their own red blood—rising like hot lava through bodies trembling with excitement about the great adventure that, at last, was now close enough to reach out and touch—that enhanced all their senses. But on 23 May, when the first of the transports steamed into the congested harbor of Brest on the coast of Brittany, the boys of the 107th Infantry Regiment were at first dazzled by color.

"Our spirit, depressed by the long trip, brightened as we saw the rolling slopes of green and yellow fields," recorded Sgt. Robert L. Peek of K Company. "The anticipation of the great adventure buoyed us up and when we landed the next day and swung along the cobbled streets of that city, we felt sensations experienced only by men who march off to war."[1]

With the eye of an artist, E Company's Pvt. Lauren Stout, the Kansas

City illustrator, wrote of the "emerald-green hills, dotted here and there with tiny thatched-roof peasant houses, the bluest of blue waters, and the fleet of sailboats of all colors, some almost toy-like in size."[2]

"As the panorama of vivid green heights with gleaming white villas unfolded, sergeants' glasses were greatly in demand," noted F Company's Cpl. Robert Waddell.[3]

The entrance into the "rock-bound harbor," impressed Sergeant Harry Mitchell. "Slowly toward anchorage rode the transports, their decks teeming with soldiers, some cheering, some merely staring. Not a whistle piped a greeting. The city snuggled white and beautiful against the rich green terraces on one side of the harbor. There was no indications of a stir."

Billy Leonard felt the same way. In a letter to the editor of the Flushing *Daily Times*, he reported, "At home we had come to think of all France as a land devastated by war, wearing everywhere the scars of war, so our first view of this wonderful country was a bit surprising. A beautiful harbor smiling in the brilliant sunshine of a May day, a rolling land of green that stretched to the water's edge, and beyond a glimpse of quaint homes with terraced lawns. A nearer view revealed that nearly every inch of land was under cultivation and the air was sweet with the smell of growing things."

Lieutenant Gow, who arrived a week earlier aboard the USS *George Washington* because he had been at home on leave when the regiment sailed out of Newport News, described, "Ridges of hills rising one after the other, a quaint picturesque old city nestling among them and running down to the water's edge. Beautiful green fields, all with hedges running around them, giving a peculiar symmetry to the landscape, like a checkerboard. Clumps of trees, and here and there, a heavily-wooded area. Sheep grazing, some old castles, with their moats and walls. Some church spires rising above the other buildings; and then the city itself."

Brest was one of two major ports on the French coast where U.S. troops disembarked. The other was St. Nazaire. Built by Cardinal Richelieu in the 1600s, the harbor of Brest was ringed by rocky bluffs. Atop the hills were ancient fortifications, reinforced with concrete gun emplacements. A medieval castle and a chateau, owned by the Countess de Rodellac du Porzic, whose father fought for the Union Army in the American Civil War, looked down on the busy harbor. Floating above the military ships

The librarian, Lt. Claude Leland.
The Seventh Regiment Fund

and fishermen's boats was a tethered observation balloon, facing toward the ocean. The evening the *Susquehanna* slipped into the harbor, 2d Lt. Claude Leland of I Company, like hundreds of awe-struck doughboys, came out on the deck of the transport for a look. "There were hundreds of ships talking to each other last night with their Ardois lights and it looked like a big gala night of some kind instead of the biggest expedition and force of men and ships the United States has ever sent forth to war."[4]

Frenchmen in small boats of every description paddled or motored or sailed out to the transports. Soldiers, leaning along the railings, peppered them with coins, candy, and cigarettes.

"An occasional 'vive l'Amerique' floated across the water from the little red-sailed fishing boats that dotted the harbor," Corporal Waddell wrote.[5] Otherwise, the welcome by the citizens of Brest was subdued. For the past six months, they'd witnessed the arrival of hundreds of thousands of doughboys—in fact, the day before the 106th Infantry had entered their harbor—until the newness and excitement had long worn out.

* * *

The 107th stayed overnight on the transports, even though the men were itching to get ashore, to feel solid ground beneath their feet once again. Lauren Stout decided to be the first enlisted man in the regiment to set foot in Brest. Somehow the E Company private swiped the uniform of a sailor, slipped into the blue bell-bottoms, and got ashore. Here he explored the city, according to Corporal Francis Miller, "to his heart's content," because his "artist temperament could not wait to absorb the quaint Brittany village and its people." Strolling merrily up the main street, "Stouty" nearly bumped into 1st Lt. William Penoyar, a veteran officer of the old First Infantry, who'd been with E Company since October. Either Penoyar didn't recognize one of his own men because of the blue uniform or he decided to overlook this brazen act of insubordination. He turned his head away as Stout walked past. Back on ship, neither man mentioned the incident.[6]

The following day, the 107th disembarked and marched to a camp-ground a few miles outside of Brest to await further orders. On shore for the first time in nearly two weeks, the regiment formed up at the quay. For the most part, the citizens of Brest continued to show little interest in the latest assemblage of Yankee soldiers. They went about their business, the clop-clop of their wooden shoes on the cobbled streets a new and strange sound to the Americans.

The route out of Brest was up a long, twisting hill to the top of the city. Dirty buildings hugged the drab street. To Pvt. Don Emery, the winding street was "lined with walls, houses and tiled and turretted structures resembling half buried castles, all relics of a bygone period, almost mediaeval in appearance though still in use by people who compared favorably with the surroundings." A few of these poor people stared from doorways or gazed out windows at the regiment. Peering over the gate of a convent, a little girl said, "Hello boys." Still, Leland noted, the men were "a little disappointed at the reception." However, Mitchell was "glad of the feel of solid earth again." L Company, he said, "swung off through town, whistling gaily. As we puffed up the hilly streets leading to the camp scores of cute French youngsters were out to meet us, crying, 'Cigaret pour Papa?' Some, kid-like, marched along with us, and one bright-looking urchin got up at the head of the column and won the hearts of us by playing 'Yankee Doodle' on a little tin flute."

Marching up the hill was "an awful pull for a man with a pack filled with junk and who still had his sea legs," remembered Leland. "A few old men and children and many black-clad women stood on the narrow sidewalks and looked at us but without enthusiasm."

Regimental Supply Sgt. Gerald Jacobson also was disappointed because the "French families watched us swing by without giving any sign of emotion." But with the children it was different. "They trickled into the street from every doorway, hailing us with shrill shrieks of welcome in a jargon few of us could understand. They followed us for blocks, begging for pennies and cigarettes. They got them too. Their welcome warmed the hearts of the men in the ranks; besides they were cute little shavers."

As Leland's company hiked through Brest, a "gamin made a hit by marching along beside a doughboy and singing in a squawky little voice, 'Hail, hail, the gang's all here!' " The gamin was actually a gamine, a little girl of five who held tightly to the sleeve of Cpl. Merritt Cutler, a magazine illustrator from Freeport, Long Island. Cutler was in the row ahead of Corporal Leonard. "Suddenly she burst into song," Leonard wrote, "a clear, childish voice, the words as distinct as any American child could utter them, 'Hail, hail, the gang's all here, so what the hell do we care now.' The whole platoon roared in laughter." F Company's Corporal Waddell remembered another "youngster at the head of the column, setting the pace by piping, 'Hail, Hail! The Gang's All Here' on a fife."[7]

Outside Brest that night, the entire 107th Infantry, officers and men, even Colonel Williard Fisk and his staff, rolled themselves in blankets and slept on the hard ground. The tents were so tight with two men in them that first night on French soil that Leonard said, "You undress by taking off your hat and maybe your shoes, and you dress by putting them on." Hardly had the doughboys closed their eyes when, at three in the moonlit morning, reveille blared from a dozen bugles. The regiment had been ordered back to Brest. There the troops would climb aboard rickety trains for a two-day trip to the mouth of the Somme River. The division had been ordered to train with the Sixty-sixth British Division, led by Maj. Gen. H. K. Bethell. His division was part of the British Third Army. As the regiment returned to Brest, it ran into a gang of German prisoners, guarded by three Frenchmen. It was the first time the New Yorkers saw the enemy. They hollered at the Germans. The Germans, in return, stared at the Americans. "Some eyed us sheepishly," recorded Mitchell.

"But there were others that scowled and sneered. Never had any of us beheld a dirtier-looking lot. Nearly all of them needed razoring."

Leonard recalled, "They were a surly looking lot. I wondered if it was prejudice in my heart that I saw the brutality in their faces. They glared at us curiously and passed low-toned remarks to each other."

Jacobson also remembered that moment. The whole city was asleep, he said. Birds were "warbling" in the trees. The setting was idyllic. But as the regiment turned the "corner of a particularly beautiful avenue . . . we saw our first Germans! We beheld perhaps fifty Hun prisoners marching between blue-clad Polius. Never could one imagine a more motley crew. They were unkempt of hair and person, shockingly in need of razoring, and their uniforms were of every cut and color ever issued in Germany." He reported that, for the most part, the doughboys "marched by the enemy prisoners in silence, merely staring at them. Here and there, however, were a few chaps who could not restrain their desire to hail them. The Huns leered at every one who yelled at them, and they seemed callously indifferent to the information, imparted by one enthusiastic Yank, that there were already eight or ten million Americans in France, and that many more were on the way."

Shortly after their first encounter with Germans, the boys met another product of the war. The French freight train that was used to transport troops. On the side of each car was written the soon famous phrase, "40 hommes 8 cheveaux." I Company Sgt. Floyd Neely later translated that "this meant that the cars were capable of holding 40 men or 8 horses. Usually the horses had been there before us."[8]

Leland noted, "Hommy cars of the usual fragrant type."

Edward Streeter, under the guise of Bill, shot off a letter to his Dere Mable. "On the doors they got painted 'Homes 40 Chevaux 8.' That's French for 40 men and 8 horses. That struck me as funny till I figgered out that they probably pack five men between each horse sos they wont rattle round so much."

The soldiers loaded into three trains and set out toward Noyelles, a two-day trip. Inside, the boxcars were even smaller than they appeared. Streeter told Mable, "The train we came down on looked like one I had when I was a kid on tracks. You felt somebody ought to get out an wind the engine every time it stopped.

"Anyone who has never ridden for two days and two nights in one of those stuffy little cars, with scarcely enough room to sit down comfortably let alone lie down, would be unable to conceive the discomforts of such a journey," Mitchell penned. "The nights were veritable nightmares. Of course everybody did his best to curl up for a few winks, but who could sleep the sleep of the just with someone's else's knees pressing against his Adam's apple and a pair of strange hobnailed brogands resting on his chest?"

Jacobson said that men "forgot the discomforts of crowded cars in the beauty of the landscape rolling by them. The quaint Arcadian farmhouses nestling snugly among their ripening acres, bits of splendid woodland, the rows of stately poplars fringing the roads—it was like gazing upon some wonderful idealistic painting." He added, "As night came the moon-bathed countryside seemed to take on an aspect somewhat ethereal, and the glowing cigarette ends inside the crowded box-cars looked like so many fireflies."

Pvt. Will Hayward from Mount Vernon, who along with his brother Ned was a private in D Company, in a letter to his parents said that trying to sleep on the train was not easy. "We had to get what we could standing or sitting, as it was impossible to lay down and stretch out there being too many in each car for that comfort." A third Hayward brother, Rob, was a Twenty-seventh Division military policeman. All three brothers, sons of a Mount Vernon alderman, had enlisted in the old Seventh before war was declared. Rob was then transferred to the 102d Military Police. In the same letter to his folks, Will said, "Have not seen Rob yet, but hope to soon. He is stationed fifteen miles from this place."[9]

Not all the soldiers were jammed into boxcars. Officers found some comfort in their quarters and were able to sit and actually stretch their legs. Leland shared a seat with another lieutenant, Dick Raven, since 1911 a K Company man from Bay Shore, Long Island. Raven's eyes were dark and intense. He wore a thick mustache that offset a balding head. His brother Robert, a corporal, was also in K Company. In fact, their father had even been in K Company, enlisting in 1884. Another brother, Edward, was currently executive officer aboard the USS *American*. And Henry, the fourth brother, a noted explorer for the Museum of Natural History, had been in the jungles of Malaysia when war was declared. By the time he got home it was too late to see any action. Leland and Raven smoked and chatted, and looked out the window.

"It was a beautiful ride through Normandy in apple blossom time," Leland wrote. "Little groups of women, children and old men stood at the stations or along the tracks and waved to us. Everything seemed so peaceful and content and we were all in such high spirits. There was big adventure in the air, but surely, the whole trip was going to be a lark. Such a picturesque country—just as I had dreamed it would be."

Corporal Arthur Church of A Company was also struck by the beauty around him. "France is at her prettiest now—flowers of every hue in bloom, large green fields and cultivated gardens. In passing through it, you find yourself feasting your eyes on a beautiful rolling country and beautiful sunsets."[10]

But the serene, peaceful setting abruptly changed when the 107th Infantry rolled into Noyelles at the mouth of the Somme. As the soldiers clamored out of cramped boxcars and fell in for another march, a bright full spring moon hung over them. The faint sweet fragrance from the apple blossoms that Leland and Raven had enjoyed seeing from the train filled the air. One soldier felt as if there ought to be "romance there on such a night as this, but war—never!" The Third Battalion marched

Lt. Dick Raven sought to avenge his brother's death.
The Seventh Regiment Fund

quickly to a British transport camp and there was fed a meal of kidney stew. The Second Battalion trailed after them, while the First Battalion was "just spilling out of the freight cars at the railhead." Dishing in a mouthful of stew, Mitchell looked up at the moon "beaming so brightly" and thought that "Jerry would have little difficulty finding his target, for all the earth was a silver sheen."

At that precise moment, a violent explosion ripped apart the quiet night. The earth trembled. Above the men the drone of planes was heard over the roar of antiaircraft guns. Searchlights scanned the sky. The boys jumped up and craned their necks to see what was going on. "Distinctly now we could hear the throb of motors," Jacobson noted. "From the sound of them, Boche sky-raiders were circling directly overhead."

"The banging of guns and the shrieking of shells was all new to us, and we were all standing and gaping heavenward," Mitchell said, "like Kansas gentlemen on a visit to New York."

K Company sergeant Roy Beyerl recalled for the people of his hometown of Malone, New York, that the battle above them so fascinated his boys that they went into a field, stretched themselves on the ground, and then "puffed calmly at their cigarettes and gazed skyward at the swift moving lights." It didn't take long for a British officer to order them to snuff out their cigarettes. "Complying with this request," said Beyerl, "the boys remained in the open watching the enemy airmen until they disappeared to the eastward."[11]

Bert Lobdell explained to his sister why most of the soldiers seemed unafraid. He began by describing the train ride. "There were 38 in our car and we spent two days and a night on the railroad. We traveled some too. When we got off we struck a little camp about dark and were greeted with an air raid first thing. We could hear the enemy plane and the anti aircraft guns trying to get it. It seems strange to think we went to sleep right in the midst of it but that ride on the train tired us out."

After the German planes flew off, the noise and excitement died down. And the boys continued their trek eastward, their minds still abuzz with their first sight and sound of war. In the dark, leading them eastward toward a half dozen villages dotting the banks of the Somme, were British guides. For the most part, the guides had poor senses of direction. The escort for the Third Battalion, although a veteran sporting the stripes of a

noncommissioned officer, proved useless. He got hopelessly lost. Marching the men around in circles for several hours, he finally struck the right
route to Favieres. Leland noted that the "British non-com [was] the first
but not the last of those good-natured 'Tommies' whose sense of direction
and knowledge of local geography were not highly developed." The
Third Battalion boys plodded on and on. Finally they stopped and word
came down the line that they'd gone four miles out of the way. "Back
along the road stumbled the battalion," Leland remarked, "saying *sotto
voce* all the uncomplimentary things it could think of about our allies."

Eventually, the 107th Infantry found the villages, scattered over a six-
kilometer radius, where for the next several weeks it would be billeted.
Headquarters was in Rue, the largest of the villages. Under the command
of Capt. Walter "Ham" Andrews, Princeton football star and grandson
of the secretary of state under President Cleveland, the Machine Gun
Company settled down in St. Firmin. Captain Clinton Fisk's First Battalion found shelter where it could in Forest Montiers. Captain Rowland
Tompkins's Second Battalion took over Morlay and Ponthoile, while
Captain Raphael Egan's Third Battalion encamped in Favieres.

As the tired men of the Third Battalion hiked down the main street of
Favieres for the first time, they saw a clean village with well-to-do-houses,
a school, and an old gray church. In the center of the village, the British
Y. M. C.A. had pitched a tent. Nearby was an *estaminet,* or little café. They
also saw K Company first lieutenant Ralph Polk Buell, a wiry, tough veteran of the Spanish-American War whose father had fought in the Civil
War, cigar clenched in his teeth, cussing like the veteran he was because
there was not much in the way of sleeping quarters for his men.

Throughout the regiment, soldiers slept in fields, orchards, or barns.
Officers shared rooms in farmhouses. As one of Egan's doughboys lamented, "Here we learned for the first time the real meaning of the word
'billet,' the company being divided into groups and assigned to shelter
in barns."

In the Second Battalion, a G Company man stated, "Part of the company was fortunate enough to get good quarters, but some were not lucky,
and had for their neighbors pigs, chickens and cows."

Lobdell, a tall, rangy lad, made the most of this unsightly situation. He explained to his father that where they were in France was "real country with cows and chickens and pigs. I'm learning to like milk. I have a big cupful night and morning twenty-five centimes (5c) a cup."

Pfc. Scott Harrison Lytle of H Company, who had tried suicide a few years earlier upon his mother's death, wrote his father, "We are at present encamped in billets in empty barns where we stay a month or so. The billets are empty barns so we are pup tenting it in the yard, as it were."

The two E Company artists, the men formerly of the Kansas City *Star*, Lauren Stout and Raeburn Van Buren, found homes in barns. Van Buren wrote to his mother, "The barn I am in is large and water proof and full of clean hay. I have never struck a better bed than the one I have on this hay since I have been in the army. The barn is part brick and part plaster and has a red tile roof. I like the interior decorations so much I would love to have a studio built on the same order in N.Y." Yet in another letter, he painted a different picture, but still kept it upbeat for his mother. "There are plenty of rats and mice about, but you soon get used to them. They don't bother you much unless they run across your head while you are asleep. I have one who lives under my pillow, but he doesn't bother me much unless he starts to move before I get to sleep."

At this time there wasn't much chance for either Stout or Van Buren, or the other soldier-artists for that matter, to put their talent on display. Every waking hour was spent training with the British. The Yanks began talking like "Tommies." Lytle reported, "The Tommies are very interesting in more ways than one. . . . We all enjoyed eating the English bacon & hard tack which they fed us with. Also tea instead of our coffee. . . . The Tommies are an easy going bunch and talk alive. Some one said they talk more than fight."

When Captain Egan made his first observation visit to the trenches on 20 June, he noticed that the British delivered food at night and that the tea was placed in two-gallon petrol tins, placed in haversacks, and then packed in hay. "This method," he wrote, "enabled the men to keep the tea hot for easily twenty hours. I personally had some tea in the front line that had been there eighteen hours and it was still quite warm and palatable."[12]

Cpl. Alfred Reeves Jr., of C Company, disagreed. "Frequently when they did bring us food it wasn't fit to use by the time it reached us. This was especially true of coffee. It would be carried up in petrol cans to keep it hot; and just when your mouth was watering and your whole chilled body longing for a cup of hot coffee, you got a cup of lukewarm stuff which had become mixed with petrol, and was fairly nauseating. Did we drink it? Oh certainly; it was better than nothing, and it doesn't take you long in the trenches to learn to make the best of what you can get."

Maj. Gen. John O'Ryan was impressed by the number of different nationalities and races that made up the soldiers of the British Empire. "Not only did one see English, Irish, Scotch and Welsh troops, but also the soldiers of Canada, Australia and New Zealand, as well as detachments of the Indian Army, South Africans, Fiji Islanders, West Indians and large numbers of Chinese coolies. There were also close by Portuguese, French and Russians troops, as well as large numbers of German prisoners."

Soon it was more than just English bacon, kidney stew, and tea that the Yanks were ordered to take from the British. The entire Twenty-seventh Division had to give up its modified Enfield rifles because there probably wasn't enough American ammunition to go around. Substituted in their place were British .303 caliber rifles. More than fifteen thousand rifles were turned in. The division's machine gun companies were outfitted with the British Vickers gun, a modified Maxim machine gun. According to Pfc. Hugh Griffiths, who hailed from the Spuyten Duyvil section of the Bronx, by the time the Machine Gun Company finished training on the Vickers gun "There was not a man in a gun squad who could not explain the sequences, strip the gun, remedy the stoppages, and give the name of every part, down to the smallest washer."[13]

"Here we were first issued that modern form of military headgear known as the 'Tin Derby,'" said Sgt. Floyd Neely of I Company, "and also drew that other article of haberdashery which was cursed every mile of the hike, yet clung to most affectionately in the trenches—the gas mask."[14]

Also, the Yanks were issued British underclothes and shoes and, eventually, British breeches and tunics. A lot of grumbling went on among the ranks, but it wasn't as bad as what happened a few months earlier when the British tried to shove their uniforms, with the crown of England on the buttons, down the throats of the 165th Infantry, the old "Fighting Sixty-ninth"—better known in New York City as the Irish Regiment.

These angry Irish Americans simply refused to put on the uniforms. Pfc. Albert Ettinger, the old Seventh youngster who had volunteered to transfer over to the Sixty-ninth, remembered how "steamed" the Irish were in his regiment. "For them, these buttons were a hated symbol of their former oppressors. Some hotheads in the regiment built a fire in the main street of the village and started to burn the British issue, and there was great excitement as one after another joined in."[15] It took an impassioned speech by Father Francis Duffy to put down the insurrection. A compromise was struck. The British buttons were pulled off each uniform and U.S. Army buttons emblazoned with the American eagle were stitched on in their place.

As training went on with the British, behind the scenes Gen. John Pershing battled for an American army. He refused to yield to pressure from the Allies to feed U.S. soldiers into the line to prop up weak and weary divisions that had been in battle since 1914. Secretary of War Baker explicitly told Pershing that the "forces of the United States are a separate and distinct component of the combined forces, the identity of which must be preserved." The Allies, however, believed there wasn't enough time for the Americans to be trained and shipped to France to be of much use. Rather, they wanted them immediately merged with their own veteran units—a kind of on-the-job training in the trenches. "The idea remained fixed in my mind," Pershing later explained, "that the morale of our troops, their proper training, and their best strategical use all demanded their concentration into an American army instead of being allotted beyond our control as replacements in the ranks of the Allied armies. In fact, every consideration dictated that our army should in no sense be in a subordinate relation with the others, but that we should plan from the start to build up our own independent organization."[16]

If that was the case, the British and French both begged that they be given American soldiers on a temporary basis while Pershing built up his own army. Early in 1918, Field Marshal Sir Douglas Haig recommended that Americans be put into the line under the command of British officers until there were enough of them to form a division, at which time U.S. officers would take over. Gen. Sir William Robertson made it clear to Pershing that without American manpower to "build up their divisions there was the possibility of the British reaching such an exhausted condition by the severe fighting in prospect that the Allies would have a very heavy task in winning the war."[17]

In fact, so depleted was the British Army that Prime Minister Lloyd George was contemplating no major offensive until 1919, or perhaps even later, the spring of 1920. Fearing the continued slaughter of his own people, he dared to hold back troops from Field Marshal Haig. Instead, he kept them home, using the excuse of a possible German attack on England's shores.[18] Finally Pershing relented, somewhat. He allowed the French the temporary use of four black infantry regiments, including the 15th New York. Those regiments stayed with the French for the duration of the war. Still, the Allies wanted more, and kept up the pressure. Pershing then bluntly let the Allied commander-in-chief, Ferdinand Foch, know that the "time may come when the American army will have to stand the brunt of the war" and that the war could not "be saved by feeding untrained American recruits into the Allied armies."[19]

This wrangling over American troops continued even as more and more doughboys poured into France. Meanwhile, the fate of the Twenty-seventh Division, like that of other newly arrived units, remained unsettled.

Far from this political intrigue, the 107th Infantry went about the business of preparing for war.

With the new British rifle in hand, O'Ryan was determined that his men know how to use it effectively. In a bulletin dated 9 June 1918, he stressed in all caps: "THE RIFLE IS THE STRONG ARM OF THE AMERICAN SOLDIER AND IT HAS [AS] MANY 'WALLOPS' AS THERE ARE CARTRIDGES AVAILABLE—LEARN TO MAKE EACH 'WALLOP' A KNOCKOUT." He added that it required fifty thousand cartridges to hit a man in battle. "Instead of belittling the value of rifle fire, this should constitute an inspiration to each soldier in the division armed with a rifle. . . . Every infantry soldier therefore owes it to himself, to his family, to his regiment and to the division to become expert in the use of his rifle. . . . DO THESE THINGS AND THE ENEMY WILL ALWAYS FEAR THE 27th DIVISION."[20]

Even in the midst of training, the Greyjackets felt like they were on vacation in France. Leland mailed a note to his parents, "France is all that I expected it to be. A more beautiful and peaceful place you can not imagine than this little corner of it." At the time he and Dick Raven roomed together in a "nice clean billet" in St. Valery-sur-Somme, where they were attending a school for officers. "There are crowds of French children everywhere and the Americans are very popular because the blamed idiots give away everything they have, food, money, everything—but equipment."

Although the doughboys gave away almost everything, they did desire one thing in return. A good home-cooked meal in one of the many *estaminets* that catered to them. Sgt. Frank Dee of I Company, later a much-decorated soldier, relied on pantomime to get food. As one of his companions recalled, "It used to be amusing to see Frank Dee saunter up to a benign-looking old French lady and scare her out of many years growth by flapping his arms wildly about and cackling. This, in Frank's words, was 'businessing' her for an egg or two."

When Lt. Buell watched his men rustle food and then gulp it down he was overheard by Cpl. Harold Mills to say, "If this bunch goes after the Huns like they do after their food, this war won't last long when we get into the trenches."[21]

In Favieres, Madame Blondin's *estaminet* was a favorite spot for the officers. Leland, Raven, Capt. John Augustus Barnard of K Company, and the burley Capt. Raphael Egan often ate there. They dined in a private room with two large windows that fronted the main street. The major course was always an omelet of a dozen or so eggs. Once, after downing an omelet, Egan, whose brothers grew into mammoth-sized men, asked Leland, who spoke some French, to have Madame Blondin whip up another omelet of "the same proportions."

"My God!" the woman said. "There are no more eggs in the village." At first, according to Leland, she was "terrified at the thought of men who ate two dozen eggs at a sitting." But when she calculated the money she might make from such great appetites, she found the eggs.

In the middle of writing a letter to his father in Mount Vernon, Pfc. Albert M. Clark of the Sanitary Detachment blurted out, "Gracious, just now I heard a rooster crow! Perhaps there are some hens about and reasoning from this, there might be some eggs."

The little coastal town of Le Crotoy was also a popular spot. "We could walk over there on Saturday afternoons or Sundays," said Sgt. Neely, "and get nicely stung at the Hotel de Commerce on one of those five and ten franc dinners. It was worth the price, however, during those beautiful days in May and June. It was apple blossom time in Picardy, the weather was fine, and the food more plentiful than in any other part of France we visited."[22]

Another diversion was swimming in the Somme. A company of men would hike down to the mouth of the famous river, shed their clothes, dive in, and bathe. On 1 June E Company, billeted in Morlay, marched off for a swim. The first into the water was Pfc. Charles Bowen, a recent graduate of Brooklyn's Erasmus Hall. He dove beneath the murky waters of the Somme and never surfaced. At first, his fellow soldiers thought he was horsing around. Then they panicked. They hunted for him, searching the banks and shallow water. At last, Cpl. Albert Brown and Pfc. Eddie Hassdenteufel pulled Bowen from the Somme. Several men swarmed over the stricken soldier, trying desperately to revive him. Bugler Charlie Coppola, an E man playing in the regimental band, ran a half-mile back to Morlay for help. He was too exhausted to continue on, and another soldier took off to find a doctor. He located 1st Lt. William Coogan of the Sanitary Detachment, who rushed back to the river. For more than an hour, Coogan tried vainly to save the young private first class. But it was too late.

"Charlie Bowen is dead!" Sgt. Nicholas Krayer wrote to his brother, Jack, who had just been transferred to the Chemical Warfare Service. "He drowned while swimming. Out last Monday with a number of other fellows for a dip he was the first stripped, and with a shout and, 'Well, boys, here goes,' he made a running dive into 15 feet of water." Krayer was in town when he heard the news. He hurried to the river's edge. "I . . . did what little I could though it was apparent that our comrade was dead. . . . We carried his body on an improvised stretcher to our billet and there we laid him out on a cot. To-day we buried him."

Bowen's body stayed in the tent for several days. A squad of E Company men stood guard the whole time. Women from the village, who had seen enough death to last them a lifetime but who were grateful for the Americans, placed flowers on Bowen's body until, according to Cpl.

Miller, "nothing was discernible through the foliage."[23] When it came time for the burial, an old Frenchman brought up from Morlay a two-wheeled cart pulled along by a mule. In the cart was a plain pine box. Bowen's body was placed in the box. Sgt. Krayer led an eight-man escort back to the village cemetery. Chaplain William McCord prayed, and afterward Frank Schwarz, a cook in F Company, sang "Nearer My God to Thee," "Lead Kindly Light," and "Abide with Me." The buglers sounded taps. The pine box was then lowered into the earth.[24]

"The old Major is a prince," Nick told his brother. "He did for Charlie all that could be done. He provided a funeral for a soldier and a Christian."

Bowen was the first soldier in the division to die in France.

Although Van Buren was in E Company, he did not tell his parents about the tragic drowning of Charlie Bowen. Instead, he was thinking of his newspaper and magazine friends now in Paris and how, if he got a transfer to that new army newspaper catering to the doughboy, the *Stars & Stripes*, he might be with them in the City of Light. Like old times in New York. Cush (Charles Phelps Cushing) was there from *Collier's*, F.P.A. (Franklin Pierce Adams) from the *Trib*, and Woollcott (Alexander Woollcott) from the *Times*—all working for the *Stars & Stripes*.

Neysa McMein was there, too. She had volunteered to be a part of the celebrity-studded American Stage and Lyceum, a Y.M.C.A. organization that during the war sent forth some thirty-five thousand people to offer entertainment at cantonments, training camps, and hospitals. Headquartered on the third floor at 10 Rue de l'Elysées, one block from the Champs Elysées, the American Stage and Lyceum eventually gave more than one-hundred thousand performances overseas—from vaudeville skits to plays staged by stock companies to one-man and one-woman shows, led by Harry Lauder and Elsie Janis, the "Sweetheart of the A.E.F." One of its organizers, James Evans, wrote, "The adventures of these modern troubadours . . . would give a deep insight into the most human side of the War. There would be tales aboard ship, nights on submarined seas, the first hours ashore at the base ports, the journeys into the bleeding heart of France, the last march on the road to battle."[25]

McMein proved to be one of the more popular performers. The siren of Manhattan knew how to make men's blood rise. Arriving in early June, she toured hospitals and camps with two other women, Anita Parkhurst Wilcox and Jane Bulley, who, like her, were illustrators. "These clever women," Evans noted, "put on one of the most original shows the boys had the good luck to see." He said that "Miss McMein was a real artist— not only with her crayon and brush, but an impresario, actress, play-wright and scenario writer, all of which vocations she employed to delight the doughboys."[26]

Before leaving for France, McMein and her two partners outfitted themselves in the latest New York fashions, believing the soldiers would get a kick out of seeing something colorful rather than the drab Y. M.C.A. outfits. She also brought other clothes and allowed the dough-boys to put them on so that there would seem to be more girls around. Neysa did a take-off on the popular Winsor McCay animated film, *Gertie the Trained Dinosaur.* While the film flickered on a makeshift screen, she played a portable organ, sang, and offered ribald remarks. Her biogra-pher believed "Neysa had managed to reintroduce into the blasted land-scape a much-needed sense of simple, silly American fun."[27]

In Paris, in between performances, McMein hung out with Woollcott and Adams, her poker-playing cronies from the Lincoln Arcade and Shropshire apartments, and got to know a young private, the bushy-haired editor of the *Stars & Stripes,* Harold Ross, later the founder of *The New Yorker.*

Van Buren was beside himself. From Cushing he heard that Neysa was in Paris. He had to let someone know the bittersweet news, so he wrote to his mother. "Cush said he had a letter from Neysa McMein telling him that she would soon be over. No doubt she is here now and Cush has had sight of her. He also spoke about having dinner with Captain Ray Ives [an insurance executive who was part of the New York literary crowd] and F.P.A. and you can imagine how hungry it made me to see these old friends after my long marooned experience." He added that Cush had quit the army newspaper so he could write magazine articles. "It seems he is free to move about as he pleases and that he gets to Paris often. Before long I hope to be in a position to do some work for the Stars & Stripes. Cush says they will make a move to get my stuff as they need it badly."

Leland was finding his experience a "holiday affair." He described how the fields, blooming with "red clover, the blue corn flower (is it?) and the poppies are so mixed that the effect is like an old fashioned garden." Food was another of his passions. "This is dairy country so we can get all the milk, butter and eggs we want at prices about the same or a little less than those at home. The good lady who serves our mess is a soldier's widow and she can cook like a Waldorf chef." He assured his parents, "We are still a good ways from the front line altho we occasionally hear the big guns. Otherwise we might think this war was only a bad dream and not a horrible reality at all, for there is no sign here of desolation or destruction." He also liked watching the airmen. "They are overhead all the time, night and day, and some of them do a lot of stunts. They like to swoop down on a column of troops on the road and scare the daylights out of them."

Gow also felt the same serenity as Leland. "The weather still continues perfect, with a cloudless sky," he wrote to his parents. "The days are hot and the nights cool—a beautiful climate. 'Sunny France' is right, but I am afraid it won't always be so." Gow fell in love with the beauty of the Somme Valley. When he told this to Thomas Janson, his wagoner, the private first class replied, "Make it your honeymoon trip, and you can show Mrs. Gow where you travelled, and tell your experiences." Gow thought that was fine idea, saying to Janson that he had "hit the nail on the head." Janson laughed, and reminded him that in the telling he had to "leave the insect pest out of the Somme travelogue."

Two men from G Company soon found out that not far away danger lurked. Capt. Maxwell Nesbitt, with the regiment since 1890, and Pfc. Walter Hauck were flown to the trenches for an overnight stay. Before they left, Hauck received a number of propositions by his fellow dough-boys to take his place. He declined them all. A scribe for the company said in the *Gazette,* "He wasn't up there very long, however, before he began to wish he had considered some of those offers as the shells were flying thick and fast. For quite a while after his trip, Houck [*sic*] would duck and jump at the slightest noise, and everyone thought he was suffering from shell-shock."

Near the middle of June, a series of blows whacked the members of the old Seventh hard. One they could get over. The other was too devastating.

First, Maj. Douglas Despard, the regiment's adjutant, was transferred to division headquarters to serve as adjutant of the Fifty-third Brigade. In civilian life, Despard, who had enlisted in K Company in 1904, was the leading importer of ivory into the United States. Over a twenty-five-year span, his company, Cowdrey & Despard, shipped in four million pounds of elephant tusks. There was hardly a piano key in the nation that was not made from ivory that came from his company.

But the blow that truly shook the 107th Infantry was made known in a letter dated 15 June and was signed by Col. Willard Fisk.

For two weeks, the old colonel, who had served the Seventh for forty-four years, suffered from a strange stomach ailment. It wouldn't clear up. By the time O'Ryan joined the Seventh in 1897, Fisk had been in a Grey-jacket uniform for more than a generation. The two warhorses, both lawyers, were great friends. O'Ryan fretted that Fisk was too ill to lead the regiment he adored. The general went to the village of Rue to see the commander. The headquarters of the 107th was in the upper floors of an old schoolhouse. Looking at Fisk, whose only son, Clinton, was now captain of the First Battalion, O'Ryan sensed an inward distress that was not evident on the kind face adorned with a rich, thick mustache.

"General, the doctors tell me I am very sick," Fisk said. "I think I shall be all right in a short while."

The two men were quiet for a moment. Then Fisk continued. "You know what I think of this regiment. Even if I were permitted to I would not by any selfish act of mine jeopardize its best interests. I am an interested party, and so you must decide my fate without an opinion from me."

O'Ryan had already made up his mind. Only a few days before he had lost his commander of the Fifty-third Infantry Brigade, Gen. Robert E. L. Michie, to a heart attack. "Colonel, you are going home," he said. "You have done a great work in the reorganization and training of this regiment. You have brought it to France and now due to your illness you must turn it over to some other man to lead it into battle."[28]

Fisk accepted his fate. He still had two more duties to perform before his shipment back to the States. The first was to prepare his regiment for review by Field Marshal Sir Douglas Haig. The second was to relinquish command of the 107th Infantry, the old Seventh Regiment.

When Haig arrived on 10 June at Le Champneuf, Fisk was unable to be at the review. His illness confined him to his billets. In his place stood Maj. Nicholas Engel, an old Seventh soldier and now the regiment's temporary commander. Meanwhile, joining the 107th were the division's fourteen machine gun companies. Twenty British airplanes circled above the troops, watchful for any sudden attack by the Germans. Accompanied by O'Ryan and Engel and with the regimental band playing martial airs, Haig walked in front of the soldiers who stood at attention with bayonets fixed. Leland thought him a "small man physically to have the whole weight of the Empire on his shoulders, but those shoulders were square and soldierly and the face, worn and pale, was businesslike." The British field marshal was meticulous in his inspection, according to O'Ryan. He talked amiably with each battalion and company commander. Then the Americans, yet to taste battle, marched by in review.

But before they reached the reviewing stand, overhead a brazen British pilot swept downward behind the men. He then gunned his engine and with a "deafening roar" buzzed over their heads, the belly of the airplane just a few feet above the tips of the bayonets. When he reached the front of the marching column, he veered straight up, waving "gaily" at the Americans. The stunt angered Leland because a few weeks earlier he had seen another British pilot showing off, only his plane had crashed, killing several spectators. "If he had miscalculated by a yard or so, as the lad at St. Valery had done, he would have cleaned up a whole company with one sweep of his wings." As the airplane barreled by, however, not a single head jerked up, a testament to the discipline instilled in the soldiers by Colonel Fisk.

"It was a very severe test of discipline to have this aerial cyclone which could not be seen by the men until it had passed, approach them from the rear and so short a distance above their heads," O'Ryan recalled. He observed that neither a head nor an eye moved.

The stony reaction of the 107th Infantry impressed Haig. "My, these are seasoned troops," he told O'Ryan. "What magnificent chaps they are!"[29]

Five days later Fisk wrote his farewell letter, addressed to his officers.

"I have been ordered to the rear," he stated. "I will always cherish . . . the recollections of the association with the officers of the Regiment, and indeed with the enlisted personnel, whose response to their officers has been so generous as to persuade me that, in the trying days to come, they will, being led by gentlemen of your attainment, make a record of which our Country will be proud. . . . I can only say good-bye—good luck— God bless you."[30]

Fisk's letter shot through the regiment like a whizbang. The silk stocking soldiers loved their commander. Jacobson called it "a great loss." He later stated that the colonel was "held in deep respect and veneration by every single man under him."

To Leland, who had been associated with Fisk for four years, the news "sobered and saddened every man of the old Seventh who had served [with him] in the pre-war days or on the Mexican border." Leland saw Fisk as a "strict disciplinarian, gruff, often cranky, unnecessarily hard it seemed on young officers—he could spot inefficiency or shirking as quickly as a hawk spots its quarry—but he was never unjust and no man who did his duty and attended to business ever had any trouble with the Colonel." His praise continued, "To have made the 107th Infantry out of several disgruntled if not inimical units of the National Guard, to have welded these elements together into a fighting machine of the highest order, to have brought this regiment through the trying period of over-training which we got at Camp Wadsworth to the battlefield of France and then to be stricken down and to see his command turned over to another on the eve of action, was a blow which only a soldier can appreciate."

Two men were considered as his replacement: Maj. Robert Mazet, the long-time Tammany Hall battler; and Maj. Nicholas Engel, an executive with John Fox & Company, a manufacturing firm that supplied New York City with most of its fire hydrants. A National Guardsman since 1890, Engel was the son of the owner of the well-known Engel's Chop House at Sixth Avenue and Thirty-fifth Street. In the old Seventh he had been among its most popular men. Engel got the post. O'Ryan selected him as acting commander because of seniority. "Everyone hoped sincerely that the senior major would get the big job," recalled Leland, knowing that assignment was temporary, but hoping that it would prove to be permanent.

Ten days later, on 28 June, O'Ryan plucked Col. Charles I. DeBevoise out of the Army School of the Line to permanently lead the 107th Infan-

Col. Charles DeBevoise replaced the ailing
Colonel Fisk as regimental commander in
June 1918.   The Seventh Regiment Fund

try. Engel, promoted to lieutenant colonel, was eventually dispatched to
the 108th. DeBevoise, who had started out in the National Guard in 1895
with Cavalry Troop C, was Brooklyn born. A stockbroker, he obviously
had the right credentials to command the silk stocking regiment.

Meanwhile, on the morning of 16 June, Fisk, the beloved old soldier,
departed for home. He left behind his son, Clinton, to carry on for him
the traditions of the old Seventh that he cherished so much.

CHAPTER 6

His Heart, I Know,
Is Back in God's Country

In mid-June, soon after the division became attached to the Sixty-sixth British Division of Gen. Sir Julian Byng's British Third Army, the 107th Infantry, now under the command of Col. Charles I. DeBevoise, began a series of marches that within a month would bring the regiment close enough to the front to see limited action. There it would suffer its first casualties. Along the way, the 107th made brief stops, overnights, to train briefly with the British. The soldiers slept in fields or barns, or if they were officers, in the comfort of a Frenchman's house. Then they were back on the road, swinging wide-eyed through the French countryside.

"We are going due east, my dears, straight for the front whether for more training or for a trick in the trenches I of course do not know," Claude Leland wrote his sons. "It looks very much like business."

"I never saw so many towns in my life," Raeburn Van Buren penciled to his folks in Kansas City. "Seems like there is a town every half mile."

East. Always east. One village after another. The names blurred. Cayeaux, Estreboef, Drancourt, Neuilly l'Hopital, Millencourt, St. Riquier, Le Meillard, Heuzecourt, Beauquemaison, Doullens.

In the *Gazette*, Sgt. John MacDonnell of M Company joked. "Shortly

After constant marching through France, the 107th Regiment jokingly called themselves
"O'Ryan's Traveling Circus." The "X" identifies Raeburn Van Buren.   Author's Collection

after we landed some of the boys conceived the idea of carving the names
of towns on their pipes; but soon realized that unless they took the hull of
an old ship and used it for a pipe bowl, their efforts would be fruitless."

Pvt. Will Hayward of D Company found that so much travel left little
time to mail letters home to Mount Vernon. "We get very little time to
write," he reminded his parents in one of his dispatches. "We are kept
hustling every minute. Tuesday at 3 A.M. we were routed and told to pack
up for a change of location on another front; fell in at 6 o'clock and hiked

four miles to a railroad station, entrained and traveled all day, reached our destination at about 7 P.M., then started to hike to a camp; stopped at 10 P.M. for supper and reached the camp at 3 A.M., just 24 hours from the start; did not bother to pitch tents, just spread them on the ground and went to sleep." Then the former three-sport star at Mount Vernon High School added, "Ned [his brother] and I are in excellent condition except for a few blisters on our feet, but they will be o.k. as our feet are hardening fast."

Ned, the eldest Hayward boy, told their parents, "We have been continually on the move, like a circus doing one-night stands, the only difference being we hike."[1]

In fact, Bert Lobdell said, "This outfit has traveled around France so much that it is called 'O'Ryan's Traveling Circus'."

Twenty-five-year-old Pfc. Angelo Mustico of L Company, whose family had emigrated from Italy to New York just before he was born and whose uncle had once been mayor of Palermo, informed his sister and brother back in Newburgh, "I would have wrote to you before but we have been on a hike for two weeks and I feel as if I have walked all over this country. We are up near the front now and can hear the big guns roaring all day and night long and they are a bother when we go to sleep. We have passed through a lot of citys and towns and most of them have been bombed from the air and very few people live in them."[2]

Cpl. Harold Mills, who found that the rigors of hiking and camping out made him sick a lot of the time, almost collapsed on 17 June. In his diary that night, he explained, "Marched all day with very heavy pack. March of about 22 miles. Nearly fell out. Ron [Pfc. Ronald Pohl] took gas mask & MacNulty [Cpl. Charles MacNulty] my rifle. Made it under difficulty. Most of our platoon billeted in orchard."

For Edward Streeter, "The worst part of the war is getting to it. I been rained on so much the last week I feel like an old sponge."

For the *Gazette,* Sgt. Robert Waddell of F Company set the regiment's wandering into verse.

We're on the hike again, boys,
Our travelling circus moves.
The French turnpikes grow level boys,
From contact with our shoes.

Our nightly stands are varied—
An orchard, field or town.
In pup tents, barns and billets, boys,
We've flopped our bodies down.

And we've been in ditches, too—
In mud and rain and damp,
Kept awake by "cooties"
And thirst and cold and damp.

Traveling mostly on foot, the doughboys passed through the strange-sounding French towns, where the inhabitants seemed always to give them a "royal welcome." Perhaps it was because they knew how free the soldiers were with their money. "They are such a queer looking people—these peasants, but good," Van Buren confided. "The only thing I have against them is that they charge the American soldier three times as much for food as they do their own soldiers."

An enterprising farmer, his wife, and daughters even offered a hot bath for the tired, dusty doughboys and charged them one franc each. When they arrived at the farmhouse, they were led into a big kitchen jammed with American, British, and French soldiers. The smell was unbearable. Large kettles of water boiled on a stove. In the center of the kitchen were two wooden tubs filled with "dirty, scummy, soapy water." A division machine gunner observed, "In each tub were two soldiers having a bath. When one was finished he got out and another got in. The room was hot, steamy and odorful. The females in the audience did not seem to mind the frolic. They were enjoying the anatomical display of the male form." The machine gunner, who grew up in Brooklyn, found the scene before him disgusting. Without taking a bath, he "rushed out the door to breathe some pure and fresh air."[3]

It was a good thing the soldiers finally received their first pay since embarking for France. Lobdell felt like a millionaire. To his father in Salem Center, he reported that after payday "all the wine shops were busy fair last night, half the camp, I guess, was absolutely assified."

When the division's affiliation with the Sixty-sixth British Division began, the Allies were still recovering from the German spring offensive that had thrown the English army back toward the French coast. The ranks of the Sixty-sixth had been so depleted that it was a division in name only. Its battle-hardened top officer, Maj. Gen. John H. K. Bethell, and Maj. Gen. John O'Ryan were the youngest divisional commanders in their respective armies. Both were in their early forties. When they met for the first time at the New Yorker's temporary headquarters in St. Riquier, the Englishman, by way of introduction, said, "General O'Ryan, I understand you are the youngest Division Commander in the American army; I am the youngest Division Commander in the British army. Look here, I think we had better get together for mutual protection." Then the two veritable youngsters sat down for tea.

Bethell invited O'Ryan to his headquarters on 20 June to meet Gen. Sir Henry Rawlinson. Because the British Fifth Army had been badly mauled by the Germans and was no longer a fit fighting force, the personally ambitious Rawlinson was in the midst of rebuilding it—under a new designation as the British Fourth Army. By the end of July he would double the size of his new command, which would include almost a half-dozen divisions of Lt. Gen. Sir John Monash's Australian Corps. His hope was to launch a counteroffensive as soon as possible. His only problem was that when he met O'Ryan, his new army was still short of men. Instead of twelve battalions to a division there were only nine. In contrast, an American division was twice the size of a normal British division. No doubt Rawlinson licked his chops when he saw O'Ryan's hale and hearty troops, even though he knew he couldn't touch them. In fact, he had recently written to Sir Henry Wilson, Great Britain's military representative to the Supreme War Council, to point out that America's National Guard troops were "desperately keen, and I fancy we shall want every man-jack of them before the summer is past."[4] However, Gen. John Pershing steadfastly refused to allow his Americans to be used as a trench fodder by the Allies, a decision that angered and frustrated not only Rawlinson but also his chief, Field Marshal Sir Douglas Haig. To make matters worse, two other sacrosanct American divisions were nearby as well—the Thirtieth from North and South Carolina and Tennessee and the Thirty-third from Illinois. At the time, all three formed the American II Corps under Maj. Gen. George W. Read. They were in the British Zone for training only; not for fighting—although from time to time they went into reserve trenches for a taste of the real thing.

Yet in spite of Pershing's hands-off policy, which Haig found "ignorant" and "appalling,"[5] within two months the fate of the Twenty-seventh, as well as the Thirtieth, would fall into Rawlinson's lap.

O'Ryan liked the tall, gangly, aristocratic "Rawley." Although he felt he was the type of general who could appeal to Americans, he found him, like most British officers of high rank that he encountered, to be "devoid of formality or in fact of anything tending to inspire awe or build up importance." At that moment O'Ryan was more concerned with Byng's Third Army than he was with Rawlinson's fledgling Fourth Army.

The British Zone where the Americans were now encamped covered northern France and northwestern Belgium. It was made famous because of the fighting there and for an immortal poem by Lt. Col. John McCrae, entitled "In Flanders Fields." To O'Ryan, who set up headquarters in Beauval, Flanders was "an attractive stretch of country." Just north of Beauval, the 107th Infantry dug in around Bouquemaison, Haute Visee, Le Souich, and several other small villages. The nearest city was Arras, roughly twenty miles east of the New Yorkers. It had been heavily shelled, and now there were mounds of rubble where buildings had once stood. Throughout the entire sector, Chinese coolies worked on trenches, digging down two to three feet and leaving the deeper work to the soldiers. It was here that General Byng feared the Germans were about to launch another offensive. He believed their aim was to capture Arras and the Vimy Ridge, a sharp rise of land that had been held by the Germans until April 1917, when it had been wrested away by the Canadians at a cost of more than eleven thousand men. A secret memorandum, issued by Byng's VI Corps, called for the Twenty-seventh Division's Fifty-fourth Brigade to be ready to defend the last of four defensive lines in case the Huns broke through. If there was a breakthrough, O'Ryan's men were to hold off the Germans until British reinforcements moved in.

The Fifty-fourth Brigade comprised the 107th and 108th Infantry Regiments and the 106th Machine Gun Battalion. Every battalion in the brigade was expected to occupy this last line of defense. On 28 June the New Yorkers moved into the trenches for the first time—even though technically they were reserve trenches nearly eight miles from the front.

Nothing happened, except at night when German artillery pounded the entire area.

Pvt. George Fetherolf assured his Aunt Mollie, who had raised him after the death of his mother, that the shellfire did not bother him. "We have grown so accustomed to hearing explosions of big guns etc that we do not notice them any more than you would notice the old switch engine in the Erie freight yard," he wrote, referring to the fact that Middletown, where he came from, was a major railroad center for the Erie and the Ontario & Western railroads.

"Yesterday put in my first day in the trenches in a very quiet sector well back of the front," Leland told his family. "All I saw of the Boche was his shrapnel bursting over a town off to our left which he was strafing. I also saw an observation balloon hit, burst into flames and come down, leaving a long black trail of smoke."

But one of the German bombs that landed far back of the Fifty-fourth Brigade struck the 105th Infantry Regiment. It came close to O'Ryan's billet, dropping into a herd of tethered horses and mules. A dozen animals went down, screaming, their legs blown away.

Another shell almost hit the division's sergeant major, Albert Breunig. He noted the near miss in his diary. "One bomb dropped in a field across the road, a fragment of which passed within a few inches of my body, burying itself in the front of the door behind me."[6]

When the danger of a German attack faded, the Americans were pulled out of the trenches. As the 107th Infantry marched back to its encampment, the unscathed boys sang familiar tunes, "East Side, West Side, All Around the Town" and "Sweet Rosie O'Grady." There seemed a trace of homesickness in their voices, Leland thought.

His impression of that brief trench experience: "We did nothing but loaf around in these half-dug trenches. Rather untidy."

Untidy was the right description for Leland. After all, at that time, he, Capt. Raphael Egan and Lts. Harrison Uhl Jr., Alan Schimpf of L Company, and Perley Gray of the Sanitary Detachment shared a rather tidy and roomy home run by a Madame Nechal. It was the finest dwelling Leland enjoyed while in France. He said so in a letter to his family. "With my usual luck I found excellent billets in a beautiful old house on the village street in front with a magnificent garden behind in full bloom. The family in the house are caretakers and refugees from the North." Madame Nechal's husband was a prisoner of war. She ran the place with her two daughters and a young son. Mess Sgt. Gerald Stanton of I Company supplied the food for the officers while Madame Nechal and her daughters cooked the meals. After dinner the contented silk stocking soldiers sat outside in a courtyard and smoked their pipes as if they were back in New York City at one of their exclusive clubs. There, according to Leland, they "swapped rumors and planned the next day's work, or visited with the family who usually joined us."

Following the short but sweet stay in the reserve trenches, training resumed once again.

Edward Streeter explained to Mable, "We got to go to school again to learn something. If I had a diploma for every school I been to in the last year my room would look like a dentle parlor."

Most of the machine-gun battalions and companies, including the 107th Machine Gun Company, stayed near the coast for their training. Here they were instructed in the use of the British Vickers machine gun. For two weeks the Americans learned the intricacies of the deadly weapon on the sandy beaches of the English Channel. Recalled Pfc. Robert Clarke of the 104th Machine Gun Company, "It was interesting and it was tiring. Lugging a 55 pound tripod or the 42 pound gun from position to position was a muscle-building job. No one had to rock us to sleep at night."[7]

Each machine-gun company was divided into three platoons of four squads. Each squad, or team, numbered eight men. The squad leader was a corporal. Every squad had a number one machine gunner. His job was to swing the tripod off his shoulder, loosen the wing nut that held the legs in place, and then position the tripod so the gun was level with the ground, no matter how erratic the terrain. The number two man placed the fifty-five-pound weapon with filled water jacket for cooling atop the tripod and locked it in place while the number three man set two boxes of ammunition belts on the ground to the right of the machine gun. Each belt held two hundred fifty rounds. The number two man then fed the first belt into the machine gun. At that moment, the number one man cocked a lever, sending the first bullet into the loading chamber. When he pressed his two thumbs forward against the trigger, the machine gun roared into action. Behind this crew, two men operated a belt-loading machine to keep the ammunition coming. And flanking the machine gunners were two riflemen. Their job was to protect the squad.

As Clarke later wrote, "It was estimated that a machine gunner's life expectancy in a defensive action was thirty minutes. He will never surrender his position or abandon his gun."[8]

Not all machine gunners were in machine-gun companies. Much to the surprise of Lobdell, he was appointed a machine gunner in L Company. To his father he said, "They say if there is anything Fritz hates, it's a machine gun. I should think he would. They call machine gun squads here the 'Suicide Club.' Don't let that cause any anxiety."

As he learned to fire his new weapon of destruction, Lobdell, like all the New Yorkers, watched from the corner of his eye the thrilling action that took place almost daily overhead. Airplanes dueled—twisting, rolling, swooping downward like raptors after their prey. "Thursday afternoon," he wrote home, "while the machine gun class was sitting on a hillside studying the gun, we saw a Boche plane. It was thousands of feet up and probably miles and miles away. We could hear the report of our guns and see the shrapnel bursting in the air around it. Talk about your fireworks! Fourth of July in the States is tame."

"This morning we saw a battle in the clouds, between two German airmen and the anti-aircraft guns," Billy Leonard reported. "It was a great sight. The Huns had come over to take photographs. It was a perfectly clear day and in the brilliant sunshine they were quickly spotted. They hid behind a cloud for a time, but that didn't long shelter them. We could see their machines—black spots against the white clouds—and shrapnel bursting all about them. They soared higher and higher, and were soon lost by our sight."

Leland also watched the skies. "We saw an air fight going on way off to the south—but didn't pay much attention to it until all of a sudden one of the planes swooped down within fifty feet us—just missed a line of trees and crashed into the next field. It was an English plane with its propeller shot away. The airman didn't get a scratch."

"Night," mused Major General O'Ryan, "was made attractive or hideous dependent upon the state of the mind of the observer, by the panorama of hundreds of searchlights scanning the skies with their accusing beams for the elusive enemy bombers, whose ominous engine throbs could plainly be heard from above. Frequently one of the beams would disclose an enemy plane. When this happened other beams were immediately turned on the aerial target while from the ground the 'archies,' as the anti-aircraft were called, belched their shrapnel into the air in an effort to destroy this most dreaded of all nocturnal disturbers. The roar of the guns, the dropping of shrapnel and shell fragments on the tiled roofs of the houses, the swinging searchlights, the occasional view of the enemy planes, the blinding flashes and severe detonations when the bombs were dropped, constituted a scene and an experience that nothing short of another such war will ever produce."

By the first of July, General Rawlinson itched for a fight. He felt his Fourth Army, refitted with six divisions of the Australian Corps, was now ready to go on the offensive. In mid-June, the new Australian commander, Lieutenant General Monash, had presented him with a modest plan to take the small village of Hamel just east of Amiens in the Somme valley. Still drooling over the untested Americans, Rawlinson figured the taking of Hamel would be a good place for them to taste blood for the first time. Symbolically, he chose the Fourth of July as the day to attack. In a letter to Col. Clive Wigram, he explained why. "I selected Independence Day, as it was the first occasion on which American troops had taken part in an actual attack alongside our own fellows. . . . " He also decided to use tanks, a first for the Americans.[9]

Of the three American divisions at his disposal, Rawlinson settled on the Thirty-third Illinois. In an end run around General Pershing, he asked General Read of the American II Corps for permission to send two companies from two of his regiments into the line. Read, apparently oblivious of Pershing's order against such a request, granted permission. The 131st and 132d Infantry Regiments, minus two companies, were then attached to the Eleventh and Fourth Australian Brigades respectively.

Meanwhile, on 1 July, General Pershing showed up at Read's headquarters unaware of what was going on behind his back. When he found out, he was livid. He told Read to take his men out of the line. He then rushed off to Paris, where he confronted Haig, telling him that the "use of

Americans at this time . . . naturally it did not meet with my approval."
Haig relented. On 3 July, Pershing called Read on the telephone to make
certain his troops were being withdrawn.[10]

The decision piqued both Monash and Rawlinson. If the Americans
withdrew, it would cause an "international incident," according to the
Australian general. "No Australian," he threatened, "would ever fight beside an American again."[11] Rawlinson, in a note to Wigram, stated, "I
was not a little put out when, at the very last moment, I got a direct order
from Pershing that no American troops were to be employed. It was then
too late to withdraw them, so I am afraid I had to disobey the order."[12]

On the 4th, the Americans "went over the top" with the Australians.
Although it was minor battle, the Allies captured Hamel. British intelligence officer C. R. M. F. Cruttwell, later principal of Hertford College,
Oxford, called it one of those "small, neat, cheap attacks" that pestered
the Germans following their triumphant spring offensive. "This little action," he stated, "was the true begetter of the great attacks in the following months, for it taught most important lessons." Those lessons he said
proved that tanks and infantry worked well together, that a creeping barrage laid ahead of the tanks kept them from being knocked out of action,
and that a battalion could attack across a wide range (one thousand yards)
as effectively as a division.[13]

Soon after the attack, a British officer strode happily into the Twenty-
seventh Division headquarters. The Twenty-seventh was then preparing
to move to another sector on the western front, this time in Belgium with
the British Second Army. Before the British officer opened his mouth, an
aide to O'Ryan, whose own officers were sorely disappointed that their
division had not been picked for the attack, said, "What about those
Yanks of the Thirty-third? Did they make good?"

"I asked the identical question a moment ago over the phone to the
Australian headquarters," the officer said, "and the Australian officer's
reply was, 'These Yanks are certainly good fighters, but, my God, they
are rough.'"[14]

The fighting spirit of the doughboys impressed Monash. The elated
Australian commander wrote, "The contingent of them [Americans]
who joined us acquitted themselves most gallantly and were ever after received by the Australians as blood brothers—a fraternity which operated

to great mutual advantage nearly three months later."[15] One of his officers who had seen the untested Americans in action reported to him, "They were a good, hardworking, keen, intelligent lot of fellows who are likely to do well in the near future." However, another officer, although heaping praise on the Americans, spotted a weakness that a few months later would cause them all great harm and the everlasting wrath of Monash. "They behaved magnificently," he reported, "but were rather too anxious to get close to the barrage—a very common fault with new troops."[16]

In other words, they were reckless.

The success of the attack on Hamel did not quiet Pershing. He ordered the Thirty-third Division out of the British Zone, leaving only the Twenty-seventh and Thirtieth to resume training, but in a place far removed from Rawlinson's greedy clutches.

"The incident," Pershing recalled in his memoirs, "showed clearly the disposition of the British to assume control of our units, the very thing which I had made such strong efforts . . . to prevent. Its immediate effect was to cause me to make the instructions so positive that nothing of the kind could occur again."[17]

But he was wrong.

On 5 July the 107th Infantry, along with other regiments and support units of the division, rode north toward the Belgium border cramped inside rundown boxcars. Staring out the window, Leland noted how the "train ran pretty close to the front for several miles and saw [how] the whole sky lighted up with the flash of the big guns and the Very lights [Invented in 1910 by Edmund W. Very, an American naval officer] and the star shells. The noise sounded like the 4th of July all right."

Training was now about to reach a different, deadlier stage.

Attached to Gen. Sir Herbert Plumer's British Second Army, the New Yorkers were to defend a stretch of the front called the East Poperinghe Line of defenses. The idea was to give each of the division's twelve battalions eight days of actual combat experience. Beginning on the night of 25 July, four battalions of the Twenty-seventh, two assigned to the British Sixth Division and two others to the British Forty-first Division, were to debut in the frontline trenches. After eight days they were to be relieved by four other battalions until, after twenty-four days, all twelve battalions had gotten their first taste of Boche blood.

The East Poperinghe Line, nicknamed "East Pop," consisted of three entrenchment systems running though Poperinghe, Dickebush, La Clytte, and Westoutre, farm villages that slouched between the medieval city of Cassel to the west and Ypres to the east. The land round about was fairly flat, except to the east, where other trenches meandered through muddy Flanders's soil, and there was a strategic hump called Mont Kemmel. It was held by the armies of Crown Prince Rupprecht of Bavaria.

Every soldier who stared up at Mont Kemmel never forgot it.

Nick Krayer recounted, "Every time a man looked over the top toward the German lines, this huge hill loomed up before him. It was a bare, bleak earthen mound; not a tree nor a bush could be observed on top. It had been a target for artillery for years, and was battered and banged as no other in France."[18]

"Mont Kemmel dominated everything in sight," stated Maj. Stanton Whitney, who during his stay in Flanders was transferred out as commander of the 107th Machine Gun Company to take over the 105th Machine Gun Battalion. "From its crest, Jerry could see our every movement; and every movement that he saw he greeted with a deluge of shells. The German was never asleep. Whizz-bangs, High-explosives, Shells, Trench Mortars and Machine Gun fire put an effective stop to any daylight movement of the Allies." Another machine gunner remembered how Mont Kemmel "reared its flat, sawed-off torso, once a proud peak, but four years of pounding by German and British artillery had given it a flat top." He added, "The more we looked at that hunk of earth, the more menacing it became. The German observers up there, it seemed to us, could look right down our throats."[19]

Another feature of the land was Dickebush Lake. A fetid quagmire befouled by gas, it gurgled and boiled like an evil witch's brew under the shadow of Mont Kemmel. Maj. Tristram Tupper on O'Ryan's staff called it a place of "many pools of poisonous water."[20]

At Steenvoorde, a French border town, the 107th Infantry detrained. The Headquarters Company and First Battalion settled down in deserted barns and shelter tents in St. Laurent, while the Second and Third Bat-

talions moved into Winnezeele, where the Fifty-fourth Brigade was setting up its headquarters. K Company marched off by itself to the outskirts of St. Laurent.

Sgt. Harry Mitchell recalled how "we hobnailed our way to Winnezeele, near the Franco-Belgium border. In Winnezeele the poundings of
the guns at the front was distinct indeed." Cpl. Francis Miller stated, "It
was here that the men heard for the first time the explosion of a shell, and
became accustomed to the whirring of them as they came over. Here they
received most of the instruction in modern methods of warfare. The use
of bombs, rifle grenades, Lewis machine guns and wave formations of attack were explained and practiced. Every other day the men were on the
rifle range."[21]

"At Winnezeele we first heard the 'zing' of the big ones," Sgt. Floyd
Neely also noted. "For the first night of our stay there the Boche shelled
us, and the next day we were ordered to dig in."[22]

Pvt. Fetherolf sent word to his "Dear Aunt" in Middletown that "at the
present time we are sleeping in tents that are sunk two feet in the ground.
We have nice fresh hay under us and make out very comfortably."

This time Leland wasn't lucky enough to find a farmhouse. Instead, he
had to pitch a tent like most everyone else. "My tent is considerably down
in old Mother Earth and as I share it with two other officers it has all the
messiness and discomforts of a front line dugout."

After getting settled, Kenneth Gow described how the regiment was
"scattered over a wide area, some of them billeted and some camped. We
are in shelter-tents. There are a dozen things I would give a thousand
francs to be able to tell you, but cannot and comply with the censorship
regulations. If I ever get back, I am going to have enough to talk to you
about for months."

In a similar letter, Billy Leonard told a friend in Flushing, "We've
hiked across a mighty interesting section of France and I've seen a lot the
censor won't let me tell. You bet some day I'll give you the story between
puffs of your excellent cigars."[23] Leonard always was hunting for a grand
story to tell with a humorous twist to it. As a journalist, it was his nature.
The ex–city editor of the Flushing *Daily Times* saw the humor in every one
of his military experiences and found them all worth writing about. From
peeling potatoes and onions while on kitchen patrol or catching pneumo-

nia and then falling head over heels for the curly haired nurse who cared for him at the Camp Wadsworth infirmary, or finding delight in the French children, who, marching alongside of him in Brest, sang "Hail, hail, the gang's all here," Billy couldn't wait to put those moments into words.

Now he couldn't wait to get into the front line. He knew a story was there waiting for him.

The 107th Infantry was not scheduled for its eight-day tour of the trenches until 10 August. But small groups of men went ahead anyway. Leonard's turn came on Sunday, 14 July. Bastille Day. Billy told his friend Sergeant Neely he had volunteered for observation duty "just to see how they do it."[24] To another friend he had stated, "The reason I am writing now is because one must grasp the opportunity when it comes. One never knows from day to day what will happen next." He then described the constant shelling that disturbed his sleep. "Every night the shells go whining over our heads. Sometimes they seem so close you'd expect to see them come in the barn door. Then 'Jerry' comes over to drop a few bombs and we open up on him with anti-aircraft and machine gun fire and there's a very hell of a racket. It's devilish hard getting to sleep again." To another Flushing friend he mused, "The nearer we get to the trenches the less we think about the war in its larger aspects. I imagine it's because we're cut off from the world, in a sense, rarely see a newspaper . . . and our own particular job fills our time and thoughts."[25]

It was a cold, wet, miserable day in Flanders, especially for the French celebrating their version of the Fourth of July, when Billy went up to the trenches. As he got ready to depart, British soldiers had finished entertaining the Americans by playing a cricket match in the rain. The Americans were ready to show them a game of baseball. And as usual above them planes fought deadly duels. With all this excitement buzzing around him, Leonard, the handsome corporal with the big, bright eyes, slung his full field pack over his back, anticipating the new adventure awaiting him a few miles to the east, and was ready to go. Leland, his pal from the Bayside Yacht Club who had enticed him to enlist in the old Seventh Regiment, remembered the moment. "He turned to wave his hand and grin at his comrades of the Second Platoon, who were offering him the usual advice—and was gone."

Later, in the veiled black of night, a British guide escorted Leonard to the trench closest to the fighting, known as Scherpenberg Hill. Beyond it was no-man's-land and Mont Kemmel, crawling with Germans. Here he was assigned to the Royal Fusiliers. The Tommies had a nightly task to perform and invited the Yank to join them. They were to slip into no-man's-land and lay down barbed wire where new gaps had been torn open by artillery fire.

At midnight, the party sneaked out of the trench and wiggled into no-man's-land. At last Billy tasted war first hand. Oh, what a story to tell back in Flushing!

No sooner had they crawled away, behind them the big British guns opened up, hurling lead over their heads toward the German trenches. The Boche answered with a terrific barrage of their own. The sergeant of the work party ordered the men back to the trenches on the double. Before they could start running, a shell burst in their midst. It instantly killed a British soldier. Fragments ripped into Billy's stomach. An officer leaped out of the trench, scooped up Billy and carried him one hundred yards back to safety. When he placed the shredded body of the American down on the duckboard he saw that the young doughboy was dead. The moment word got back to the 107th Infantry, Leland sat stunned in his shelter tent. "No one imagined he was going into any danger for as yet the war hadn't really hurt any of us. It was sort of a joke—the whole business. But Billy never came back. He was our first loss and it shocked and sobered Company I inexpressibly. Gallant, light-hearted Billy Leonard killed? Impossible! There was surely some mistake!"

"We couldn't believe it at first," wrote Neely. "War at this point had not been an affair in which people were killed. Now it came home to us. Billy's smile and his cheery words had often dispelled the 'blues' in camp or on the march. He was one of the mainstays and chief supporters of the company spirit. His loss was a great one to all of us, but the memory of Billy's wonderful personality and his noble death will always remain in the minds of his comrades."[26]

Hit the hardest in the regiment was Billy's younger brother, Eugene, at that moment assigned to Headquarters Company. To their mother, the heartbroken New Yorker wrote, "The English did everything possible for him and brought up a chaplain from ten miles behind the lines, and buried him with all the honors of a brave soldier."[27]

Billy Leonard was buried almost where he fell, next to the British soldier who had died with him. Leland recalled, "They were buried, side by side, on the slope of the Scherpenberg—the immortal ridge against which the high tide of German invasion broke and could not pass." In a letter to William Holmes, the commodore of the Bayside Yacht Club, one of Leonard's favorite hangouts at home, Leland sent word, "Long before you get this you will doubtless hear that Billy Leonard has 'gone west.' He was our first casualty and you can't understand how hard it was to lose him unless you have been through what I've been through with these boys—most of them young enough to be my sons.

"Well, what more can I say, except that while his body lies out there on that desolate, iron-swept hill, his heart, I know, is back in God's country, with his loved ones."[28]

CHAPTER 7

I Want … to Keep These Fellows Over Here Cheerful

etting over the loss of Billy Leonard, the first soldier in the division to be killed in combat, was not easy. Yet by the end of August, when the 107th Infantry left Belgium for the Hindenburg Line, death within its ranks would be commonplace. At first death was distant, hitting other regiments, but sparing silk stocking soldiers. Pfc. Otto Koch of the 105th Infantry died on 15 July, a day after Billy had "gone west." Cpl. William Davidson of the 108th Infantry was killed on 16 July. And so was Pfc. Percy Sweet of the 105th Machine Gun Battalion. Two other 108th Infantrymen fell on 23 July. Soon afterward, grim news of old Seventh Regiment graduates, as the *Gazette* referred to its former members, began filtering in. Among the casualties on the western front were 40 of the 350 men who had been transferred to the Sixty-ninth Regiment, now the 165th. Pfc. James G. duB. Tiffany and Pvt. Philip Schuyler Finn, the son of the late Tammany Hall sachem, "Battery Dan" Finn, were killed. Before his death, Finn wanted his brother, Joe, to know that someday he would be able to "relate some of my experiences to you, and then you will look upon me as a real soldier." Malcolm Troop Robertson went down at the Ourcq River, nicknamed the "River O'Rourke" by the

Irish soldiers, on 30 July, felled by a shell while rallying his platoon against a German counterattack. A day later, Sgt. Joyce Kilmer took a bullet in the head. Cpl. Vanderbilt Ward, great-grandson of Commodore Vanderbilt, gassed in the battle, embellished Kilmer's death in a letter to his mother. "When we attacked we moved so rapidly chasing the Huns that the artillery had no chance to catch up. Poor Joyce Kilmer was one of the first to fall, with five machine gun bullets, one of which went through his heart. He, as you remember, volunteered, and was transferred with me from the 7th to the 69th. When it came to a close-up with the Huns we remembered Leo and Joyce and the others, and I want to say that we treated them rough."[1]

Perhaps the hardest death to hear about was Maj. James McKenna Jr., who after eight years with the old Seventh had in 1916 transferred to the Sixty-ninth so he could receive a commission. The son of the postmaster of Long Island City, McKenna was a lawyer and had been one of the Seventh's renowned athletes. As a leader in the Irish Regiment, he commanded the Third, or "Shamrock," Battalion. On the 28th, a shell hit McKenna. An officer remembered hurrying him back to an aid station. "His pulse was still flickering, the same faint way. The doctor immediately gave him an injection of strychnine, but two minutes afterward the pulse beat ceased." When the boys of the old Sixty-ninth lit after the Hun at the Battle of Ourcq, they roared, "Remember McKenna!"[2]

Maj. Gen. John O'Ryan's headquarters was now in Oudezeele, an ancient Flemish town of stone and brick houses. Here the general organized a Divisional Theatrical Troupe. He believed that entertaining his men would certainly help take their minds off the brutality of war now bursting all about them in ever-increasing intensity. Thus, he reunited the talented men throughout his division who had earlier written, produced, and staged the play *You Know Me, Al*, which debuted in Spartanburg and then ran in New York. He ordered them to erect a stage in a field opposite his headquarters and every evening between eight and ten put on a show as good as any on Broadway.

From the start, the theatrical troupe was a success, playing in the open field jammed with cheering, whistling, laughing Americans, Australians, New Zealanders, Englishmen, Scots, and Irishmen as well as the dumbfounded local residents of Oudezeele who knew not a single word of English spoken on the stage.

Kenneth Gow, who had taken his mother to see *You Know Me, Al*, told her about his trip into Oudezeele. "These men are doing fine work. There were between two and three hundred British officers at the show, and they certainly enjoyed it. It is strange to see this organization performing at a point where a 'Jack Johnson' or some similar bird might land at any minute and spread performers, stage and audience all over the landscape."

In the *Gazette*, Sgt. John MacDonnell compared the divisional show to "as fine a vaudeville bill as ever graced Broadway. The songs that one learns there are resung on hikes, all the jokes and witty sayings rehearsed with the result that the burden of the hike is forgotten—lost in the memory of evenings that were well spent."

"Altho low in spirit at times," Pfc. Scott Lytle enjoyed the female impersonators and let his father know that some of the jokes were "soldiers' jokes, ever side-splitting."

D Company's Will and Ned Hayward also took in the show, and were joined by their brother, Rob, a military policeman. "Believe me, Ned and I were glad to see our brother," Will wrote home. "He looks fine and says he's 'living the life of Riley.' We talked for over two hours." He added that "we all enjoyed [the show] very much."[3]

Not only did soldiers pack the field, but every night Flemish children sat in the front row, enthralled at the vaudeville antics and bawdy songs of the entertainers. "At first they gazed in almost dumb wonderment at the nonsense of the clowns or the dancing of the 'girls' and listened intently to the divisional jazz band and the popular Broadway songs," recalled O'Ryan. "Before the division had been at Oudezeele a month one could hear the boys of the village whistling such songs as 'Wait Til The Cows Come Home,' 'My Heart Belongs to The U.S.A.,' 'Mother Machree,' and other melodies. In two months they were singing the songs in English."

In Oudezeele, the soldiers also found other entertainment. Even though it was a modest farming village, it sported dozens of *estaminets*. One of them was on the main street right across from O'Ryan's headquarters. It was an old-fashioned inn that, in due time, according to one colonel, would "become the Manhattan Club for elite doughboys, meaning conquerors at the various 'crap' games that grow and multiply everywhere."[4]

Don Emery described how he and several of the boys "drifted into town and made for certain quarters known as '*estaminets*' and there we mixed with other soldiers from every quarter of the Globe—English, French, Canadian, New Zealander, Australian, Belgian, Highlander and American blended, or rather joined their voices in a noise to drown that of the bombardment only a few short kilometers away." He added, "The wine here is excellent let me say and there seems to be no scarcity of it, in fact water is much more difficult to get than either 'Rouge Vin' or 'Stout.' Madame says 'L'Americane is tres large and has ze thirst and ze appetite to match.' 'Tres correct, Madame' we reply, 'and proud of it.' "

MacDonnell believed that "if you've seen one [*estaminet*] you've seen them all. They sell light wines and beer, the wine being the other name for 'coca-cola,' while the beer resembles the original only in name."

E Company soldiers, when avoiding their own army food, dined on eggs, chips, and coffee at Julie's. "The place was a shanty to be sure," commented Cpl. Francis Miller, "and the people for whom it meant daily bread were very dirty and some said, questionably loyal, and the forks with which the men ate were covered with fat, but it was the only place around, and Julie always wore a smile, and showed an attempt to look clean. She was cheerful, exchanged bright repartee with the men, who liked the way she said, 'No compres!' "[5]

A Company Cpl. Arthur Briggs Church urged his mother to "be sure the kitchen range is in good shape for you will have your hands full feeding me when I come home for that long vacation I'm going to have."[6]

Gow fared better. His meals were "just as one would want anywhere." He had fresh butter every day, cheese, and homemade beer. "The French," the lieutenant noted, "can fry potatoes such as I have never tasted before, real French fried." He also found billets in an enormous farmhouse outside of Oudezeele, owned by a wealthy farmer. Inside was a piano, and one night he heard someone playing what he thought was Chopin's "Fifth Nocturne." He went in and saw a girl of fourteen. "She played for me for an hour and [a] half. She played several pieces that Marj. used to play, and it all reminded me so much of her."

Raeburn Van Buren lolled about his pup tent one day, writing a letter to his mother. "Our band is now playing in a field on the other side of a hedge back of my tent and it sounds good. Way off in the distance the rumble of big guns can be heard and a few aeroplanes are in the air over our field." And then he thought of Neysa McMein, knowing that she was now in France somewhere entertaining the troops. "I hope to goodness to get a squint at her." A few days later he wrote to his sister, Vea, whose husband was on the staff of the New York *Herald*. "The weeks pass so slowly in this game. They seem like years and our work is very hard and monotonous. . . . We are very near the front now (news to be kept from mother) and there is much activity tonight. Sometimes the ground seems to tremble. We have been within the sound of the big guns so long now we hardly notice them. They lull me to sleep every night. From here we can see the flashes of them all along the line and now and then a big dozy comes whistling over our heads." And his thoughts drifted back again to his old apartment in New York and to McMein. "You would be surprised how pretty she can look in an evening gown after a good dinner and an afternoon nap. God I would love to see her. Guess she is in France now but I am so isolated here I never hope to see anyone until after the war."

Not only did he miss McMein, he missed his mother. "Mother dearest," he wrote on 27 July, "This is one of those old wet Sundays that makes a soldier want his mamma. Mud everywhere. I wish you could see my shoes they are so heavy I can hardly move in them. . . . I haven't had my uniform off for about ten days. We only take them off when we have a bath and baths are as hard to find around here as hair pins and lace."

He was right about the rarity of a bath. There were just too many soldiers and not enough water. However, at the opposite end of the field in which the stage for the division's theatrical troupe had been erected, crude showers were built. Sgt. Harry Mitchell never forgot his first "field wash" at Oudezeele. "A small tank had been reared in a field over a little cylindrical stove. It held between ten or fifteen gallons of water, and about ten men could bathe at one time under pipes that released a tiny trickle that was barely sufficient to allow a flow to work up a lather and rinse off. Besides, each man was allowed but three minutes for his scrub, and all the while a couple of men had to be working a pump that sucked water from a nearby creek."

Will Hayward wrote to his family, "This afternoon we fell in with towel and soap and hiked to the village for a bath. Was it good? No, it was great!" He also was able to wash his clothes. "I'm a good washerman," he said, "but don't know anything about ironing. I'll get that when I reach home."[7]

Bert Lobdell reassured his mother that all was well with him. "Feel fine and dandy all the time and happy. We're kept so busy we don't get time to get homesick and it's hard to even find time to write. I'm with a great bunch of fellows and as long as the war goes on I wouldn't want to be satisfied anywheres but with them. A number of them from White Plains. Of course I know them all."

Toward the end of July, the weather turned hot, muggy, and oftentimes wet. "Just the kind of weather to make you sweat from head to foot," Van Buren complained to his sister. Claude Leland let his family know that Flanders "had a lot of wet weather recently and of course plenty of mud which makes it very disagreeable soldiering." Pvt. Angelo Mustico informed his siblings in Newburgh that "I have never seen such changeable weather as we are having here. It rains for a while then the sun comes out."

The awful heat in July and August, mixed with rain, bore down on the men. It struck the boys of E Company especially hard. The company had been ordered to dig trenches deep enough to bury cables so they would not be destroyed by artillery fire. "Working all day, digging through the clay of Flanders to a depth of six feet," stated Corporal Miller, "they laid hundreds of yards of cable. There were no slackers, everybody took a crack at using a pick or a shovel. Corporals and sergeants took turns, for there was rivalry between the various squads."[8] Pfc. William White of Cornwall-on-Hudson found the work ironic. His father had run the steam plant that powered the equipment that dug the tunnel under the Hudson River for the Catskill Aqueduct. Now he was digging by hand in the blistering heat. Seeing him and other boys in his squad pant and sweat, Sgt. Anthony Farina, in civilian days a foreman at the du Pont Fabrikoid Works, among the largest employers in Newburgh, told them to shed their woolen shirts. This relief did not last long. O'Ryan happened by with his staff. He ordered Farina to have his men put their shirts back on. The sergeant saluted the general and told his boys to don their shirts.

Then he watched O'Ryan motor way. The moment the car disappeared from sight, Farina barked out, "Okay boys, you can take off your shirts again!"[9]

But the real heat came at night—the seemingly endless German artillery shelling. To keep themselves as safe as possible in their two-man shelter tents they hollowed out shallow indentations in the clay soil and slept in them. The holes were two feet deep and only wide enough to hold one body. Pitched in unmilitary disarray, tents were scattered here and there, wherever the ground gave the most protection. As Capt. Harry Hayward of E Company described to a friend, "Instead of regular rows of tents, tents are placed wherever there can be obtained concealment—along hedges, under trees, etc. with no regard to regularity. Deep holes are dug under the tents and the earth banked high up to protect against the burst of high explosives."[10]

Another captain in one of the other regiments wrote, "By dark the landscape for miles around was dotted with stabbing flames of big gun discharges, each followed by an air-shattering report and the diminishing roar of the shells. They flamed and bellowed hour after hour until it seemed there must be a limit and when one paused to consider how the human made tornado had hurled tons of steel each hour of each night for month after month the mind just failed to grasp it."[11]

It was on such a night of endless shelling that Col. Charles L. DeBevoise's 107th Infantry at last moved up to the front line. From mid-July to mid-August, three infantry battalions and one machine gun battalion occupied the East Poperinghe Line. For the rest of August the regiment dug in around Dickebusch Lake.

The orders were simple. Hold the line. Rumors were rampant that the Germans planned another offensive and would sweep down and around Mont Kemmel to drive the Allies back toward the Channel ports once again. For the Machine Gun Company, the orders sounded extreme. Where they were going, the gunners had been told to hold their position to the last. "In case of attack, the gun crew will remain at their posts until gun is out of action, after which they will defend the position with rifles, bayonets, revolvers, grenades, clubs, stones and other novelties. If any members of the crew cannot remain here alive, they will remain here dead. Finally, this position will be held."[12]

Before its stint in the line, however, the Machine Gun Company underwent a change in command. Then-Captain Stanton Whitney, who had started his military career with Squadron A, another of New York City's elite National Guard units that was on par with the old Seventh when tapping into high society for its men, was transferred to the 105th Machine Gun Battalion. Capt. Walter Gresham Andrews, an ex–First Cavalry officer from Buffalo and grandson of Walter Q. Gresham, secretary of state in President Grover Cleveland's cabinet, was sent over from the 105th Machine Gun Battalion. Lieutenant Gow, one of eight machine gunners from Summit, New Jersey, liked his new commander. "Capt. Andrews is fine and very efficient," he said in a letter to his father. "He is the famous Ham Andrews of Princeton, the football player. I saw him play once in a game between Princeton and Yale. He is twenty-one."

Ten days after Andrews became commander, the Machine Gun Company headed toward the line for the first time. It was 27 July.

Recalling that moment, New York City resident Pvt. Patrick Merrigan of the First Platoon wrote, "I was carrying the pack up to our position when I heard a whistle and wondering what strange bird could be out on such a clear morning, I heard a deafening explosion and saw a house go up, twirl and come down in debris which could make some big wrecking companies green with envy."[13]

Like all companies within the regiment, the machine gunners didn't move into the trenches until night. The following experiences are representative of what it was like for all the doughboys of the 107th Infantry as they reached their final positions under the eerie shadow of Mont Kemmel—whether it was the "East Pop" line or the Dickebusch sector.

"Night had already fallen when we unloaded and the darkness was emphasized by the grim silence," noted Sgt. Joseph Robins of the Machine Gun Company's Third Platoon, a New York City resident. "The guides were met and the party was divided into several reliefs, each going to a different position. The consensus of opinion was that, in order to be a guide, one must be the fastest walker on earth, and also have the instinct of an animal to come from a place in darkness and return to it. Our walk to the position was more of a trot than a walk, and how anyone could find the way through such a maze of trees, ruts, fox-holes and ruins of all description was a puzzle to us. In the distance we heard the 'put put' of machine gun snipers."[14]

Sergeant MacDonnell envied the guides. "Would that I had the owl-eyes of a guide! I imagine they were all brought up in the country and, being used to traveling over dark paths, have that advantage over us fellows from the city."

"Who among us will ever forget that night along shell-torn roads," wrote Cpl. Drew Hill of B Company; "the deafening roar of our 'heavies,' the ceaseless rumble of the ration limbers as they rolled past us in unending numbers, the sudden flares of Jerry's Very lights, the barking rat-a-tat of machine guns and the intermittent crack of snipers' rifles."[15]

Overhead the "Steenevoorde Express," as they called German shells in honor of the village in which they were encamped, whistled past, and the Greyjackets instantly became "loyal members of the Shell-Duckers Union."

Pfc. Harold Chasmar of the Sanitation Detachment, who had enlisted in the old Seventh from Port Chester, told his parents, "We entered our position at night and as we wound our way in the dark a strange feeling seemed to creep over us. All was quiet and the steady tramp, tramp of the marching men was all that broke the quiet, except now and then a suppressed word from one stumbling over a wire or slipping in a shell hole. As we neared our position the batteries opened up and it seemed as if —— had been let loose."[16]

"All the horrible havoc of brutal warfare lay in the path that led to the outermost posts of civilization," is how Sgt. Gerald F. Jacobson put it. "Enemy shells shrieked and exploded ahead and behind and on either side of the advancing groups of each battalion. The march forward, of course, was made in small detachments so that loss of life would be minimized should enemy shells find their targets."

As the boys followed their guides through the darkness, they spoke in low whispers, each trying to convince the other that they were as brave as seasoned veterans. MacDonnell remembered running in single file. "Certain points must be passed quickly—on the run, with a fifteen pace interval between men. The head of the column halts, being under cover, to allow the rest to catch up. All gas masks are placed in alert position. Two blasts of a whistle followed by a long one means to continue the march. It is real dark, not a star in the sky." The nearer they got to the trenches, the sound and smell of war wrapped tightly around their very being like a choke collar. They took in the "sweet, sickly, pineapple odor" of phosgene gas—a shell-encased carbonyl chloride mixed with chlorine. A deadly gas, it attacked the respiratory system, killing its victims within forty-eight hours. Jacobson recalled the "sharp, hateful staccato of machine guns sounding amidst the louder, more ferocious barks of the opposing artillery. It seemed so dark and ghostly up in that region of death and destruction. The sky was constantly stabbed and streaked by the vivid flashes of the heavy guns, and now just ahead could be seen the rocket-like flares of the very lights."

"We seemed to be moving into a new world," another soldier stated. "Terrible and grand beyond all description."

Cpl. James Throckmorton Vought of K Company, who had once taught school at the Summit Academy in New Jersey, a Harvard graduate and member of the Knickerbocker and Whist clubs in New York City, was one of three men detailed to lug the mail up that first night. As they moved, stooped down through the utter blackness, one of them dropped a heavy mailbag into a filthy water-filled shell hole. They had no choice but to wade in after it. When they had climbed out, hauling the soaked mailbag with them, their company had disappeared. "We were absolutely lost in a strange place which was once a forest," he told his brother, Grandin. "We began to go along when suddenly machine-gun bullets began ripping through the wood uncomfortably close. Shortly some shells began to fall right near us. It was several hours before we located our men. We found out later that we had spent most of the night wandering the famous Scottish Woods. They were always heavily shelled at night and raked by machine-gun fire, for the Huns knew that all men and supplies went to and fro through those woods."[17]

MacDonnell described the "enemies' bullets cracking over our heads. We press on, hugging the ground, taking advantage of all the cover that affords itself. The man in front of you drops in a prone position and you 'follow suit.' The same is continued all along the line. 'Pass the word for the stretcher bearers' goes from mouth to mouth. 'Keep your feet out of my face' whispers someone to the man in front of him. 'Keep your face away from my feet,' he answers back. The stretcher bearers have gone forward and are now returning carrying someone on a litter."

Will Hayward recalled how D Company had to wait before it could enter the trenches. "Going nearer to the front on the march we could hear the shells singing over our heads. At times it seemed as though they were fired right at us. We got to the trenches a few hours later, but could not go in them as they were full of water. This particular section is noted for this condition. We took scattered positions in an open field to avoid shells. Soon got used to the noise, lay down and had a good sleep."[18]

Once the doughboys hit the trench that led them to the front, they followed it on the run, keeping low. The Very lights exploding overhead illuminated the ghastly landscape. Every time one of the lights went off, the New Yorkers froze. For every Very light the Germans sent up, the Allies sent up two.

"Why the brightest spot on Broadway is but a shadow to any sector in No Man's Land," MacDonnell wrote.

In charge of the machine-gun squads of his company, MacDonnell made certain each squad was at its designated post the moment they reached the main trench. With head down, he hurried from post to post, checking on his men. He also spotted a shell hole "fifty paces" in front of the main trench, in no-man's-land. To him, it was a good spot for one of his squads to hunker down with a machine gun. Ordering a squad to follow him at five-pace intervals, he rolled out of the trench and onto his back, the heavy machine gun resting on his chest. One hundred pounds of equipment pressed down on him. "Unless you have muscles of steel and sinews of iron, the result of hard physical training, you'll find it an exhausting task to move even the distance of a few yards." Slowly, he and the squad waggled toward the shell hole. Safely there, they assembled the machine gun. He then crawled back to the main trench. "All night long rifles are cracking, machine bullets are whizzing," he wrote, "and for every one the enemy sends over we give him five for good measure."

During their stint in the trenches of Flanders, the soldiers kept their heads low during the day and their eyes open wide at night—ready for a German assault. They mingled with the British, learning from them what to do. "We were mixed up with the Tommies, who had been holding this sector for some time," Corporal Hill said. "They began immediately to teach us the rules of the game according to Hoyle."[19]

Private First Class Chasmar explained to his parents, "Sleep all day and on the job all night. Just reverse the day and I have adjusted myself to

In Flanders, the men of the 107th await their first trip into the trenches. National Archives

the change. Am sleeping on two boards with my pack as a pillow, rats as bed fellows and mud for good measure."

Pvt. George Fetherolf boasted to his aunt and uncle back in Middletown, "I have learned how to make a smokeless fire out of an old tin can, a piece of sandbag and a candle. You wash your hands in a shell hole of water in the bottom of which there may be a dead German, for they are lying about in most places."

The trenches the men now lived in were not elaborate underground systems. Vought called them "mainly shell-holes connected up with shallow ditches and you were really in the open all the time."[20] Mustico reported to his family in Newburgh that the trenches "were only two feet wide and hardly any place to sleep and not deep enough to stand upright in some places."

Still, the trench system was a confounding maze of twisting trails. It was easy to get lost. A wrong turn could lead into enemy lines. Capt. Thomas J. Brady, regimental intelligence officer, noted that the best way not to get lost was to memorize the locations of the graves of the Allied soldiers who had been buried where they fell. "There were no other guide posts aside from the names of the dead painted on the neat crosses and headstones set up by the French and British. No matter how hurried they were they found the time to care for their dead. In going back and forth in groups of two and three we would remember that Private Clearly, for instance, was buried along what had been the pathway to the Hague Farm. Private Wilkinson's grave always showed me how to get to Micmac Farm. I'll never forget the graves with the poppies waving about the crosses."[21]

Getting lost was the least of the worries for the soldiers burdened with hauling supplies and ammunition to the front. Their route took them over ground that the German artillery pounded nightly. Every midnight 1st Lt. John A. Korschen, an old First Infantry hand from Middletown, worked his way up to the trenches with supplies for I Company. "Believe me it is not the nicest job on earth to go up there with wagons and horses," he assured his hometown friends. "I lost two men and one horse. But then I consider that very fortunate for we have no means of cover like the boys in the trenches and when the shells come we have to dodge the best way we can and at times the traffic is badly congested." Korschen added that after making his deliveries, he then had to report to battalion headquarters to "find out if there were any bodies to bring back and if there were I would bring them back in the wagon and turn them over to the burial officer. The bodies are sewed up in burlap, placed in a grave with a small wooden cross, the man's name and organization on the grave."[22]

Another of the boys charged with bringing up supplies was Gow, who, like Korschen, had to haul rations and ammunition for the men and guns now in the trenches. "The Boche harasses all roads and communications with his artillery continuously, and we have to run this gauntlet of fire. Last night he let loose with everything he had—whizz bangs, shrapnel, high explosives and gas right on us, and we were in perfect hell for fifteen minutes," he penned his mother after a few days in the front line.

Gow also let her know, "My ears are O. K., which is a consolation, as many men get their eardrums punctured by the detonations."

For the most part, the men in the trenches slept in bivvies. These were small dugouts, mere shelter holes gouged out of the sides of the trenches. Cpl. Alfred Reeves Jr. of C Company explained to New York City newspaper reporters that bivvies was "short for bivouacs, you know. It's a name we give to the shelves dug out on the sides of the trenches which serve us for beds. We sleep in our clothes, of course, sometimes we don't have them off for four and five weeks at a stretch. Over the bivvies are galvanized roofs covered with dirt to make them level with the edge of the trench. Sometimes, when an enemy attack is on, you hear the bullets pounding on the galvanized roofs, and it certainly does make you feel queer. It's a merry dance for the bullets, but not quite so cheerful for you underneath them."

Pfc. Bob Helstern of the Headquarters Company, a Newburgh native, after climbing into his bivvy, used his coat and ammunition belt as a pillow. Once, when he had not yet gone to sleep, a German shell exploded within a few feet of his head. The concussion knocked him out. Shrapnel struck his ammunition belt. Thirteen rounds in the belt went off. His bivvy collapsed on top of him, burying him from his waist up to his head. The shell killed one British soldier and wounded seven Americans. "They thought I was a 'goner' but mother I fooled them all when I dug my way out and rolled down the bank without a scratch. I am the talk of the place now! I happened to be the nearest man to it and the only one not wounded." Every piece of his personal property was torn to shreds. Inspecting his helmet afterward, Helstern noticed that it had been pierced by two pieces of shrapnel.[23]

In the letter to his aunt and uncle, Fetherolf explained what it was like in the trenches. "I have experienced the wide awake nights when to even doze off is nearly as good as death. When it is necessary to stand motionless for hours at a time in one spot else draw the enemy's snipers' attention and get an explosive bullet in some vital part of your entirely too large anatomy. When gas comes creeping slowly toward you and you feel for your gas mask that dear old thing that you cussed up hill and down. . . . I have experienced the sensation of how heavy the tin hat is when you first put it on on the way up to the line and the farther you get the lighter the old head shell feels and then perhaps a shell bursts nearby and shrapnel flies around you and that tin hat gets as light as an egg shell and about the size of one, so you think when you try to crawl under it."

Private First Class Chasmar, in a letter home to Port Chester: "We dare not 'nose' about much during the day, but work at night. I am sitting here among debris and ruins writing this, so when you read this, try and picture where I was when writing. The boys and Tommies are sitting near me talking about 'shows' and amusements." He also said that after set-tling down, his detachment was "waiting, waiting for a call for medical men. Thank God no call came." He assured his parents that he was "calm and trusting in God and am having an experience never to be forgotten."

Cpl. James M. O'Toole of H Company, writing of his experiences to his family back in Mount Vernon, at first complained. "When we first went into the trenches I was taken away from my Lewis automatic gun and placed in charge of another gun under an English corporal." But af-ter a fit of shelling, he added, "I must say that I was very fortunate because my side partner who was left in charge of the other gun [Lewis] had both of his legs torn with shrapnel."[24] Later on, another shell landed close enough to O'Toole to bury him in dirt.

Cpl. Burrell Hoyt of the intelligence section of the First Battalion re-membered his "first taste of shell fire and our first whiff of chloropicrine and mustard gas."[25] While his unit was in the trenches, his commanding officer, 2d Lt. Ford Terry, was pulled out of the line and replaced by D Company's 2d Lt. Oscar Hellquist from Summit. "After working under Terry's capable direction . . . we did not welcome the change, but liked Lt. Hellquist from the first. Later we learned to love him for what he was—a gentleman and an officer of rare good judgment, great enthusiasm for the work at hand, and absolute devotion of duty. He proved himself a friend to all of us."

Hellquist, the Cornell graduate, and his men constantly put their lives on the line by crawling into no-man's-land nightly to gather information, to be the eyes of the artillery. As Hoyt put it, "We trailed along to snipe and observe and scout. The 6th British Division had been holding this sector for some weeks but was hanging on for a few days before withdraw-ing to 'break the Yanks in.' Jerry's outposts were less than two hundred yards away and our snipers put the fear of God into every Hun who showed his head for the fractional part of a second. We carried on in the approved manner, drumming up a dixie of tea with our Tommy mentor-friends every night as soon as the burlap bag of rations and petrol tin of water came up."[26]

Nightly, Hellquist and two other lieutenants in the Intelligence Sec-tion, Marsh S. Lockyear, a regular army veteran of ten years, and Harry

W. Robinson, formerly of the Third New York Infantry, "went over the top," said their commander, Captain Brady, "crawling on their stomachs, wiggling through the barbed wire, twisting about like snakes. They sometimes lay for hours in observation posts exposed to machine gun fire. One patrol spent 24 hours in a tower, during which time the enemy poured in a steady stream of exploding shells around the place." Hellquist always led these patrols. Brady called him a "fearless, modest, keen soldier, always willing to go on any mission." When he talked of Hellquist and Lockyear and Robinson, he said, "Too much cannot be said about their nerve."[27]

In his letters home, Hellquist never mentioned his adventures in no-man's-land. He did tell his little brother that because he was the youngest officer he drew the worse part of the trenches. Instead, he wrote about all the tea he had to drink. "I suppose you think we're out for tea parties."

Another soldier new to intelligence work was 2d Lt. Earle Grimm, the yachtsman, public relations expert, and former four-year veteran and sergeant of E Company. On 9 August, Grimm was named Second Battalion

Advertising wizard Lt. Earle Grimm tormented the
Germans during his first battle on the front line.
The Seventh Regiment Fund

intelligence officer. The Troy, New York, native possessed a diabolical sense of humor. While in the Dickebusch sector, he built a huge billboard of wood and canvas. Then in German, and in large letters, he copied on the canvas brief accounts of Allied victories. At midnight he and several compatriots slipped into no-man's-land, dragging the billboard with them. When they had crawled within a few feet of the enemy's barbed wire, they raised the bulky billboard upright, secured it into the ground and slipped back to their own trenches. A sergeant in K Company stated, "By morning, every German soldier in that section had read its bad news, news they would never have learned from their own command. This typical example of 'Seventh' daring and imagination drew many chuckles from the British troops, and a volley of plainly heard curses from the opposite trenches."[28]

About the time the billboard was erected in no-man's-land, obviously a strange sight amongst the almost unchanging routine of trench warfare, another weird sight popped up close to the trenches. A huge, white beach umbrella. As Capt. Tristram Tupper described it, "just an inoffensive, sit-in-the-sand-by-the-sea, green-lined white umbrella."[29]

It belonged to the famous portrait artist John Singer Sargent.

The prime minister of England, Lloyd George, had commissioned Sargent, a sixty-two-year-old expatriate American whose society paintings gained him international fame, to capture battlefront cooperation between the United States and Great Britain. When he recruited Sargent in the spring of 1918, Lloyd George had high expectations that the portraitist would be able to commemorate the war with a "number of great paintings, one of these paintings in which British and American troops are engaged in unison." Perhaps the prime minister had an ulterior motive—to shame Gen. John Pershing into assigning several of his divisions to Douglas Haig's battered armies. Sargent left England in July, garbed in an officer's uniform. By the time he caught up with Tommies and doughboys fighting side-by-side it was August. The doughboys were New Yorkers, and belonged to O'Ryan's Twenty-seventh Division.

Tupper likened Sargent's beach umbrella to "a giant mushroom" that sprung "unheralded overnight out of the mud and mire of things." When the expatriate arrived with his umbrella and art supplies, the division was hunkered down in a place where "everything else was warlike, every-thing was hard, serious, tense and determined, for this was at battle head-quarters on a hill, overhanging the lines." O'Ryan and his staff were holed up in a Nissen hut, a squat corrugated hovel. It was an ideal spot for an artist to capture the realism of war. But Sargent had no idea what war was all about. He thought that on Sunday there was no fighting, that the soldiers on both sides actually rested. He failed to realize how much dan-ger he was in, sitting out in the open, shielded only by his glaringly white umbrella. Obviously, the Americans feared for their visitor. It took some arguing, but they at least got permission from him to camouflage his ob-trusive umbrella.[30]

Meanwhile, O'Ryan invited Sargent to live with him for a few days.

"Mr. Sargent . . . became a member of 'A' Mess," recalled the young general. "It soon developed that his idea of seeing something of the American troops involved a search for appropriate subjects amid the scenes of front line activities." O'Ryan said that with difficulty he "dis-suaded him during the first few days of his visit from going farther for-ward than the Division Headquarters."

Meanwhile, as Sargent, much like a hungry animal in search of a meal, prowled behind the lines hunting for suitable subjects he instinc-tively knew he couldn't find, deep in the Dickebusch sector E Company settled into the trenches. Soon the artistic paths of one of the company's doughboys and Sargent would cross. But first this doughboy and his close companions had to endure life at the front.

Sgt. Nick Krayer related how E Company moved up at night, after tea: "On all sides and in all directions came the roar of guns and the crash of bursting shells. The German Very lights thrown up from outposts and pa-trols seemed very near yet were more than a mile away. Then the troops moved in single file, following paths and trenches now filled with water." To Krayer, "The men were engrossed in thought. They were entering upon the greatest experience of their lives. None knew how much longer he had to live. Everything became an uncertainty."[31]

In Kansas City that night, the service pin worn by the mother of Rae-burn Van Buren, who was then celebrating her forty-eighth birthday, sent out an eerie warning to her that he was now in danger. A Christian Sci-ence practitioner, she immediately began to pray for the safety of her only son. Later, he wrote to her, telling her how thrilling the trip to the trenches had been. But also how he had come out unharmed. Almost a month later he received a letter from her about the service pin. It sent shivers through him.

Company commander Capt. Harry Hayward let the child of one of his best friends know what it was like on the front. "Just now I am writing from a . . . headquarters dugout up in the front line. I wish I might send you a picture of it—underneath a demolished brick house, it looks like anything but a headquarters from the outside. But inside it is not too bad—lined with heavy corrugated iron, with a table, three chairs, a telephone, and a box spring bed salvaged from the house. The more the shells knock the house down above us, the better protection we get from the shells, because the brick and mortar falling on top make the top thicker. It is upside down here—everything that man has built is in ruins. We work all night and we rest by day. Nights are one continuous show of brilliant fireworks with death lurking everywhere."

To the child's father, he wrote, "The line which we occupied was hardly a trench, but more an outpost line, resulting from the constantly changing front nowadays. Therefore all communication had to be by night and by day there was no movement and no communication to the rear, everything had to go over the top. You can take it from me that it is some strain to be in command of a company on a line like that with an active enemy in front—a couple of hundred yards away."[32]

Shelling of E Company's position was endless. Yet for a few days, no shell landed among the boys. Pvt. Chick Leghorn of Newburgh was dumbfounded at their luck. "Everybody can't be where they ain't hitting," he said.[33]

Oddly, the first casualty was Pvt. Raymond "Sunny" Jones, who on 14 August accidentally shot himself in the foot. On the same day that "Sunny" shot himself, Cpl. Frank Shade and Pvt. Bill Roberts where sitting next to a British soldier, their backs pressed against the trench wall, the Tommy between them. Without warning, a shell tore through the ground. Although it failed to go off, its sudden force sent equipment flying everywhere. It ripped Shade's rifle out of his hands so that the weapon struck him in the face. The point of the shell tore right through the chest of the British soldier, killing him instantly. Roberts was so unnerved that he had to be sent back behind the lines.[34]

Also, on the 14th, 1st Lt. William Penoyar suffered mustard gas poisoning. As he staggered away, a shell landed four feet from him. He saw the
flash and, as he explained to a friend in Newburgh, "the next thing I
found myself some distance away from where I had been standing. The
side of my face felt as if a million bees had stung me and my left leg came
in for a share." Penoyar reeled back toward a dressing station. In the dark
he stumbled into a tangle of barbed wire. The sharp prongs tore up his
legs. Then another shell exploded nearby. This time shrapnel burned into
his chest and left shoulder. Because of the concussion, he lost the hearing
in his left ear. The lieutenant had to be evacuated to a British hospital. Although he wanted to "get back again with the boys," for Penoyar the war
was over.[35]

The bloodiest day in the trenches for E Company came on the 16th.
Sgt. Anthony Farina's squad was assigned to hold an outpost in no-man's-
land. Farina was the sergeant who against O'Ryan's direct order had allowed his boys to take off their woolen shirts while digging ditches in the
unbearable August heat. Farina, twenty-three, had been company clerk
before his promotion to sergeant, but begged to be put in the line. His
brother Nicholas was a corporal in the same company. Late at night a
shell came shrieking toward the New Yorkers. This time it hit them where
they were. Pfc. George Crawford, twenty-four, of Newburgh, and Pvt.
Stephen McCaul were killed. Pvt. Joseph Pilus and two other privates
were wounded. Shell fragments cut into Sgt. Farina's head and chest. He
was knocked to the ground, bleeding profusely. Pfc. William White of
Cornwall-on-Hudson, unhurt in the explosion, lifted Farina into his
arms. White stood only five-feet-five. Around him he heard the vicious
"pop-pop" of the German machine gunners and the continued threatening whine and whump of bursting shells. The trenches seemed far away.
Yet White carried Farina back to the safety of the line. He then went back
and brought in the rest of the wounded.[36]

For this heroic action in front of Mont Kemmel, White earned a divisional citation for heroism from O'Ryan.

Van Buren was one of the lucky boys. He found a place to sleep underground, safe from heavy bombardment. He shared his cavelike shelter
with several other doughboys. Thick timbers held the muddy walls and
ceiling in place. While keeping his head out of sight during daylight, Van
Buren used a shard of glass and, in the flickering candlelight, went to

work half-drawing, half-carving one of the timbers into the comely shape of a woman. Back in New York's world of magazine illustration, he had picked up a reputation for drawing beautiful girls. In a letter to his mother he had once told her, "I want to do all I can to keep these fellows over here cheerful." He had started off making life cheerful at Camp Wadsworth with his gag pictures in both *The Gas Attack* and *Gazette*. But there were no magazines in the trenches. His only artistic outlet now was this piece of timber. So he worked long and hard on the woman. And when he had finished, the fellows from E Company, as he called them, found cheer among the carnage.

It didn't take long for word of Van Buren's woman to reach O'Ryan's hut back at divisional headquarters. It was night, and John Singer Sargent sat with O'Ryan and his staff, working on a portrait of the general. In an article for the *New York Times*, Tupper observed, "His long, unusual hand was steady as it guided a crayon over white drawing paper."[37]

While he sketched O'Ryan's portrait, Sargent decided he wanted to see this woman of the war. He later admitted that he was finding it impossible to capture American and British troops in "unison." In a letter he moaned that fact, stating that "the farther forward one goes the more scattered and meagre everything is. The nearer to danger the fewer and more hidden the men—the more dramatic the situation the more it becomes an empty landscape." Still, there might be something worthwhile down in the trenches. Thus, he ignored O'Ryan's admonition not to venture beyond divisional headquarters. He talked two officers into accompanying him forward; surprisingly they were Lt. Col. J. Leslie Kincaid, the division judge advocate who should have known better, and Capt. James Wadsworth, the billeting officer. Tupper decided to tag along. To him, it was "an evil night to look for a dugout where a young soldier artist by the name of Van Buren had drawn on the wall . . . a remarkable picture of a woman."

The trek to Dickebusch Lake lasted two hours. "Many things moved along this road like shadows to the accompaniment of the big-throated guns, to the flash of their fiery tongues and the whistle of the shells as they spat toward the enemy," Tupper wrote. The ground they covered smelt of toxic gasses. With the group was a messenger dog. When a shell hit close by, the dog tore from its leash and bolted away.

Near where Van Buren had carved his woman, there was a stinking marsh, and the stench from its poisonous pools of water filled their nostrils. Tupper thought "it a strange place for a young artist to have dreamed of a woman and stranger still that he should have transcribed his dream from his mind to the rough wall." The four men descended twenty steps below the ground where they entered a short gallery and then into Van Buren's dugout home, dark and deserted. "The senses," Tupper noted, "are distinctly affected by three things, first, the decreasing sound of artillery fire, the next, the seeming thickness of the darkness and, finally, the strange odors of the earth."

Sargent was appalled. "There's nothing here! There's nothing here!" he said. "No artist ever worked in a place beneath the ground like this!"

A candle was flamed to life and in the glimmer of its light Sargent and the three officers looked at the sensuous work of art. "On the wall," Tupper wrote, "a woman had been drawn with seeming carelessness—a creation of the war." It was suggested that they cut out the timber and bring the carving of the woman back to divisional headquarters for safe keeping.

"This is the only frame that suits it," Sargent said. "It should be left here."

And it was, said Tupper, "the woman of the war."

Meanwhile, Van Buren's mind had already switched to another woman, a real flesh and blood girl and also to a different art form. This time his thoughts were not on Neysa McMein, the darling of the New York set, but on his gal in Kansas City, dark-haired Fern Ringo. And so he penned a poem to his sweetheart.

Does the water still flow in the Hudson
Are there any more chocolate creams?
Are oranges and peaches within people's reaches?
Was the Past just as good as it seems?

Do people still dine around tables?
And order food that they please?
Or when they want taters and juicy tomaters
Do they have to eat crackers and cheese?

Are the taxis and street cars still running?
Do fashions change twice every year?
Are dances and dinners still blue ribbon winners
On nights that are balmy and clear?

And, by the way, now that I'm asking
Please, tell me, are you really real—
A live human being I once was a'seeing
Or dream girl my waking hours steal?

CHAPTER 8

He Was Their Gunga Din

S hortly before the Greyjackets made their first trip to the frontline
trenches, Capt. Fancher Nicoll, the rather melancholy commander
of L Company, and his old first sergeant, the upbeat Claude Leland, now a second lieutenant in I Company, took a rare, long walk. They
had not seen each other since landing in France. The evening was quiet
as they strolled down the street of a small village. They passed restau-
rants, small shops, and churches. The sweet smell of apple blossoms was
now gone and the heat of summer had been turned up a notch. To the
east they could hear the constant rumble of distant gunfire. In this surreal
tranquillity, the friends reminisced about the old Seventh Regiment,
their days at the armory, and their adventurous times in Texas and
South Carolina.

Nicoll came from two well-known Walden, New York, families: not
surprisingly, the Fanchers and Nicolls. He traced his military lineage
back to the Colonial Wars; in fact, he was a member of the Society of Colonial Wars because one of his descendents had been a Capt. William
Lawrence from Flushing. History meant a lot to Nicoll, compelling him
to serve on the executive committee of the New-York Historical Society.

Capt. Fancher Nicoll with his children during more peaceful times.   Jeffrey Nicoll

His father, James Craig Nicoll, was a well-known painter who specialized in watercolors. Although Fancher probably inherited his father's sensitive, artistic eye, he had instead become an attorney, and was a partner in the New York law firm of Harris and Towne, the same law firm that also employed 1st Lt. Richard McIntyre of regimental headquarters. Both he and McIntyre had gone to Williams College. Nicoll had enlisted in the Seventh in 1900 and was promoted to his captaincy in 1913, a few months before Leland joined the regiment. He was nearing forty years of age.[1]

Eventually, their conversation turned to other things. "Fancher and I were not given to talking much about serious matters," Leland later wrote, "but somehow we did that evening and in a way I have never forgotten. We spoke of our family affairs and of how harder it was for those we had left behind than it was for us with new scenes and experiences ahead every day." At the time, the two men were the fathers of two children, although Nicoll had lost an infant son in 1915, who was buried in Brooklyn's Green-wood Cemetery.

As they talked, they passed a church. "You know," Nicoll said to his friend, "I feel as much at home in one of these old churches over here as in my own back in New York. I think nothing of going into one of them for a few minutes of prayer, something I seldom did in the U.S."

The two soldiers walked until it "grew so dark we could barely see the road and then turned back toward the village," Leland wrote. Recalling that brief moment, he wondered about the captain's spells of dejection, as he put it. "While he never said as much to me, I think [Fancher] was pretty sure that he would not live through the war. But for that matter, few of us in the infantry had many hopes to build on." What Leland probably did not know at that time, however, perhaps because his friend had not told him, was that Nicoll's father had died only a few weeks earlier, at age seventy-one.

And if Nicoll did in fact have a premonition about his death, he certainly did not share it with his older sister, Emily, the matriarch of the family. In a letter to her, about the time he and Leland had their evening walk, he assured her, "I am a bit surprised to find that am not scared to death by either shells or air raids and have every expectation of coming through O.K."[2]

To date, most of the casualties suffered by the 107th Infantry had been from grenades and artillery fire, or from the bullet of a hidden sniper. It had been deadly, but impersonal. Now all that was about to change. On 12 August, when the Third Battalion, comprising I, K, L, and M Companies, took its turn in the trenches, the Germans had decided to test the Americans with a small-unit attack. And they had singled out Captain Nicoll's L Company.

Sgt. Harry Mitchell, the L Company journalist, recalled how, "With the regimental band playing one stirring martial air after another, we marched off with the rest of the battalion that afternoon in the direction whence sounded the booming chorus of the guns." He added that the "trip ended at midnight with our being separated into small groups and led through the ghastly remains of Ridge Wood and into the front line of the Dickebusch salient." When the battalion got close enough to the front line, it halted to await the guides that would lead them in. Nearby, British soldiers were unloading limbers. "There was an air of suppression about the place," Mitchell noted. "And as we were thinking of all that it meant, we were startled by the blast of a whistle. Instantly every man within sight stopped dead in his tracks, and a voice rang out just loud enough for all to hear:

"'Jerry's up! Stand fast!'"

An enemy plane droned above them, searching for activity below upon which the pilot would then call in the artillery. The plane flew on. Nicoll and two of his lieutenants then showed up with "mum, grim-faced" guides, and L Company headed into Ridge Wood, a forest of stumps, twisted, leafless trees that had simply withered away in the years of battle. All kinds of splintered, rotting, and rusting debris were scattered every which way—a wretched earthen dumping ground. Ridge Wood separated L Company from I Company. The men had to skirt Dicke-busch Lake before reaching Ridge Wood. To Mitchell the lake was a "murky sheet of water [that] seemed silent as death itself. Not even a bull-frog croaked from its depths."

I Company, without a captain to command it because Raphael Egan had recently been put in charge of the battalion, moved into Ridge Wood, too, dropping into position to the left of L Company. Taking over the helm of the company was 1st Lt. Percy M. Hall of Montclair, New Jersey, and an old Seventh hand since 1908. Leland, in charge of the second pla-toon, felt him the most popular officer in the regiment. "Other officers," he said, "let the vicissitudes and hardships of campaigning get on their nerves—not Percy Hall. He was always seeing the funny side of every-thing, always had a smile and a jibe for the most untoward event or the most difficult situation. To have him around was tonic to the whole outfit; and for the purposes of morale Perce was worth two hundred ordinary men."

Both companies were attached to battalions of Sherwood Foresters, mostly miners from Nottingham and Derby. Cpl. Hal Mills of K Com-pany found the Tommies with whom he shared a "dirty, stinking hole" as "mostly very young or very old, 2 Marne veterans."[3] For two days and nights the doughboys would serve with these battle-scarred Brits, whose ranks were noticeably thinned by the bloody spring offensive that had al-most driven England from the war. On the third day, the companies would be on their own. From Mont Kemmel, German observers of Prince Rupprecht's army had watched the New Yorkers from L Company enter the trenches under cover of darkness. Immediately, a Boche raiding party, armed with bombs, slithered across no-man's-land—not waiting for these newcomers to get settled. The Germans reached a section of trench where Cpl. Julius DeWitt Williams and privates Frank J. Fitzsimmons and Johnson Titus Watkins of White Plains, known as "Young Watty" so as not to be confused with Sgt. Charles "Watty" Watkins, had just taken up their positions. While the threesome got acquainted with their English counterparts from Robin Hood's hometown, the Huns jumped to their feet and lobbed five "potato-masher" grenades into the trench. When the grenades exploded, everyone miraculously escaped unhurt. Williams's squad opened up, firing round after round into the night. The grenade attack stopped. In the dark of no-man's-land they heard three shrill blasts from a whistle—the German signal for stretcher bearers. They knew that at least one Hun had been hit.

That night Pfc. Charles B. Terrell and several other L Company boys had been assigned to carry messages back and forth from the trenches to battalion headquarters. Every time they sprinted out of the trenches, German snipers tried to pick them off. Finally, Terrell begged a machine-gun corporal to give them cover. As he wrote to his parents in Newburgh, "We had to go over the top some distance before we could get into the trench again. It was a full moon and very bright." On their way to headquarters, they were about to jump into a trench just as a German machine gunner opened up on them. The German then ran up to the trench, raking it with machine-gun fire. He ran along the edge of the trench blasting away. Yet Terrell and his comrades got away safely. "In a few minutes I started again, for the first platoon. The snipers again tried to get me but they did not succeed. Soon I heard a whistling through the air and saw a rifle grenade coming for me. I rolled into a trench and lay with my face to the ground. The grenade exploded about six inches from me, and in front. My helmet saved me that time, but I was covered with dirt." Terrell finally made it back to headquarters. But he was still not safe. A whizbang struck five feet away, fragments struck him in the knees and arm. "It wasn't bad," he added, trying to calm his folks. "But I had to have the needle in my chest to prevent blood poisoning. I still am alive and happy."[4]

As morning broke, another raiding party hit the New Yorkers. Cpl. Herb Winslow of Hastings-on-Hudson, who had joined the old Seventh on 13 April 1917, had his Lewis machine-gun squad ready for any Hun marauders. Among the boys under his command were privates Billy "Kit" Carson from Newburgh, Jack Flynn from Beacon, Billy McGraw from Albany, Charlie H. Schneider Jr. from Rutherford, New Jersey, and Otto P. Schultz from Milwaukee, a new replacement who had joined the company a week earlier. Even though they stared straight into no-man's-land, they missed a squad of eight Boche bombers moving silently along a communications trench. The Germans closed quickly, tossing grenades at Winslow's surprised men. This time their was aim was deadly. Winslow, admired for his "quiet, sincere and thoroughly determined personality," said Mitchell, died instantly when the grenades hit. Fragments struck Schneider in the body and face, putting him out of action. Carson was also wounded and put out of action. Flynn and McGraw scrambled for the machine gun, wheeled it around, and mowed down three of the enemy. The other five fled.

Herb Winslow was the first L Company man killed in the war. According to Mitchell, his death "cast a pall of gloom over the boys when they learned about it back in reserve." On the other side of Wood Ridge, Leland, who had commanded the corporal when he was company first sergeant, felt that Winslow's loss was "a blow over the heart to every old Company L man. Quiet, good-natured, dependable, handsome Herb was loved by every one who knew him. A straighter, cleaner, up-standing boy never breathed." Leland recalled how Pvt. Maitland Rice, Winslow's best friend, came out of the line brokenhearted. Later that night, stretcher bearers went past Leland and Sgt. Washington Irving Clayton with Winslow's body. Leland and Clayton climbed up an embankment to let them by. They watched the "mournful procession vanish in the dark with a heavy heart."

Raids continued. Privates Hughie Daley from Newburgh, who had been with the First Infantry since early in 1916, and Owen Wheeler from Stockdale, Texas, like Pvt. Schulz a recent replacement, were both captured on the night of 21 August. It was the last anyone ever saw of them.

Two New Jersey boys, Cpl. Charles "Hobey" Hoblitzel from Jersey City and Pvt. Frank Monks from Orange, were detailed by Nicoll to carry the message of the capture of Daley and Wheeler back to battalion headquarters. The harassing fire and shells that the duo were forced to dodge had them running and crawling and diving behind any shelter they could find. They both made it through safely. "But at the end of the trip," Mitchell wrote, "Monks' nervous system just seemed to snap, and he was sent to hospital."

Because of the capture of two of its men, the Third Battalion was ordered to spend two more days and nights in the trenches. In his little pocket diary, George Fetherolf jotted down in telegram-terse prose, "Two more deaths & 4 wounded—patroled all night. Slept all day. Not relieved because two prisoners taken—48 hours more of this dirt."

While the Germans tested L Company they also had their eyes on I Company. A raiding party of bombers hit the third platoon on 20 August. "This platoon was badly shot up by trench bombs," Sgt. Floyd Neely reported.[5] One bomb landed in a fire bay and killed Cpl. Paul McLeod and Pvt. George Leary and wounded six others.

These skirmishes proved minor. The Germans had a bigger party planned for the early morning of 22 August. Their main target was L Company.

Cpl. Randall Henderson from White Plains had charge of an eight-man squad in an exposed outpost position at Ridge Wood. At five o'clock, the Germans opened with an artillery bombardment. Next they laid down a severe trench mortar and machine-gun barrage. The moment the barrage stopped, a raiding party of forty Huns stormed across no-man's-land just to the left of Ridge Wood, "grunting and yelling like mad men." Vastly out-manned and out-gunned, Henderson's squad tried to repulse the attack. In a twinkling, six of his boys were cut down. That left only Henderson and Pvt. George Delahay from Beacon to defend the outpost.

As Sgt. Mitchell recalled after the fight, "These two found themselves overwhelmed in numbers, but they stuck it out there, heaving Mills hand grenades as fast as they could swing their arms." In the desperate fray, Delahay went down with a wound. Henderson fought on alone.

In the midst of the assault on this lone outpost, the Germans launched another, yet bigger attack on the main trenches held by I and L companies. Word was rushed back, "Enemy assembling in large numbers!" Was this at last the expected major assault by the Germans to push the Allies back to the Channel ports?

I Company hit the charging Germans with everything it had. Sgt. Neely remembered how Sgt. Clayton "treated the raiders to a hot rifle and Lewis gun fire which discouraged them." At the exact time Clayton's squad held off the attack against I Company, on Neely's right flank the Germans hemmed in L Company with a box barrage. "One platoon in L Company was literally blasted out of its trench and through a mistake in command fell back a little."[6]

Lt. Hall ordered Neely and another sergeant, Frederick H. Brown, Jr., and their first platoon to support the reeling men from L Company. The swift support of I Company rallied the battered doughboys. Still alone in no-man's-land, Henderson and the wounded Delahay continued to hold off the attackers on their position. Mitchell believed that Henderson's resistance "broke the nerve of the surviving attackers. They turned and scurried like scared rabbits for their own line, with our chaps banging away at them with such telling effect that barely a third of the number that started got back untouched." Leland agreed. "Henderson stuck to his piece of trench and bombed the party of Boche who were rushing to it so effectively that they turned tail and ran the other way." Mitchell added, however, that while the groans of the German wounded filled no-man's-land, the groans and wounded "filled our own trench as well presented a sad spectacle."

In the meantime, at company headquarters, Nicoll and 1st Sgt. Theodore W. Todd, a relative of Teddy Roosevelt, grabbed their rifles and rushed forward to fight alongside their boys in the line. Todd was every bit a silk stocking soldier. His grandfather had joined the old Seventh Regiment in 1841 and had fought in the Civil War. His father had been an old Seventh veteran, too. Teddy had enlisted in 1910. The family owned the Todd Salt Company, at the time one of the oldest businesses in New York City.

"While the fight waged hot Capt. Nicoll displayed the greatest coolness, walking along the trench among the men and reorganizing gaps in the defense as fast as they occurred," Mitchell wrote. "And it was while accompanying him and lending every aid that 1st Sgt. Todd was killed."

Sgt. Edmund Breusch of H Company in a letter to his wife told her that their old friend Teddy Todd and several of his men had actually gone over the top to meet the charging Boche troops head on. "They were able to inflict some serious casualties on the Germans, but were outnumbered and fell back on the Company behind. Being reinforced they advanced again and drove 'Jerry' back to his own lines." When the Germans faltered and there was a momentary lull, it was discovered that Todd was missing. "One of the boys in the trench volunteered to go over the top and into No Man's Land in broad daylight to see if Teddy was out there."[7] Although the name of that soldier is lost, Nicoll gave him permission to find their first sergeant. After crawling around no-man's-land for awhile, the soldier located Todd's body and then crawled back with the news that he had been killed.

Todd's death shocked Nicoll. To Teddy's father, he wrote, "He was not more than ten yards from me at the time [he lost his life] and I can testify that he died as he had lived, cleanly and bravely, with his face toward the task that was his." Todd was twenty-nine.

"Not many minutes passed before rumors came back to the effect that L Company had been wiped out," Leland jotted in his memoirs. "On the heels of this, stragglers drifted back . . . some wounded, some dazed and unable to account for themselves. They said that . . . Todd had been killed outright and that the company had been blasted out of one trench and badly cut up."

With the Americans now in the brawl of their lives, British artillery thundered shells down on the German positions.

As the bullets, bombs, and grenades flew like gritty sand in a raging desert storm, Don Emery of the Sanitary Detachment tended to the wounded and dying of two platoons. "To get from one to the other meant a precarious trip in the open across ground subject to severe and sweeping machine-gun fire," Mitchell reported. Emery was unarmed and weighted down with his medical supplies and dressings as he jumped from one fallen doughboy to the next. "'Twas on the fateful morning that we suffered most of our casualties, and Emery literally seemed to be everywhere at once. He'd kneel over each patient and apply the bandages with all the outward calm of a commuter reading a newspaper, and then with a word of cheer for the wounded man, dash off to where the next one lay."

Because the fight took place during the day, the wounded had to stay in shell holes, in the blazing heat and without water. "The sun seemed to burn into the trench with a vengeance and there was nothing more cruel than heat to a man with a torn and lacerated body," was the way Mitchell described it. "They went through more or less torture during that interminable day, yes—but Emery helped them a lot. He was their Gunga Din. He brought water and cigarettes to them, and did everything possible to ease their pain."

Pfc. Angelo Mustico was their Gunga Din, too. The Newburgh soldier continually sprinted back behind the lines under constant enemy fire to a wrecked house where a well had been discovered. Here he filled canteens with precious water and, evading enemy fire, carried them back to his parched comrades. Pfc. Wilbur Cathcart also spent the morning dodging bullets as he raced back and forth from the trenches to battalion headquarters and from platoon to platoon to deliver running accounts of the fight.

Pfc. Angelo Mustico's heroics in Belgium earned him a divisional commendation.   Frances Smith

I Company, and especially K and M Companies, which had been in support, escaped the fight with slight casualties. One of I Company's wounded was Pvt. Frederick O. Brown, from Flushing, a boyhood friend of Billy Leonard. A hunk of shrapnel crashed into Brown, but miraculously struck a pocket mirror. Instead of plowing into his chest, it was deflected, ripping a hole in his right arm and breaking it.[8] But in L Company, sixteen men were hit, three killed. For their heroism on that day, Cpl. Randall Henderson and "Doc" Emery earned the American Distinguished Service Cross. "Ran" was the first soldier in the division to receive the D.S.C. He and Emery also got the British Military Medal and the French Croix de Guerre. Henderson was then reassigned to division headquarters. Emery was sent to officer's candidate school and later assigned to the Thirtieth Division as a second lieutenant. For the wounded Delahay, there were no medals. Instead, O'Ryan handed him a divisional citation for bravery. Another divisional citation for bravery that day went to Private Mustico.

In a letter home, Mustico was nonchalant about his role in the fight. "We had plenty to eat but very little water," he said, leaving out his bit in the action. "We managed, however, to get water at an old knocked down house just back of the trenches." He admitted that he had "quite a narrow escape from death while 'up there,' but a 'miss is as good as a mile,' so don't worry as I will take the best care of myself."

For Bert Lobdell, the attack had taken place considerably to the right of his squad. During the whole morning, he had not seen a single Hun. But he had heard the fight, and knew Henderson's squad was in trouble. "My blood was boiling and my knees shaking and later in the morning after things had quieted down I noticed that both my wrapped puttees were down around my ankles. I've been trying to figure out every since whether it was my boiling blood or my shaking knees that caused them to come loose. I have my suspicions!"

Division Sergeant Major Albert Breunig entered in his diary on the 23d, "Dickebusch Lake sector—much fighting. Many of our men killed & wounded. Much shelling near division headquarters."[9]

To his parents, Leland said, "My luck is still good and I have a four-leaf clover in my pocket—so have no fear." He later added that while he was in the trenches he read one of his mother's letters by the light of a "candle well shaded from the Boches. It was such a strange sensation to hear from home in that place, and such a comfort,—and it surely brought me good luck for your sonny got out without a scratch,—out of a very warm place indeed. I felt that my mother was very near me through it all,—and will be through all the other trials ahead."

John L. MacDonnell of M Company chronicled the marksmanship of Cpl. Ray Collins. He claimed that Collins "copped off" thirty-two German snipers. He stated that "Ray is an expert and when he pulls the trigger 'good night Hun!' " MacDonnell reported how Cpl. Eddie Murphy, on the night of the big attack, boasted of stopping a squad of Germans that had turned tail seconds after leaping out of their trenches because of the deadly fire from his machine gun. Pfc. Bill Corey quipped that the Huns had jumped right back into their trenches because "mess call sounded." The right "wing" of Pfc. Ralph Kretschmar, MacDonnell stated, was "sore from hurling bombs and he rubs it with his left hand to alleviate the pain. Still one never can tell—it may be the 'cooties' he's chasing."

On the night of the 23d, the Third Battalion was relieved and gratefully slipped out of the trenches. Moving along in single file, the four companies retraced the steps that more than ten days earlier had brought them into the Dickebusch sector. After every ten paces, the soldiers stopped to await the brightness of a Very light to pass. "Should one man in the column move," MacDonnell wrote, "it would be a signal for the enemy's machine guns to turn loose." Once out of the maze of trenches and into the relative safety behind the lines, the companies halted. The tired boys slumped by the roadside, their packs were unslung, their steel helmets dropped at their feet. Soon, the red embers of lit cigarettes glowed in the dark.

"While we sit and talk and laugh," MacDonnell recalled, "three shrill blasts of a whistle sound. 'All lights out' passed from one Platoon to another. We listen and can hear the motor of the enemy's aeroplane over us. Should he see us, we all know what it means. His machine is equipped with a wireless and that wireless talks to his artillery, and his artillery answers within thirty seconds after the receipt of the message. We put on our packs and continue to move along in the dark."

In I Company, Fetherolf found the whole experience "surprisingly exciting," especially the "moment during Jerries' barrage when you are straining your eyes to see him coming and it seems to be an eternity before you can see anything of him. Then last but not least comes that hour of darkness when the new relief comes creeping in your trench and you creep out bound for the rear and out where the air's pure and you sleep at night and stand up straight when you walk."

Mitchell recorded that for L Company the day of its relief "passed like an eternity, but eventually night and the hour of our relief did come, and wearily but happily we started the tramp toward more restful places." Tramping back to their rest zone, the men heard the frightening roar of an incoming shell. It struck I Company. Fortunately, there were no reported casualties. L Company resumed its march, hiking through the pitch black, empty remains of the village of Ouderdom. Overhead, a German plane spotted them. "The pilot . . . began to signal to an enemy battery, for we could hear him circling over us like a bird of prey."

Anxiously, the soldiers looked up and waited. One of them was Pvt. Bronson Hawley of Bridgeport, Connecticut, who had enlisted in the Seventh on 9 July 1917. He came from one of the oldest Connecticut families. He had attended St. Paul's School and Yale University. He loved the outdoors and would hike from Bridgeport to Kent Hollow, a distance of over thirty miles, where his mother owned a farm. Here he kept "Meander," his horse, and "Billy," his dog. Here, in the woods, he collected birds' eggs, which he later gave to Yale's Peabody Museum. Bad eyesight kept him from being an officer, and so he joined the Seventh. Now a private, he and the other boys from L Company listened for the roar of a German artillery shell to come hurtling their way. They did not wait long. It came whistling in, striking Hawley's platoon. Men were bowled over like duck pins. Hot shrapnel cut through Hawley's steel helmet. He flew off his feet and was dead before he hit the ground. He was buried in Abeele, alongside all the others from the 107th Infantry who had been killed in the East Poperinghe Line and the Dickebusch sector. For several years afterward, his old horse and his old dog still waited for him to come home. In 1920 Hawley's two brothers went to Flanders, dug up his body and shipped it home. He was reburied in Kent Hollow. And when "Meander" and "Billy" also died, they were laid to rest near their master.[10]

CHAPTER 9

That Country Was Full of Gas and Dead Englishmen

The day after the Third Battalion left the trenches, Gen. John Pershing traveled to Bombon, thirty miles southwest of Paris, to meet with the Allied commander-in-chief Marshal Ferdinand Foch. He strode into the headquarters of the seventy-seven-year-old generalissimo, excited to be there to discuss the coming campaign in the St. Mihiel sector in which his army, the American First Army, would at last make its long-awaited entrance into the war. He was, nonetheless, as stubborn as ever about the deployment of any of his troops with the British or French armies, having spent the better half of the month fending off fervent British requests for American divisions.

On this point, Foch sympathized with him. But the man who looked more like a professor than a soldier did not agree with Pershing, for he knew how desperately Great Britain needed men. In the very halls of British power, ruling politicians and the military's top brass battled over the use of the soldiers still left to carry on the fight against Germany. Sir Douglas Haig's job as Britain's commander in chief was in jeopardy. Prime Minister Lloyd George was reluctant to send him any more men for fear they would be slaughtered, as in the past.

And for Haig, if he couldn't have more of his own men, then he wanted the Americans.

For a year, Pershing had fought long and hard to keep his American troops intact. He had stood fast against the desperate pleadings of Haig. As recently as 12 August, Haig had begged him to keep just five American divisions that were training with his armies. He wanted to know if he could count on using them for an attack that the British were then planning for the end of September against the Hindenburg Line. But Pershing had already decided to withdraw those divisions.

In his private papers, Haig noted, "I pointed out to [Pershing] that I had done everything to equip and help those units of the American Army, and to provide them with horses. So far, I have had no help from these troops (except the three Battalions which were used in the battle near Chapilly in error). If he now withdraws the five American Divisions, he must expect some criticism of his action not only from the British troops in the field [but] also from the British Government."

When Pershing turned him down, Haig lamented that all he had wanted to know was "definitely" whether he could count on the American troops for the September attack. "Now," he wrote in his diary, "I know I cannot do so."[1]

Even before facing down Haig one more time, Pershing met with George V. The English king was familiar with the Twenty-seventh Division. He had reviewed Maj. Gen. John O'Ryan's troops on 6 August. According to Pershing, the king explained that although he was "not a politician and did not see things from their point of view, [he] thought it would be advantageous to have some Americans serving [with] his armies."The American general countered that his country was "forming an army of our own and would require practically all of our troops as soon asthey can be brought together." Undeterred, the king asked for at least "some divisions," knowing that the New Yorkers were still in the British Zone, as was the Thirtieth Division. Pershing said he could not make any promises. But as soon as he left the king, he ordered that all divisions training with the British must be removed, and that the request for their relief should be sent to Foch, who would then pass along the order to Haig.

But pressure continued to build for Pershing to give in—even if it was only for one or two or three divisions. In Pershing's visit to Georges Clemenceau on the 13th, the French premier, known as the "Tiger," thrust into Pershing's hand a telegram from the British prime minister. In part, Lloyd George had asked Clemenceau to intervene so Haig could have just a "few" American divisions held in reserve. He said that he did not consider his demand "excessive for it must not be forgotten that the greater part of the American troops were brought to France by British shipping and because of the sacrifices made to furnish this shipping our people have the right to expect that more than five divisions of the twenty-eight now in France should be put in training behind our lines."[2]

For once, Pershing softened his stand. But it was hardly noticeable. On the 15th, he notified Haig, "approving [his] request that 27th and 30th Divisions remain with the British temporarily to function under our II Corps."[3]

Now ten days later, meeting face-to-face with Foch at Bombon to go over the battle in which the American First Army would enter the field at St. Mihiel, Pershing was taken aback at the way the pipe-smoking generalissimo steered their conversation around to the divisions still in the British Zone. Pershing recounted their exchange. "He [Foch] considered it important, he said, to have them ready to assist if necessary the British operations then in progress. I replied that not only were these troops needed with our own army but they were eager to serve under their own flag. Moreover, it had been clearly understood that they should join the American Army when it was formed."[4] Foch agreed. As he later recalled, he told the general, "No one desired more fervently than myself the constitution of American corps and armies and sectors in which American troops would fight an American battle, and that my best efforts were being directed at this end. I was, indeed, firmly convinced that the soldiers of any country only give their best when fighting under their own leaders and under their own colours. National self-esteem is then engaged."[5]

However, Foch, whose blue-gray eyes had a way of showing there was a lot of fight still left in the old soldier, felt it was important to the Allied cause that the two divisions were to be "counted on" to fight with the British.

At last Pershing gave way. "I felt that if our divisions should once become engaged in battle as part of another army it would be unlikely that they could be withdrawn, yet under the circumstances, I accepted the military emergency as the real reason for the request and assented, with the understanding that these divisions should not remain with the British indefinitely."[6]

In his memoirs, Foch wrote, "We . . . came to an agreement regarding the employment of certain American divisions in the Allied armies. Two divisions (27th and 30th) were to remain under the orders of Sir Douglas Haig and to take part in the operations in the British zone."[7]

That very next day, not knowing of Pershing's decision, Haig bitterly noted in his diary, "The last American Division started to entrain to-day. What will History say regarding this action of the Americans leaving the British zone of operations when *the decisive battle* of the war is at its height, and the decision is still in doubt!"[8]

Yet the Twenty-seventh and Thirtieth Divisions did not leave the British Zone, as Haig thought. However, when the field marshal realized he had won his case against Pershing, he was too ensnarled in a political brouhaha with his prime minister to savor the temporary gift of those two divisions for his attack on the Hindenburg Line. Lloyd George and his cabinet had for more than a year lost confidence in Haig, appalled at the catastrophic loss of life on the western front. Almost three-quarters of a million British soldiers would eventually fall in battle. The prime minister, as one noted British historian put it, schemed to "give Haig enough rope to hang himself."[9] In other words, if another horrific bloodletting of British men took place, then Haig would be gone. On 29 August, Haig commented, "The Cabinet are ready to meddle and interfere in my plans in an underhand-way, but do not dare openly to say that they mean to take responsibility for any failure though ready to take credit for every success!" He felt that Lloyd George would try to cover himself if the next offensive ground to a halt. "If my attack [on the Hindenburg Line] is successful, I will remain on as C. in C. If we fail, or our losses are excessive, I can hope for no mercy! . . . What a wretched lot of weaklings we have in high places at the present time!"

He then received a letter on 1 September from Gen. Sir Henry Wilson, the British military representative to the Supreme War Council, in which he, Wilson, stated, according to Haig, that the "Cabinet were anxious I should not sacrifice many men in attacking the Hindenburg Line." In part, Wilson's letter warned, "Police strike and other cognate matters make Cabinet sensitive to heavy losses, especially if they are incurred against old lines of fortification." In his diary, Haig blasted everyone while justifying himself. "How ignorant our present Statesmen are of the principles of war. In my opinion, it is much less costly in lives to keep on pressing the enemy after several victorious battles than to give him time to recover and organise a fresh line of defence. The latter must then be attacked in the face of hostile artillery and machine guns, all carefully sited."[10]

Yet this time the field marshal, well on the way to earning his reputation as a "butcher," did not have to throw all of his own soldiers against the Germans. In Gen. Sir Henry Rawlinson's British Fourth Army, he had five Australian divisions, four Canadian divisions, and one division of New Zealanders at his disposal. And now, thanks to Pershing, he could add to that army two American divisions, each twice the size of a British division—more than fifty thousand unseasoned doughboys to attack the center of the dreaded, heavily fortified Hindenburg Line!

The first of the "several victorious battles" that Haig had referred to in his diary had started in Amiens on 8 August, the time that O'Ryan's division, seventy miles to the north, was in the midst of learning the hardships of trench warfare.

At Amiens, Rawlinson's men, particularly the Australian Corps led by Lt. Gen. Sir John Monash, drove the Boche from the city to an outer defensive line. German casualties reached over twenty-six thousand. Some eighteen thousand men were taken prisoner. Erich Ludendorff, who with Hindenburg was guiding German war policy, called the defeat at Amiens "a black day for the German Army in the history of this war."[11] It dawned on him that victory in the field was now impossible. The best Ludendorff could hope for was to retreat to the Hindenburg Line, where he believed he could hold off the Allied forces, at least through another bitter winter, and there negotiate favorable terms for the end the war. After all, his armies still held most of Belgium and a huge portion of northeastern France, and were a menacing fifty miles outside of Paris.

For England, the victory at Amiens heralded the beginning of what was later termed the "Hundred Days' Campaign," and would prove to be the most successful series of battles in British military history. But that's getting ahead of the story.

* * *

Up in Flanders, where the fate of the Twenty-seventh Division to fight with the British Fourth Army was yet unknown, the bloodied boys of the 107th Infantry had on 24 August been removed to the safety of rest areas behind the lines to lick their wounds. Of the 580 battle casualties suffered by the Twenty-seventh since landing in France, including 118 killed, 180 were inflicted on the silk stocking soldiers through the end of August. Of that number, beginning on 14 July with Billy Leonard, the newspaper editor from Flushing, and ending with Bronson Hawley, the nature lover from Bridgeport, Connecticut, thirty-two had been killed or had died of wounds.

On the 25th, the regiment's three battalions rested safely out of range of German artillery. Scott Lytle reported home, "We came out of the trenches two days ago & the boys are taking a rest. I guess we lost a dozen men and quite a pile of wounded. A boy in our squad was nearly buried alive, his helmet was knocked from his head & his rifle completely smashed. He was unhurt. I tell you the men were all tired out & our company considers themselves lucky in getting off without any serious losses. I can't describe the awfulness of the war. As most of the men say, it is not war, it is slaughter."

Pfc. Albert Clark wrote in the *Gazette* of the awfulness of war. To his father he said, "You cannot conceive of the suffering, the wreck and ruin for miles and miles. Love seems to have vanished from the face of the earth." He confessed of his own fear during his turn in the trenches. "Those machine guns strike terror to any man's heart, but I shall carry on and try to be cheerful about it. Only I wished I were born with a steadier set of nerves and I would be able to stand the ordeal better, but as it is I let my mental powers bring the best of me into play."

Lobdell never mentioned the recent scrap with the Huns. Instead, the day he came out of the trenches, he cabled that he was well and happy. Then in a letter he said the cable had been foolish to use the words well and happy. "Foolish," he wrote, "not because I'm in such good health but because I know you won't believe I'm happy. How can anybody be so far from Salem?"

Raeburn Van Buren sent off a letter to his mother, telling her that E Company was "located in a beautiful piece of woods and are taking life pretty easy just now." He explained that there had been a lot of rain. "To-day the sun came out and gave us a chance to dry our blankets and clothes. These little pup tents we use are poor shelter from a down pour of rain." In the letter he drew a portrait of himself slogging through thick mud, his smiling face turned toward his "dear" mother. And then he wrote, "How long we will be here is a question I can't answer."

Leland described to his mother the "wonderful weather [we had] during our first tour in—no rain—and moonlight which is fine once you are in. . . . Since coming out to rest up we've had a nice mud puddle to wash in—after going days and days without taking our clothes off. You would think there was water enough in Europe but it's nearly as bad as Texas."

"Water?" laughed Cpl. Alfred Reeves Jr. "Why water was the scarcest thing in all Europe. There were whole days when we'd be given no more than a cup of it, for drinking and washing. Frequently the water like the coffee was full of gasoline."

In his terse style, George Fetherolf scribbled into his diary, "Hiked around for a bath but got none." In a more verbose letter to his aunt, he moaned about the lack of water. "I just stopped to figure out when I washed last in it. About two months ago I heated up a cupful of water to shave with (a luxury) and washed my hands, arms, face and neck in it. I think I remembered my ears on that momentous occasion. All our baths have been taken in cold water since then."

Although they lacked water, they had an abundant supply of lice. To his aunt, Fetherolf said, "When we came out of the line we had a big hunt for cooties. I found fifteen and a million eggs. I guess the record was forty-five but I am just as will satisfied that I do not hold the record."

Van Buren wrote on a Sunday, "The boys have spent the day boiling their clothes to kill off the 'cooties.' We have all had a pretty fair crop this month."

Cpl. Hal Mills, the agricultural researcher who had shaved his head on the Fourth of July, entered in his diary, "Found my first cooties. 3 of 'em."

"Every time we come out of the trenches the company has a big cootie hunt," Kenneth Gow detailed in a letter to a friend in Summit. "A cootie, as you probably know, is what the vulgar call a louse. Every man throws a tuppence, or possibly as much as half a franc (if they have just been paid), into a pot, and the man who finds the biggest one wins. Cooties are at the same time both the funniest and the most unpleasant pest we have to put up with. They are all colors and sizes, and bite like a fiend incarnate. The only consolation one has when they make a sortie on one's person is the knowledge that they are no respecters of rank, file or station in life. They will tackle a field marshall or a lieutenant-general as quick as a buck private." In a note to his family, he said, "The company has come out with the finest assortment of grandfather cooties you could imagine. The men are on the hunt now, with a pot up for the man who can exhibit the biggest." He closed by letting them know, "Everyone from Summit is O.K."

One of the boys with a Summit connection, K Company's Cpl. James Throckmorton Vought, who had taught at the Summit Academy for two years after graduating from Harvard, complained to his brother, "The cooties were bad and bothered me terrifically. We called them seam rabbits and ranked them private to colonel according to the number of stripes they had. I was so badly affected by them that at one time they wanted to send me to the hospital. They poisoned my blood and I had a great number of boils. After I was wounded the boils bothered me more than the wound itself."[12]

John L. McDonnell assured the men holding down the armory on Park Avenue that "Over here it is no disgrace to have the 'cooties.' An itch to a General and a scratch to a soldier is one and the same thing, both being prompted by the same cause. Imagine how one feels to go about without having to scratch—of course after you've worn your fingernails off for the past month or so. So the bath here is the blessing divine. A night's rest without being awakened every half hour to scratch for an unwelcome 'visitor'—the soldier's paradise."

In between wearing their fingernails down to the quick, hunting for enough water for a body scrub, and writing letters home, the soldiers also trained hard. For them there was no letup. O'Ryan was a strict disciplinarian who knew that for his troops to be effective in battle they had to be ready—physically and mentally. Their recent trench experience was just one stage in their endless training sessions.

"Instruction," O'Ryan once told an interviewer, "must be repeated and repeated until the mechanics of the movement and action of the soldiers come automatically."

O'Ryan was such a hard-liner that when his division was still in New York he had his own men arrested if he found them walking the streets in their uniforms with cigarettes dangling from their mouths. Summoned to their regimental court, the soldiers' defense was that they had no idea smoking was illegal in New York City. O'Ryan, who later became police commissioner under Mayor Fiorello LaGuardia, scoffed. "I told the court to ask them if they'd ever seen a New York policeman with a cigarette in his mouth—never mind about on duty—going home from the precinct? They never had. I never had—not when they were in uniform. That was discipline."[13]

On 27 August, Fetherolf confided in his diary, "Drilled today, 4 1/2 hours." The next day he wrote, "O'Ryan around all day." On the 30th he added, "Inspection this morning—got thro' o.k." Then his entry for the 31st reflected big news for the Fifty-third Brigade. "Laid around all day. Report Kimmel is taken—Germans retired 6000 yds."

On that day, a Saturday, O'Ryan had another thing on his mind besides discipline. His division had been ordered to go after Prince Rupprecht's German army, which, it seemed, had apparently deserted Mont Kemmel, and was retiring eastward toward the Hindenburg Line. For the next three days, the Fifty-third Brigade took part in the Battle of Vierstraat Ridge, a low-lying chunk of land that bordered Dickebusch Lake. On the eve of the battle, Ransom Hooker Gillett from New Lebanon Center, New York, arrived from Paris. A lawyer and Yale graduate, Gillett had enlisted as a private in December 1917 but six months later had been promoted to major. O'Ryan assigned him to lead the First Battalion of the 106th. Gillett hiked all night in the darkness to catch up with his new command, then poised to fight at a place called Cross Road. "We fought over that cussed Cross Road for two days and three nights and lost quite a lot of men," Gillett wrote. "That country was full of gas and dead Englishmen, and Frenchmen, and some Americans, and any quantity of Boche. I'll remember that smell to the day of my death."[14]

On 2 September, the British Forty-first Division relieved O'Ryan's troops. The Fifty-third Brigade took "a number of prisoners and had captured considerable booty in the way of machine guns, anti-tank rifles, grenades, ammunition and other supplies," the general reported. He also reported that 40 of his own boys had been killed or later died of wounds, another 276 were wounded, and 33 gassed. The total casualty list for the three days numbered 349.

For the Empire Division, the magnitude of the killing on the western front was beginning to hit home. Now it would only get worse.

CHAPTER 10

You Are Being Fattened Up for the Next Killing, You Know

Once again the Empire Division was on the move.

After clamoring aboard another troop train on 4 September, Raeburn Van Buren summed it up best when he warned his father, "I am now going to lose myself again because we are already started and we understand we're going a long distance by rail." He added, "Our moving will keep us out of the trenches for some time, and I'm glad because they are not very alluring."

In a letter to his sister Emily, Capt. Fancher Nicoll wrote, "This will have to be a short note as it's after dark and I am not supposed to be keeping a light going owing to the possible air raids—Jerry still flocks over at night—and lays a few 'eggs' none of which seem to hit anything worth while, but which are quite annoying if one is a light sleeper. We are about to head out to another sector, but where we know not. I suppose the German withdrawal all along the front makes changes on our part a necessity."

From its bloody stint in the East Poperinghe Line, the Dickebusch Sector and the Vierstraat Ridge in Belgium, the division was headed in a roundabout route to Doullens and nearby villages for still more training.

A new wrinkle would now be thrown in. The doughboys would get to know how to fight alongside tanks, more and more the favorite weapon of the British.

Doullens was a supply depot halfway between Amiens and Arras, about seventy-five miles from the center of the Hindenburg Line near Cambrai. Doullens was a familiar town to Maj. Gen. John O'Ryan's troops, because it was near it that the division had been encamped when in July Gen. Sir Henry Rawlinson had planned his attack against the Germans at Hamel, using Americans for the first time despite Gen. John Pershing's orders forbidding such use. This time, however, the area around Doullens fell under the command of Gen. Sir Julian Byng and his British Third Army.

"Three months before, on our first halt there [Doullens], the inhabitants were few and the troops were many," recollected Capt. Henry Maslin of the 105th Infantry Regiment. "Now we found business resumed, very few troops, and the people moving their furniture back to their homes. It was like coming back from Hades to heaven."[1]

Just before piling into the several trains that were to take it from Belgium to Doullens, the 107th Infantry, according to Jacobson, was "a-tingle with expectation, for most of the men believed that we were now on our way to join the American armies further south. The men were by no means tired of fighting by the side of the British, but a great many of them had a most natural desire to fight side by side with their own countrymen."

Sgt. Harry Mitchell agreed. "Rumor had it that we were going to the American sector, and there was a heap of rejoicing among the men. Not that they didn't like fighting with the British. Not at all. But most of them felt that they would much rather be with the rest of the American army."

The day before pulling out, Cpl. Harold Mills entered in his diary that he had found a four-leaf clover outside his tent.

Although the 107th Infantry headed south, it had actually set out with no intentions of joining up with Pershing's new American First Army. Its fate was still unknown. Rumors aboard the trains had the troops off to Italy. Or maybe it was Russia. And so in a way, Van Buren was right. His regiment seemed lost as it wound its way across the battle-hardened northeast corner of France. Pvt. George Fetherolf jotted in his diary on 4

September, "Left for the south about 4 p.m., but seem to be going north." The trains loaded down with the New Yorkers, in fact, went north where the slow-rolling cavalcade then followed the French coast southeast, passing through Dunkirk, Calais, Boulogne, and Etaples at the mouth of the Canche River. Here it turned eastward, rolling another fifty miles before reaching Doullens at midnight.

Gerald F. Jacobson recalled "chugging straight into Calais and then swerving southward along the English Channel coast through Boulogne and swinging back to Doullens, which town we had left [in] July." To him, the trip was fascinating. Outside of Calais, "mountainous piles" of quartermaster's supplies dotted the landscape. The trains creaked beside supply depots, dog kennels, and makeshift hospitals. "Some [hospitals] were merely clusters of large and small tents, and others groups of crude frame buildings or shacks," he wrote. "And painted on the roofs of all these hospitals or etched out on the ground with whitewashed stone or brick were huge white crosses that were intended to serve as a protection against German bombing planes. But at least one hospital camp proved that these crosses were of little avail when the Hun flew aloft with a cargo of bombs. Several of the frame buildings were reduced almost to splinters by enemy bombs dropped during air raids."

In Doullens at last, Kenneth Gow described how "At the end of our train ride we had to unload in the dark, harness, get our limbers straightened out, unload the mules and start off out of the big city to our destination at which I arrived with the transport at 5:15 the next morning, riding all night. I had to go through country I had never seen before with a guide, on the compass bearing only the name of my destination. During the night there was no one on the roads to help you out."

A few days later, Claude Leland told his family, "We have made a big jump since I last wrote, and are now in a typical old French town that escaped the ravages of war." He also mentioned how the Third Battalion rolled into its new town "hot, hungry and ready to drop."

For Leland, the town was Beauquesne, where most of the regiment bedded down. Next door was Terramesnil, the new home of the Machine Gun Company and the First Battalion. "We '40-hommed' to Doullens," noted Cpl. Drew Hill, "and from there to Terramesnil. To this day, there is none of us who claims to know the correct pronunciation of the name of the town."[2] Pfc. Bert Lobdell had problems with Beauquesne. "Dear Pop," he wrote on 7 September, "Censorship won't allow my telling you where we are. I couldn't spell the name of the place anyway and besides you couldn't find it on a map with field glasses."

Terramesnil was an unattractive little hamlet that squatted among the hills outside of Doullens. Gow reported that it was "very dirty when we came in, but the regiment had policed it from limit to limit. Men were sent into every yard and corner to sweep and clean. They carried out some 150 truckloads of debris—old cans, dead dogs, cats and rabbits, and a thousand other surprising things, and now we have a spotless town. The inhabitants were utterly amazed."

Beauquesne was beautiful in comparison. "By far the best town we had been in or near for any length of time since our arrival in France," reported Cpl. Lauren Stout.[3] Nick Krayer found Beauquesne pleasurable. "Quiet, peaceful, French!" he wrote. He later noted, "Here [E Company men] met the first French civilians that they had any opportunity to meet and learned for the first time what French hospitality is. Band concerts and performances of the divisional show were frequent."[4] Another E Company man, Pfc. William White assured his aunt in Cornwall that in Beauquesne he found "the most beautiful church I ever saw. All the fellows are good Catholics over here and most of us go to communion every Sunday while we are out of the lines."

At first the troops slept in fields and orchards, scattered about Beauquesne and Terramesnil. The apples were still green, and within hours of pitching their tents, E Company men, according to Krayer, had "sampled every apple tree near it."[5] To his parents in Mount Vernon, D Company Pfc. Jack Lydecker likened his outdoor quarters to the family summer camp at "Lake Orange, as we are situated in a dandy apple orchard." He went on to state, "Old Mother Earth is as soft as a feather bed and I sleep like a top."[6]

The men of the Third Battalion pitched tents on the western edge of Beauquesne, with K Company settling down in an orchard atop a knoll. The officers slept in houses. Third Battalion commander Raphael Egan, now acting major, made his headquarters on Beauquesne's main thoroughfare, dubbed by the New Yorkers as the "Street of the Ditches." Directly across this street, L Company's Nicoll and his second in command,

Lt. Robert A. Byrns, found their sleeping quarters. Nicoll and Byrns had been good friends for more than twenty years. Next door to them, Lieutenants Leland, Percy Hall, and Griswold "Tot" Daniell, another old K Company veteran whose family ran the well-known department store in lower Manhattan, John Daniell & Sons, set up a "very high-class eating place." Boasted Leland, "The family which lived in our house gave us their dining room, and our cooks selected from I and K set up a kitchen in a shack out in the farmyard. Our good hosts loaned us their china and napery and we lived in style." And then to rub it in, he added, "We were very comfy and quite cozy."

For Sir Douglas Haig's armies there wasn't time to get comfy or cozy. All along the British front, the Germans were in retreat. Chasing the Hun took the English and Dominion soldiers across familiar battlegrounds that in the early spring had belonged to them. By 1 September they had pushed the enemy east out of Mont St. Quentin and Peronne, in some places slogging through the waist-deep marshes of the Somme River. It was a small, yet sweet victory for Lt. Gen. Sir John Monash and his Australian Corps. Rawlinson was "overjoyed." He later wrote that the capture of Mont St. Quentin "was indeed a magnificent performance and no praise is too high for [the Australians]."[7]

There was no doubt the Germans were on the run; heading back to the sanctuary of the Hindenburg Line. A good sign of that came on 3 September, when Byng's Third Army and the Canadian Corps attacked behind a creeping barrage. After the smoke had lifted they had found the battlefield eerily empty. The enemy had slipped away in the night.

Throughout the first half of September, the chase continued. It was essential that this hot pursuit, according to Rawlinson's chief of staff, Maj. Gen. Sir Archibald Montgomery, be "maintained with unabated vigour in order to prevent [the enemy] from destroying the roads and railways west of the Hindenburg Line during his retirement." He stated that in one sector, the withdrawal had been so sudden that the Allies had "lost touch" with Germans for several hours.[8]

Haig was obviously thrilled with the advance of his troops. He now wanted to break the famed Hindenburg Line and any other German defenses that stood in his way. To that end he committed his armies to Marshal Ferdinand Foch. At the time, the Allied commander was planning an all-out attack on the Germans that would also include Pershing's newly created American First Army, from the Meuse River to the North Sea— one crushing blow to end the war. Haig's commitment fit perfectly with his own plans. Foch's grand assault was to be launched on 26 September, with a combined Franco-American force hitting Verdun and then moving through the Meuse Valley in an effort to capture a vital supply center and railroad junction. On 27 September the British First and Third Armies would move toward Cambrai. On the 28th troops under the command of the king of the Belgians in Flanders would push eastward from the North Sea to Lys. And, finally, on the 29th Rawlinson's Fourth Army, supported by the French First Army, would storm the center of the Hindenburg Line between Cambrai and St. Quentin.

But as Foch finalized his all-out attack and Haig reveled over his easy victories, on 8 September the German resistance began to stiffen. The weather changed, too. Rain came pouring down in torrents. Pursuit slowed to a crawl. "This change," Montgomery pointed out, "hindered the advance of the troops."[9]

The heavy rain drove the enlisted men of the 107th Infantry indoors.

Before giving up his tent, Lobdell described the weather to his sister as rotten. "So much rain everything is damp. There are drops dropping now right through my pup tent onto my paper."

On 10 September Gow announced to his family that "everything is literally floating in mud and water. It rained steadily for five days, and the outlook for clear weather is bad."

Nicoll sent word to his sister Emily, "We have been having the usual September weather with heavy showers coming out of a clear sky, high winds and occasional perfect days. Fortunately we have been back behind the lines and in good billets so we have been enjoying the good days and not worrying much over the bad ones."

To his "Mother Dearest," Van Buren wrote, "We are billeted in barns and houses instead of those little tents which helps some because we have been having rain for about ten days and everything is pretty well soaked."

To his aunt in Cornwall, William White confided, "Three other fellows and myself are living in an old barn, but the roof is good and we have cleaned the place out, and have plenty of straw to sleep on."

Leland felt that along with the rain it was the "coolness" of the September nights that had forced the doughboys into any kind of building they could find. "Our men were finally placed under roofs, 'locked in the stable with the sheep.' At best, none of them were too far removed from the fragrant manure pile the size of which the peasants measure their prosperity."

The division had been brought to Doullens and the neighboring villages for a period of what was officially termed as "rest." After spending time in the trenches, troops were pulled out to a "rest area" far enough behind the lines to be safe from enemy artillery and bombs. As the New Yorkers found out, the term "rest" was a misnomer. They were there for more training. H Company's Cpl. James O'Toole explained the situation in a letter home to Mount Vernon. "Our division is now out on rest and I do not know where we will have to go in the trenches again. When I say rest, it does not mean that we do nothing but eat and sleep; far be it from such, because we have close order drill and maneuvering for six hours every day. In order to best the Hun a fellow must keep in good physical condition, and that is the only way it can be done."[10]

Mitchell also explained that "resting did not mean all the word implied." He added, "A system of trenches had been constructed just outside the town and we began to use them practicing such offensive tactics as rushing machine gun nests. Furthermore, a squadron of heavy tanks were used to teach us the latest ways in which those ponderous machines of war were being used against old Jerry."

C Company Pvt. Albert Ingalls from Watkins Glen stated that while resting "we drilled, practiced going over the top with the tanks, of which five were put at our disposal, made tactical maneuvers and thus prepared ourselves for the push soon to come."[11]

To Cpl. James Throckmorton Vought, the maneuvers were "very interesting, as they simulated actual battle conditions and we went over the top preceded by real tanks."[12]

Drew Hill remembered when some of those tanks first arrived. "One day," he wrote, "four lonely-looking British tanks rolled into town. From then on B Company had the muddy task of showing the rest of the division how to advance in an attack with tanks."[13]

Jacobson wrote that resting consisted mostly of "daily maneuvers, machine gun practice, and practicing, with the aid of tanks, the latest methods of wiping out enemy machine gun nests."

In a war where speed to get across wide-open no-man's-land mattered greatly, the British had only recently found that tanks could effectively tear holes in the tangled web of barbed wire. The infantry then followed the tanks through the holes. Not only did tanks flatten barbed wire and thus speed up an attack, according to one British military historian, they also took over the "psychological role" of the creeping barrage.[14] Tanks could even knock out concrete pillboxes and other fortified strong points as well. Yet the infantrymen, with their Lewis guns, rifle grenades, and mortars, were just as effective in wiping out machine-gun nests. In the meantime, training in the conventional methods of trench warfare also continued for the Empire Division. According to O'Ryan, the Third Battalion demonstrated how "under a creeping barrage the line gets ragged and salients are developed." He said, "This battalion became very expert." Later, in front of Maj. Gen. George W. Read, commander of the American II Corps, and Maj. Gen. Edward M. Lewis of the Thirtieth Division, the battalion showed the "incorrect ways of attempting an advance against hostile machine-gun fire and finally the correct methods."

Krayer recollected the tedious days of training. "Nearly every day there were field maneuvers of some kind. Always combat formations were given the important periods of the day, in fact, many wave formations. Many hours were spent practicing operations against supposed machine gun nests and heavily manned trenches. The different approach formations and wave formations were practiced until every man thoroughly understood them!"[15]

Bronx native Sgt. Hugh Griffiths wrote, "We learned the most secret workings of the Vickers. We went on maneuvers. We visited machine gun ranges, rifle ranges and pistol ranges."[16] In a letter to his aunt, Fetherolf insisted, "I wouldn't part with my dear old Lewis for the world. That's the thing that gives Jerrie his iron rations when he tries to come over. It never fails to stop him. One really has quite a responsibility for he is depended on to be able to take the place of twenty-five riflemen."

As the days of September flew by, the ultimate destination of O'Ryan's division remained unknown. Before leaving Belgium, it had been transferred to the British Third Army sector. And there it waited.

Meanwhile, with his British armies hounding the Germans at every turn, Haig and his staff were busy putting the finishing touches on a grandiose plan to attack the Hindenburg Line. In the end, when their plan had been finally hammered out to the satisfaction of the Allies, it would include the American II Corps. For the moment, Haig was putting his trust in Rawlinson, his most aggressive officer, who in turn counted on, among others, an Australian Jew of German descent. On 12 September, meeting at Monash's headquarters over a "cup of afternoon tea," he accepted a scheme by the short, heavy-set general to beat the Germans at the very ramparts of the Hindenburg Line.

The plan was simple enough.

A series of five defensive lines made up the Hindenburg Line. The British were familiar with two of those lines because they had once belonged to them. However, before reaching the main Hindenburg Line system, they first had to cross those two lines plus a third held by the Germans—the old British reserve line, the old main British line, and the Hindenburg Line outpost position.

"These were all natural strong positions, and had been very much strengthened with wire, trenches, and dug-outs both by ourselves and the enemy," Montgomery explained. "This was the line the enemy was now holding in considerable strength and he showed no signs of giving it up with out a struggle."

Because the third line of defense—the outpost position that stood in front of the main Hindenburg Line—ran across high ground, the key to success was for its immediate capture. "So long as it was held by the Germans," Montgomery reckoned, "we were denied all observation over the Main Hindenburg Line." He went on to state that the importance of the observation this line afforded was "so obvious that it had been materially strengthened and had become part of the outer defences of the Main Hindenburg Line."

The first goal then was for the British and Dominion forces to capture the outpost position, to gain the high ground. And to capture it quickly. "Every day's respite given to the enemy was of inestimable value to him," Montgomery wrote. "Further, should it be decided to attack the Main Hindenburg Line, our troops would need a short period of rest in which to reorganize. It would be advisable that this interval should take place after the capture of the outer defences of the Hindenburg Line, rather than before, so that advantage might be taken of it for reconnaissance, for the systematic organization of the artillery arrangements and for the other important preliminaries that would have to be carried out before an attack on a large scale could be undertaken."

The plan was divided into three stages. The first stage called for the British Fourth Army and the XXXVI Corps of the French First Army on its right flank to take the first line of defense, known as the old British reserve line. The second stage zeroed in on the next line of defense, or the old British outpost line. The third stage "consisted of gaining a footing in the last of the outer defences of the Hindenburg Line," Montgomery noted. Part of that section passed through three extremely fortified places just west of the fortress village of Vendhuile—The Knoll, Guillemont Farm, and Quennemont Farm.[17]

"Picked German troops held these positions," Tupper wrote. "The entire outer defense system bristled with light and heavy machine guns, minenwerfers [German mortar] of various sizes, anti-tank guns, and carefully concealed field pieces. A vast amount of enemy artillery was in support, and at Guillemont Farm there were powerful flame throwers. On a rising ground in the rear of this formidable series of outworks was the main Hindenburg system of field fortifications based on the underground tunnel carrying the St. Quentin canal."[18] O'Ryan described The Knoll as "a great flat-topped rise of ground, nearly every part of which can be dominated by fire from the heights northeast of Vendhuile, which from Vendhuile itself reinforcements could be conveniently fed when counter-attacks were to be made." O'Ryan's assistant chief of staff, Lt. Col. William T. Starr, remembered those strongholds as "a high ridge of hills devoid of trees, with a perfect field of fire for machine guns, and there was one mounted in the trench about every twenty to twenty-five feet, to say nothing of the artillery in back."[19] And Col. Franklin W. Ward, commander of the 106th Infantry, whose regiment would soon attack these strongholds, recalled, "The sector of country which the fortress covers is open, knobby and gently rolling. . . . A field long and thin longitudinally, rather than deep from west to east, with no foliage now, other than that found in narrow gorges, and little sunken groves. Everything has been cut down, root and branch, by hostile artisans, plus shot, shell and small arms fire. A tremendous field, in which to become lost is an easy matter, be-

The St. Quentin Canal Tunnel. The Seventh Regiment Fund

cause zig-zagged trenches run everywhere, dug slowly by men with light picks and shovels; with wide holes yawning between, dug instantly by rending projectiles. A shaggy, monster field that can swallow twenty thousand men with the same ease an elephant swallows a peanut."[20]

It would be here, at Guillemont Farm and The Knoll, that at the end of the month Rawlinson would order the 107th Infantry to capture, and then for the Americans to continue on to breach the main Hindenburg Line, which included the St. Quentin Canal Tunnel.

Rawlinson chose 18 September as the day for his army to attack the outer defenses. His front was fourteen miles wide. Monash's Australian soldiers were assigned the center, a front of seven thousand yards. To the left, the Seventy-fourth British Division had been given a front of two thousand yards while the Eighteenth Division took over a stretch of fewer than two thousand yards. On the extreme left, the Twelfth Division held a line of only seven hundred yards.

At five-twenty on a rainy, gray, sodden morning, supported by seven-hundred-fifty 18-pounder guns and 228 4.5-inch howitzers and with a limited number of tanks, twenty-seven thousand men of the British Fourth Army began their assault on the outer defenses of the Hindenburg Line.

Even as the British launched their preliminary attack, the fate of the New York division was still unknown. A British officer, dining in Doullens with Capt. Maslin, dropped a hint that something might be up. As Maslin remembered their chat, the officer said, "You are being fattened up for the next killing, you know. We always know something is coming when we are sent to rest in a big town for a few weeks. In about another ten days you will be up again."[21]

While O'Ryan's men cooled their heels, word drifted in that Pershing's First Army had at last entered the war. On 12 September, it attacked the St. Mihiel salient—550,000 doughboys from ten divisions, including the Forty-second, stormed a weakened German defense. By the 16th, some 2,300 enemy had been killed or wounded, 13,250 more taken prisoner, 443 guns and 752 machine guns captured, and two hundred square miles of French territory freed from the iron grip of the Hun. The cost to the Americans had been seven thousand casualties. St. Mihiel turned out to be the biggest battle an American army had fought since the Civil War.[22]

On the morning of 15 September, while Haig plotted and Pershing fought, Ken Gow jumped on his horse and rode over the French countryside. The rain had finally stopped. The sun burst through the retreating cloud cover. The foliage seemed as fresh and green as when Gow first set foot on French soil. Urging his horse off the road, he galloped across the lush fields. "I don't know when I've enjoyed myself so much," he wrote his father that day. "I love the country and its people."

Raphael Egan also loved to ride horses. But he was a giant of a man, almost six-and-a-half feet tall, much too big for the smaller horses that had been requisitioned by the division. Knowing this, 1st Lt. Hiram Taylor, a veteran of the old Seventh who had just been appointed supply officer, came up with a solution. He purchased a horse from one of the local farmers. It was a Percheron, a rugged draft animal. Leland claimed the beast weighed "at least two tons, one of those sturdy French farm animals with whiskers on their feet." Taylor outfitted the Percheron with a pair of cavalry saddles and then presented it to Egan. Pleased at the gift, the hefty Newburgher swung his great bulk atop the first saddle. Taylor then hopped up behind Egan onto the second saddle. Thus aboard, they rode the horse up and down Beauquesne's "Street of the Ditches" like two farmers at a county fair.

About the time Egan and Taylor were riding the big Percheron around the village, 1st Lt. Ralph Polk Buell, a descendent of President James Polk, had been assigned to C Company. He sensed that soon all hell would break loose, and so from his lonely billet, he penned a love letter home to his wife, Mary, on her birthday. "Every night I say to Our Father that I am in his hands, to do with as He wishes. I do not ask his help for my own safety, save only that through Him I may walk straight, without fear whatsoever. I do give unto His loving care, my little Mary. And so my beloved, over the many miles of land and sea that keep us apart, and perhaps from beyond the stars, I hold out my arms to you and holding you close; Oh, so very close; I kiss your dear lips, and in your ear I whisper, 'A happy birthday sweetheart."[23]

Bert Lobdell sat on an old Harvester tractor that was rusting outside

Lt. Ralph Polk Buell was a veteran
of the Spanish-American War.
The Seventh Regiment Fund

a brick barn, writing letters to his family. Chickens, ducks, and a few pigs scratched the ground near him. He had just gotten over a painful sty, the fourth he had suffered while in Beauquesne, and now because of it was handling clerical work for L Company's first sergeant. He said that it made him look like "I'd been walloped a good one in the eye and everybody wishes they could see the other fellow." Along with fighting the sty, at the time he was also fighting the "grippe." He said to his mother not to worry. He had caught it in time. To his father, he explained about his ten-thousand-dollar life insurance policy. "We've been requested to advise our families of our serial numbers so that in case it ever becomes necessary to write to the War Department for any information you would refer to me as Private First Class Albert J. Lobdell, Jr., 1211903, Company letter and organization."

Although the flu spared Lobdell, it struck Cpls. Henry I. Ingersoll of K Company and Arthur Briggs Church of A Company. Ingersoll died on 15 September. Church, a New York City attorney, wound up in the hospital. "Nothing more than the old-fashioned grippe," he guaranteed his family. When he got out he claimed he was in excellent shape. "I didn't have a very enjoyable time at the hospital, but thank the Lord I am out of it, and until you have been away from your company you don't realize how much you have become attached to it and the close ties of friendship and affection you form with men by whose side you have fought."[24]

Sitting on a stone doorstep that led to the courtyard behind his billets, Fetherolf mused about friendship, too. It was dusk. A harvest moon, "big and yellow" lit up the sky as brilliantly as a Very light or artillery flash. "Duke Doolittle [Cpl. Aaron W. Doolittle, also from Middletown] is the only one of my intimate friends left now," he wrote his aunt. "We stick together and manage to hit the trail very good. He is the boy whose wife gave me a jar of pickles to take to him when I was home on my furlough." In fact, Doolittle's wife went all through grade school with Fetherolf, even sitting next to him in class.

Lobdell thought about his friends in L Company, especially Cpl. Wetherill Palmer, perhaps because "Weth" always looked out for him. "The other day Weth went out and bought two steaks and then took them and me to a house where the woman cooked them for us. Gosh make out it wasn't good," he informed his Mom. And then again, "There is nothing I enjoy as much though as the pipe Weth gave me when I can get Velvet or Prince Albert, and most every place we go now there is an American Y. M.C.A. so have no trouble getting it."

Van Buren and Stout, however, had a falling out. The two best friends from Kansas City, where they had been sketch artists on the *Star,* went their separate ways. According to Van Buren, Stout had done something he had not liked, but he never said what it was. Now his best friend in E Company was Cpl. Robert "Jeff" Davis. Yet in mid-September, Davis was selected for officer's school. "I hate like the dickens to see him go because I like him better than any one in this company," he bemoaned to his mother. "It will be just like loosing a brother because he has been every bit of that to me for twelve long and lonesome months."

Ironically, the day Jeff Davis left for officer's school, 9 September, Van Buren was named company historian. "I feel very puffed up over being picked out of this company of 250 men for such a responsible job. I know I can do the work and will slip one over on the other companies in the regiment by illustrating my history." A week later a divisional staff officer bumped into Van Buren, remembered his pulp-magazine work, and introduced him to O'Ryan. The general then ordered the gag artist to take over illustrating the division's history. Thrilled, Van Buren wrote home, "I am attached to the division headquarters from now on until my work is finished. I am to make portrait sketches of all the high officers from the general down to the Majors in this division and war sketches at the front and back behind the lines. All my work will be reproduced in this History which will be a book that will last for the ages."

Earlier he had been sought out by one of the editors at the *Stars & Stripes,* John Tracey Winterich, to be an illustrator for the fledgling army newspaper. Because several of his New York friends, including Charles Phelps Cushing and Alexander Woollcott, worked on the paper, they had wanted him to be part of the staff. But at the time he turned them down, not wanting to desert the boys in his regiment. Now that he was no longer an infantryman, but safe at division headquarters, shivers of guilt coursed through Van Buren. He felt he was leaving his comrades behind. Trying to justify to himself this sudden good fortune, he scribbled a long letter to his mother. He explained, "I could not bare the thought of working on The Stars & Stripes without first doing a turn in the front line trenches. I loathe those swivel chair 'soldiers' who are doing their fighting with a pencil in some comfortable little room in Paris or Washington while we fellows are out here running the risk of war and living in filthy places crawling with body lice and rats. I've been through the mill and can now take one of the soft jobs without feeling one bit conscious stricken and I'm going to do it." And then, as if sighing, he finished up. "You & my friends will never know what a hell this is no matter how long it lasts. I went into the trenches without the least bit of fear and came out untouched. I gave Fritz his chance and he let me go so now for a while I can take on this work and at the same time look the world in the face."

The British attack on the outer defenses of the Hindenburg Line had gone well, for the most part. The night before the assault the Australians were in "bounding spirits," according to C. E. W. Bean, the official war correspondent of the Australian government. As they got ready to rush forward, however, "showers of rain, swishing down the iron roofs of their huts, many hearts sank." But when the rain stopped, a dense fog fortunately hid Monash's troops so that they were able to reach the German outposts without much resistance. They pushed the Hun back almost five thousand yards. From their new vantage point, the Australians now saw the St. Quentin Canal and the water in it. They saw the entrance to the tunnel. The position they held, Bean reported, "was on the final line of exploitation and the importance of it for any force attacking the Canal was obvious at a glance."[25]

But the success of the Australians was tempered by obvious disaster on their flanks, most notably the northern flank. There the advance had been held up. The British III Corps—the Twelfth, Eighteenth, and Seventy-fourth Divisions—had been stymied. Each time they pushed the Germans back, a counterattack drove them off their newly gained ground. For two days the III Corps hammered at the entrenched Germans, unable to wrest the high terrain from them. The Knoll, Guillemont Farm, and Quennemont Farm stayed in the hands of the Hun.

Because III Corps had not reached its objective on the 18th or the 19th, the attack continued. "It was essential," Montgomery later reported, "that all objectives of the 18th should be secured as early as possible, with a view to future operations." On the 20th, Lt. Gen. Sir Richard Butler of

III Corps ordered a combined attack for the following morning at five-forty, with the Eighteenth and Seventy-fourth Divisions and the First Australian Division on their right to take The Knoll, Guillemont Farm, Quennemont Farm, and Willow Trench, which ran from The Knoll to Guillemont Farm. Four tanks were added to the attack. Yet by two P.M., the British divisions, after gaining some ground, had been repulsed and were now back at the original start line. This failure worried Montgomery. "The chief importance of these places to us was that, so long as they were held by the enemy, it would be very difficult to support our attacking troops with an efficient barrage beyond the main Hindenburg Line."[26]

When drafting his plan, Monash believed the entire length of the outpost line would be in the hands of the British Fourth Army for the storming of the main Hindenburg Line. Now that was not to be. And to make matters more strained he had already informed Rawlinson that his First and Third Divisions were to be taken out of the line. "The wastage of their battalions had gone on faster than the inflow of fresh drafts or the return of convalescent sick and wounded," he later explained. "The two Divisions contained the original sixteen battalions who had immortalized themselves in 1915 in the landing at Gallipoli. My hope was that, if these Divisions could be allowed to rest over the winter, they could be sufficiently replenished by the spring of 1919 to be able to maintain all sixteen battalions at a satisfactory fighting strength."

With the loss of those two divisions, he then worried, "I would thus be left with insufficient resources to maintain an immediate continuance of the pressure upon the enemy."[27]

After Monash explained the situation to Rawlinson, the British general asked him if he would like to take on the responsibility of commanding two American divisions so that operations could continue. He said he could get the American II Corps, which meant, of course, the Twenty-seventh and Thirtieth Divisions. Monash's eyes lit up. Back in July, at the Battle of Hamel, he had seen how feisty the Americans were in combat. "It was true," he later said, "that this new American Corps had no previous battle service, but measures were possible to supply them with any technical guidance which they might lack." He did not hesitate in accepting Rawlinson's offer of fresh fodder. He then planned to submit a new proposal for, as he put it, "a joint operation to take place towards the end of the month by these two American and the remaining three Australian divisions, with the object of completing the task so well begun, of breaking through the Hindenburg defenses."[28]

While the British battled for the outer defenses of the Hindenburg Line and Monash pondered how he might survive a diminished Australian Corps, on 19 September, the Twenty-seventh and Thirtieth Divisions held a joint exercise near Beauquesne. On that day, Read informed his two divisional commanders that it was likely they would soon be called upon to join the British in a major attack. Two days later, orders came down for the New Yorkers to depart the Doullens area on the 23d and 24th for Peronne, where they would then march to Haut Allaines.

As they prepared to leave, Read informed O'Ryan that his troops, along with troops of the Thirtieth Division, would be attached to the Australian Corps in a subservient role. But according to O'Ryan, Read added that before he turned over his men to Monash he had decided to assign the Twenty-seventh to the northern sector of the St. Quentin Canal Tunnel because "that in all probability the difficulties to be met there would be much greater than in the southern sector." He explained that because the British had been unable to capture the outer works in the northern sector, and that because of the strength of the Germans there, the Twenty-seventh would be asked to undertake a preliminary assault on the Hindenburg Line outpost line—the very piece of high ground that the British Eighteenth and Seventy-fourth Divisions had just failed to capture.

Finally, the months of endless training were coming to end.

Back in Beauquesne and Terramesnil life went on as usual for the boys of the 107th Infantry.

A favorite hangout for the New Yorkers lucky enough to be encamped around Beauquesne was a green-colored *estaminet* on the "Street of Ditches," next to Capt. Egan's mess. A beautiful, charming, and mysterious girl ran the tavern. Leland, who lived across the street and visited the place as often as he could, remembered the girl, whose name he said was Andrée (although other soldiers remembered her as Alaine or Elaine), as "very pretty and attractive." She and her family were refugees from the north, he said. "A better-mannered, more refined and more proper girl would have been hard to find anywhere; and yet she kept a saloon and sold wine to all kinds of soldiers. She was a good little sister to all of them, and while they were all probably in love with her, no one ever got gay with Andrée. If anyone had been the least bit disrespectful he would have had his block promptly knocked off."

Every night the *estaminet* was packed with soldiers, singing and "whooping it up." Andrée had one large room for enlisted men and another, smaller room for officers. She always served the doughboys first, then the officers. Her place was lit with candles and kerosene lamps. A blue haze of cigarette and pipe smoke hung over the boisterous soldiers. Van Buren, whose creation of a woman on a dugout wall in Flanders had drawn John Singer Sargent into the trenches, basked in her beauty, as did scores of other soldiers. After eating one of her meals of boiled chicken, soup, potatoes, strong beans, coffee, and cookies, he and his E Company companions insisted that she sit down with them. "After several shrugs of the shoulder and No, no, nos, she consented and seemed to have the time of her life. She is the best looking girl I have seen in this town and has quite some class for small town stuff."

Nick Krayer, a sergeant in Van Buren's company, was also taken in by her. He called her a "little barmaid who was so pretty, and as dainty and *tres chic* as she was good."[29] Van Buren's estranged friend, Lauren Stout, another illustrator with an eye for pretty women, wrote, "Yes, we saw beautiful girls occasionally. They were the kind we had always heard and read about at home. Everyone agreed that Elaine, who served in the green estaminet, was a prize beauty."[30]

Andrée went to church every Sunday, dressed in black. When she strolled along the street "every head popped from every window to watch her pass by," Leland wrote. "She was surely good to look at."

Andrée kept a large autograph book for her favorite soldiers to sign. Her book dated as far back as 1916. Along with hundreds of signatures, it was crammed with verses and caricatures and sketches from Australian, French, English, and Scottish soldiers, many of them a fine lad, as Leland later recounted, "whose bones were rotting on the Somme." One night Leland and two other lieutenants, Carey Walrath and Harry Robinson, both from M Company, autographed Andrée's book. Also endorsing the book with little illustrations, according to Leland, were I Company artists

Merritt Cutler and Harold Kunkle. Like many of the signatories before them, several of these silk stocking soldiers would soon be buried somewhere in the Somme valley.

Yet Leland, the bookish librarian, sensed there was more to Andrée than met the eye. As he later surmised, "She was such a superior and refined sort of girl in a place where you would least expect to find one, that we rather suspected that she might be employed by the British secret service. A clever woman who knew all the officers and men could hear so much in an estaminet that would interest headquarters. But we were always looking for spies."

One day while he was not eyeing the mysterious beauty, Leland spotted a bicycle messenger pedaling like the wind up to Egan's quarters next to Andrée's *estaminet*. The messenger darted into the building. A moment later, Egan came out. He signaled to Leland and several officers nearby.

"Orders have arrived," he told them. To Leland he said, "Take your sergeant and report back to headquarters as soon as possible. You will go with the advance party."

When Van Buren heard that the regiment had been ordered toward the front, he sent off a letter to his mother. "We have been in this little town for several weeks," he wrote, "but our rent is due so we will move out tomorrow or the next day."

Raymond "Mickey" O. Blauvelt, an H Company private first class, penned a letter to a friend back in his hometown of Nyack, New York. "Expect to move either tomorrow or Monday and God knows when I will get a few minutes to myself." Mickey's brother Charles, serving with the Seventy-seventh Division, had been killed on 30 August. But Mickey did not mention the death of his brother in the letter. Instead, he closed by stating, "We have the Huns on the run and if the weather will only stay good he will be drinking water out of the Rhine for coffee. The American battle cry is 'Heaven, hell or Hoboken by Christmas,' so here, hoping to see you by Xmas."[31]

In Terramesnil that night, the Machine Gun Company took over an entire *estaminet*, knowing that training was now over. "The estaminet was jammed," Sgt. Griffiths recalled. "There were speeches and drinks. Closing time came—and went. Finally, in the small hours, the party broke up.

"The next thing we remember were the ruins of Allaines."[32]

CHAPTER 11

We Were Up Against
the Line Itself

Before the regiment embarked for Tincourt by train, bus, horse, and lorry, and then from there to Allaines on foot, Lt. Claude Leland had a final task—to make sure his I Company boys hadn't stiffed Andrée. Or maybe he wanted to see her one more time. He went into her *estaminet* for the last time. It was Saturday night, and the tavern was deserted. Andrée was anxious to hear where the New Yorkers were going. She was told that they were probably headed for the front.

"I am sorry to learn that, Monsieur," she said, tears flooding her soft eyes.

Leland asked her if there were any unpaid debts.

"Oh, no, Monsieur," she said, "they always pay too much, these Americans. And they are such nice boys; well, good-bye, Monsieur. Good luck in the war."

Early on Sunday morning, Leland and 1st Lt. Stephen M. Schwab of E Company, as part of the advance party, got aboard a bus parked in front of the church. Joining them were 1st Lt. Edwin Munson, the regimental gas officer; sergeants George Rowe of I and Walter Farley of L; and Pvt. James Page of K. Because it was a bus they were taking, the soldiers felt like they were off to Coney Island instead of the front. Although Leland never said, when the bus pulled away from the church and rumbled out of Beauquesne, never to return, certainly every head was pressed against a window as all eyes looked longingly for Andrée to see if she might happen by on her way to Mass wearing her pretty black dress.

"There must be several broken hearts left behind from what I gather," K Company Sgt. George Ely II confided in his diary. He also hated to leave Beauquesne, for he added: "If the French girls do break hearts, I hope we do go back sometime."

For Kenneth Gow there was no bus ride. Leaving from Terramesnil, the machine-gun lieutenant rode on horseback. "It was the most fascinating and interesting and at the same time depressing trip I have ever made. The regiment came by rail, and the transport hiked—that is, the mounted and wheeled detachment of the company—under my command. I was in the saddle for thirty-six hours and travelled only at night, under a full moon. It rained torrents for four hours the first night, but it has been clear since. It is very cold and consequently uncomfortable." In the same letter, which he had been anxious to put in the mail, he wanted his family to know, "If it is my fate to go this time, remember you have given a son to a great cause. Pray not for my welfare, but that I may have the strength and courage to do my duty and not fail those who depend upon me. I am your son and brother, and have done nothing you would not have me do."

Ely found himself crammed aboard a train with 741 other doughboys of Raphael Egan's Third Battalion. In his diary of 25 September, he wrote, "Here we are up in the line again. The trip was bad. We hiked to the train and rode twelve hours until two this morning."

Cpl. Alan Eggers, one of the "Jersey Gunners," described that "wherever the railroad ran through a cut we could see deep dugouts in the banks made by the Germans. On both sides of the tracks stretched flat fields full of shell holes and littered with old guns, ruined tanks, busted aeroplanes and other wreckage of war. We passed through many small towns and some large cities, all of which had been shelled and reshelled until there was hardly a house standing in any of them."[1]

Pfc. Jack Lydecker from Mount Vernon found the trip by train "72 hours of hard riding."[2]

* * *

It was indeed a "hard" ride. The entire regiment took as much as three days to reach Tincourt. Most of the soldiers rode in three trains, crushed in like fans at a sold-out baseball game at the Polo Grounds. When they were let loose, they then had to march to Allaines and Haut Allaines, side-by-side villages east of Tincourt and also to Longavesne and several hamlets to the north. For the past several days, the division's other regiments had been tramping into the sector held by the British III Corps. The division's orders were to relieve the battered Eighteenth and Seventy-fourth Divisions. Tristram Tupper reported to his wife, "Our boys started to steam in that evening [no date given]; guides had met them at the railroad some miles away and now the regiments which were to move into the line the next night, relieving the British, were marching past at the close of a drizzling day to the fields, the hills and huts we had [picked] for them. They should have been marching into palaces for many of them had but one more day to live. Instead they marched, slipping in the mud, bearing forty pounds upon their strong young backs, cheerfully to wet fields, there to pitch their little shelter tents."[3]

The land the doughboys crossed still smoldered of battle. Signs of the recent fighting were everywhere. The landscape was out of an H. G. Wells novel. "We passed through Albert," Lydecker wrote, "and you can't imagine what the place looks like. Can you picture a city like Mount Vernon and one house left that has not been blown to hell. An earthquake would have done less damage. It was a sight I would not have missed for the world."[4] Cpl. James Throckmorton Vought told his brother back in Rochester, "The most smashed up place possible to imagine. There was not one brick on top of another." He said that "desolation was absolute and complete—no sign of life anywhere."[5]

"The rolling countryside was eloquent with the signs of the struggle so recently waged across its face," noted Cpl. Robert Waddell.[6]

When the bus carrying Leland, Schwab, and Page pulled into Allaines, the librarian found "fields strewn . . . with German equipment. Along the road on both sides were hastily constructed trenches or machine-gun pits, tin huts badly punctured and now and then a dead tank. Everywhere there were mounds with rough wooden crosses above them."

The ruined countryside stunned Harold Mills. "Dead men and horses are strewn all around, bloody trenches, discarded equipment, many shell cases and pieces of shells. All the marks of great fighting. We are going to be busy for some time now."

Nick Krayer also saw all the terrible "evidence of bitter fighting." The men of E Company, he said, slept under "crosses of heroes who gave their lives to gain this ground." He added that "live shells, bombs and rifles and thousands of rounds of small arms ammunition littered the countryside. Battered trenches marked the hillsides. The men investigated all of them and all day long could be heard the explosions as the men threw German potato masher bombs. And as dusk approached the sky was ablaze with German signal lights sent up by the more adventuresome of the American soldiers."[7]

Even Ely described piles of rifles, ammunition, helmets, "scarred" British tanks, and unused artillery shells. In his diary of 26 September, he remarked, "Last evening I had to walk over three battlefields. There are graves all over. Jerry's thistle or bayonets stuck over them, and Australians with their little white crosses. And there are Jerrys without graves. One was found with nothing in a dug out. It being a novelty, so they tied a rope around his ankles, hauled him up the steps, went over him for souvenirs and they used him for a target for potato mashers."

L Company's Cpl. Bernard Thomas Hunt from Albion, New York, a 1913 graduate of the United States Naval Academy and former ensign before enlisting in the old Seventh in 1917, found Allaines "a shell of its one-time self, and even the shell had been still further shattered. On every side were unpleasant reminders that Jerry had lately passed through, as he headed for home."

Lydecker alarmed his parents, "Where we are now the Germans just left and the entire village is mined. The other day a lad and four pals were hunting souvenirs; they picked up a German helmet and were blown to bits. Some others stumbled over a German dead body; it was wired and now these poor fellows have gone west." The Mount Vernon lad also reported that German prisoners "are coming in fast, so many of them that we just put up sign posts and they go right to their prisons; they are glad to be taken." He mentioned one prisoner who had once owned a bakery on New York's Third Avenue. "In 1914 [he] decided to get strong with his folks, so he joined his fatherland's army. He knew of the 'Seventh' regiment and several old members. It seems the boys used to trade in his shop. He is glad now that he is safe in our hands."[8]

What bothered Fancher Nicoll the most was that too many officers from the regiment were being pulled out of the line, many then sent to schools all over France. He now felt there were no longer enough officers to go around. In a letter to Leo Knust, the former captain of E Company who had resigned in the spring because he had not been allowed to accompany his men to France, perhaps owing to the fact that he had been born in Germany, Nicoll lamented that the "old crowd of officers is going fast. Major Engel is the only field officer left, Sherman having been sent to another Division. Capt. Heylman has been made Personnel officer, an office job; Blythe has broken down and is out; Stratton wounded & out; Fisk going off to staff school, Hayward still on the job; Nichols present, Nesbitt going to Line School next week, Tompkins on the job, Egan present, Bernard sent to U.S.A.; Nicoll about to go to school and Coleman out. I lost six Sergts in one week, two casualties and four to O. T. S., so you see how things change."

The reference in the letter about himself going to school was a fact he had mentioned to his sister Emily in a note to her dated 20 September. "I am selected to go to school for three months course commencing in about a week and am looking forward to it though it will take me away from the regt for that time at least and probably for ever if I make good." He then closed with an odd comment for a soldier who had been with the old Seventh since 1900. "I will not feel so badly about leaving."

After setting up divisional headquarters on the 23d in a "hutment camp" in the shelled village of Bois de Buire near Tincourt, Maj. Gen. John O'Ryan received orders to report to Lt. Gen. Sir John Monash. Awaiting the arrival of O'Ryan and Maj. Gen. George W. Read of the American II Corps and Maj. Gen. Edward M. Lewis of the Thirtieth Division, the commander of the newly organized Australian-American Corps mulled over the disappointment that his plan to capture the high ground in front of arguably the most fortified point of the Hindenburg Line had not gone off as perfectly as he had hoped. The British III Corps had fallen short. The outpost strongholds of The Knoll and Guillemont Farm that overlooked the northern end of the St. Quentin Canal Tunnel were still in enemy hands. Therefore, in a last attempt to wrest away these strongholds before the attack on the Hindenburg Line, set for 29 September, Monash and Gen. Sir Henry Rawlinson decided to use one American regiment where two British divisions had failed. After securing the strongholds, every regiment in both American divisions would then take part in the final assault on the German fortifications. Upon the arrival of O'Ryan, Lewis, Read, and their staffs, Monash explained his amended battle plans. He told them that he wanted one regiment from each division placed in the line with six regiments held in reserve. The Twenty-seventh would face the northern section of the canal; the Thirtieth the southern sector. On the 27th, only one New York regiment would attack the outpost strongholds, ensuring that they would be in Allied hands by the end of the day so that on the 29th the main attack could off without a hitch. He next outlined the assault for the 29th.

"It was a plan which had, intentionally, been reduced to the simplest possible elements," Monash recalled. "It was to be a straightforward trench to trench attack, from a perfectly straight 'jumping off' line to a perfectly straight objective line, under a dense artillery and machine-gun barrage, and with the assistance of a large contingent of tanks. . . . The advance was to be at a deliberate pace, and if due regard were had to a few elementary precautions, should prove a simple task for the American infantry." After the St. Quentin tunnel had fallen into Allied hands, Monash's own infantrymen would leapfrog the doughboys, driving the Germans back and thus capturing not only the main Hindenburg Line, but also a reserve line further east known as the Beaurevoir Line for the village through which it ran.

The ground that Monash hoped to capture on the 29th had been sectioned off into three lines—each line, or objective, designated by a color. The Blue Line was the original starting point that he had hoped to be in Allied hands before the main assault, but, as already chronicled, was still held by the Germans. Six thousand yards to the east, across the St. Quentin Canal Tunnel, ran the second objective, designated the Green Line. It formed a long arc, running south from the village of Vendhuile and then along the eastern outskirts of the fortified villages of Le Catelet, Gouy, and Nauroy. It was up to the Twenty-seventh and Thirtieth divisions to capture this Green Line by midmorning on the 29th—in Monash's mind a "simple task." Of course, the tunnel was the heart of the Hindenburg Line defenses, and considered impregnable. The Red Line (the Beaurevoir Line) was the third and final objective. Some forty-five hundred yards further east, it was the least protected of the German defenses. Easy pickings. But it was not to be attacked until after the Americans had secured the Green Line. Monash's plan called for the Twenty-seventh to swing to the north once it reached the Green Line and the Thirtieth to swing to the south, opening a wedge so that two Australian divisions, the Third and Fifth, could pass through and take the Red Line.

Naturally, it all hinged on whether on 27 September one American regiment could seize the outpost strongholds so that, in fact, there was a "perfectly straight jumping off line" that Monash called crucial to the success of the attack set for the 29th.

As Monash remembered his meeting with the American generals, a "rain of questions" soon deluged him even though his presentation had been, according to him, brief and simple. He was not used to being questioned at length by his Australian subordinates. The pestering Americans seemed to have annoyed him. "With blackboard and chalk, maps and diagrams," he whined, "I had to speak for more than three hours in an endeavour to explain methods and reasons, mistakes and remedies, dangers and precautions, procedures and expedients."[9]

O'Ryan did not recollect it that way at all. He believed that only four or five questions had been asked, and not until after Monash's presentation. "His conversation and explanations were so detailed and lengthy," he countered, "that there did not seem the necessity to ask many questions." What concerned O'Ryan most, however, was that Monash's plan was "based upon the assumption that the outworks of the Hindenburg Line would be in possession of the Fourth Army prior to the day of the attack." It had been made very clear to the young general that the mission his untested boys were about to take on called for "one regiment . . . to do what two divisions of the British III Corps had been unable to do after repeated efforts and heavy losses."

The general picked the 106th Infantry for the task. In support, he chose the 105th Infantry. For the main attack on the 29th, he had decided to rely on the 107th and 108th Infantries. The division's judge advocate, Maj. J. Leslie Kincaid, recalled that O'Ryan had "made up his mind that, if it was humanly possible to do it, the line before the division was going to crack and crack hard."[10]

And so on the night of 25 September, the 106th Infantry, two thousand strong, advanced to the front—the first of the division's regiments to try and crack the Hindenburg Line. Each man in the 106th carried two hundred rounds of small arms ammunition, six grenades in pockets, four sandbags, a pick or shovel, and an extra water bottle.

"Everybody thought we were in contact with the outpost positions of the Hindenburg Line, but as a matter of fact, and as subsequent developments proved, we were up against the line itself," argued Maj. Ransom Hooker Gillett, commander of the First Battalion, 106th Infantry. "And a lousy, dirty dangerous place it was."[11]

"Hooker's" battalion with three companies in the line and one in support had been assigned the right flank that faced the stronghold of Quennemont Farm, more than three thousand yards distant. In the center, staring ahead at Guillemont Farm, the Second Battalion under the temporary command of Major Kincaid, took up its position, two companies in the line with two in support. On the left flank, Capt. William E. Blaisdell's Third Battalion, with three companies in the line and one in support, fronted The Knoll. Also part of the assault was the regimental machine gun company led by Capt. George E. Bryant and twelve British tanks. Lined up behind Blaisdell's Third Battalion, there to provide flank protection, were two companies of the 105th Infantry.

In the night before the attack, strips of one-inch-wide white tape were stapled to the ground in a straight line in front of each battalion. "The white ribbon to more clearly signalize the jump-off line in the darkness," Col. Franklin W. Ward explained. Zero hour had been set for five-thirty in the morning. An hour before, the troops were on the tape. A heavy ground mist hovered over the battlefield.

Ward remembered being in the midst of a "tomb-like silence of a cold September dawn, a single fieldpiece is discharged! A moment later a burst of fire from the guns of the . . . British artillery is the answer to the signal, and all along the front coalescent sheets of exploding flame bounce, seethe and creep forward."[12]

At exactly five-thirty, the American machine gunners opened with a thick barrage. "The output of these ninety-six machine guns," wrote O'Ryan, "must have sounded like the buzzing of millions of wasps as they passed over the head of the infantry lying at the start line." Ward was there on the front, where he heard the "twangs and whines" of the "wasp-like buzz of a barrage of copper-nosed bullets from ninety-six machine guns, each of which fires two hundred rounds a minute."[13] Meanwhile, nine brigades of British field artillery pummeled the Hindenburg outpost line—the eighteen-pounders fired at a rate of three rounds per minute while the 4.5 howitzers dropped their shells at a rate of two per minute.

With smoke from the bombs mixing with the morning mist, the boys of the 106th leapt to their feet and, behind the protection of a creeping barrage, charged the strongholds of The Knoll and Guillemont Farm. Every three minutes the barrage rolled ahead of them—one hundred yards at a clip. In this thunderous wake, the doughboys steadily advanced against the enemy. The moment the awful noise of crashing artillery and the death rattle of machine guns reached the 107th Infantry, crouched far back in a reserve line, the silk stocking soldiers let out a roar of support for their New York comrades.[14]

With the 106th Infantry advancing across no-man's-land in the heat of battle, there was no rest for the 107th Infantry. Col. Charles L. DeBevoise ordered his boys up to the front and into the trenches, per O'Ryan's instructions.

At a meeting of K Company's noncommissioned officers, among them Sergeants Ely, Roy Beyerl from Malone, Robert Peek, Harmon Vedder, and Philip DeMilhau Vosburgh from Staten Island; and Corporals Joseph R. Cushman and Van Strycker Mills and his older brother Hal, all from Manhattan; H. Lonsdale Scannell, known as Lonny, and his brother John, Cornwall-on-Hudson residents; Long Islander Robert Raven, whose brother Dick was a lieutenant in E Company; and James Throckmorton Vought, listened as their commander George B. Bradish explained the regiment's role in the coming days. A native of Malone and veteran of the old First Infantry, Bradish had just earned his captain's bars. "After the meeting, we stood about in groups, talking it over, every man's face bright with anticipation and excitement," Peek reminisced long after the battle. "Those of us who remain can look back on that evening as the last time the old bunch were together and can remember the light of the campfire playing on the dear faces of men with whom we had lived and worked for a year and many of which we were not to see again."[15]

When orders came to move out, the doughboys had to turn in their shelter tents, poles, and pins, and all personal property not needed. "Extra clothing and odds and ends were wrapped up in the shelter tents and turned in," Krayer wrote. "They were all plainly marked by the names and numbers of the owners so that those fortunate enough to come out of the fray with the company might regain them. Blankets were turned in too."[16]

Among the personal belongings turned in by Captain Nicoll were one silk comforter, a pair of slippers, four pairs of pajamas, twenty-three pairs of socks, nine towels, one whisk broom, eighteen handkerchiefs, seven white shirts, two black ties, a set of gold cuff links, and a mirror.[17] He had earlier explained to his sister, after telling her of a recent three-day leave to the seashore, that his sojourn away from the war had made him realize how "immensely" he enjoyed civilized life. "I shall not find it any effort to shake off my uniform and to try being civilized again." Also among his belongings was one hunting knife sheathed in its case.

Noted Cpl. Drew Hill, "Hasty preparations were made—packs, consisting only of a mess kit and slicker—were rolled. Then we set off for the big push. We had heard that we were 'going over' with the Aussies, and that helped to keep our spirits up."[18] Bernard Hunt, now a corporal with the Third Battalion Intelligence Section, agreed with Hill about the Australians. He knew their fighting reputation. "Glad we were to hear that we were to be with such good company as the 'Aussies' during the coming great attack," he later stated.[19] Ely scrawled in his diary on 26 September, "It seems we are to work with the Australians in our next big push and it is a compliment and a privilege for us. I have never seen a finer lot of men."

All day on the 27th the Greyjackets marched toward the roar of artillery and heavy guns, the smell of battle deep in their nostrils. The muddy road they trod was awash with ambulances, ammunition wagons, and supply trains grinding toward the front. The closer they got to the fighting the more they realized that where they were headed the recently departed East Poperinghe Line and Dickebusch Lake would seem like mere child's play.

* * *

At first, the desperate fight that raged in front of the 107th Infantry had
gone well. In just over an hour, the Fifty-third Brigade had battled its way
to The Knoll and Guillemont Farm. One hundred fifty prisoners were
rounded up. By nine forty-five A.M., an additional one hundred and thirty
prisoners were in the hands of the doughboys. But then the brutal fighting
around the three strongholds slowed the advance. O'Ryan believed that
his men had, in fact, reached their objectives early in the day, yet were unable to consolidate their gains "for there were many casualties en route,
which sadly thinned the line." A vicious German counterattack drove
Blaisdell's Third Battalion off The Knoll. Twice the Americans tried to
dig in and recapture this vital high point, but each time they were pushed
off. "In many instances," O'Ryan wrote, "the groups which gained their
objective line held on with the greatest tenacity and courage against great
odds. In some cases . . . where the fighting was heaviest, some of these
groups were surrounded, bombed into submissiveness and taken prisoners. Other groups counter-attacked, destroying them, or where possible, taking prisoners."

To the right of the Second Battalion, Gillett's First Battalion faced stiff
opposition near Guillemont Farm. Behind him in reserve, waiting to be
called up, was a company of the 105th Infantry, commanded by Capt.
Henry Maslin. Orders from a frustrated Gillett told Maslin to have his
men take the Farm. Gillett's words, as Maslin remembered them, were
blunt. "Get this done quickly!" Maslin, the Irish-born veteran of the
Spanish-American War, was elated. Fighting hand-to-hand sure beat getting passively hit by shellfire.[20]

First Lt. William Bradford Turner sprinted up to a German machine-
gun pit and wiped out the entire crew with a pistol. The Long Island native left the dead slumped over their gun and dashed twenty-five yards to
another machine-gun pit, killing one member. By this time, he was
joined by several of his own men and they finished off the Germans.
Then, in an extraordinary display of bravery, they continued moving forward in a swarm of flying bullets, putting one machine-gun crew after
another out of action. Several bullets tore into Turner, but he kept going.
And when his pistol ran out of ammunition, he picked up the rifle of a
dead soldier and jumped into the middle of yet another machine-gun

crew, bayoneting its bewildered members. He then leaped out of the pit and ran to another. This time he was surrounded and overwhelmed. The Germans killed him on the spot. For his gallantry, Turner earned for O'Ryan's Twenty-seventh Division its first Medal of Honor.

Sgt. Reidar Waaler of the 105th Machine Gun Battalion also won the Medal of Honor that day. A resident of Manhattan, Waaler saw a tank explode and burst into a ball of flame. A few moments later he spotted several men crawling toward him in the confusion of the fight. At first they looked as if they had on red underwear. As they neared, he realized that their clothing had been burned off and what he saw was their broiled skin. The sergeant knew that other members of the crew were still trapped inside the tank. Creeping through a sheet of machine-gun fire and exploding artillery shells, he climbed into the burning tank, understanding that at any moment another explosion could annihilate him and anyone still in the tank because of the live ammunition stowed inside. He found three men. One of them was the driver, and he was beyond help. Waaler's captain remembered afterward seeing the "burned mummy of the driver still grasping the wheel and peering through the slit in front of the tank." As Waaler freed the surviving two soldiers, his slicker caught on fire. By the time he got them outside, it had burned off. Satisfied the soldiers were safe, he went back to killing Germans.[21]

"In spite of barrage, in spite of smoke, in spite of bullet, bayonet, butt and hand grenade—the enemy fire never slackens," Ward wrote. He then described how the "nonce" of civilization had given away to primeval instinct. "The crapshooters are all here, but now they are tossing the bones with death!"[22]

By nightfall, the 106th Infantry had not captured the strongholds. The survivors were ordered back. Once again, the Germans had held. Dead and wounded soldiers were scattered over the battlefield. The living clung to the ground where they had fallen—in shell holes, in and around machine-gun pits, in the open atop the blood-soaked Knoll, or by the ruins of Guillemont Farm and Willow Trench. Trying to get to them was impossible. There was nothing to do but to peer through the night and wonder how many of the boys out there in no-man's-land were still alive.

The cold facts were that on that entire day the division lost 262 officers and men killed, 537 wounded, 128 captured, and 80 reported missing. Of the 1,153 casualties, the 106th Infantry alone had suffered 910 killed, wounded, gassed, captured, or missing. A tally by Gillett showed that when his First Battalion entered the line, there had been about nine hundred men and ten officers. "We came out with four officers and less than a hundred men. Three Company Commanders were killed and one badly wounded."[23] He stated that he had been "comparatively safe and managed to reorganize what was left of the Battalion and bring it out." A similar count by Maslin recorded that before the battle, B Company of the 105th Infantry had 2 officers and 138 men. Two days later, only twelve men were left.[24]

O'Ryan had to have been stunned by the loss of men. In one telling moment, he stated, "No reports of the battle were made by company officers of the 2d Battalion after the battle for the reason that all of them had been killed or wounded." Yet he believed that if he could have been given the chance to launch a second attack with fresh troops from the Fifty-fourth Brigade, he would have successfully cleared the field of "fatigued German survivors of the day's battle and would have secured all points of resistance before they could have been secured by fresh German troops."

Unfortunately, Monash never issued such an order. Instead, he, too, was stunned. But not by the number of casualties. As a veteran of the slaughter on the western front, as well as at Gallipoli, he was inured to such awful numbers. Rather, he had counted on O'Ryan to capture the outpost line, and therefore had gone ahead with plans for the main attack on 29 September. "To await the result of the operation," he reasoned, "would have allowed insufficient time to complete the necessary maps and to distribute them before nightfall on September 28. There was no option but to assume that Gen. O'Ryan would succeed in capturing the northern section of the outpost line still in enemy hands and upon that assumption to fix the artillery 'start line' as falling east of that objective. For the first time I had to gamble on a chance."[25]

Afterward, Monash admitted that he was "considerably embarrassed" by O'Ryan's lack of success, especially the failure of his troops to "mop up" during the course of the battle. Mopping up was the key to consolidating gained ground—otherwise the Germans that had been passed over could then regroup behind the advancing Americans or jump from hidden tunnels, resume fighting, and catch their foe in a deadly cross fire.

Although he admired the "fine spirit" of American soldiers and their "magnificent individual bravery," he found them woefully lacking in "war experience, in training and in knowledge of technique. They had not yet learned the virtues of unquestioning obedience, of punctuality, of quick initiative, of anticipating the next action."

Now the Australian commander had another thing to fret about—the number of men still alive on the battlefield. "The knowledge that a number of American wounded were still lying out in front, and in suspicion that some of the American troops had succeeded in reaching Guillemont Farm, precluded any alteration of the artillery plans for September 29, even if there still had been time to do so without creating untold confusion," he wrote. "To have brought the artillery start line, proposed for September 29, back to the start line of September 27 would have brought our own barrage down upon these forward troops of ours."

The dilemma that faced Rawlinson was whether to lay down a creeping barrage on the 29th and risk slaughtering the wounded Americans still strewn over the battlefield or to let the 107th Infantry attack across this deadly killing ground in front of the Blue Line or of the strongholds of The Knoll, Guillemont Farm, Quennemont Farm, and Willow Trench, unprotected. Monash wanted to delay the main attack by a day—not for the humane evacuation of the wounded, but to gamble on yet another attack to take the Blue Line.

"I hastened to the Army Commander [Rawlinson] and suggested a postponement for a day to give this Division [Twenty-seventh], which had ample resources in troops, another opportunity of retrieving the position." (If, as O'Ryan had suggested, a second attack had been launched immediately on the heels of the heavy fighting of 27 September then in all likelihood the Americans would have captured all three strongholds and straightened out the start line.) Rawlinson rejected Monash's request for a day's delay. He explained that "it was too late to alter the programme because three whole Armies were committed to the date first appointed. He agreed that additional tanks, out of Army reserves, should be placed at my disposal so that I might allot them to the 27th to assist them in passing over the 1,000 yards which would bring them up level with the artillery barrage. I hoped that this would enable the Division to catch up with the southern half of the battle."[26]

As strange as it seems, however, Rawlinson had failed to warn Monash that the British had, in 1917, planted mines in the ground over which the 107th Infantry would make its charge. Each mine was now a potential death trap to tank crew and infantryman alike. Neither the Australians nor the Americans had any idea that such danger lurked on the field of battle. In fact, even the 106th and 105th Infantries had been ignorant of the presence of land mines when attacking the strongholds, although there was never any mention of casualties caused by the buried explosives. It was later believed that the tank that exploded and burned in front of Sergeant Waaler, the Medal of Honor winner, had rolled over a mine. And there was an added peril to go with the mines. For the first time in the war, Sir Douglas Haig had decided to use mustard gas. The lethal mixture, known as the "Yellow Cross," burned through clothing and skin, wiped out vision, and choked out life. More than thirty thousand rounds had been allotted for the attack on the 29th.

Meanwhile, with hundreds of wounded Americans still in no-man's-land, Monash and Rawlinson had not ruled out a creeping barrage that, if it were allowed to take place, would certainly roll over the defenseless troops. Meeting with O'Ryan for the last time before the big attack, Monash callously asked the American commander how he felt about subjecting his men who were sprawled between the Allies and the waiting Germans to a creeping barrage. There was no doubt many of them would be killed. But at least the fresh troops dashing forward would be protected. O'Ryan cringed. He believed that his boys still out there had every right to expect to be saved, even if it meant sacrificing some of the boys of the 107th Infantry. "To voluntarily assume the risk of destroying them [the wounded in no-man's-land] because of a decision to increase the security of the 54th Brigade, no matter how logical it might be in the tactical sense, would be repulsive to the mass of officers and men of the division, and destructive of morale."

He told Monash that there was to be no protective creeping barrage to cover the 107th Infantry. Capt. G. H. F. Nichols, whose British Eighteenth Division had been unable to advance the start line, remembered the decision not to use artillery protection—a decision, he later wrote, that "sealed the fate of the 27th American Division."[27]

What this decision meant was that all the Allied troops massed at the start line in front of Germany's main bulwark, including the Thirtieth Division on O'Ryan's right flank, would have the advantage of a creeping barrage the moment the attack set for the 29th was launched. Although artillery shells would rain down in front of the New Yorkers, the shells would be too far ahead of them to provide much protection. Instead, the 107th Infantry would have to across twelve hundred yards of proven impregnable defenses to catch up to the barrage. And Monash hadn't given the regiment much time to catch up.

"We were to have something like four minutes in which to catch up with our barrage before it started to move," growled Sgt. Harry Mitchell. "Fancy it! Twelve hundred yards in four minutes over a terrain that was literally pockmarked with shell holes, deep and shallow—and with nobody knew how many machine gun nests to put out of business as we went along. But it had to be done. After four minutes that curtain of exploding shells would start forward, jumping a hundred yards every four minutes and we all knew it was safer for the doughboy to be as close as possible to the barrage clearing the way for him." Once across, the 107th Infantry would join up with the other Allied troops on its flanks and push on over an additional five thousand yards—through the main Hindenburg Line—covering more ground than any Australian division had ever tried to cross in the entire war! And that seemed highly unlikely. If Pickett's charge at Gettysburg in the Civil War had proven to be folly then so, too, would the charge of the silk stocking soldiers.

"The task thus allotted to the [Twenty-seventh Division] by Monash was at least as great as any that he had ever set for Australian divisions, if not greater," C. E. W. Bean, the official Australian war correspondent, later argued. He then pointed out that as far as he was concerned, given the task handed to the 107th Infantry, the regiment never had a chance of success. "To its original task of penetration, 'deeper,' as Monash said, 'than we have ever had before,' there had since been added what surely no Australian divisional commander would have attempted—a preliminary advance of 1,200 yards against the Hindenburg Outpost-line without a barrage."[28]

CHAPTER 12

It Was an Awful Time

Throughout the night and early morning of 27 and 28 September, remnants of the 106th Infantry and the Third Battalion of the 105th staggered back to their own sheltering trenches, now occupied by troops from the Fifty-fourth Brigade. The men were blood-splattered, wounded, dazed, and dead tired. Behind them, the groans of the wounded and dying left on the battlefield sent a dreadful chill through the 107th. The soldiers knew that within twenty-four hours, it would be their turn to be out there fighting for their lives. In fact, as they had moved up to the front line, they were taunted by veterans of the British III Corps, assigned to protect their left flank. Their task was impossible, the Tommies had shouted. The only result was sure death.

The boys of the 107th were strung across a fifteen-hundred-yard front. Like rabbits, they hunkered down in muddy furrows that cut in front of the waiting Germans hidden deep in their concrete machine-gun nests. Every few hundred yards along this north-south slit scratched into the earth listening posts jutted into no-man's-land. The names of these listening posts held meaning to the hardened Australian and British soldiers, survivors of past battles on this scarred land. Soon they would mean something to the unseasoned Americans. Doleful Post and Duncan Post, which faced the ruins of Guillemont Farm; Egg Post; Lempire Post; Yak Post; and, in the extreme left flank, Fleeceall Post, which looked toward The Knoll. Near Pimple Post, Col. Charles L. DeBevoise had his makeshift regimental headquarters. Heaps of stones marked the ruins of once-prosperous farms. Sart Farm to the west of Doleful Post; Tombois Farm on the regiment's left flank, near Fleeceall Post; and atop the high ground in enemy territory, the German strongholds of Guillemont Farm and Quennemont Farm. Even the trenches bore names—Fag Trench, Causeway Lane, Island Traverse, and none more ominous, of course, than Willow Trench, which linked The Knoll to Guillemont Farm and was still in Boche hands. It was along Willow Trench, where Macquincourt Valley starts its run eastward toward the northern entrance of the canal tunnel, that the Allies had twice failed to capture Monash's coveted start line, and where in a last-ditch fight the 105th and 106th Regiments had just been beaten back. And one hundred yards east of Willow Trench ran Lone Tree Trench, another German bastion.

By four A.M. on the 28th, 749 officers and men of the First Battalion, led by Capt. Clinton E. Fisk, the son of the former commander of the old Seventh, had taken over the regiment's left flank, relieving the Third Battalion of the 105th Infantry. The trip up to the front was like New York City at rush hour. "A two-line road upon which four lines of traffic attempted to move," described Cpl. Ben Franklin of A Company. "Infantry moved up—column after column of them; artillery going forward, artillery of our bosom friends, the Australians; kitchens clattering along and empty caissons returning for ammunition—every possible inch of road space was in use, and yet there was no great confusion. The unity of purpose was too fixt in every man's mind."

Gen. Sir Henry Rawlinson's chief of staff chronicled that each day, from 26 September to 4 October, as many as fifteen supply trains had to be unloaded and that eventually over three million rounds of artillery ammunition were then "moved forward by lorries, which often as not, were delayed by the congestion of the roads."[1]

Sgt. Gerald F. Jacobson of the 107th was struck by the endless stream of ambulances that were working their way to the rear. He knew that inside were wounded soldiers of the 106th Infantry. "It was an impressive contrast," he thought, "on one side of the road a moving column of robust, normal fighting men in the pink of condition, and on the other side of the road an apparently interminable train of ambulances moving slowly to the rear with men who only a few hours before had been as these men now advancing toward the front—strong, virile, hopeful."

A cold drizzle fell on the soldiers as they hiked forward. "Penciling shafts of light from brilliant search-lights pierced the sky for the enemy's planes, the noise of which was quite prominent above the creaking of the gun limbers and the curses of the drivers," Franklin wrote.

His A Company was only five hundred yards away from its journey's end when a shell landed in its midst. Six men were killed and thirteen wounded. Cpl. Arthur Briggs Church was among the dead. A few hours earlier he had written to his aunt. "Keep up courage and don't you ever worry about me. I have been lucky so far and there is a lot of good campaign left in me yet."[2]

With hate now boiling in his heart, fellow A Company corporal Theis Roberts vowed that there was yet "another debt to be wiped out."[3]

Rising directly opposite the First Battalion's front was The Knoll. Here

Capt. Clinton Fisk, the son of the former
commander, led the First Battalion.
The Seventh Regiment Fund

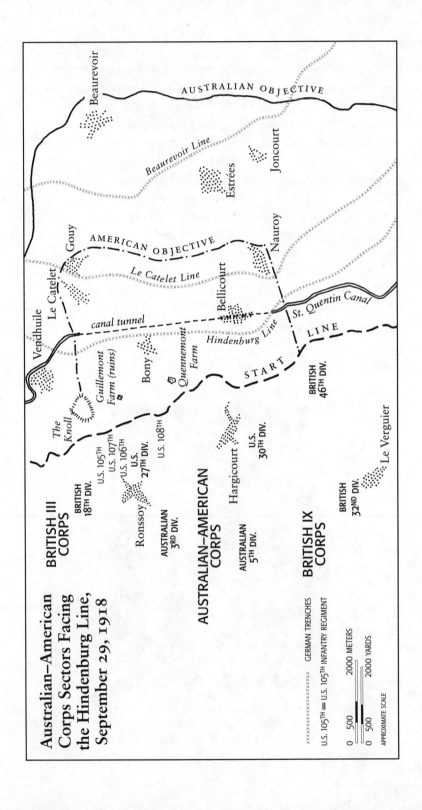

Australian–American Corps Sectors Facing the Hindenburg Line, September 29, 1918

Beaurevoir

AUSTRALIAN OBJECTIVE

Beaurevoir Line

Joncourt

Estrées

Gouy

Nauroy

AMERICAN OBJECTIVE

Le Catelet

Le Catelet Line

Bellicourt

Vendhuile

St. Quentin Canal

canal tunnel

Hindenburg Line

START

LINE

The Knoll

Guillemont Farm (ruins)

Bony

Quennemont Farm

Hargicourt

BRITISH 46TH DIV.

Le Verguier

U.S. 105TH

U.S. 107TH

U.S. 106TH

U.S. 27TH DIV.

U.S. 108TH

BRITISH 18TH DIV.

Ronssoy

AUSTRALIAN 3RD DIV.

U.S. 30TH DIV.

AUSTRALIAN 5TH DIV.

BRITISH 32ND DIV.

BRITISH III CORPS

AUSTRALIAN–AMERICAN CORPS

BRITISH IX CORPS

xxxxxxxxxxxxxxx GERMAN TRENCHES

U.S. 105TH = U.S. 105TH INFANTRY REGIMENT

2000 METERS

2000 YARDS

0   500

0   500

APPROXIMATE SCALE

Fisk positioned companies B and C along London Road and Fag Support Trench that ran south from Tombois Farm to Egg Post, a distance of about five hundred yards. B Company was in the hands of 1st Lt. Samuel Crump Jr., while 1st Lt. Ralph Polk Buell had responsibility for C Company. In support, just behind them, at Sart Lane, Fisk placed Companies A and D, under the charges of 1st Lts. Frederick D. Conklin and Thomas G. Simpson. He then set up battalion headquarters at Lempire Post.

In support of the First Battalion was the Machine Gun Company, about two hundred fifty men commanded by Capt. "Ham" Andrews. Because of the congested roads, the machine gunners trudged into the line much later than scheduled. They finally settled down after ten P.M. Although there were a lot of boys from the Utica area in Andrews's company, there was also that knot of close friends from Summit, known as the Jersey Gunners—Lts. Edward Willis, Kenneth Gow, and Paul Gadebusch; Cpls. Alan Eggers and Thomas O'Shea; and Pfc. John J. Mallay Jr. Back home, all but Eggers had sung in the choir of Calvary Episcopal Church.

Gow, in charge of the transport, knew he was not going to see his friends until after the battle. Gadebusch remembered that "Kenneth had brought up the limbers and came over to see me to say good-bye. It was in a sunken road almost on the very front line. Artillery were coming up into position, and both our men and the infantry were making their preparations for going over. The only light was the occasional flash of a burst shell. It was in this setting, amidst almost constant bombardment, that the finest friend a man could have came up to say good-bye."

According to O'Ryan, the First Battalion had the "hardest task imposed upon any unit in this great attack. Not only were they to advance against the open cut of the canal, between which and their start line lay that formidable position known as The Knoll, but they were to constitute the left flank guard of the division in its advance." Because the task was so dangerous, the division commander had decided to find enough able-bodied survivors from the 106th Infantry to pull together a regiment of five hundred to six hundred men that would follow Fisk's battalion through no-man's-land. The job of this piecemeal regiment was to mop up the enemy first and then assist in the capture of Vendhuile, the village near the northern terminus of the Green Line.

In the meantime, 754 officers and men of Raphael Egan's Third Battalion moved in on Fisk's right flank. On the way up, the soldiers passed

Capt. Rowland Tompkins, Second Battalion
commander, was an engineer in civilian life.
The Seventh Regiment Fund

a burning ammunition dump. Flames rose over two hundred feet. "The illumination made a dazzling scene and soon invited more fire from the Germans," wrote Sgt. Roy Beyerl of K Company.[4]

In front of the Third Battalion stood Guillemont Farm. Egan picked Duncan Post for his headquarters. Around Doleful Post, 1st Lt. Murray E. Cramer's M Company had ducked down into shell holes and trenches. To their south, K Company, commanded by Capt. George Bradish, had also dropped into shell holes and trenches. Companies I and L, led by 1st Lt. Percy M. Hall, at the very moment burning up with fever, and Capt. Fancher Nicoll, respectively, took up support at Sart Farm and Kent Lane.

"A few shallow shelters had been dug into the side of [Kent Lane]," recalled Sergeant Harry Mitchell, "but they were not nearly sufficient for the number of men there. So, except for the men on sentry, all hands huddled together in groups, like animals trying to keep one another warm. We didn't even have a blanket to wrap in."

K Company's Cpl. James Throckmorton Vought also remembered how crowded the trench was and that it was "rainy and no sleep was possible. No food could be brought up under the fire and we lived on the rations we were provided with."[5]

Sgt. Floyd Neely of I Company spotted small "tin bivvies" cut into the side of Kent Lane in which his men could climb into for a few hours' sleep. "Several of them [were] already occupied by dead Tommies," he later recalled, "as I found by kicking the feet of one poor chap and trying to waken him."[6]

Orders called for the Third Battalion to attack across Willow Trench, capture Guillemont Farm, and fight its way over the canal to the Green Line.

Capt. Rowland Tompkins's Second Battalion, 740 officers and men, went into support behind Egan's Third Battalion. E Company, commanded by Capt. Harry Hayward, found itself in Shamrock Trench, a long ditch that ran past Ronssoy. There he held a meeting with his noncommissioned officers. He gave them their final instructions. "It was the last time these men gathered together," Sgt. Nick Krayer recalled. "It was the last time many of these men saw their officers."[7] In Thistle Trench, Capt. George P. Nichols's F Company had settled down right behind Hayward's men. In another nearby earthen trough, named Rose Trench, huddled G Company, led by Capt. Marston E. Drake. And finally, 1st Lt. Arthur J. McKenna's H Company moved into Yak Post.

The Second Battalion, in support, was to follow the Third Battalion over the canal to the Green Line, mopping up the enemy.

On the right flank of the 107th, in front of Quennemont Farm, the 108th Infantry had also been readying itself for the coming attack. And further to the right the American Thirtieth Division had dug in as well.

Opposing the two U.S. divisions were four German divisions, roughly sixty thousand soldiers, although these divisions were certainly understrength. Thousands of the Germans, many of them crack Prussian Guards, were hidden inside the St. Quentin Canal Tunnel itself—deep enough where the pounding of artillery had no affect. Others were sheltered safely beneath the ground in camouflaged concrete pillboxes with rooms big enough to hold squads of machine gunners. A number of the rooms had subterranean passages that led back to the main tunnel. In the coming battle, no matter how many times the Americans might think they had mopped up, the enemy had plenty of reserves it could keep pouring out of the ground.

In total, eight German divisions faced the entire British Fourth Army, from the village of Tronquoy in the south all the way past Vendhuile in the north, a distance of about ten miles. Six more divisions were held in reserve.

And the freshest of all the German divisions was the Fifty-fourth. On The Knoll and Guillemont Farm and all the thousands of little concealed places in between, its deadly machine gunners trained their sights on the silk stocking soldiers.

There they waited. And watched.

Knowing there would be no creeping barrage to lead the assault, Brig. Gen. Palmer E. Pierce, commander of the Fifty-fourth Brigade, sent into no-man's-land on the 28th daylight patrols to probe the ground in front of his regiments. One mission was to advance the start line as far forward as possible. That meant eliminating all the machine-gun nests that stood in the way. Also, his men had no idea what was out there. Where, in fact, were the German machine-gun nests? How many? How thick was the barbed wire?

One soldier of the 107th had already been out all night, reconnoitering. First Battalion Intelligence Officer, 2d Lt. Oscar E. Hellquist, another Summit native, had not only checked German defenses, but he and his patrol guided wounded men from the 105th to safety. When the tired and dirty Hellquist slithered back into the trenches at four A.M., other patrols slipped out. Captain Bradish led one of the patrols. Some of the men with him were Sgts. George Ely and Philip Vosburgh; Cpls. Van Strycker Mills, Christopher C. Malone, Robert S. Raven, Lonny Scannell, and Buchanan Tyson; Pfc. James J. Page; and Pvts. Hugh J. V. Morrison and Edward G. Romaine. Weighted down with German potato-masher hand grenades, because they needed to save their own Mills grenades for the following day, the men lumbered from one shell hole to another. Instantly, they came under heavy attack. To their right, a patrol from M Company, commanded by 1st Lt. Carey Walrath, was stopped cold after advancing two hundred yards. Bradish's men pushed on, gaining three hundred yards. As they worked their way forward, machine-gun bullets whined and whistled and zinged past them, kicking up clods of earth. The closer they got to the Germans the worse the fire. Bullets struck Scannell. The Cornwall soldier dropped to the ground as if his legs had been yanked out from under him. Bob Raven also caught a bullet. He pitched backward, mortally wounded. Chris Malone was killed. Jim Page was killed. Ed Romaine fell, too, and died out in no-man's-land. Buck Tyson suffered severe wounds. Fourteen other men in the patrol were also wounded. Seeing his men shot up, Bradish ordered them to retreat. Phil Vosburgh wasn't about to follow orders. Instead, the Staten Island resident sprinted to the edge of a shell hole, where one of his comrades lay wounded. Machine-gun bullets ripped into his right thigh. One of them rocketed downward along the femur, tearing blood vessels and nerves. It then shattered his knee. As he toppled into the shell hole, Vosburgh still had the presence of mind to drag his comrade in with him, saving his life.[8]

When the survivors of the shot-up patrol at last scrambled back into their own trenches, they knew they had to go right back out into no-man's-land. They weren't about to leave their wounded among the Germans. Sergeant Ely, Corporal Mills, Pfc. Roger "Monty" Montgomery (a cashier for the Seaboard National Bank in Manhattan and cousin of B Company's Bill Breck, the illustrator of the "Dere Mable" letters) and Pvt. Hugh Morrison from Poughkeepsie volunteered to bring them in. Back out they went, lugging a single stretcher. When they reached Scannell, he begged them to help the others first, even though he was badly hurt himself. Back in the ranks of K Company, his brother John watched nervously. He had lost one brother a few years earlier in a sledding accident. He didn't want to lose another.[9]

The Germans hounded the rescuers with unrelenting machine-gun fire, bombs, and gas grenades. One by one the wounded men were brought in. Monty was the first to reach Vosburgh. "He looked after me like a mother looks after her child," Vosburgh later wrote. "He emptied my pack and stuffed all sorts of things into my pockets. I was not much interested in that at that time but he insisted, 'Oh, you'll need them all right when you get to the hospital.' And later on I was indeed glad to have them." The last time Vosburgh saw Monty, he was peering over the parapet. As stretcher bearers carried Vosburgh away, Monty waved. "Good luck," he said, "and a pleasant trip to Blighty." Vosburgh's knee was so horribly shattered that later his leg had to be amputated. "Four hours from the time I was hit I was on the [operating] table. Of course, the leg had to come off just above the knee." He predicted that with luck he would be home by Christmas with his "cork leg" and that "as for the leg you'll never notice it." For his heroism that day, he won the American Distinguished Service Cross.

Carrying a soldier back behind the lines, Mills inhaled gas. It nearly crippled him. But he pushed on and reached the security of the trenches. Morrison personally got four men to safety, and later received the Distinguished Service Cross. When Scannell arrived on a stretcher, after waiting four hours in no-man's-land, his brother was there to meet him. Night had fallen. John bent over Lonny, and his brother whispered to him what had happened. Oh, what heroism, thought John. It will never be surpassed. He then took Lonny personally to a first-aid station. Afterward, he sent a letter to his aunt in Cornwall. "I cannot tell you what the outcome will be," he warned, "but I am in great hopes of his recovery, brave and clean-lived—that's what counts in a situation of this kind." Three days later, while John battled the Germans along the Hindenburg Line, Lonny, who had enlisted in the Seventh in 1916 and had served on the Mexican border, died of his wounds. He was twenty-two.[10]

Harold Mills wrote in his diary that night, "Patrol goes out. Bob Raven, Page, Romaine & Malone are killed. Tyson and Valles wounded & others. Shell drops on trench 1 ft. from my head. Sitting under an iron strip. Completely buried." He did not mention his brother's bravery for which he earned a divisional citation.

Pfc. Phillip C. Jessup, who was spared going out on patrol, later looked back and commented, "Our battalion lost a number of men on a useless patrol in the afternoon, but the other companies suffered only from shell fire, which was constant. The hill opposite us bristled with machine gun nests, some of which we located through the glasses and put out of action."[11]

In his diary, George Ely commented on the difficulty of the patrol and the rescue afterward. "I was out in a post with four men some 400 yards beyond our lines until 4 A.M. Sunday morning trying to locate the wounded, who couldn't get back, and the dead. It was an awful time. I was short men, had only one stretcher and there were Jerry patrols out. It was ticklish. When I got back I was told we went over at 5:50 A.M."

While Bradish's patrol had slipped into no-man's-land on the morning of the 28th, back behind the lines at Villers Faucon, Maj. Gen. John O'Ryan paid a visit to what was left of his 106th Infantry. He felt that if he was to crack the Hindenburg Line, he needed at least one able-bodied battalion from this regiment to support the 107th Infantry. Col. William A. Taylor had his battered and bloodied boys assembled by the time O'Ryan arrived. "The prospect of organizing an effective battalion looked at first most unpromising," O'Ryan wrote. What he encountered that morning were mud-splattered, blood-encrusted soldiers sprawled or stretched over the ground, many of them in a "stupor of sleep." He saw that that those not sleeping suffered from shell shock. The strain of their fight showed visibly in their faces. "They presented an appearance that would have appealed to the sympathy and indulgence of almost any heart," O'Ryan recollected. "They were silent men. But in spite of their apparent exhaustion the faces of most of them . . . wore looks of inquiry mixed with surprise." The general sensed that "these men had done all that men should be called upon to do, and that they suspected that some additional and impossible demand was now to be made upon them." They were right. They were needed the next day to follow the Fifty-fourth Brigade, to mop up. The moment O'Ryan told them what he wanted, he realized that the fight had gone out of them. He had to say something that would win them over, to persuade them to go over the top one more time.

"Men, you must not forget that scattered about in the fields around The Knoll, Guillemont Farm and Quennemont Farm are numbers of your pals still lying there wounded," he said. "You don't propose to abandon them do you? I think not; not even to the willingness of the 54th Brigade to look after them. You are going to get them yourselves. One other thing. If I know the 106th Infantry they will do even more than that. They will mop up in such manner that their work will leave nothing to be desired by the comrades lost in the attack yesterday." Then O'Ryan picked out one of the biggest soldiers. "How about you?" he said. "Do you prefer to hang around here and sleep, or will you be one of those to get out behind the 107th and tear things up?"

All eyes turned to the soldier.

As tired and bloody as he was, the soldier faced his commanding officer. He told him that he had killed plenty of Germans, but that his job was not yet done. He promised to follow the 107th or go "anywhere else to get another crack at the Hun."[12]

The men had been won over. Maj. Ransom Hooker Gillett was placed in command of the provisional battalion, and ordered it to get ready for the main attack on Hindenburg Line.

That very noon Lt. Gen. Sir John Monash lunched with Australia's official war correspondent C. E. W. "Charles" Bean, W. E. Berry of the *Times of London,* and Sir Arthur Conan Doyle, the creator of Sherlock Holmes. He explained the nature of the attack to the two newspapermen and the famous author. When he was finished, he had obviously impressed Berry. To his readers, Berry reported that the Australian "gives you at once the idea that efficiency is the keynote of the success with which his troops have engaged the enemy." He also pointed out that the Australian had a "keen sense of humor," adding that everywhere within Monash's headquarters, there was "a cheery optimism, not only as to the immediate objective, but as to the future generally." Monash, he wrote, was "the idol of those brought into close contact with him."[13]

Bean did not share Berry's seeming adoration of the general. He even came away with a different view of the "cheery optimism" in the Australian camp as described by Berry. Bean stated that Monash's narrative of the coming attack was "as usual, an absorbingly interesting account," mainly because he, Monash, found it necessary to "talk like Alexander the Great—to be painted among bursting shells and dead men's helmets and to spout grandiloquent phrases about the bayonet and the front line."[14] In fact, Bean had the impression that Monash doubted the Americans would succeed. "It struck all of us that John was hedging against a possible defeat in which case he would be able to throw the blame onto the Americans."

For the day of the attack, Monash, despite his possible misgivings about the Americans, gave permission to Bean, Berry, and Conan Doyle to get as close to the battle as they could. This thrilled Berry especially, because not only was he in the company of the legendary novelist, but he was to go forward with Bean, who had already established himself as a legendary war correspondent. "Bean," Berry said, "is a man whose faith holds very strongly to the accuracy of the proverb that 'seeing is believing,' and appears to roam battlefields as a countryman does his fields."[15]

CHAPTER 13

How in God's Name
Can Anyone Live in This?

St. Michael the Archangel, defend us in battle; be our safeguard
against the wickedness and snares of the devil. May God rebuke him,
we humbly pray. And do you, O prince of the heavenly host,
by the power of God, cast into Hell Satan and all the evil spirits
who prowl about the world seeking the ruin of souls? Amen.

—*St. Michael the Archangel Prayer*

Sunday morning, 29 September. The day that was to turn out to be
the bloodiest for a United States regiment in any war[1] dawned in
irony. It was the day that Christians celebrate the Feast of St. Michael the Archangel—God's champion who drove Satan out of Heaven.
For the men of the 107th Infantry, the army of Satan was a few hundred
yards away, barricaded behind one of the strongest defenses ever designed. And like St. Michael, the resolve of the silk stocking soldiers was
to drive this evil army out of France.

Throughout the miserable, cold, damp night, they had readied themselves for the assault on the Hindenburg Line. Watches and compasses
were rechecked. The men were to head on a bearing of eighty-five degrees northeast. A number of the boys gave their rifles a last cleaning,
wiping the bolt mechanisms with oily rags. Sgt. John C. Latham, the horticulturist from Windmere, England, who would much rather have had

his fingers dirtied by potted soil than gun oil, recalled how the men in his Machine Gun Company constantly "took their guns apart, oiling them and cleaning them."[2] Iron rations were distributed along with grenades and extra ammunition. Cpl. Ben Franklin stated that each man was handed three grenades and two extra bandoliers of rifle ammunition.[3] Shovels and picks were given out so that once the men reached their destinations they could dig in against counterattacks. Officers made certain that everyone had their first-aid packets.

At midnight, stew was brought up in large covered pails—a last meal for many of them. Mess Sergeant Harmon Vedder, who had enlisted in the Seventh in 1916 while a sophomore at Columbia University, dodged enemy shells all night long to bring stew to his own men in K Company. His younger brother, James, was one of the company's machine gunners. Latham felt that the "soup kitchens served extra large portions on the theory that we might not get another square meal for several days."[4] For some the stew was impossible to eat, particularly for the men of L Company. A gas shell had exploded near them. Sneezing and wiping tears from their eyes, they dropped their mess tins and donned gas masks. When they thought it was clear, the masks came off and they started to eat again. Then another cloud of gas floated over them. Masks were pulled over their heads again. "For half an hour we were so annoyed and when we turned again to our stew we found that it had changed from a steaming delicacy to a thick greasy mass that served to only fill a void," chronicled Sgt. Harry Mitchell. "You could have almost made candles out of it."

After supping on stew, most of the men then tried to sleep amid the constant pounding of artillery. While they dozed, patrols laid down white tape marking the start line in front of the First and Third Battalions.

Father Peter Hoey, the Catholic chaplain, set up a little altar. More than one thousand soldiers "received the Saviour's most precious gift," he stated, and those who later perished in the fight "died with the Blood of Jesus still fresh upon his lips."[5]

Toward dawn, the artillery quieted down. Once in awhile, a shell exploded nearby. Because it was night, Sgt. Jerry Stanton of I Company found the sound of those shells deceptive. "The shriek and burst of shells comes from you know not where. They may be bursting a mile away, but to you it seems out in the back yard." An occasional shell flare also lit the sky. To keep the Americans on edge, German machine gunners intermittently fired off a round or two. In the meantime, the grinding clatter of armored vehicles shook the ground as the 301st American Tank Battalion rumbled slowly toward the front. To muffle the noise of the advancing tanks, scores of airplanes buzzed about in the sky—now and then dropping a bomb on the Boche trenches.

Last-minute meetings were held between officers and their noncommissioned officers. They went over final instructions for the attack. In most instances, companies were down to only two officers. Sgt. Mitchell commented that Capt. Fancher Nicoll and Lt. Robert A. Byrns were the only officers left in L Company. "Lieutenant [Alfred] Schimpf had long since been detached to manage the Third Battalion transport and Lieutenant [Allen] Reagan was away at some specialty school." Sgt. C. Edgar Burton pointed out, "We had but one officer with our [A] Company, and I had command of the second half of the Company when we went over."

As earlier noted, the lack of officers bothered Nicoll. To go into battle so badly understaffed was a grievous blunder. And compounding this error, too many sergeants had also been pulled from the ranks, to be sent to officers' candidate schools.

Abetting the shortage of officers, fever had dulled the body and quick wit of the commander of I Company, 1st Lt. Percy Hall from Montclair, New Jersey. A veteran of the Seventh since 1908, he spent the night shivering beneath a blanket in a dugout in Kent Lane. Claude Leland urged him not to go forward with his men. "[His] cold had grown worse," Leland recalled. "He had a high temperature. I did my best to get him to go back to Regimental and let the doctors fix him up. . . . He laughed in his usual way at my efforts to find excuses for him and, though he was undoubtedly depressed at the thought of taking the company into a fight while he was in such a wretched physical condition, there was little outward indication of it. He was the same old Perce, with a smile and a sarcastic jibe at the world in general."

Perhaps it was Hall's illness, but according to Lt. Francis Gould, the lieutenant had a premonition that he would not come back from France, much like Nicoll. "He was not morbid about this," Gould stated, "and probably very few people knew of it. However, the idea was firmly fixed in his mind."[6]

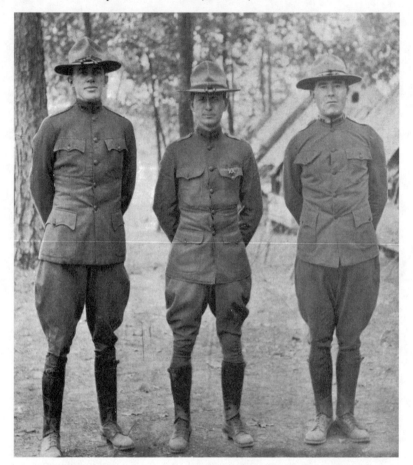

*I Company comrades: Lt. Percy Hall (left), who led the company after
Capt. Wade Hampton Hayes (center) was assigned to General Pershing's staff.
The other man is Lt. Francis Gould.*   The Seventh Regiment Fund

Hall and Nicoll were not the only officers in the 107th who sensed that
in France their days were numbered. B Company's 1st Lt. Samuel Crump
Jr., a former Poughkeepsie newspaper reporter, had that night written to
his mother in Verona, New Jersey. He told her that he did not expect to return from the battle alive, yet he was not afraid to die.[7] It was the same
kind of message that Kenneth Gow had sent to his parents the week before. He even repeated it in a letter he had just finished writing to a friend,
Walter, in Summit, dated 28 September. "If I'm destined to go, it is for a

cause worth a dozen lives. My best to the family, Walter, and my keen appreciation of a friendship which has been an honor."

If the enlisted men had any premonitions about death, they kept it to themselves for the most part, not wishing to burden the folks back home. An example was the letter Bert Lobdell sent his sister, assuring her that when he got back home he would tell her about his experiences, and "you will see how very useless and foolish any anxiety, for my welfare was. Honest and truly, the greatest part of the time I'm having a fine time."

Sgt. Richard Dean Hamilton of the Machine Gun Company boasted to his mother in Mount Vernon, "No German will ever get me alive, nor will he get my gun!"[8]

Cpl. Alan Eggers "woke up cold and for minute I had a sickening feeling as I realized what we were about to do, but almost immediately we heard our barrage start and then got the order to go over."[9]

Pvt. G. Carroll Coll of I Company handed his family Bible to his supply sergeant, Tyler Johnson, with the request that if something happened to him to make certain it was returned to his aunt in Dorchester, Massachusetts. The Bible had been given to his grandfather, Michael Coll, an orderly in the Sixty-ninth Infantry by its commander, Col. Michael Corcoran, in 1861 when the Irish Regiment left New York City to fight in the Civil War. Coll had then carried the Bible with him in every battle the Sixty-ninth fought. Now his grandson did not want to lose the Bible—if he should fall in battle in the Great War.

In contrast, several of Coll's companions in I Company kept their Bibles with them. Cpl. Harold Kunkle, the young illustrator from Brooklyn, slipped his inside his tunic. And so did Pvt. George Fetherolf. That night he scribbled in his diary: "Read the 91st psalm and feel secure for the ordeal ahead."

Around four-thirty, in the predawn dark, the First and Third Battalions were ordered up to the start line. Support companies moved up behind them. Also moving up were the 105th Infantry, which was to help defend the 107th's left flank, and the provisional 106th Infantry of fewer than four hundred men, which was to mop up behind the Second and Third Battalions and to bring back the wounded. Also in support was the 105th Machine Gun Battalion. Maj. Kenneth Gardner, a Manhattan lawyer who had been with the Seventh since 1907, was now in command of the machine gunners.

Clutching their British Enfield rifles, the first wave of assault troops crept toward the stark white tape. Grenades bounced quietly against their bodies. Gas masks rested on their chests, in the alert position. They carried a day's ration of food. Some of the boys slipped into shell holes. Across no-man's-land, Germans opened sporadic artillery and machine-gun barrages. Very lights soared overhead, illuminating the moonlike landscape. Hundreds of craters and trenches pocked the ground. Barbed-wire entanglements looped and twisted every which way, sharp-edged, rusty tentacles ready to ensnare the Americans. On the division's extreme left flank, B Company, First Battalion, lined up at the tape, five yards between each man. Lieutenant Crump walked among his Greyjackets, encouraging them, giving his platoon leaders last minute instructions. Behind them, A Company slid into place. "We lay 20 yards behind Company B in a line of squad groups," wrote Cpl. Theis Roberts. "Everything quiet except an occasional shell or star-flare."[10]

Further back in support, the Machine Gun Company spread itself over a width of a hundred yards. On the right flank, 1st Lt. Paul Gadebusch readied his first platoon. In a letter to his father, he described how his men were spread out along the road and how he had to "walk continuously from end to end to see that all are ready, that all keep down until the final moment."[11] In the center, 1st Lt. Harry Adsit from Buffalo commanded the second platoon. Adsit carried a cane, and with a big cigar clenched between his teeth and his square jaw jutting heroically forward, Sgt. Clarence E. Gurley from Rome, New York, boasted, "Who wouldn't follow him."[12] Covering the left flank and rear, 1st Lt. Edward Willis, the nephew of the mayor of Summit, had charge of the third platoon. Stationed to the right of Adsit's platoon was company commander Ham Andrews and his staff, including 1st Sgt. Charles Veitch from New York Mills, and four stretcher bearers carrying only two stretchers between them. Meanwhile, twelve men from H Company, Second Battalion, had been assigned to the Machine Gun Company as ammunition carriers. Each soldier was then attached to one of the undermanned machine-gun squads.[13] The task of Gow, company supply officer, was to keep mules packed with rations and then to continually lead them up to the front.

The moment the men of the 107th Infantry got into place, the cold whipped against them like a March wind blowing off the Hudson River. Reported Cpl. Charles S. Lloyd Sell, "We lined up behind the crest of a hill, hidden from the Hun and nearly froze to death, waiting patiently for the zero hour." Franklin never forgot how the "cold cut through to our marrow." He wrote later, "Taking it all in, it was a perfect setting for the hell that was to follow."[14] Fetherolf felt the "cold damp fog, and that with the nervous tension made me shake like a leaf. About then a fellow begins to wonder how he is going to make out and is having a nice little scrap with himself trying to be convinced that he is (or isn't) a bit scared."

On the way to the start line, Cpl. Harry A. Burke of H Company was surprised to see the road "full of dead men and horses, broken wagons and shell holes." He remembered, too, how the shells dropped all around his company. "You would think that the men would be a little frightened and nervous those last few moments, knowing that their chances were as good as 50–50, considering the proposition that was before them. . . . It was surprising to see how cool the men were, getting into position just as though they were at drill." In fact, one shell hit nearby, killing a number of soldiers. Another corporal in H Company told how the "shrieks and moans of the wounded chilled my nerves to a standstill—it was odd to me to feel a less degree of apprehension coming over me. All I wanted was to get going where I could kill something."

In the Third Battalion, L Company dropped into shell holes, grateful for the refuge, according to Mitchell, "and then [we] began the trying wait for the signal to attack. We were to move forward simultaneously with the first roar of our barrage."

Next to L Company, I Company was having difficulty getting to the start line. The great hulk of Raphael Egan appeared out of the dark. He told Leland to hurry up and follow him and an Australian intelligence officer attached to the battalion. They hastened over four hundred yards of land that dipped toward the east, the Australian hunting as they went for strips of white paper that he had put down as a guide. Finally, he stopped.

"This is the left of the battalion line," he informed the platoon officer. "Look out for the troops on your left!" And then he disappeared into the night. Leland brought up his platoon as quickly as he could.

It was now almost five-fifty—zero hour!

"In the mirk and mire and waxy mud of a cold dark September morning, everything is ready again," wrote Col. Franklin Ward. "Artillerymen are tightening their short lanyards, machine gunners have their fingers on the triggers, tank pilots are ready to roll and the doughboys toe the tape!"[15]

"Things were still quiet as the gray dawn of early morning was becoming evident," wrote Ham Andrews. "As dawn and zero hour approached the light became brighter, when finally word was passed around that the men could smoke, there being no further danger of detection through the lights showing, and every one availed themselves of this opportunity."[16]

Then a long ribbon of red sunlight appeared across the eastern sky.

"Ever so gradually," Mitchell said, "our eyes began to make out dimly certain objects on the landscape ahead of us."

In the dawn's faint light, the men saw a heavy mist draped over the frosty, sodden ground in front them—ready to swallow them up. Another obstacle in the way.

"One moment all was silent except the whispered mutterings of commands passed back and forth along the line of waiting men," Franklin recounted. "The next moment it seemed as if the fury of hell was let loose."[17] Pvt. Albert Ingalls of C Company recalled that at first "a single gun barked; then another; then a thousand."[18]

Behind the Twenty-seventh and Thirtieth Divisions, British and Australian artillery units went to work. Twenty-three brigades of field artillery, ten heavy brigades and five siege batteries opened up a fierce bombardment on the German defenses that shook the ground along the front like an apocalyptic earthquake. Eight hundred eighteen guns and howitzers sent steel shooting over the heads of the Americans. In the case of the New Yorkers, the shells landed more than a thousand yards ahead of them. If they were to break through the Hindenburg Line they had to catch up to those shells and then, using them as a shield, follow them over the tunnel canal to their objective—the long Green Line, looping just beyond the villages of Gouy, Le Catelet, and Vendhuile. The British general, Sir Archibald Montgomery, wrote, "The guns continued relentlessly battering the enemy's positions, and above the noise of the guns could be heard the drone of the tank engines moving forward in the darkness over the slippery ground. Persistent and distinct from the gunfire, and not unlike the drone of the tank engines, was the rhythmic throb of the aeroplanes patrolling overhead. Occasionally these dropped a bomb on the enemy's trenches."[19]

To Mitchell, the heavy bombardment created a "soul-shaking roar, sounding for all the world like the crack of doom . . . shrieking like ten thousand mad women."

"The moment," he said, "had come."

Captain Nicoll leaped to his feet, a wooden walking stick grasped in his hand. With it, he signaled his L Company men to follow him. Just over the head of the doughboys, machine-gun bullets from their own men streamed past them toward the entrenched Germans. "Like an echo to that opening crash of our barrage old Jerry's artillery swung into action, and now that we were under way his shells were splashing round us fast and furious," Mitchell wrote. "His machine guns were spitting hate and death squarely into our faces, and as we pressed on we noticed curiously the vast number of rockets that were sputtering skyward over his lines, signals no doubt to his artillery."

I Company had just gotten into place when the attack started. Leland, a cane in his hand, was still dispersing his platoon at five-pace intervals. Sgt. Washington Irving Clayton, one of the heroes in Flanders, stood next to him when "all the great guns on earth and all the shrieking little ones broke into a perfect inferno of a barrage. We're off! Pass the word to keep interval!" Lieutenant Hall could hardly stand, his body racked with fever. The sudden blast from a shell knocked him backward. It took only a moment for him to recover from the shock. Then he staggered forward, leading his men up the first rise toward Guillemont Farm, with Leland off to his left doing the same. German flares lit the sky and his "green over green S.O.S. flares" were already warning the troops back in the canal tunnel to get ready to counterattack. The Boche scurried through their maze of underground grottos, bolted up concrete steps that led to the surface—set to pour out of the ground like killer ants and catch the Americans in a cross fire.

Ahead of I Company, the boys from K started their charge. The millionaires' sons from Manhattan were now mixed in with the appleknockers from upstate. "I'll never forget the noise in all my life," Pvt. Oakley Rhinelander penned to his father on Fifth Avenue. "It was a wonderful sight to see our battalion advance in the dawn."[20] Oakley's company commander, Capt. George B. Bradish, said that his men had started "swinging along light-heartedly, stopping a moment to light a cigarette and then running to regain their places, bantering with each other, singing snatches of old familiar tunes. They seemed to scorn the shells that screeched overhead or burst in their very midst."[21]

Over in L Company, Mitchell claimed that he "saw mere boys pause out there in the midst of that inferno, casually light a cigarette and then go on with no more outward show of agitation than a baseball fan hurrying on his way to the Polo grounds."

To the left, the First Battalion rose up. "All right, boys!" yelled Lt. Crump of B Company, "Let's go!"

Behind them, A Company stood, cheering. Before they followed the first wave, the men who smoked, like those in K Company, lit their cigarettes. Then they all took off, shouting, "Mineola! Mineola!" They did not run. Instead, as Franklin described, "Slowly we advanced at a leisurely walk."

Cpl. Merritt Cutler of I Company, another of the old Seventh's cadre of artists and illustrators who, along with Corporal Kunkle, had signed Andrée's autograph book back in Beauquesne, said, "Walking at a very slow pace—my what a sensation—I felt cold all over and very weak, particularly around the vicinity of my knees, but then I saw 'Jerry's' head sticking over the parapet in front and forgot everything but the desire to smash one or more of them."

Regimental Supply Sgt. Gerald F. Jacobson watched the attack from the rear. "The entire regiment promptly moved forward, some of the men cheering," he later wrote. "The interval between the men was regular—the attacking waves straight and steady. All moved forward at a fast walk."

"What a sight," recalled Pvt. Harold W. Simmons, also from regimental headquarters. "It was just starting to get light. We got over about a hundred yards before we saw the first Huns."

The sight before him also impressed Alan Eggers. "There was a slight rise in front of us, and as we started up at a walk it was just light with a mist over everything. I could see our own infantry advancing in wave formation in front of me, and over the hill I could see all different colored lights and rockets going up from Fritz's lines. These were his S.O.S. signals calling for a counter barrage to protect him. Almost immediately his machine guns opened fire on us, and the fire increased as we went on."[22]

And Leland, urging his men forward, looked off to his right and watched in awe as "four long waves of the old regiment, which the 'knockers' of New York said would never go over the top—went to its death as steadily and beautifully as it ever marched up the [Fifth] Avenue on parade." He told his family that no man in his outfit hesitated—clerks, orderlies, runners, adjutants, from the poorest soldier to the snappiest sergeant—all took their medicine. "On they went over the first hill and down into the valley, with no tanks ahead of them and no barrage to prepare the way."

From the start line to the strongholds of The Knoll and Guillemont Farm, the First and Third Battalions had to traverse one thousand yards of pitted land and barbed wire, where not a twig of vegetation had been left alive. When the regiment started off, most of the enemy's machine-gun nests were too far back to be knocked out. Trying to reach them was a bloody nuisance. Meanwhile, any Germans hidden between the Americans and the strongholds either surrendered or were bayoneted.

With the aid of fifteen tanks from the 301st American Tank Battalion, attached to the British Fourth Brigade, to plow ahead of them, the early going had not met with much resistance. The tanks ripped apart the barbed-wire barricades, opening gaps through which slipped the New Yorkers. The tanks also tried to take out enemy machine-gun nests and light artillery. Eggers wrote, "As we advanced we could see the tanks ploughing along ahead, and cutting the barbed wire and firing into the Germans."[23] However, as the tanks pushed forward, they soon ran into trouble. B Company Pvt. Constantine C. Roeder saw three tanks "put out of action immediately, one of them breaking open just like an egg." Because he, the entire regiment, and especially the tank crews had no idea the battlefield had been laced with forgotten British mines, he believed "Jerry had the place mined and as the monster machines came over— 'Blooey' they went up in the air."

"Our tanks were in advance," reported Pvt. Edgar C. Sharp of C

Company, "and before they covered 500 yards all but one had been smashed. So we 'carried on' without them."

Five tanks never made it past the start line. Because of the fog, several tanks drove into shell holes and were ditched. Only two tanks made a true fight of it, one of them commanded by 2d Lt. Earl Dunning who believed that a black cat, found the night before in the woods where the tanks had been hidden from German airplanes, had actually brought his crew good luck. Dunning was right. Only his tank survived to pierce the Hindenburg Line, reaching the village of Le Catelet.[24]

But in the meantime, without the creeping barrage and now without tanks, the regiment was left exposed in the open like jacked deer caught in the glare light of a hunter. As Pfc. Phillip C. Jessup of K Company put it, "When we reached the crest of the hill we formed clear targets against the dawn, and few crossed the ridge with the first wave."

Although the fight had quickly broken down into a wild free-for-all of point-blank pistol and rifle fire and hand-to-hand bayonet duels, the Knoll and Guillemont Farm were now within reach. And so were the hundreds of sheltered machine-gun nests, swarming with Huns. The barrage from these experts in the art of rapid fire, where six hundred rounds per minute spit forth like a torrential thunderstorm, momentarily stopped the regiment in its tracks. The soldiers hid in shell holes as bullets rained over their heads.

In the First Battalion, Lt. Ralph Polk Buell of C Company decided to charge The Knoll virtually single-handedly. He had already led his men forward, but at a faster pace. Within moments, he was thirty yards ahead of them. Alone, the veteran of the Spanish-American War, New York lawyer, and Princeton graduate stood with an automatic pistol in one hand and yelled at C Company to follow him. He knew that if he faltered now his whole company might not get going again. Frantically, he opened a path in the wire entanglement while straight in front of him an enemy machine-gun crew, secured in a trench, attempted to take him out. To his left, more machine gunners fired at him. Hundreds of bullets zinged past his head. Behind him, several squads from C Company, led by Sgts. Gilbert C. Clark, Thomas W. O'Connor, and John W. Schwegler, reached the cut wire. Their arrival diverted the fire of the Germans, allowing Buell time to scramble up to the first trench. Standing on the edge of the parapet, he fired down into a swarm of Germans. But he had hardly pulled the trigger of his pistol when Boche machine gun bullets finally found their target. Buell's men saw him spin around like a top and fall. Doggedly they pressed forward and in a fierce firefight destroyed the machine-gun nest. All three sergeants suffered severe wounds. The survivors of the fight pressed on, believing Buell had been killed. They left their company commander where he had fallen.[25]

In that fight, an explosive bullet struck a grenade that Cpl. Morris Bannister from Newburgh had put in his pocket. "The bomb didn't explode," he wrote to the mother of fellow Cpl. Edwin Standring, who was killed only moments later, "but the bullet did. The concussion was right on my hip bone that it stunned me for a moment. I dropped to my knees and I yelled to Ed and Roy [Bettes] that I was hit. They stopped to assist me but I told them to get what shelter they could. Machine gun bullets and shrapnel were flying around. I took shelter in a shell hole for a minute to get my wind. Ed and Roy never made the next trench. Ed was killed. Providence sparing him all pain."[26]

B Company crossed the first trench in front of The Knoll and moved unwavering toward the second. In front of Ben Franklin, a German officer jumped up, blood-smeared and with one arm hanging uselessly by his side. But the other arm was raised at Franklin and the young corporal found himself looking into the barrel of an automatic pistol. "To be truthful," Franklin recalled, "his appearance had been so sudden that my heart jumped into my mouth and it seemed as if I was powerless to move for the fraction of a second—an eternity in the mat[t]er of life and death." Franklin spotted an Iron Cross around the Hun's neck. In that instant, he fired from the hip. The hero of the German army went down. Six more Germans appeared, yelling, "Kamerad! Kamerad!" One of them dangled a gold watch and chain, an offering to spare his life. Another threw money at the American. Franklin sent them to the rear, as prisoners of war. He then reloaded his rifle, wondering all the time how come the dirt in front of him was kicking up earth clods. Then out of the din of battle, he swore he heard three distinct shots. "Crack! Crack! Crack!" Next, he felt the pain. He had been hit in the shoulder, above the right eye, and in the left cheek. He sank to the ground, certain he was dead.

"My pal, Hunter Leaf, jumped over to me, and at the risk of his own life, pulled me into a shell-hole, where he bandaged my face and made me comfortable." Leaf left Franklin there and continued forward. Franklin passed out for a few minutes. The trembling earth and a grinding noise shook him awake. Bearing down on him was a tank. With all his strength, Franklin raised up his right leg and waved it back and forth. "It was impossible for me to move my body back and forth, the loss of blood having weakened me to such an extent, and I shut my eyes in terror, expecting to feel the cold steel on my skull." The tank swerved to the left. As it rolled along the edge of the shell hole, the tank loosened enough dirt to partially bury the wounded soldier.[27]

The ground fog had not let up. In fact, with all manner of shells exploding all around, particularly smoke bombs, the regiment was virtually lost in a cloud so thick that Captain Andrews remarked that it was "very difficult to see even our own men at a greater distance than ten yards." In some instances, soldiers got disoriented.[28]

"I could not see three yards about me as a very dense smoke screen had been laid," described A Company's Sergeant Burton. He had just been hit as he bolted from a shell hole, running sideways toward a trench. An explosive bullet blew through the upper part of his right arm and into his shoulder blade and then exited his back. Burton thought the wound lucky. If he had been running forward, he believed the bullet would have killed him. He knew he had been shot because his arm went numb.

One of the corporals in Burton's company, Charles S. Lloyd Sell, found that he and his squad, now down to four men, had become separated from the rest of A Company in the dense fog. That meant that he was also out of touch with his brother, Edward, a private in the same company. Sell ordered his men into a trench in front of The Knoll. He checked his compass, discovering that he had been moving forward at a seventy-degree angle, not the eighty-five-degree angle calculated by Monash's tacticians as the route the regiment had to follow to reach the Green Line. He quickly made the adjustment and moved on, all the time repeating to himself, "Tho' I walk through the valley of the shadow of death I shall fear no evil, for Thou art with me."

While B and C Companies led the assault, D Company had the crucial task to protect the left flank of the battalion. In support of D Company, the British Eighteenth Division, which a week earlier had failed to nail down the start line, was also charged with covering the battalion's left flank. Its assignment was to thwart the Germans from hitting the Americans with enfilading machine-gun fire and to mop up. The British soldiers had been told to keep pace with the advancing U.S. troops all the way to the canal. However, action of the British III Corps, according to General Montgomery, was "entirely dependent on the progress of the battle on its right . . . with the object of securing the left flank of the enemy. It was not to undertake a general attack but whenever the situation permitted was to endeavour to gain ground along the whole of the front."[29] Capt. G. H. F. Nichols knew his Eighteenth Division had a rough chore keeping pace with the Americans, for he had seen how worn down his men were by all the constant fighting that had started on 8 August.[30] Perhaps that is why when the division commander, Maj. Gen. R. P. Lee, saw the New Yorkers in a desperate fight in front of both The Knoll and Guillemont Farm, he held back his troops, ordering them to stay where they were. This timid action, although warranted by his orders, exposed the left flank of the 107th Infantry's First Battalion to a furious counterattack by the Germans.

Machine-gun bullets now flew in every direction. Germans popped out of the ground from their secret tunnels and caught the Americans from behind. Mopping up had proven to be a disaster. "The air is full of sizzling red hot things—millions of bees are buzzing in our ears! How in God's name can anyone live in this?" Leland thought.

In this inferno, D Company fought frantically to protect the regiment's left flank.

Pvt. Frank Petrie took a bullet in the left jaw. It smashed his jawbone, ricocheted down inside his neck perilously close to the jugular and came out his body through the left shoulder blade. Another bullet winged his leg. Pvt. Philip Kearney Mindil Jr. was shot in the heart. Mindil was the son of the drama critic for the New York *Tribune*. His grandfather had twice won the Medal of Honor in the Civil War, and served on the staff of General Philip Kearney, for whom Mindil was named. Three brothers, sons of the city clerk of Mount Vernon, all corporals, fought like devils. One of the brothers, Peter Collins, did not like the fact that his squad had been held up. Collins ordered his men to follow him around to the left of the Germans. There he found a trench teeming with Huns. Firing his Lewis gun, he jumped into their midst, killing many them and forcing others to surrender.[31]

Twenty-three-year-old Pvt. Michael Valente, who had come to America recently from Cassino, Italy, felt his comrades were not fighting hard enough. And when one of his friends went down, his anger rose up like Mount Vesuvius. Lt. Oscar Hellquist, the battalion intelligence officer, saw "our Italian boy" finally erupt. One of Valente's fellow soldiers characterized his state as "frenzied!" He'd had enough of the murderous machine gunners that were everywhere. Alongside of him, another private, Joseph Mastine, a bartender and cigar maker also from Ogdensburg, was equally stirred up.

What then took place has many versions.

Valente rushed into the open, armed with his Enfield rifle and a bunch of hand grenades. Dropping to one knee, he drilled a Hun machine gunner through the head. He fired into the nest until he was out of ammunition. Then he jumped to his feet and charged more hives of machine gunners. Running along a trench teeming with Germans, he tossed in one grenade after another. Dozens of the enemy threw down their weapons, raised their hands and yelled, "Kamerad! Kamerad!" The diminutive Mastine, who was only five-feet-six-inches tall, followed Valente step by step, firing as he went. The Boche who did not surrender scrambled out of their trenches and fled back toward the Hindenburg Line. One eyewitness said Valente was jumping from trench to trench when he was shot through the left arm. The wound infuriated him even more. He knocked out four machine-gun nests, bellowing at the cowering Germans the whole time. When his anger was finally spent, he had captured over twenty prisoners. Mastine then herded the infidels back behind the line. (Eleven years later, the U.S. government got around to awarding the Medal of Honor to the Italian immigrant, who was described by one of his Ogdensburg friends as a modest man with an "unassuming grace." Mastine received the Distinguished Service Cross and the honor of having a cigar named after him, "The Mastine.")

The responsibility of protecting the left flank did not belong solely to D Company. Also fighting to preserve that flank was the Machine Gun Company, the Jersey Gunners along with a contingent of men from Utica and other parts of New York. Corporal Eggers remembered how the machine gunners advanced slowly at a walk for fifty or sixty yards at a clip and then jumped into shell holes for a quick rest. Their guns were heavy and easily tired them out. They moved along in squads, single file, with corporals in front. Eggers stated that the squads advanced "calmly and steadily, although men had already started to drop. I know I had no sensation of fear, whatever, but had a rapidly rising hatred for Fritz and a desire to get at him, and I think we all felt the same way."[32] With all compasses set at eighty-five degrees, the machine gunners blasted their way up to The Knoll and to Willow Trench, even at a walk. The Third Platoon, which was on the extreme left, came under the heaviest fire. Yet it breached The Knoll. Stretching away to the east was Macquincourt Valley and, at the far end, the canal tunnel. One of the machine-gun sergeants, Arthur R. Beyer, a salesman from Bayonne, New Jersey, described how they "crossed over a ridge and dropped down into a little valley." Here grew a covering of vegetation. "When I think of how ['Jerry's'] bullets cut the weeds and grass all around us, I wonder at our luck in getting through," Beyer added.[33] Leading the assault, Lieutenant Willis pushed his men on. Eggers described how the "Fritzies had come out of their dugouts now, as our barrage was far ahead, and were sending a perfect hail of shots at us from machine guns and snipers." He went on to state that the Machine Gun Company crossed two German trenches that had been hastily abandoned. The machine gunners then entered the valley. "It was about this time that our artillery started sending over a smoke cloud intended for our left flank to screen us from the Germans there. But the smoke was unfortunately blown down into the valley and bothered us a lot."[34] After pushing on for more than a mile, the machine gunners became "bewildered and lost" because of the thick smoke and dropped into an enemy trench. "Here we stayed until the smoke cleared and it was possible to determine just where we were," Beyer wrote.[35]

To the right of Willis, the First Platoon lost its commander. Lieutenant Gadebusch had also reached the top of The Knoll. Like Buell in C Company, he had moved too fast and was alone in front of his men. Seeing a "nice path" through the tangled wire, he continued on by himself. Then he felt a sledgehammer blow to his left shoulder. The impact of the machine-gun bullet spun him around twice. His steel helmet tumbled off his head. His automatic pistol flew from his hand. He pitched face down into a shell hole. Pvt. James Hartley from Watertown, the platoon runner, dropped into the shell hole next to him.

"Why didn't you go with the platoon?" Gadebusch barked as he turned over his map case to Hartly. "Go join them now!"

"You must go to the rear, sir," answered Hartley, handing Gadebusch his helmet. At that moment, a bullet crashed into Hartley's hand. The private now had to go to the rear as well. Helping Gadebusch to his feet, they started back. But Gadebusch proved unable to travel. He ordered Hartley to leave. The lieutenant then staggered a few feet and found refuge in a German trench. In the bottom was sprawled a dead Hun. Once in the trench he passed out. When he awoke, he found himself in a brutal cross fire between his own men and a Boche machine-gun company. Six inches over his head bullets whined, zipping past in two directions. He tried to move. But his body was almost totally paralyzed. The only way he could move his head was with his hands. After a bit, he saw a man standing at the edge, blood seeping from a leg wound. It was one of his own sergeants.

"There are two stretcher bearers over the hill," the sergeant told him, all the while ignoring the roar of machine guns. "I'll go get them." The sergeant turned and as he moved away from the trench, Gadebusch heard the "crack, crack" of two shots. He never saw the sergeant again.[36]

He never saw several of his boyhood friends from Summit again, either. Lieutenant Willis, married at Camp Wadsworth, had started

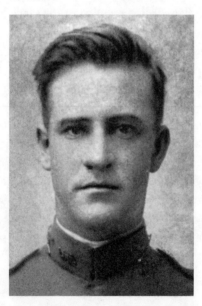

Lt. Edward Willis was the nephew of the mayor of Summit, N.J. The Seventh Regiment Fund

down into the Macquincourt Valley when he was gut shot. Even while he lay dying, Willis tried to encourage his Third Platoon to push forward. Nearby another Summit friend, Pvt. John Mallay Jr., the baseball star at Seton Hall High School, suffered gun shots to the abdomen and left leg, and died out on the battlefield. Cpl. Nicholas Kelly went down, too. Willis, Mallay, and Kelly were not the last of the Summit boys to die that day.

Three noncommissioned officers in Gadebusch's Machine Gun Company, Sergeant Latham and Cpls. Thomas O'Shea and Eggers, had been blasting the German defenses with their Vickers gun for most of the morning when they got disoriented in the fog and smoke and cut off from the rest of their men. At about that time their gun was struck by bullets and shattered beyond repair. "We threw ourselves into a fairly deep shell hole," Latham said, "figuring we might be able to weather the fight until nightfall or until reserves moved up in a new attack."[37] Eggers wrote to his parents in Summit, "We were on the slope on the right side of the valley and ran into machine gun fire all around us. So we went into shell holes again until we [got] our bearings."[38]

Virtually unarmed, the trio hugged the sides of the crater until they figured they had to do something. Nearby, another of the ill-fated tanks had either rolled over a mine or had been struck by artillery. It was equipped with a heavy Hotchkiss gun, an automatic weapon for opening gaps in the barbed wire and for knocking out light artillery batteries. If Latham, Eggers, and O'Shea could cross the open ground and dismount the Hotchkiss gun from the tank, they then had a chance against the Germans.

Slipping out of the shell hole, Eggers saw "Germans on three sides of us, about three hundred yards away." As they started working their way toward the disabled tank, Latham heard groans coming from inside the steel hulk. They had only gone a few steps when Eggers was hit in the back of the neck. He dropped into a shell hole, dazed. "My wound was very slight, but it jarred me a lot." Latham stayed with Eggers while into the smoke and fog O'Shea went on alone. A moment later, Eggers felt he was all right to go on. "We kept going and reached the tank," Latham said. "Eggers crawled in while I crouched down outside. He handed out two injured men. Then we dismounted the Hotchkiss gun." To his parents, Eggers told them that Latham had gotten the weapon to work, but then they "had to stay in the shell hole all day under fire from Fritzie's machine

Three Medal of Honor winners. Cpl. Alan Eggers (left) and Sgt. John Latham (center) were both in Machine Gun Company, 107th Regiment. The third man, Sgt. Reider Waaler, was a member of Machine Gun Company, 105th Regiment. The ceremony took place in January 1919, two months after the armistice. National Archives

guns and snipers, with Jack pegging back at them with the old Hotchkiss machine gun."[39] Latham described how he "saw two Boche gunners laying their machine gun on our shell hole. They were uphill and had the drop. I swung our gun and let 'em have it, and I could see the bullets cut them in two. It was a close one. A second later and we'd have been dead mice."[40]

Eggers meanwhile prayed that O'Shea was only missing and that his best friend would soon appear out of the heavy smoke unharmed.

On the right of the First Battalion, the Third Battalion was also experiencing blistering machine-gun and trench mortar fire from all sides—from the front and back and from both flanks. Capturing Guillemont Farm was proving just as difficult an assignment as The Knoll.

Egan, whose imposing size made him an easy target for German snipers even though he was in the center of four advancing companies, crashed to earth with a wound in the right leg just above the knee. The first thing that flashed into his mind was that the Huns were not fighting fair. He assumed that they would not shoot him because he was an officer. Two British soldiers, who had been with the battalion when it attacked, lifted up Egan and carried him back to a dressing station. They had a hard time. The American was so much larger than most Tommies. When they finally staggered up to the dressing station, one of them muttered under his breath, "My Gawd, he must weigh eighteen stone!"[41]

Before Egan went down, Cpl. Bernard Thomas Hunt, the United States Naval Academy graduate, said that the battalion commander's voice "could be heard bellowing encouragement in tones well calculated to reach the utmost flankers." Now with Egan out of the fight, Capt. Bradish, K Company commander, was put in charge of the Third Battalion. In Bradish's K Company, Cpl. James Throckmorton Vought, who had stuffed his Mills grenades inside his tunic instead of hanging them correctly from the outside where they were handy, described to his brother how "We went forward under a terrific fire and the casualties were heavy from the start. Some of the companies lost all their officers as they were going over. We ploughed into the trench and all Germans in sight were killed or captured. Another fellow and I found a small separate trench which had two dugouts in it. We called on the Huns to surrender and about eight came up. Those we took prisoner and turned over to a slightly wounded man who was taking a batch of prisoners to the rear. We then bombed the dugouts to clean out any Huns who had not come up."

Vought ran on, shooting two Germans. Then he knelt and took aim at another Hun three hundred yards away. Next to him enfilading machine-gun fire hit a soldier in the head. Vought felt a "sting and sizzle" in his chest. He did not know if he was shot, but the grenades inside his shirt scared him because he thought they might go off. He yanked them out and threw them forward as far as possible. Looking down at his chest, he saw blood spreading across the front of his tunic. "The Hun riflemen were using explosive bullets," he said. "The shot that hit me was a clean one and went clear through my right lung. It was ten minutes of eight then." He rolled on the ground for twenty yards until he reached a shell hole. He slid in and dressed his wound as best as he could. Also in the same shell hole was his friend Roger Montgomery, the company mail clerk who the day before had saved the life of Sgt. Philip Vosburgh.

"Montgomery [had] a terrible wound in the stomach. He must have died shortly after I left, for he was in bad shape. Whenever he moved, or I did, it caused him great pain, so I wanted to get out of the shell-hole and into one right back of it where our machine gun was, and I waited my chance until it should stop firing." He added, "From now on I looked only after myself; it was all I could do, and Monty was too far gone for me to help him." Vought then began working his way back, running and walking, toward a dressing station.[42]

When K Company pressed on and reached the edge of Guillemont Farm, a bullet ripped into the right leg of Pfc. Oakley Rhinelander. Crawling into a shell hole, he wrapped up his leg and hobbled back to where several wounded comrades were huddled. A shell dropped among them, killing most of them and shredding Rhinelander's face with hot shrapnel. Blood streamed into his eyes. He staggered farther back, a gory mess, looking for a medic, when yet another shell burst next to him. This time, fragments tore open his side. By now, one of Rhinelander's wealthy friends, Cpl. Joseph Cushman, while trying to move his machine-gun squad closer to the enemy, had been struck down and killed. Cpl. Alexander Menard of Malone detailed three men to go with him to bring back some of the wounded. As they sprinted into a hail of machine-gun fire, Menard was himself mortally wounded. Pfc. James O. Vedder, brother of Mess Sgt. Harmon Vedder, died instantly when a shell exploded on top of him.

In this melee, the boys fired their rifles wildly. Bradish reported that now and then a sergeant or a corporal would get a small group of men together and would attack a machine-gun nest, capturing or killing every German in sight. But the officers were unable to direct the movement of their units because of the dense smoke and fog. Runners carried messages, or when there was a clearing in the smoke, the officers signaled by waving their arms.[43]

Sgt. George Ely did not remember much about the attack. What he did recall was that "Jerry had their wind up. His machine gun bullets were coming over by the hundreds of millions. How my body lived thru' that mainstream it is impossible to understand. I paid my regard to six Fritzers, about ten I think! I have lost my best friends. Oak Rhinelander, Bob Raven, Jim Page, Joe Cushman, Adolph Bussel, and too many others are gone." Harold Mills, one of the corporals in Ely's company, entered in his diary, "107th badly damaged, especially 3rd Bat., which got to canal. Bush & Cushman killed. Cushman's last words, 'Carry on with the squad, Hal, write home & tell them I died game & with a smile on my face.' "

Also in front of Guillemont Farm, L Company, which had taken the brunt of the regiment's casualties in the Dickebusch Sector, came under fierce fire. A machine-gun bullet split the skull of Captain Nicoll. He fell into a shell hole, blood pouring down his cheeks like tears. His company clerk, Sgt. John Aloysius Kennedy, dropped next to him, wounded too. Just before he died, Nicoll, the father of two young children, tried to comfort Kennedy. A moment later he was dead. In his hand, he still clutched his walking stick. His second in command, Lt. Robert A. Byrns, was also hit in the head. He refused to go down. Sgt. Mitchell watched the Staten Island native, recalling that "with blood streaming across his face as he pushed on, he appeared to those around him as an inspired avenger, and the lads at his beck and command could but emulate his high courage." A second bullet smashed his left arm. At last the loss of blood weakened him too much and he was taken to the rear.

Forced to take over command of the company, 1st Sgt. Edward Scott of Westchester, already wounded in the arm, "led his men with a dash and coolness that made a worthy successor to those whose places he filled." Scotty had been in the Seventh for a long time, and had been drilled often by Captain Nicoll inside the armory on Park Avenue.

Bert Lobdell from Salem Center, who had told his sister not to worry, that he would certainly come back with lots of tales to tell, was silenced forever by machine-gun bullets. Also killed was Pvt. John Howell Westcott, a direct descendant of Plymouth Pilgrims John and Priscilla Alden.

"We had gone about four or five hundred yards when I saw Major Egan drop in front of me," Pvt. James Duffy wrote in a letter home to White Plains, where many of the boys from L Company came from. "A little further on I recognized Walter Farley and Allen DeNike going down. I could see fellows dropping all around me but it was just breaking dawn and you had to look straight ahead. I was unable to recognize any of them as White Plains boys. I understand that Ralph Tompkins was hit somewhere in the forehead, just put up both hands over his face and dropped dead. Don Hunnewell was hit, tried to get up but could not. Later he started to make his way back to a dressing station when a shell hit him.

Walter Williams was wounded and put in a trench for shelter. A shell landed in the trench and finished him. Edwin Paul was wounded in the stomach and died just before reaching the first aid station."[44]

Sgt. Andrew Todd from Newburgh had reached the first band of barbed wire when a German machine gunner found him. An explosive bullet burrowed into his elbow joint and his whole right side froze up. He hit the ground and crawled toward a shell hole. The moment he wiggled into it, machine-gun bullets struck the top just above his head. Todd thought that he was finished. Then, wave after wave of his comrades passed over him. "The casualties in that day's fighting were very heavy," he later recalled, "and all about me I could see the dead and wounded."[45]

Adrian Kissam, the Vanderbilt scion and Sergeant Ely's cousin, was mowed down in the legs. As blood gushed from his wound, Pvt. Angelo Mustico, one of the heroes at Dickebusch Lake, appeared along the edge of the shell hole in which Kissam squirmed in agony. The two Newburgh men had had a violent argument abroad ship on the way to France. Mustico had warned Kissam then not to turn his back on him once they got into combat. As a sporting man who had not yet worked a day in his life, Kissam was a crack shot with a rifle. Mustico's threat had never worried him. Now their argument was a distant memory. Mustico's arms hung helplessly by his side. He had been riddled with bullets.

Looking into the shell hole, Mustico cried out, "Ad, is that you?" Then he moaned, "Ad, I'm hit in both arms and I can't move either one of them!"

Although badly wounded himself, Kissam was appalled at the blood flowing from Mustico's limp arms. There was nothing either of them could do to assist the other.

"Ad, I'm going to try to make it an aid station and get help."

But Mustico never made it to an aid station. He died on the way. Kissam had to wait for help while around him the battle roared on.[46]

Albert H. Corrigan from Pelham, a law student at New York University and a private in I Company, had his hand "mangled" by a sniper. He still had four grenades and jumped into a trench and captured four Germans. One of them was a Red Cross volunteer, who bandaged up his hand. Corrigan ordered the Germans to transport him and several of his wounded friends back to a first-aid station.

During the assault on the Hindenburg Line, machine-gun bullets raked Pvt. Adrian Kissam's legs. Robert V. Kissam Sr.

One of the luckiest Greyjackets turned out to be the ex-navy man Cpl. Bernard Thomas Hunt. As his platoon moved up the hill at "slow double time," on all sides "comrades were falling, and when near neighbors were hit the sickening spat could be heard. Above all was the minor whine of the machine guns and the deafening roar from the artillery of both sides."[47] In this commotion of hell, a bullet smacked into one side of Hunt's head, right between his temple and eye. It then traveled behind both his eyes and came out on the other side of his head. Yet he survived.

Mount Vernon Cpl. Irving J. Savage of H Company also had a close shave. "A couple of bullets passed through the sleeve of my coat, one through the knee of my pants, two through my pack, right through my toilet kit and rations. My gun sling was cut to ribbons and my gun was riddled with bullets. So you can see how lucky I was. I think I got at least ten Jerrys and four others threw up their hands crying for mercy and pulling out a loaf of brown bread to show that they had their rations."[48]

In I Company, Leland described how his men just kept going from one shell hole to another. "The wire catches our coats and leggings, but we tear ourselves loose and keep on. My walking stick saves me from several nasty falls. The fire is hotter from the left as we go up the slope into the farm." The barbed wire ripped the clothing of one soldier so badly that he caught chill. Lt. Percy Hall, although feverish and shaking himself, took off his coat and draped it over the shivering soldier's shoulders.

Ahead of the company a group of frightened Germans bolted from their machine-gun nest. In Leland's squad of Lewis gunners, only two men were left: Pfc. Harold Tuthill and Pvt. Earl Van Peer, both from the old First Infantry.

"Can you shoot from the hip?" Leland yelled at Tuthill.

"I haven't a strap, but I'll try it, Lieutenant."

Tuthill stood up and sprayed the trench, while next to him Leland fired away with his automatic pistol. The rest of the company closed over the trench, the men tossing in Mills grenades. An Allied airplane then buzzed over them firing into the trench before a shot brought it crashing down fifty yards away. "There were plenty of dead machine gunners in the trench we passed over," Leland later wrote. "One who was sitting on the stool at his gun had been hit on the head by a grenade."

Close by, Lieutenant Hall caught a bullet and flopped down into a shell hole. Lieutenant Gould remembered that he was "unable to speak, while the shells shrieked and the bullets hissed about him and the fight went on. Moving with difficulty he reached across to a wounded doughboy by his side, grasped his hand, smiled and then settled back and breathed his last."[49]

Above the shell hole, Cpl. W. Vincent Lawder from Middletown took a bullet in the chest. It stopped short of his heart because it had first struck a shaving kit that he had left in his pocket.[50] Cpl. James L. Fottrell, a printer from Flushing, was shot in the shoulder, face, and through the mouth, where most of his teeth were knocked out. Another Flushing lad, Pvt. Norbert Filan, the son of the fuel inspector for the New York City

Board of Education, took a hit in the right side. The bullet passed through his body and ripped out his back. The wound left him paralyzed on the battlefield.

Private First Class Fetherolf gripped his Lewis gun with one hand and his automatic pistol in the other. "One might call it armed to the teeth," he wrote. He jumped into a trench and there spotted a doorway and a steep flight of stairs leading down into a dugout. He peered into the dark tunnel and peering back at him were five Germans. "They were shaking to beat the band with their hands up yelling 'Kamerad.' Did I say yelling, I mean they were 'whooping it.' They had lost their voices from fright. Just then it dawned on me that I must be rather a formidable sight, and with a machine gun on my left arm and revolver in my right then and there. It was so funny, the expression on their faces, of fear and intense desire to understand me. Then a whole bunch [of I Company boys] jumped in together so I don't get the credit of capturing them. However as soon as they came up out in the trench I had to go and leave them with the fellows who were mopping up."

In the second wave, the Second Battalion followed the Third.

Nick Krayer recalled that when E Company reached the first wire, "a terrific fire from German machine guns on the extreme left of the divisional sector hit the company and men fell dead and wounded."[51] Rushing ahead of his men in E Company, Capt. Harry Hayward, who loved the woods of his native Maine, caught a string of explosive machine-gun bullets in the groin. The lawyer pitched into a shell hole, his intestines oozing out of the gaping wound like a knot of live worms.

Sgt. Arthur Bancker and 1st Lt. Benjamin Hammond from Dutchess Junction, referred to by his men as Uncle Ben, crawled up to Hayward. The sergeant tried to dress his captain's horrible wound. Yet he and Hammond knew there was nothing more they could do. They knew, too, that they had to go forward. Hammond stood and looked down at Hayward and then said to Bancker, "Follow on!" At that moment Uncle Ben fell backward, shot in the chest. As Bancker watched the thirty-seven-year-old soft-spoken lieutenant go down, a bullet zipped into his abdomen. It raced upward into his chest and then hitting bone bounced back down into his abdomen. He slumped into a shallow hole and fainted. After a bit he regained consciousness. "I laid very still for about two hours. 'Jerry' was playing his machine guns all around me and I was covered with dirt and mud from the shells landing close by."

One of those shells caught twenty-four-year-old 1st Lt. Stephen Schwab, a native of New York City, in the head. When it exploded, he lost half his face. He later died. Sgt. William Drabble from Summit was hit in the chest by machine-gun bullets. The gaping wound left him clinging to life in a shell hole. Meanwhile, several men tried to bind up Hammond's wounds. Frustrated at losing one of their endearing officers, they swore uncontrollably. Just before he died, Uncle Ben begged them to stop their cursing.[52]

Up ahead, E Company Pvt. James Borgia reached his first enemy trench. Cowering inside where six "pitiful" Germans. "They could not get away and were shaking all over and you could not blame them. They just threw up their hands and yelled 'Kamerad.' " But one Hun made a dive for freedom. "You should have seen that dive. It was the funniest

Righteous 1st Lt. "Uncle" Ben Hammond did not like his boys to curse.
Mortally wounded by a bullet in the chest, he continued to urge his boys
not to use foul language with his dying breath. The Seventh Regiment Fund

thing I have every seen over here. They were glad to be taken prisoners and to get out of the war." Borgia and his fellow E Company boys were not always so merciful. "We had some Germans trapped in a dugout and hollered to them to come out. I guess that they were too scared to come, so we threw them a couple of hand grenades to divide among themselves so they would not starve. I don't think they will ever come out now."

Another E Company soldier recalled, "We hit him so hard, so fast and so often there was not much shooting, but we surely did put the old bayonet to them. For two and a half miles you could not walk three feet without stepping on a Hun."

Cpl. Morgan S. Baldwin of G Company, the son of the private attorney of Tammany Hall "Boss" Charles Murphy, took a terrible wound and fell. He tried to hold on while the fighting roared past him. "There sure was some excitement" where H Company's Pvt. Michael Houlahan was engaged. The Mount Vernon native "got it in the leg." As he said, "Nothing to worry about. Got two Germans before I got it."[53]

Lt. Stephen Schwab, who had enlisted in the old Seventh Regiment in 1912, died of wounds received during the fighting around Guillemont Farm.
The Seventh Regiment Fund

Corporal Burke, also of H, remembered having to cross a sunken road. He easily slid down one side, holding his Lewis gun over his head. "But I had a tough time getting up the other side. When we got there we were in a curtain of German machine gun fire, and the boys were beginning to drop fast. We were into it then and the excitement made us forget everything but fight, and how the boys did fight. I never knew until then what American spunk amounted to. [E]very man kept going straight ahead, killing as he went."

Among the fallen lads was Cpl. Perry Breck from an old Mount Vernon family and considered one of the best amateur tennis players in Westchester County. Another of the dead was Cpl. Dean Hamilton, who had promised his mother that no German would ever get him alive. The step-grandson of the brother of President Benjamin Harrison, Scott Lytle, who had tried to kill himself a few years earlier because he had blamed himself for his mother's demise, also went down. This time the angel of death won out.

Not all casualties of the silk stocking soldiers were among the killed or wounded. Many of the New Yorkers were taken prisoners and were marched quickly back behind the Hindenburg Line. One of the captured men was a hero at Dickebusch Lake, Pfc. William White from E Company. Another prisoner was 1st Lt. Richard McIntyre of Headquarters Company, an attorney in the same law firm as Captain Nicoll and who had been in the Seventh since 1909.

The only officer in the division to be captured, McIntyre had charge of a squad of trench mortarmen, attached to the First Battalion. Almost at the moment of attack, he noticed that the battalion seemed headed too much toward the south instead of pushing eastward. He then spotted a platoon of men he felt was headed in the right direction. He ordered his mortarmen to get behind that platoon. However, barbed wire held them up until a tank rolled by, opening a hole in the entanglement. When finally they got going again, McIntyre had lost sight of the platoon in the thick fog and smoke barrage.

"The concealment didn't bother me then," McIntyre wrote to his wife, "because it concealed the whole outfit from the Germans and I reckoned that the advance could progress without much hindrance until we got actually with the enemy in his trenches. But I realized that I was on the flank of and not behind our troops, so I started leisurely forward bearing considerably to the right, in the expectation of running across either the laggards of our first line or the troops in the supporting platoons."

McIntyre was now lost. And as he and his orderly, Pvt. William J. Cairns, "pushed on" alone they felt like Columbus. "Cairns feeling more particularly like those sailors of Columbus who thought the discoverer had gone crazy." Indeed, Cairns figured that they were nearing Berlin. The lieutenant now believed that they had to turn around and go back if they were ever going to be of any assistance to the battalion. Starting back, they ran into two Germans. One of them surrendered. The other melted away in the smoke. Their prisoner was just a boy. "His capture," McIntyre felt, "was disconcerting to me because it was reasonable now to suppose that we were actually behind the German lines." The boy told them that the area ahead was "thick" with Germans. Soon more Boche came toward them out of the mist. McIntyre and Cairns started amassing a sizeable collection of prisoners.

"I could not understand the absence of the Americans," McIntyre confessed to his wife.

He did not have to wait much longer. About six or seven doughboys trooped out of the fog, escorted by a single German. "We hailed them to make a break and we would knock down their guard. With appropriate profanity one of them urged us to look around us and judge our chances. As if this was the signal for the raising of a curtain on the climax act of a high tragedy, the mist and smoke disappeared with astonishing rapidity and our situation was disclosed." McIntyre was in the middle of a company of Germans. Machine-gun crews had their weapons aimed at him and Cairns. Just to the east were lines of trenches, command posts, field artillery guns, and the canal tunnel, and everywhere spike-helmeted Huns, "each one close enough to represent grinning death."

McIntyre and Cairns took off, sprinting south. Bullets flew at them, "each ball of which seemed to be plowing through my neck." Cairns fell. McIntyre dove into a shell hole and quickly buried his maps and pistol. He then "tamely" gave up. "Cairns miraculously popped up when I surrendered and quite disgustedly threw away his rifle and joined me."[54]

As combatants who had actually been fighting at the time of their capture, McIntyre and Cairns had become unwittingly, and arguably, the first Allied soldiers to pierce the Hindenburg Line.

CHAPTER 14

Lads Here, Lads There, Torn Almost Limb from Limb

eports on the progress of the attack started coming into the Twenty-seventh Division headquarters fifteen minutes after the troops from the Fifty-fourth Brigade broke from their start lines. Each regiment had been given a code name. The 107th Infantry went by "Tuve." The 108th was called "Tumo." The code name for the Fifty-fourth Brigade was "Fuzu." One of the first messages to reach Maj. Gen. John O'Ryan read: "Tuve got off to a good start. No reports from Tumo." By eight A.M., two hours into the fight, O'Ryan was informed that Tuve was "fighting its way forward successfully."

Messages sent to Lt. Gen. Sir John Monash were also promising. The stout commander's battle plans were going well. Not only was the Twenty-seventh advancing on schedule, but also so was the Thirtieth Division. And on the right flank of the Americans, the British Forty-sixth Division was unstoppable. Reports indicated that more than one thousand Germans were already prisoners and that the 107th Infantry had captured Bony. "It looked as if everything was going strictly to schedule," Monash recalled. "That morning the stream of messages pouring into my headquarters from special observers, from the air, from the line divisions, from the artillery and from my liaison officers with neighbouring Corps, exceeded in volume and import anything I had met with in my previous war experience."[1]

With such good news, Monash confidently moved up his own Third and Fifth Divisions to get them ready to leapfrog the Americans.

It was about this time, perhaps a little after eight, when C. E. W. Bean, accompanied by W. E. Berry of the *Times* and Arthur Conan Doyle, left the Australian Corps headquarters and headed for the front. Except for the mist, the weather seemed perfect for an all-out attack along the western front. "Our own batteries were barking away from several miles back, and grew louder and more numerous as we progressed," went Berry's dispatch in the *Times*. "Presently round a corner in the road we came upon the first token of the fighting ahead in the shape of one of the first batches of prisoners to come down the line."[2] Conan Doyle wrote that those prisoners were "pitiable enough, and yet I could not pity them, weary, shuffling, hangdog creatures, with no touch of nobility in their features or their bearing."[3]

As the trio neared the fighting, they came across several destroyed tanks. Also, lines and lines of backed-up Australians. Bean's trained eye noticed right away that the diggers, as the Australian troops were known, were not moving forward as ordered. That meant that possibly the American attack had bogged down and his Australians could not get to the front. The war correspondents climbed to the crest of a hill. "From here we could see the valley to the slope on the opposite hill, where the advance was held up near a farm," Berry reported. "A moving mist and the smoke of the guns made detailed observation difficult, and stretching away to the left round a hill Bean pointed out to us the German defences which had fallen to the attack only an hour or two before. On the other side the Germans were keeping up a perfect storm of shells, and the line of the ridge was permanently hidden in the smoke and debris kicked up by the shells, many apparently of large size."[4]

Conan Doyle then went off on his own with a young Australian captain, where they found an immobile tank. He scrambled atop it for a better view. From his new vantage point, and perhaps knowing, too, that this day belonged to Saint Michael—a day of "retribution" Conan Doyle called it—he jotted down that "under our very eyes was even now being fought a part of that great fight where at last the children of light are beating down into the earth the forces of darkness. It was there. We could see it. And yet how little there was to see."[5]

While the war correspondents had gone toward their observation post on the hill, back at the Twenty-seventh's headquarters, O'Ryan hurriedly scanned the messages from his two regimental commanders, Cols. Charles DeBevoise of the 107th and Edgar S. Jennings of the 108th. Jennings's men seemed to be fighting well. A message from DeBevoise stated that at nine A.M. the Australian Third Division, which was to pass through his regiment, had been halted in Kent Lane. Although the general did not know it then, the 107th had met stiff resistance at The Knoll and Guillemont Farm. A counterattack had been launched. Germans had gushed out of their secret tunnels and underground warrens, and threatened to throw the Americans back, as they had done first to the British and then to O'Ryan's own Fifty-third Brigade. One of Monash's nightmares was about to be realized. The failure to mop up. The Australian feared that the inexperienced Americans, "eager to show their mettle, would be carried away in the excitement of the moment, and would rush headlong forward, regardless of the dangers that lurked behind them. So indeed it happened."[6]

One of the first indications that this was the case came in a midmorning message, this time from brigade headquarters. It stated, according to O'Ryan, that the "situation on the front of the 107th Infantry obscure and that reports being received were conflicting; that the leading battalion . . . had gained their objective, but were compelled to withdraw." The counterattack was not only coming straight toward the division, but also on both flanks and from the rear. The ensuing enfilading fire cost the 107th Infantry dearly on its left flank, particularly where the missing British Eighteenth Division had been expected to defend. And the Americans had to turn around and fight backward, over ground they thought they had just won.

Tristram Tupper, among O'Ryan's personal observers at the front, reported, "Enemy reserves, who had been held in the tunnel carrying the St. Quentin Canal, attacked fiercely on three sides, while a terrific counter attack was launched against the left flank of the division from Vendhuile in an effort to roll up this flank and crush the whole attack."[7]

Father Francis A. Kelley of Albany, a divisional chaplain on the battlefield, described how difficult it was for the boys to mop up. "We found, in many cases, that the Germans had left behind certain of their numbers hidden away in dugouts and trenches with the idea that as our lads advanced they should spring up behind them and attack them from the rear."[8]

Lt. Col. J. Leslie Kincaid explained how roused and angry the soldiers became when, "no sooner had they conquered one area than fresh German troops would rise out of the ground behind them and fire from the rear. They came up through the underground passages, connecting them with the tunnel, and, armed with machine guns and bombs, attacked our boys from behind as they were advancing. The men of the 107th, with Germans in front of them and the Germans behind them fought like so many devils. It was a battle against terrific odds. Time and again they made attempts to mop up the line and clear the ground that the advance had gone over. But the constant surging of the Germans behind them made it a grim task."[9]

Col. Franklin W. Ward of the 106th Infantry described what his sister regiment, the 107th, was going through as "murder, hell-to-breakfast carnage." He pointed out that the silk stocking soldiers had to "trek into and over deep enemy ditches then through the wire. Reaching Willow Trench the work with bullet, bayonet and grenade is rough and bloody." He reported, "In the crash and smoke they cannot hear their own rifles—the recoil against the shoulder being the only proof it is pumping lead. They drain out trenches only to have them fill up again from some unseen bunghole."[10]

Observers tried to make sense of the fight so they could send accurate reports back to the corps commander. The Australian diggers had been held up behind the Americans, and were champing to get at the Germans and press the attack. No one knew exactly what was happening. As Monash noted, "The situation was confused and uncertain." Monash claimed that he had personally rushed forward to hear from the divisional commanders. "I soon formed the conclusion that . . . once again the 'mopping up' procedure had been neglected. The enemy had reappeared in strength from underground behind the Americans, and was holding up the advance of the two Australian Divisions to the second phase of the operation."

Monash was upset enough that he then blamed the Americans for what he perceived as a "miscarriage of plans," as Bean surmised he would do.[11]

Two observers confirmed that O'Ryan's New Yorkers had been stopped, even though Brig. Gen. Sir James E. Edmonds, in his definitive history chronicling British military operations in the Great War, pointed out that owing to the fog, the specially trained divisional observers could see nothing. And he added that where the Twenty-seventh Division was engaged, "The fog prevented much of what was going on from being seen."[12]

However, according to the historian of the Australian Flying Corps, an Australian pilot from the Number Three Aero Squadron, on reconnaissance, reported that the left flank of the Twenty-seventh—namely the 107th—was "held up almost entirely" and that the "attack had dissolved into lost fragments." He went on to report that he "found no American line at all, but only bewildered bunches of men, rather lost in the fog and dismayed by hostile machine-gun fire from almost every side."[13]

Another observer also thought the Americans were lost and, even worse, unable to think for themselves.

Frenchman M. Paul Maze, fighting with the British, somehow got himself mixed up with the Twenty-seventh while in the very midst of the raging battle. His account of the doughboys was condescending. The son of a wealthy merchant, friend of the first lord of the Admiralty, Winston Churchill, Maze was an obvious dilettante, who had studied art with some well-known painters. In his memoirs, *A Frenchman in Khaki*, he recalled the first time he came upon Americans. It was "at night, at a time when a barrage was making a fearful din, and I thought they were all talking at once, but on closer inspection it turned out that they were only chewing gum." Maze apparently wandered into a "battalion" dugout in front of The Knoll as if he owned the place. "At a table sat a Colonel and two staff officers, in stiff jackets with high collars facing a map at which the Colonel kept glancing through tortoise-shell glasses attached to a silk cord, which he kept putting on and taking off his big nose." Maze did not identify the officer. In any case, the dilettante continued: "They had no news of their attacking regiments. 'Waal,' he [the colonel] drawled, adjusting his glasses, 'I have no news yet of how the boys have gotten on, but they went over at skeduled time, and I am confident that they have done their dooty.'" Maze told the colonel what he ought to do, turned on his heels and strode out of the dugout. He hopped on his motorcycle and took off toward The Knoll. When he could no longer ride, he ran. He next described doughboys retiring from the fight "simply because they were not in touch with anybody; they had no news and most of their officers had been killed in the advance. I made some of them stay where they were and place their machine-guns facing the battle, then ordered the rest to go forward and rejoin their comrades, which they immediately did. They were not in any sort of panic, but had merely sauntered back for want of instructions." Maze then hustled back to "battalion" headquarters, where he found that it had been leveled and "three corpses lay there partly covered by a sack." The colonel, he said, was "down below," alone, "mopping his brow."[14]

Written sixteen years after the battle, Maze's memoirs are a stretch. Not once does his name appear in any literature about the Twenty-seventh; not in O'Ryan's history of the division nor in any of the regimental or company histories nor even in one letter or diary written by the soldiers themselves. Yet there is a ring of truth to the confusion he described. Colonel Ward, who was indeed there, put it best. He called it a "black fury" that engulfed the 107th. "There is no battle line now," he wrote in the present tense; "it is a force of groups rather than the formal fighting movements of platoons and companies. Each man is his own captain."[15]

Such confusion and conflicting reports forced O'Ryan out of his own headquarters. Like Monash earlier, he had to get close enough to the fighting to see for himself just what was happening. In fact, O'Ryan made it a habit to go back and forth to the front quite often, alternating the trip with his chief of staff, Col. Stanley H. Ford.

"The best way to get information firsthand is from the walking wounded," he told an interviewer from Columbia University years later. "If they're good enough to walk, they're good enough to talk, and you can judge in a couple of seconds whether they're too dumb to tell you anything." One of the first soldiers O'Ryan met was walking briskly along, sobbing hysterically. He called him over. Mud covered the soldier from head to foot. He kept saying that he had been shot through the brain.

O'Ryan rubbed off the collar to his uniform so he could read the insignia pinned there. The soldier was from the 107th. Still trying to clean him up, O'Ryan looked closer at what he thought was a piece of dirt clinging to his forehead. "[It] was the man's brains coming out, so I took my handkerchief and stuffed it in the hole."

O'Ryan stopped another trembling solider.

"I'm not a coward, sir," the dazed doughboy cried when he recognized O'Ryan. He wiped his face and held out something in his hand. "Do you know what this is? Look at it! Look at it, general, please!" O'Ryan saw, too, that it was brains. "How did that happen?" he asked. "You look all right, otherwise." "General, they're not mine!" He told O'Ryan that he was next to his best friend when a shell "shot through the top of his head and spilled all his brains over him."

However, O'Ryan was able to flag down enough wounded soldiers who were drifting back to the first-aid stations to get a clearer picture of the battle.[16]

Despite the seeming confusion of what was taking place within the shroud of fog and smoke and clouds of mustard gas as well as the godawful reports that the Americans were too bewildered to act on their own (Bean wrote that an Australian officer came across some Americans in a shell hole doing nothing, and that one of them was "calmly cleaning his gun"[17]), O'Ryan discovered otherwise. Although the losses among his officers in the 107th Infantry were so numerous and "the system of shell holes and demolished trenches which the troops occupied were so complicated, and the shelling and machine gunning so constant, that it was only with greatest difficulty, amid the tangle of trenches, wire, corpses, wounded and fighting men, that the surviving officers were able to establish any kind of dispositions in depth. And this latter action was imperative, because even the soldiers in the ranks then knew that the mission of the battalion was no longer to continue to attempt the impossible, but to provide at any cost for the security of the left flank of the corps."

O'Ryan also learned that leading elements of the 107th had "swept into and through Willow Trench" and then continued east to Lone Tree Trench, and in some isolated pockets threatened to breach the canal— hardly the actions of a bewildered regiment of fighting men.

Now feeling a bit more optimistic, the general returned to divisional headquarters. There he had a chance to interrogate a captured German officer. The officer bragged that he hoped the Americans would reach the canal. "For in that event," he warned, "it would mean the destruction or capture of all attacking troops by reason of the ability of German forces to roll them up by flank drives from Vendhuile which nothing could stop."

For the 107th Infantry, forcing its way beyond The Knoll and Guillemont Farm and then on toward the canal was proving to be an almost hopeless endeavor. The enemy was everywhere. Fighting was hand-to-hand. Bayonets, pistols, and grenades. In one sector, the Germans had formed a human chain, like a bucket brigade, and passed grenades forward where the lead men then threw them at the Americans. Bodies were blown apart. Limbs littered the ground.

"It was not surprising to find lads here, lads there, torn almost limb from limb by the fearful work of the high explosives," wrote Father Francis A. Kelley, who later won the Distinguished Service Cross.[18]

Bugler Ralph Kretschmar knew exactly how one of the Huns' potato mashers worked. "The head is filled with high explosives and there is a cap at the end of the handle which unscrews and a long piece of fuse is pulled so that in seven seconds it goes off," he explained in a letter home. He had been firing at gray-clad figures from the hip because he wanted to keep his bayonet handy. Out of the thick smoke a grenade hit his right shoulder and went off. "The explosion was so great my steel hat flew off. My gun flew out of my hands and I hit the ground like a ton of bricks." Metal imbedded itself in his shoulder, smashed his collarbone, and broke three ribs. He found a shell hole and slid in to wait for help.

One of those high explosives, perhaps a hand grenade, landed near Cpl. John McClave Granger of M Company, the grandson of John McClave, the former police commissioner of the City of New York. Granger had just captured four Hun prisoners. The explosion blew off his left leg and smashed his right one. The prisoners were not hurt. Nor did they run off. "Pvt. Chauncey Entrott of Ogdensburg rushed up with a stretcher," Granger was later able to tell a New York reporter. "But just then a second shell came and smashed his [Entrott's] leg, so he was nearly as helpless as I was myself." Ironically, Entrott also lost a leg. Still, the two severely wounded soldiers had the presence of mind to order the German prisoners to carry them back to a first-aid station.

"A huge shell burst nearby," said 2d Lt. Arthur Brundage of E Company, "and I heard one of the boys scream. I turned to help him and then I remember no more. We were half buried in mud and stones. When I came to I was covered with a blanket which the boys had put over me."[19] A German "stick bomb" landed next to F Company Cpl. D'Alby Brown while he was in a shell hole. "Not having time to pick it up and throw it back, I put my rifle over it and started to get away. When I was about 2 feet away it went off, up I went into the air and my gun was blown to pieces. You could not find a piece of the gun to make a match stick with it. The bomb wounded me in five places."[20]

Cpl. John F. Foley of B Company got it in the head. A hole was blown open in the roof of his mouth and his upper teeth and right eye knocked out. His stomach and one leg were split open. Already struck once by a whizbang, Cpl. Harry Burke and four of his fellow men in H Company were hit by another. The force threw them back against the wall of their trench like scarecrows in a cyclone. "When I came to my right ear was in terrible shape. I thought my ear drum was broken and I had a jumping headache that had me almost blind."

A shell knocked I Company Private William Miller into the air. When he crashed back to the ground, he was half buried by dirt. Claude Leland said that he lay there unconscious for some time, "came to, tried to follow the company and in a dazed condition wandered into the German lines." The regiment listed him as killed in action. Instead, he had been captured, and one day soon after the Armistice shuffled into the company's orderly room "a sick man," Leland wrote, "but very much alive."

Pfc. Dutch Wilbur from Otisville, who had enlisted in I Company with his best friend William "Bunny" Stanfield while they were still in high school and had recently turned nineteen, caught a bullet in the lung. He had no idea what to do, and so he started walking. Blood ran down his body, soaking his uniform. It then ran down his legs and filled his boots. "I sloshed on in my own blood," he said to his family after the war. He kept pushing on, over the canal tunnel and deep into German-held territory. Finally, too weak to continue, he found shelter in a shell hole. Fearing that he would get shot, he pulled four or five heavy German trenchcoats over him that he had found. He then hoped that his trigger-happy Americans would not find him under the coat. He knew that they would shoot first and ask questions later.[21] His friend, "Bunny," escaped getting wounded. When the war ended, Bunny would break Ernest Hemingway's heart by marrying the very nurse who had tended Hemingway after he suffered wounds on the Italian front, Agnes von Kurowsky. She would be the model of the heroine in his novel *A Farewell to Arms.*

The Germans often tricked the inexperienced doughboys into thinking they were surrendering. Sgt. Theodore Tyler, whose job was to bring up "the grub," related how one Hun held up his hands to surrender but "worked a machine gun with his foot, but that lasted only a second until he got a bomb in the face." One ruse, according to Corporal Burke, had the Huns sticking up a white flag of truce. When the Americans got to them they discovered "about ten Germans throwing hand grenades for all they were worth." Burke and his men "charged right at them" and they threw up their hands, pointing at the white flag. "We killed every one of them." The closer they got to the canal they started finding Germans

Pfc. Dutch Wilbur wandered for several miles
behind enemy lines with a bullet lodged in his lung.
Virginia Cairns

chained to their machine guns. "I don't know whether their officers did it or it was a ruse of their own, but by that time the boys seemed to have decided that they would take no prisoners." Burke and his machine-gun crew later got pinned down in a shell hole. The second the Boche stopped firing, Burke figured they were reloading. "I started out of the hole with my No. 2 man alongside me, as I got to the top of the hole a 'Whiz-Bang' shot past my gun and hit alongside my partner, killing him instantly, taking half his head off; it knocked the gun flying out of my hand and threw me into the next hole badly shaken up."

An infuriated Pvt. Constantine Roeder and his equally enraged compatriots in B Company refused to let the Germans surrender to them. Their anger pushed them beyond the accepted laws of warfare even in a pitched battle as bloody as their assault on the Hindenburg Line. "We didn't take any prisoners," he confessed in the *Gazette*, "for we saw the dirty way in which they fight, and when we saw a couple of them deliberately shoot down a couple of our stretcher bearers who wear red crosses on their arms and carry no arms, the blood did boil I tell you and every one of them that came up with his hands in the air with this 'Kamerade—Kamerade—Mercy Kamerade' stuff got a bullet or the business end of a bayonet without any ceremony at all."

Roeder stated that when he reached the Hindenburg Line, his company was halted for "a while, because the Huns had the place just packed with machine guns and took a stand there. The unfortunate machine gunners had to, as we found out later when we had bombed them out, for there they lay chained to their guns—like dogs—they couldn't run."

Pfc. Albert Clark of the Sanitary Detachment watched in horror while a sniper tried to pick off his stretcher bearers. "He failed—but he fired just the same. Another wounded man was killed on his litter and a bearer killed by a sniper."

Pfc. Edward A. Pierce of C Company decided to give the Germans some of their own devious medicine. He put on a Boche officer coat and helmet, slipped his Lewis machine gun under the coat, and then walked toward the enemy. They let him get close enough, and then he opened up. "Many a 'Jerry' went west till a stray got Eddy in the leg," reported Cpl. Gardner Adams. After suffering a wound, Pierce went back to killing

Huns with a pistol and "cleaned up [a] little flock of 'square-heads' in a dangerous bay."

By the time Pvt. George Fetherolf got up to the canal, he still clutched his smoking Lewis machine gun and automatic pistol. He could actually see the canal and the tunnel entrance. But a Hun machine gun had forced him to take cover in a shell hole. He emptied his Lewis gun at the Germans. Then he ducked down and reloaded. When he poked his head over the edge of the shell hole, he spotted four Jerries "jump[ing] out of the back of the canal directly behind their gun. I cut loose on them and poured 45 rounds in the four. They dropped. When we climbed out on the other side I passed over the four who were dead."

Fetherolf dropped into another shell hole to reload again. This time, when he peered over the edge, a German sniper shot him in the head. "Ping! Right through my old steel hat one of his bullets went," he wrote to his aunt. "It parted my hair on the girl's side." The bullet not only creased his hair, it drilled a deep groove into the hard bone of his skull. A little lower and it would have split the skull wide open. At first he had no idea he had been shot. Then the left side of him "went out of action" and he started to flop around in the shell hole like a fish out of water. The number two man on his Lewis gun, Pvt. Vincent Dillon, bandaged him up and sent him toward the rear. A moment later, Dillon was killed.

Cpl. Merritt Cutler, also in I Company, recalled how the Boche streamed out of the smoke barrage on his left flank. This assault by the Germans sweeping down out of Vendhuile had come to pass—just the way the captured Hun officer had crowed to O'Ryan that it would happen. "We heard them coming," Cutler said, "and stood up and fought." The air was thick with bullets and he could feel them hitting his trench coat. "I felt like the man in the circus must feel, who has some one throwing knives which outline his shape on the wall, only not as safe." All about him he saw his men falling fast. Cpl. Alexander Kin rushed the attacking Boche, yelling, "Come on, let's go!" A bullet struck him in the head and killed him. A grenade hit 1st Sgt. Dill Werley and Pvt. William C. Dunlap, both from Middletown, blowing them into a German trench. Dunlap died. Werley fell among a pile of dead Huns, where he lost consciousness.

Stated Cutler: "A great many of the 40 with me were wounded or killed, but we stopped 'Jerry.'"

Observing that fight, Tupper saw that Cutler was right, the 107th and one battalion of the 105th had indeed stopped the Germans. Tupper described how the enemy "had come unexpectedly from the left, where the British had been unable to come up. The counter attack was defeated and, despite the odds, elements of the division reached the main line and occupied parts of the St. Quentin Canal. These elements held on, bombing dugouts and positions of the main defense system and capturing more prisoners than their own strength."[22] Lt. Col. William Starr, O'Ryan's assistant chief of staff, confirmed Tupper's observation that after beating back the German counterattack elements of the 107th then penetrated the Hindenburg Line. He added, however, that once through the line, the New Yorkers "[found] large numbers of Boche coming up in their rear, and shooting them in the back with machine guns as they oozed out of this tunnel. They crossed this line and had to fight their way back to the line again and mop up. Thinking they had mopped up, they moved forward again, only to be shot in the back again. It required the assistance of the 105th Infantry at that time to protect our northern [left] flank, which was being heavily enfiladed from the north by both machine gun and artillery fire."[23]

When the 105th Infantry came up to help the 107th, Capt. Raymond F. Hodgdon nearly wept as he advanced over the dead, dying, or wounded Greyjackets. "Some [of] them looked at us in a dazed sort of way while others weakly appealed for aid."

After the counterattack, Cutler and Leland found themselves lost in the soup, each cut off from their company. At that moment, Cutler, alone, but within sight of the canal tunnel, felt it was time for him to retreat.

"So I jumped up and beat it for another shell hole back a little further. Immediately the firing became terrific. They were evidently waiting for some one to get up, but I flopped in safely and right on top of one of our boys, named Blanckett [Pvt. George E. Blanchette], who had both hips smashed by bullets and simply howled when I landed on top of him." [Blanchette had actually pushed on by himself past Lone Tree Trench toward the canal before getting hit. He was cited for his heroism.] Cutler decided to stay with the wounded private until help could be found.

Leland, on the other hand, had gotten himself mixed up in a trench with several men from A Company of the First Battalion, including 1st Sgt. Charles H. Adrean from Utica. A happy-go-lucky sort, Adrean had been shot in the head. Blood seeped through his bandages and streaked his face. He could hardly stand. Leland asked him where the Third Battalion was. Adrean said it was somewhere off to the right. Leland then ordered him to go back and get medical attention. The first sergeant refused, telling the lieutenant that all the officers in A Company had been killed or wounded and he would not leave his men.

"I'll stay with the gang as long as I can stand up," Adrean said.

Leland left Adrean and the few survivors of A Company. As he moved off, the wounded sergeant went forward, looking for the remnants of his company. Those he found he reorganized into a line of defense. He went forward again, searching for more men. This time an explosive bullet thudded into his shoulder. The new wound put him out of action, and he later died.

Leland worked his way to the south, the right flank of the regiment, where he hoped he would find I Company. The trenches he described were "nothing but masses of churned up earth. More dead Boches were lying about. I passed smoking dugouts with dead men choking the stairways." Keeping to the south, he passed over wounded men, one of them an American, who pleaded, "For God's sake help me out of this, will you?" Unable to help the wounded doughboy, he moved on until he reached a road. Machine-gun bullets flew over the road so thick and heavy that he figured a "field mouse could not have crossed alive."

On the other side of the road more trenches zigzagged row after row in the direction of the canal tunnel. The dead were scattered everywhere. Wrecked machine guns littered the ground. Further back he saw on a slight rise of land what he took to be the village of Bony and just beyond that the canal tunnel. Then Leland's eyes caught what at first he thought was a huge bloody bandage draped over a parapet. Using a pair of field glasses, he focused in on the object. It was an American flag pinned to the ground on each corner by a stone to keep it from blowing away. "This was the only time during the war that I remember seeing the colors on the field," he wrote. The flag out there near the canal "put heart and hope in me. It was a good omen."

CHAPTER 15

The Best Names
of the City of New York

Lt. Gen. Sir John Monash wanted a quick, clean, decisive sweep through the Hindenburg Line—an astonishing advance of over eight miles. He had ordered the Empire Division to angle northward, capturing the northern entrance to the St. Quentin Canal Tunnel as well as the villages of Bony, Gouy, and Le Catelet. He had the Old Hickory Division curving southward, taking the southern entrance to the canal tunnel and the villages of Bellicourt and Nauroy. Then his battle-hardened diggers from the Third and Fifth Divisions were to shoot through this gap all the way to the Red Line, overrunning the villages of Beaurevoir, Estrees, and Joncourt. He believed the Hindenburg Line would be in his hands before dark on Sunday, 29 September, and that by the next day the newly gained ground would be firmly secured. In this daring attack, according to C. E. W. Bean, Monash had given his men "strict orders not to become entangled in the Americans' task but to keep to themselves for their own."[1]

Between seven and eight-thirty A.M., the Australians left their encampments that were scattered close to the booming artillery guns to carry out their role in this daring drama. Monash expected the Green Line, the objective of the Americans, to have been reached by ten A.M. or earlier. By eleven A.M., the Australians were to cross the Green Line and be on their way to the Red Line, the last of Germany's organized defenses in France. At that time the Americans were to be relieved, refitted, and within a few days, ready to rejoin the Allies in chasing the Germans out of France.

But ten minutes after eleven, the Australian commander received his first report that something was amiss. His Australian Fifth Division was "hung up" behind the American Thirtieth Division. Two minutes later, word from his Third Division, which was bunched behind O'Ryan's New Yorkers, stated, "We are dug in on the west side of the tunnel. Americans held up in front of us."[2]

"Evidences rapidly multiplied that all was not going well," Monash grumbled. The Australians now had to fight their way forward, over ground that he felt ought to have already been won by the Americans.[3]

Out on the battlefield, Bean reported that the diggers had run into small parties of retiring Americans who "said they did not know what had happened except that they had failed; they had lost their way in the smoke, were without officers and did not know what to do, and were anxious to find anyone who could tell them. German anti-tank guns blazed at the retiring Americans from down the valley, as did other field-guns behind Guillemont Farm on the ridge. These and machine guns caused tragic loss as the untried troops scrambled out of this or that trench to shoot and then make a run back up the valley, heading towards Willow Trench in the hollow or up the bare knoll of it."[4]

Claude Leland, still lost and seeking I Company, nearly got "plugged" by an Australian officer who was working his way forward with several men. Leland asked him if he had seen any troops from the 107th Infantry. "I have lost touch with my Company in the smoke and I can't find them."

The Australian officer then gave the librarian the bad news. "I am afraid you have been badly cut up. What is left of the 27th Division is holding on and our division is coming up to support you. If you go back there a ways, you will find our battalion headquarters near a dressing station and the Colonel can tell you probably where to find your regiment." Leland hurried back to the Australian aid station. There he met the colonel of the Fortieth Battalion, Tenth Brigade, "damning everything." The colonel glared at Leland. "Your troops have been repulsed," he snapped.

"We are going to prepare right here for the counter attack which is probably on its way now. One of your officers is collecting all the Americans he can find. I want you to man and hold this line of trenches here on the left."

Looking around, Leland spotted 1st Lt. Charles Graham-Rogers from B Company. He and handful of 107th men were hunkered down in one of the trenches. Graham-Rogers gave Leland more bad news—Capt. Fancher Nicoll had been killed. He said that Capt. Harry Hayward had been killed, too; and so had been 1st Lt. Samuel Crump Jr., and that Lt. Ralph Polk Buell was mortally wounded. As they talked, Ham Andrews, captain of the Machine Gun Company, came toward them in the trench. He was wounded, and his company decimated. He had grim news, too. First Lt. Edward Willis had been killed, 1st Lt. Paul Gadebusch wounded, and Cpl. Thomas O'Shea missing.

Leland climbed out of the trench to look for more 107th men. In his search, he heard wounded Germans crying for help. He had not gone far when he found several boys from the Headquarters Company and brought them back to the trench. Counting heads, he had twenty-five men. The Australian colonel showed up and said that at three P.M. they would attack Lone Tree Trench. When the time came, Leland's provisional company moved out with the Australians. The Aussies worked their way around to the left and began bombing a Boche trench. The return machine-gun fire and artillery barrage stopped them cold, and the Americans were also halted.

In the midst of the fight, Cpl. Merritt Cutler suddenly appeared out of the heavy smoke and hail of bullets, sprinting toward them.

As mentioned earlier, Cutler had been pinned down in a shell hole with Pvt. George F. Blanchette. Wounded severely in both hips, Blanchette had begged Cutler to drag him back to a dressing station. Every time the private moved, Cutler heard his smashed bones grating against each other. When the machine-gun fire finally died down, he pulled Blanchette from the shell hole and for the next two hours, as bullets whistled over them from both directions, they inched back fifty yards where Cutler thought he would find help. But Blanchette's cries were too much. The private was now delirious. Cutler had to find a stretcher bearer. Keeping low, he ran through the smoke. Ahead of him he eyed a company of Australians. They pointed for him to drop into a trench. Following their directions he dove in next to Leland and his men. But he did not stay long. He found an Australian stretcher bearer and led him back to Blanchette.

"I took one end [of the stretcher] and an 'Aussie' the other," he recalled, "and we went out in front and brought poor Blanckett [*sic*] in."

After rescuing his wounded comrade, Cutler rejoined Leland. But now neither the Americans nor the Australians were able to move on. "We stayed in the trench until night," Cutler stated. Leland noted that the "shell fire grew hotter and a cold drizzle added to our discomfort." He also remembered how before dusk Cutler went out again to bring in more wounded, braving hostile machine-gun bullets to save several of the boys. His deed that day earned him the Distinguished Service Cross, the British Military Medal, and the French Croix de Guerre.

When it finally grew dark, the Australian colonel ordered Leland, Cutler, and the rest of the doughboys back to the support line, telling them that he had enough of his own men to carry on the fight.

Not all the silk stocking soldiers were ordered back and, in fact, those who were disobeyed such commands and fought on with the Australians.

In one instance, the Australians pressing forward saw "a number of figures of which one was clearly waving them back," Bean commented. "They [his Australians] went on, however, and reaching the mound at 10:50 found several Americans along the bank and dugouts. These men could say only that something was wrong ahead. Looking thither the Australians saw a few more Americans in the ditch of a light railway 300 yards out. Just then bullets swept viciously from the north along the rear side of the mound."[5]

Messages reached Monash's command that the Twenty-seventh Division had, according to Bean's account of the battle, "undoubtedly reached the Tunnel mound, but how much further they had gone was unknown."[6] Both American regiments, the 108th and the 107th, had become so mixed up with the Australians that Arthur Conan Doyle claimed it would "tax the industry of some Antipodean historian to trace each unit, Australian or American, and define their relations to each other."[7] Bean reported that about one hundred doughboys entered the same trench as the Forty-first Australian Brigade and captured five machine guns and seventy prisoners. An airplane observer reported that Americans had reached the tunnel.[8] Sgt. Roy Beyerl from Malone, assigned to the Third Battalion Intelligence Section, reported that K Company had actually "dashed across the aqueduct." He said that here the battle raged more fiercely, if that could be. "Dugouts equipped like subterranean mansions were blasted with hand grenades, and their fleeing occupants were picked off on the run. The tunnels and trenches gave up their teeming hordes."[9] From the sky, ground flares were seen in Gouy, along with the village of Le Catelet one of the 107th Infantry's primary objectives.

"If the air report was true," Bean stated, "the 27th Division, despite repeated warnings, which Monash had begged the leaders to impress upon their troops, had made the same mistake that it was believed to have committed on September 27th—dashed to its objective without thoroughly mopping up the trenches left behind."[10]

The Australian brass believed that the Americans had rushed ahead recklessly because of international rivalry—they wanted to be the first to break the Hindenburg Line and not the Aussies.[11]

"While this was happening," Monash published two years later, "the Third Australian Division, deprived of the assistance either of artillery or of tanks and in broad daylight found themselves confronted with the difficult problem of carrying out the whole of the task which had been set for the Twenty-seventh Division because of the reappearance of the enemy upon the ground successfully passed over by some of the Americans earlier in the day nullified all the value of that success." Monash was ignoring the very fact that under a worse situation he had sent the Americans on an undeniable suicide mission. The commander then had to abandon the original plan, "which had taken so many days and so much labour to prepare," so that his troops could secure the gains of the day and prepare for another day of fighting.

Thus the Australians were ordered to push on over ground that still held pockets of Germans, blast them out of their hiding places and then link up with those Americans still believed fighting at the very barricades of the canal tunnel itself. According to the Australian general, "air observers continued to report the presence of American troops between the Hindenburg Line and Le Catelet, and also in the latter village. Late that night [29 September], an Australian liaison officer managed to make his way back into our lines with the story that he had actually advanced with a battalion of Americans into Le Catelet, and that they were still there, although partially surrounded."[12] The American colonel, Franklin Ward, stated that it was Capt. Clinton E. Fisk's First Battalion that, with the support of the 105th Infantry, had indeed reached the tunnel mouth. And in doing so, he wrote in the present tense, "they are protecting the left flank which has nothing to fasten to, for the troops of the Third British Corps on the north have not come up."[13]

German prisoners, herded back toward the Australians, admitted that the Americans had crossed the Hindenburg Line.

Conan Doyle reported, "For a thousand yards north of the interdivisional boundary, near the village of Bony, they [the New Yorkers] got into the main line, and from point to point, all along the front bold parties pushed forward as far as Gouy and Le Catelet, many of whom never got back."[14]

Lt. Col. J. Leslie Kincaid stated, "The tunnel was taken and the retreating Germans were spewed out of the ground in hordes. Airplanes flying over the battleground reported that the areas behind the tunnel were thick with running men."[15]

In his history of the Fourth Army, Montgomery wrote of O'Ryan's men, "Only the most fearless and self-sacrificing troops would have faced the fire to which they were subjected from the moment the attack started, and it is to their undying credit that they achieved what they did and broke the backbone of the tunnel defences."[16]

When C. E. W. Bean's official war history debuted in 1942, he was convinced that the Americans had not penetrated the main Hindenburg Line, or of if they did so, it was in small, isolated groups of lost men. He even discredited the Australian liaison officer's eyewitness account that he had accompanied a battalion of Americans across the line and into Le Catelet. Yet when reporting the battle for the newspapers in 1918, Bean wrote, "There is not the slightest doubt that, in their first assault yesterday, the Americans reached Gouy." He went on to acclaim the New Yorkers, as well as the men of the Thirtieth Division, fighting on the right flank of the Twenty-seventh. "Some day, when the full story of the American attack yesterday can be told, the American people will have every reason to thrill with pride at those magnificent troops upon whom the tremendous task of yesterday fell. Never in this war have I seen keener or braver soldiers or more intelligent and high-minded men."[17]

Monash was not so praiseworthy. He found the "situation . . . profoundly disturbing." And so on the night of 29 September, he issued orders to the American II Corps to "withdraw all advanced troops that could be reached, and to concentrate their regiments for rest and reorganization, so as to be ready as soon as possible for re-deployment." What Monash discovered, however, was that the Americans could not be "induced" to "withdraw from the fighting and to rejoin their own units, so keen were they to continue their advance."[18]

Throughout the night and for the next two days, obstinate remnants of the Twenty-seventh fought alongside the Australians. The wounded and dead were scattered ahead of them as they advanced against the Hun. One doughboy, Pfc. Edward A. Pierce, who had earlier donned a German officer's coat and walked up to the enemy and machine-gunned them, hooked up with the Aussies as they crossed over the canal. He stayed with them until he was killed.

Pvt. Harold W. Simmons of the Headquarters Company described how he and a lost bunch of the boys spent the night "standing to waiting for 'Jerry' to come over. To help things it rained all-night and freezing. No coats on. We had to dig in the side of the trench to put the wounded and dead in, to get them out of the way. But the trench wasn't big enough for all. Nearly all the wounded died during the night from exposure. We thought it was our last day on earth. But dawn appeared and saw some figures come over the hill behind us. The Australians came up and relieved us."

Bugler Ralph Kretschmar, who had been struck down and nearly paralyzed by a potato masher on Sunday, his right shoulder torn wickedly open, had also spent the night in a shell hole. The following day, "When noon approached I thought I was about to cash in. I had no water. Well, I stayed there until the afternoon and then the Australians went by and one of their medical men put some rum on his fingers and let me lick them. This put some strength in me and I felt better. Then some of our men put me in a blanket and carried me to a more sheltered position." Kretchmar lay where he was left for the rest of Monday and through another night until midday on Tuesday. "I was finally found in pretty bum condition as the shell hole was pretty wet and my wounds kept bleeding."

It was not until that Tuesday, 1 October, when the last of the bloodied and bone-weary doughboys finally left the field of battle while the diggers continued on. In the end, on a front of almost six miles, a wedge of six thousand yards had been driven into the feared Hindenburg Line. The Germans were now in retreat, moving back, then reforming into hurried, makeshift defensive positions where they continued to cause heavy casualties. On 6 October the German chancellor sent a message to President Woodrow Wilson, requesting an armistice.

A day later, Lt. Kenneth Gow wrote, "We took part in the great attack launched against the Hindenburg Line, at one of the strongest points, if not the strongest. And, Weakie, we smashed it, smashed it into a shapeless ditch. We went over the top with the Australians, the cream of Britain's fighting men, behind us, and when our objective was reached they went through us and carried on what we had made possible."

Pvt. Frederick R. Toombs of the Headquarters Company, who had been working as a guide to the patched-together 106th Infantry so its men could mop up and was later cited for his bravery by O'Ryan, neatly summed up the chaotic battle in the *Gazette*. "Confused momentarily by a heavy smoke barrage sent by the British as an aid, consisting of shells that gave out dense clouds of smoke bursting, our boys rallied and assaulted the machine gun nests in a manner actually sublime. They went at 'Jerry' from the front, and from the flanks. No matter who dropped, others there were to 'carry on.' They worked around in the rear and jumped into the nests with fixed bayonets. They caught him overhead by throwing hand grenades and shooting rifle grenades. 'Jerry' was attacked from every possible direction.

"Before noon he was giving way. He began to break. Our boys went over his machine gun nests, rushed his trenches, forced their way through his elaborate wire, cleaned out the reserves from his big tunnel, drove him across the canal. We had started from the town of Ronssoy, about which our trenches were constructed. We gained our chief objective, the town of Le Catelet, after the Germans were pushed farther on."

Sgt. George Ely of K Company bitterly noted in his diary of 3 October,

"We Americans opened up the way for the English and Australians so that they have since been able to go forward about ten kilos. Of course, they get the entire credit for it."

If Bean had an American counterpart, especially when it came to being a keen observer of warfare, it was Lt. Col. Wade Hampton Hayes. The slightly built, thirty-nine-year-old Virginian was the only National Guard officer to serve on the staff of Gen. John Pershing during the war. Like Bean, Hayes had been a journalist, working as Sunday editor of the New York *Tribune* for six years. He next switched over to Wall Street and a more lucrative career as an investment banker. He traced his military lineage back to his father, two grandfathers, and nine uncles, all of whom had fought for the South in the Civil War, and where the names Wade and Hampton are still cherished in places like Virginia and South Carolina. Hayes himself had fought in the Spanish-American War with the Fourth Virginia Volunteers. When he moved to New York to study political science at Columbia University, he joined the Seventh Regiment. As a proud I Company Greyjacket, he rose through the ranks, and was a captain in the guard in the spring of 1917 when the United States declared war on Germany. On 10 June 1918 he was assigned to Pershing's staff.

Hayes held a fascinating job. Basically, he was the commander in chief's eyes and ears up and down the entire western front. He went to almost every battle, sending back detailed reports. He boasted that within a five-month period, he had traveled close to twenty-two thousand miles, and that he had witnessed engagements involving eleven American divisions, four French divisions, and two British divisions. When Pershing was bogged down in the Argonne Forest, trying to push his American First Army through the Meuse Valley, early and confusing reports from the Hindenburg Line reached his headquarters. He wanted to know what exactly happened. He dispatched Hayes to find out.

"The few stray facts about the recent battle in which they [107th Infantry] were engaged that reached these headquarters [AEF] indicated that something unusual, even for this war, had happened," Hayes penned to his friend George W. Chauncey on 28 October. Chauncey, who had joined the Seventh back in 1872, was chairman of the board of directors of the Mechanics Bank in Brooklyn. "The General . . . decided that he wished more complete information on the subject so I was called in from the Argonne-Meuse front where I happened to be at the time and sent north for the special purpose of making a detailed report on the entire operation. . . . Of course my investigations related to the entire Division but the part in which you will be most interested relates primarily to the old Regiment."[19]

As the letter indicated, Hayes was indeed more concerned about *their* old regiment and the fate of their silk stocking friends than he was about the rest of the division. But he was determined to write a complete and, under the circumstances, unbiased report, and in doing so let the chips fall where they may. For two days, he made "a most careful reconnaissance," he assured Chauncey. He personally interviewed Monash, O'Ryan, and Sir Archibald Montgomery, the chief of staff of the British Fourth Army; Maj. Gen. George W. Read and Maj. Gen. Edward M. Lewis, commanding officers of the American II Corps and Thirtieth Division; brigade and regimental commanders; and dozens of other officers. He walked over the battlefield and "personally got down into at least one-hundred gun emplacements in order to sight their field of fire." Already knowledgeable about most of the battlefields of Belgium and France, Hayes professed that *nowhere* [his italics] "could one find a position that could with greater reason be considered more impregnable than that strip of ground over which those wonderful men swept like an avalanche." He carefully added that, of course, "I would be prejudiced in favor of these fellows; who could have been associated with them as long as I have and know them as well as I do and not be, yet what I am saying to you I said in my official report where exaggeration would not be tolerated; and no statement I have ever made on any subject has been more completely justified by the facts."

Hayes submitted his report and supporting documents to Pershing on 15 October. In it, the former newspaper editor detailed how the British III Corps had failed in its mission to reach the predetermined jumping-off line, putting the New York Division at a distinct disadvantage for the attack on 29 September. He described the Hindenburg Line, the deep dugouts and underground galleries, and the canal tunnel with barges converted into barracks able to house two German divisions. He recounted the preliminary attack of 27 September and how the Fifty-third Brigade of the Twenty-seventh Division had to mop up holes, dugouts, and tunnels repeatedly, and that the only success that day was the severe losses in killed or wounded enemy. He noted that when the actual assault took place, the Allied artillery barrage landed more than one thousand yards ahead of the New Yorkers, offering little protection, if any.

"The ground over which the 54th Infantry Brigade had to attack without artillery assistance," Hayes wrote, "was literally seething with machine-gun nests, and almost every square foot of ground was completely enfiladed with machine-gun fire." He described The Knoll and Guillemont and Quennemont Farms. It was at these strongholds that the Germans made the "supreme effort to stop the attack." In almost every instance, he stated, he found dead Boche still lying about their machine guns and that almost without exception they had been killed by the bayonet. "Very few of the enemy dead appeared to have been killed by rifle or shell fire," he wrote. He discussed details of Monash's plan—how the two Americans divisions were to open up the center of the Hindenburg Line, pushing out the right and left flanks so the Australians could leapfrog them and reach the Red Line. He mentioned the British III Corps' failure to guard the Americans' left flank and the quick destruction of the tanks.

He concluded that, even though the Twenty-seventh Division lacked barrage protection, advanced elements "reached their final objective (the green line east of Goy-Le Catelet [*sic*])." But once there he explained how the Germans poured through their underground passages and hit the New Yorkers from behind. "The maze of tunnels and underground galleries permitted the Boche to continue conveying troops to positions well in the rear of these advanced elements in such great numbers that they were enabled to supply sufficient machine gunners and infantry to the west of the canal to hold up not only the support elements of the 27th Division, but also the Australian troops following in the rear." He even mentioned the confusion that suddenly swept over the battlefield. But he added that after three hard days of fighting and mopping up, the Australians, in fact, had "accomplished that part of their mission in passing through the 2d American Corps and having established themselves, the 2d American Corps was withdrawn a short distance to the rear to refit and reorganize preparatory to their participation in operations now in progress."

Hayes addressed the question of mopping up as well, claiming that to have done so properly would have required all the troops that were in the attack. "This is borne out by the fact that it required an Australian Division and a part of the 27th Division most of two days to complete this mopping up." He said that the unrelenting attack of the New Yorkers kept the German army too busy to thwart other advances along its front.

"The whole fighting on this part of the front," Hayes stated, "appears to have been a free-for-all, in which everybody was fighting everywhere throughout the width of the contested area without there being any well-defined front."[20]

When Hayes got to Ronssoy and then proceeded to the start line of 29 September, what was left of the Empire Division was still coming off the battlefield. He hurried forward, searching for silk stocking survivors, most especially the men from I Company. Standing on the roadside, he at last spotted the 107th Infantry, the old Seventh. It marched past him in columns of squads. He noticed how the men held their heads up with a proud spirit. As they neared him, he "detected a bit more elasticity in their step as they came swinging down the road with characteristic touch of the elbow and arm swinging across the front of their bodies just as we have so often seen when they were on parade. Of course I thought of General Dan [Appleton] and longed for him to see his beloved Grey Jackets as I saw them."

Looking closer, Hayes saw that their faces were grim with seriousness. Then he caught sight of K Company. He was stunned to see only three squads of what was left of the millionaire boys and their upstate apple-knockers. Right behind them swung just two squads of I Company. Hayes stepped in and trooped beside his former company with a touch of the elbow.

"I simply had to march along with that old Toujours Pret crowd until I had shaken hands with every mothers' son of them and when they had passed out of sight I hated myself for not having given way to my impulse to hug each and every one as well."[21]

Also joining the march off the field was Mess Sgt. Theodore Tyler, who described the I Company boys as an "awful forlorn looking bunch, filthy and just completely all in. I was never so sorry in all my life."

Hayes then went out on the battlefield. Here he found dead doughboys and slain Germans. Burial parties from both sides had not yet appeared, although makeshift graves were everywhere. Many of the Boche had bayonets still in them. One bayonet had gone clear through a Hun's chest and had pinned him to a dugout timber. At first he wanted to yank the weapon out. But he felt it better to leave the blade in so another visitor could also thrill in seeing how the enemy had been killed.

Trodding across the hills and shell holes and crumbled-in trenches, standing on The Knoll and in the ruins of Guillemont and Quennemont Farms, and gazing out past the St. Quentin Canal Tunnel to the villages of Gouy and Le Catelet, he was at last overcome. "I will never forget that bleak October morning when under leaden skies I found on a hillside in northern France the final resting place of some of the best friends I ever had in my life," Hayes confessed to Chauncey. He came across the place where Percy Hall, the commander of I Company, had been killed. His body was in a shallow grave. Hall, who had the led the charge while ill with fever, had been Hayes's first sergeant in Texas, and later his first lieutenant when they drilled inside the armory on Park Avenue or at Central Park's Sheep Meadow.

The slender Virginian, now more a New Yorker than ever a descendant of the Southern aristocracy, knelt over Hall's grave. Tears swept down his cheeks. "I loved that boy as a brother," he wrote, "for he was one of the sweetest natured men I have ever known."

Percy Hall was among 349 of the 2,500 officers and men of the 107th Infantry who were killed or died of the wounds they had suffered on Sunday, 29 September—the day of the Feast of St. Michael, the Archangel. It was the highest casualty rate ever of a U.S. regiment on a single day. There was a total of 1,062 casualties among the silk stocking soldiers who had left the start line on that cold, mist enshrouded morning. The Third Battalion, under Raphael Egan, was hit the worst. One hundred twenty-two of his men lost their lives while more than three hundred, including Egan himself, were wounded—a casualty rate of almost 60 percent. On the entire battlefield, counting the other regiments and units of the Twenty-seventh Division, 686 New Yorkers died and over 2,000 were wounded, gassed, captured, or listed as missing in action. From 28 September through 2 October, 393 Greyjackets lost their lives.[22]

The 107th Infantry won four Medals of Honor, the most by a regiment for a single day's action in the war. D Company's Pvt. Michael Valente, the Italian immigrant from Ogdensburg, got his medal for his angry assault against several machine-gun nests. Three "Jersey Gunners" with Summit connections, Sgt. John Latham and Cpls. Alan Eggers and Thomas O'Shea, earned theirs for saving a tank crew and then holding off constant attacks against them. Recommended for the Medal of Honor was Ralph Polk Buell, who had rushed alone through the German barbed wire when his company had gotten bogged down by machine-gun fire. Although severely wounded and believed killed, Buell survived. He was one of sixty-four silk stocking soldiers who were honored with the American Distinguished Service Cross.

Remembering the heroes of the 107th, O'Ryan, who had begun his military career in the old Seventh, remarked in his memoirs with a touch of sadness because of his long relationship with the regiment and its officers and men, and because he was one of them: "The roster of the dead contains the best names of the city of New York—best in the sense of family tradition and all that stands for good citizenship in the history of the city."

CHAPTER 16

We Keep Moving . . . Deeper . . . into the Darkness of This Dream

I t was not until two P.M. on Tuesday, 1 October, two days after the assault had begun on the Hindenburg Line, that the 107th Infantry was officially relieved by the Australians, although sporadic fighting was still going on as Lt. Gen. Sir John Monash's diggers pushed east toward the Red Line. The Americans marched back to Peronne and eventually to the small village of Doingt to rest and to be refitted for more combat.

Now safely behind the lines, Kenneth Gow wrote home. "You have never been so close, Mother, as you are tonight. I feel as though I wanted you as I never have in all my life before."

While Gow was writing this letter, the entire length of the western front was ablaze. But all was not going as smoothly as the Allies had hoped, although the Germans in front of Sir Douglas Haig's armies were now pulling back from the Hindenburg Line. French president Georges Clemenceau was enraged at Gen. John Pershing's interminably slow progress through the Argonne Forest and Meuse Valley.[1] The valley's steep, hilly terrain coupled with heavy German reinforcements almost thwarted the Americans. Yet they punched forward like a battering ram, and grudgingly the Hun gave way. On the Belgian front, north of the British, King Albert's men found themselves bogged down in the muck of Flanders. As the German armies systematically retreated, Ludendorff planned to establish new defensive lines on the border of his country, where he felt he could hold out through the winter. In doing so, Germany could demand peace terms that in the end would justify four years of horrible bloodshed.

In subsequent letters to his family, Gow broke the news of the death of Lt. Edward Willis and the others from their hometown. He told them the Dartmouth track star, Sgt. Bill Drabble, also wounded on the 29th, had died. A month later, Bill's younger brother, Phillip, a gunner in the 105th Machine Gun Battalion, would die from influenza. Yet Gow did not tell his parents of his own heroism for which he would later be awarded the Distinguished Service Cross and the French Croix de Guerre. All through the battle, the young lieutenant had brought supplies up to the men by mule, braving continuous machine-gun and shell fire.

From Doingt, Oscar E. Hellquist, the daring intelligence officer from Summit, sent a letter to his mother. "If you could have seen us when we finally came out," he wrote. "I was filthy. Hadn't washed or shaved for a week and was mud from head to foot and dead tired from constant running around and lack of sleep. But I'm grateful to be here."

In another homeward-bound letter, Claude Leland, after stating that by some strange chance he was alive and well and without a scratch to show what he had been through, echoed Hellquist's sentiments. "If you could only have seen me that day. It would have made a picture 'no artist could paint.' I was all mud and glory including a week old beard. My leggins and trousers were torn to shreds on the wire—my good trench coat ripped and stained and ruined. A more forlorn looking warrior probably never came out of a fight."

To his mother, Raeburn Van Buren, who as division artist had been spared from taking part in the attack, assured her "that I am safe and sound and that there will be no more reason to worry for some time to come. I have felt the effect of your C. S. [Christian Science] work a thousand times and feel so sure that it will continue to help me thru this trouble. I would be willing to stake my future on it. No, there is no need for worry because we will soon be back again in a quiet place, far from the noise of battle—back where we can see a woman and a building that hasn't been shattered away from its original shape."

Even while unscathed survivors, like Gow, Hellquist, Leland, and Van Buren regrouped in Doingt, there were silk stocking soldiers still on the battlefield, most of them desperately wounded, pinned down in shell holes or simply adrift among the dead and dying. At the time, Maj. Gen. John O'Ryan had no idea what his losses totaled. He immediately sent the 107th's Headquarters Company and what was left of its Machine Gun Company to scour the killing ground for casualties and to salvage any usable matériel.

Throughout the night of 29 and 30 September and for days later, the wounded worked their way back, one by one, or in small groups, even though Boche snipers tried to knock them off and an enemy machine gunner suddenly appeared from an overlooked dugout, firing away.

Lt. Paul Gadebusch had been hit early on in the fight and lay in a shell hole all day on the 29th, knowing that another twenty-four hours without medical help and he would perish. His best bet, he figured, was to work his way back at night. His wound and the frightful loss of blood made it impossible for him to run or crawl. He had to walk upright. As dusk settled over the western front, Gaddy flexed his stiff muscles. He realized that even though his brain told him he could do it, his body argued otherwise—it was, he thought, rebelling at every suggestion, because it was "discontented, physically exhausted, stupid, heavily laden, scarcely able to move about." When it finally got dark, "after years of interminably waiting," and a lull in the machine-gun fire seemed to have settled in, he yelled at himself, "Come on! Get up you fool!" Urging himself on as if he were still an athlete at Princeton, he wobbled to his feet: "There are only the last forty strokes, the last quarter! Everything when really needed!" Machine guns rattled in the night. Step-by-step he staggered back.

In the dark an American voice shouted at him. "Hands up! Who is there?"

"An American wounded!" he hoarsely replied.

"Get him into a trench," the voice ordered to someone.

Gaddy tumbled into a corner of the trench, now unable to move. Yet he felt his heart singing. To himself he said, "I got away with it!"[2]

Farther out on the battlefield, Dutch Wilbur, blood seeping from his mouth after a bullet had passed through his lung, remained hidden under a pile of German overcoats. By late afternoon on 1 October, he wondered if he might bleed to death. Somewhere nearby a machine gun kept up a steady barrage. He feared the Boche would soon return to retake the shell hole. His chances for survival were not good. Voices sounded above him. Risking it all, he peeked out from under the overcoats. Several Australians peered back at him.

"Hello, Sam, are you winged?" one of them asked.

"Yes," Wilber said, thankful that they were not Germans.

"Can you walk?"

"Yes."

"Well, you just wait a minute until I take care of that machine gun nest out there and I will take you back to a first aid station."

The Australians then silenced the machine gunners and returned to take the private first class from Otisville back to safety.[3]

Pvt. August Engler, whose parents were from Bavaria, had been riddled with bullets and too weak to crawl out of his shell hole. He desperately wanted a cigarette. Along the edge of his shell hole two Boche loomed big as death. In German he quickly asked them for a cigarette. One of them dug a cigarette out of his tunic, lit it, and stuck it between Engler's lips. The Utica machine gunner inhaled the sweet smoke and passed out. When he awoke he found himself safe in an Australian first-aid station. His German saviors were gone, prisoners of war.[4]

Cpl. Ben Franklin hated the rain and the way the wind changed and blew harder and that all around him he had to listen to the pitiful moaning of his fellow soldiers with their "arms and legs blown off" as they begged for stretcher bearers. "The poor fellow next to me, who had lost both his legs, was delirious all the time and toward morning his spirit passed into the keeping of the God of battles." Franklin was not discovered until midmorning on the 1st.[5]

Sgt. John L. MacDonnell lay out near the canal tunnel for three days until an Australian came up to him, bent down, and asked, "Hey, Mate, are you dead?" MacDonnell groaned that he was not yet dead. The Aussies also found the body of I Company's Cpl. Harold Kunkle, the promising Brooklyn illustrator. Kunkle still clutched his Bible.[6] Another of the I

Company dead was Pvt. Carroll Coll, who had given his family Bible that had gone through the Civil War to Supply Sgt. Tyler Johnson for safe-keeping. Later, Leland sent the Bible to Coll's aunt in Dorchester, Mass.

The Aussies, it turned out, were looking for more than the dead and wounded. They wanted souvenirs. Not only did they want German bayonets and pistols and helmets. They coveted American money and jewelry. Cpl. Alan Eggers complained to his parents that, although the Australians were the most wonderful fighting men he had ever seen, on the battlefield they were so at home "some of them were seen looking for souvenirs while they were waiting to advance and while the machine gun bullets were thick, to say the least."[7] The worst of them carried gunnysacks to stow their loot in, and eagerly rifled through the pockets of the dead Americans. Letters were ripped up and thrown away. In a confidential report to Pershing, dated 18 December, O'Ryan protested. "Bodies of our dead were systematically looted." He even mentioned that "In one case the finger of an officer who wore a valuable ring was cut off for the purpose of removing the ring." He added that such action "aroused" criticism among his men, and that if the Australians themselves had not been so praiseworthy of the fighting spirit of the doughboys the bitter feeling toward them might have gotten out of hand.[8]

With the rescue of the wounded under way, burial parties, accompanied by chaplains, marked and identified the dead; stuck their rifles into the ground, bayonet down; and tied white rags around the gunstocks so the stretcher bearers could find them. The dead were carried to a freshly dug cemetery close to Guillemont Farm, across the way from a first-aid dressing station. The graveyard was cut into a hillside. Here they were placed in long rows, awaiting burial. In the end, over 160 men of the 107th would be buried there. More than 130 others would be interred in another cemetery in the nearby village of Bony.

Hellquist and Sgt. John Latham joined one of the search parties. "Yesterday [2 October] I went back to the lines with a volunteer detail to search for bodies," Hellquist wrote, "which were in obscure places and might possibly be overlooked." While they were out hunting for the dead, O'Ryan showed up on horseback. He asked Hellquist what his name and the name of his regiment were. When the sandy-haired lieutenant answered that it was the 107th, the division commander "just beamed." According to Hellquist, he then asked "if the men realized how wonderful their work (the fighting of the regiment) had been." Next O'Ryan gathered the party around him, Hellquist boasted to his mother, and told them that what they had done "was a deed that would go down in history. And when he says such things you can believe that something unusual took place. But we all knew that when the test came the men would show up true blue." Cpl. Harold Mills was there, too, and put down in his diary that night, "Gen. O'Ryan met us & said he was proud of us. Did work Ozzies were afraid to do. Work of 3rd Bat. was wonderful."

Among the regimental chaplains attending to the dead at the cemetery at Guillemont Farm were Edwin F. Keefer, Hugh Stewart, and Father Peter Hoey. Keefer, a Lutheran, recalled, "Here we laid fifteen, some of our own regiment and some of the engineers and other units—Jews, Catholics, and Protestants—side by side. Chaplain Hoey read his service, Chaplain Stewart and I our own. But what was to be done for the Jews? No Rabbi had yet come to the Division; and the Jewish boys declined to officiate. Borrowing a Jewish Prayer Book, I read the translation of a burial prayer over the same grave, and I believe that our Divine Master approved the act."[9] It was not until several days later that the first Jewish chaplain arrived at the division.

As the chaplains went back out to search for more bodies, the Germans opened an artillery barrage. Latham suffered a wound in the attack that quickly "became so violent," Keefer said, "that we returned to Headquarters just in time to escape a very heavy shelling." Three men were killed and seven wounded. This attack filled Father Hoey with such hate for the Hun that two weeks later he confessed that he was praying to "erase the stain from my mind and soul. Oh, how I have aged."[10] Gow, also part of the burial party, was as incensed as Father Hoey. "God punish the Kaiser and the fiends he has collected around him. They wouldn't even let us bury our dead. They fired on our stretcher-bearers with the Red Cross insignia, the symbol of mercy. They fired with machine guns on our wounded who were crawling back. As there is a just God in heaven, they will pay for their atrocities."

Corporal Eggers, Latham's comrade, had also volunteered—not to bring in the dead, but to salvage any equipment. He also had another reason to volunteer. When he was getting his neck wound dressed at a first-aid station on 30 September, he learned that his best friend, Cpl. Thomas O'Shea, had been wounded, but not brought in. The next day he was informed that O'Shea was still missing, that there was no record of him. "When the company moved up again to bring in the dead," he later wrote to O'Shea's parents, "I got permission to go out again and look for Tommy. I was unable to find him." Even when O'Shea was listed as missing, Eggers wrote, "I couldn't give up hope that he would be found at one of the hospitals."[11]

At least Sgt. George Ely received good news concerning one of his best friends. He entered that news in his diary on 3 October: "I just heard that Oak was not killed, but was seen on a stretcher on his way back. We still have details picking up the dead. It was an awful massacre."

Pfc. T. J. Oakley Rhinelander had endured severe wounds, the last ripping open a deep gash in his side. In a letter to his father from the Australian military hospital in Rouen, he explained that he had been hit so early in the fight that he never had a chance to see a "Fritz," only the wounded and dead all around him. He said that after his third wound, all he remembered was "being terribly jammed in ambulances and passing through different dressing stations. Each one said 'Get this case to the rear right away.' Then there was the train ride till I got here."

Rouen was one of many hospitals the wounded were shipped to. In a lot of cases, they were sent on to England, or as they called it, "Gone to Blighty."

Cpl. James Throckmorton Vought recollected his trip to Blighty. He had taken an explosive bullet through the lung. Somehow he had walked back in the thick fog and low-lying fumes of mustard gas when he emerged into brilliant sunlight. It was midmorning on the 29th. Australians were lined up behind four tanks, ready to advance against the Hindenburg Line. Vought staggered up to them, seeking help. One of the Aussies pointed to a white tape on the ground and told him to follow it back for about two miles and he would find a dressing station. As he struggled on, he began to grow faint. A lieutenant spotted him and led him into a trench, explaining that if he stayed in it and walked back three hundred yards there would be a dressing station. The trench, the officer said, would protect him from shell fire. The moment the word shell fire reached his ears, Vought tuned into the noise exploding about him. Shells dropped too close to him. Then the Australian artillery answered. "It was a terrific shock to me, and I had just strength enough to climb out of the trench and reel around when one of the gunners saw me and picked me up. They called for a stretcher and pretty soon I was at the dressing station. My first aid card was marked at 10 A.M."

The medic thought the Yank was done for, and he was put in a room with the cases that were not expected to live. "Men—English, Scotch, Australians, and Americans—died all around me that night. For breakfast the next morning I asked for porridge; but all they had was sausage. So I ate it." Later that day he was shipped to Rouen. He believed that a major there, named Kingsland, saved his life. "He aspirated my lung—removed the loose blood—and gave me the best care possible. He worked for days without rest on the forty cases under his charge." On 6 October Vought was shipped to England, the beginning of a series of misfortunes. On the way, his ambulance broke down. Trying to fix the engine, the driver left the motor running. Vought inhaled gasoline fumes. His throat and lungs became irritated. When he finally got on the train to carry him to Le Havre, it got stuck in the tunnel leading out of Rouen. By the time he reached the coast, the hospital ship was packed with wounded men. Vought had been promised a bed, but there were none left. He tried to bribe a sergeant major to find him a bed. No bed turned up, and thus he languished on the litter for forty-eight hours, using a life preserver for a pillow. "They tried to make me wear it, but I wouldn't." He finally arrived at the Canadian military hospital in Taplow, England. He spent a month in Taplow and then was sent to the American hospital near Winchester.

"Finally, the good news came that we were to be sent back [to America], and on December 3 we went to Liverpool and boarded the *Leviathan*." Vought arrived in Hoboken, New Jersey, on 16 December. He was placed in the Columbia War Hospital. Eventually, he made it home to Rochester—in time for his sister's wedding, although at the time he was suffering from influenza.[12]

Cpl. George Delahay, one of L Company's heroes in the Dickebusch Sector of Belgium, was among the scores of Americans to die in Blighty. The Beacon native, raised as an Episcopalian, caught pneumonia after being wounded. Just before he died, he converted to Catholicism. After his body was shipped back to the States, however, his funeral was conducted at St. Andrew's Episcopal Church in Newburgh. Delahay was buried in a cemetery outside the town of Fishkill.[13]

A Company sergeant C. Edgar Burton, who on Sunday had taken an explosive bullet in the shoulder that exited his back, had his wound first bandaged in a sunken road. He was then taken to an Australian field ambulance station, rebandaged, and given the best cup of cocoa he ever tasted. He was put aboard a narrow-gauge rail train and evacuated three miles back to a casualty clearing station. That station was too crowded with wounded, and so he was driven by truck to another one. There he received a new bandage. He was placed on a stretcher. He stayed on the stretcher until Tuesday, when he was finally loaded onto a Red Cross train and transported to the hospital at Rouen. He got a bed and meal and was there for two days. On Thursday he was moved to Le Havre, where wounded soldiers were met by Red Cross workers who handed out cigarettes and newspapers. Burton was then taken aboard a hospital ship that carried him to Southampton. There was another train trip in Blighty. He did not arrive at his final location, the hospital at Brighton, until Saturday. His journey had lasted a week.

Cpl. Charles S. Lloyd Sell, also from A Company, who had tried to keep an eye on his brother, Edward, during the battle, was gassed. Charles was sent to a dressing station, where he lost track of his brother. From the dressing station, he boarded a bus and was driven to another first-aid station. Next, he and the other wounded were carried aboard a narrow-gauge train that, after starting on its trip to Rouen, jumped the track. In Rouen, Charles got the "scare of my life." A wounded man in his company dropped a bombshell. He said that he had heard one of the Sell brothers had been killed. Then the soldier left the hospital. "This got me crazy," Charles proclaimed in a missive back to the *Gazette*, which he wrote while still in the hospital. He then started hunting for Ed. But it was impossible to get any information. Later, he was moved to a convalescent camp in Rouen. There he heard that Ed was in a hospital and was not expected to live. He had a tracer sent out, with no success. Because he had been gassed, Charles took a turn for the worse. His eyes and throat burned, and he was shipped to another hospital overlooking the harbor at

Le Havre. Charles later learned that Ed had never made it to a hospital. He had been killed during the assault on the Hindenburg Line and was buried in the cemetery at Bony.

In Doingt, a heartbroken 1st Lt. Richard Raven, adjutant of the Third Battalion, searched the cemetery there for his brother's grave. Robert had been killed while on patrol on the 28th. But he had been buried elsewhere. The cemetery was in an old churchyard. The civilian section, which was closer to the church itself, had been torn up by shell fire. Splintered coffins and bodies had been blown out of their final resting places. After seeing the cemetery, even though he did not find a marker for his brother, Raven requested to be placed in a line company. He was given command of E Company, which had lost its leaders, Capt. Harry Hayward and 1st Lt. Ben Hammond, on the 29th. Witnessing Raven's actions for the remainder of the war, Sgt. Nick Krayer recalled that he was "imbued with a severe and intense hatred for the Germans that led him to the execution of deeds almost impossible."[14]

Several cemeteries were dug in Rouen for Allied troops. A Red Cross Episcopalian chaplain there, Arthur B. Rudd, thought the cemetery at St. Sever, where almost 50 boys of the 107th and more than 125 others from the division were buried, was truly beautiful. It was in a little valley near the old part of the city, where five centuries earlier Joan of Arc had been burned at the stake. Rudd recalled an autumn afternoon when he officiated at the burial of six Americans, among them Cpl. Clarence J. Osterhoudt of the Headquarters Company. The air was heavy with the scent of sweet alyssium that had been planted on the neighboring graves, he wrote Osterhoudt's father in Cornwall-on-Hudson. "At the grave I used the burial service of the Prayer of the Episcopal Church, and as the last volleys were fired and the sound of the bugle sounding 'taps' for his last long sleep died away our thoughts went out to you in love and sympathy. You have the great loss to bear while your loved one sleeps in this beautiful land of France that he died to deliver from the hand of the oppressor." Rudd added that the young soldier now "rests in ground that I blessed (though I feel that all France has been consecrated by the blood of our boys) and we trust his soul is in that bright land where all sorrow and sighing are done away."[15]

Closer to the battlefield, Father Hoey conducted a service in a cathedral that had been built in 1783. Almost eight hundred doughboys received Holy Communion and another one thousand crammed inside the ancient church to hear the service. The regimental band was there, too. "Two non-Catholic lads, fine, manly fellows," Father Hoey noted, "played Gounod's 'Ava Maria' on the violin and violin cello for an offertory piece and they played it so beautifully that a good many of us were deeply affected. Another lad who had been in the grand opera, sang a solo, 'O Jesus I Am Not Worthy,' as a communion piece, and the whole congregation sang the 'Holy God.' Believe me, the rafters rang with harmony and the Padre felt like hugging every one of the boys because they can fight like the devil when need be, and when that is done with them they can kneel in boyish simplicity and pour out their souls in song."[16]

In the hospitals, meanwhile, the wounded were grateful for their treatment and newfound comfort.

For one thing, there were no more cooties.

Dutch Wilbur, after a fifteen-hour train trip, a twelve-hour voyage across the English Channel, and a bumpy ambulance ride to the American hospital near London, wrote home, "Good eats, nice bed and kind nurses make me the most contented chap in the world. My wound pains me but little, so it's quite comfortable."[17]

George Fetherolf, who had been hit in the head by a machine-gun bullet, wrote to his aunt that his hospital train had "nice clean bunks with a sister and an orderly in charge of each car to see we were comfortable." His trip to the coast took four hours. German prisoners carried him aboard the hospital ship. "We received a nice hot meal on the boat and then I fell asleep."

Pfc. Clinton Roosa, in the same company with Fetherolf, told his family in Middletown, "Just a few lines to let you know that I am alive, and having the time of my life for the past two days. Have been in bed for a week because the Hun got me with some gas. I was blinded for about four days but my eyes are gradually getting better and I hope to be able to see clearly within another week. It is great to get in a clean pair of pajamas and between white sheets to say nothing about the nurses."[18]

When Sgt. George "Scotty" Campbell of the Machine Gun Company, whose wound was classified as "GSW TNT," meaning "Gun shot wound through and through," had a surprise at the South African General Hospital No. 1 in Abbeville, France. A Red Cross nurse had taken off the Utica resident's socks when "something fell on the floor and the orderly picked it up and handed it to me. It proved to be a bullet. It must have been the bullet that put me out of the fight."[19]

Penned Pvt. James Borgia, "England is more like home than France and is a much nicer place, I think. It is quiet here, and that is what one needs after a good fight. I expect to be laid out here for three or four months, and it looks like as though the war would be over by that time. Our slogan is 'Heaven, hell or Hoboken by Christmas,' and it looks like as if it were coming true."

But before they were to reach Hoboken by Christmas, the New Yorkers still had one more battle to fight.

At first, the worst fighting assigned to the Americans after the main attack on the Hindenburg Line went to the Thirtieth Division. The boys from North and South Carolina and Tennessee had little time to rest. After being relieved by the Australian Fifth Division on 1 and 2 October, they were ordered out again on 5 October. For the next week, in what was known as the Battle of Montbrehain, they advanced in successive operations eastward. To their right was the British Sixth Division and to the left the British Twenty-sixth Division. O'Ryan's Empire Division was held in reserve. In the village of Brancourt-le-Grand on 8 October, the Old Hickory Division met stiff resistance. In a bloody encounter with the Germans that day, five doughboys earned Medals of Honor. Throughout the bitter advance, the division amassed ten Medals of Honor and its total of eleven was the most by a division in the entire war.

In the meantime, the 107th Infantry cooled its heels in Doingt. From a strength of 80 officers and 2,865 men going into the line on the morning of 28 September, it now carried on its roster 63 officers and 1,629 men. The weakest battalion was the Third, with just 6 officers and 291 men. As late as 6 October, O'Ryan's daily reports still did not carry the regiment's total losses for the 29th. The list was incomplete. All the divisional commander knew was that so far the Fifty-fourth Brigade accounted for 10 officers and 210 men killed, 14 officers and 921 men wounded, and 1 officer and 109 men missing.

Soon the regiment was on the march again, leaving Doingt for Bellicourt nine miles to the east. It was a tough march, according to Leland, "and everybody in the outfit was dead beat from the roughness of the road and the inability to avoid obstacles in the dark." From Bellicourt, the 107th moved east again, this time eight miles to Montbrehain, where up ahead of them the Thirtieth Division was locked in battle with the retreating Germans. On the night of the 8th, Van Buren found shelter in an iron shed. "The rumble of guns is at my door and the old iron walls of this little 'studio' quake now and then," he told his grandparents. He signed his letter with a cartoon of himself fleeing from a huge bomb with the words, "Must Go Now!"

The division kept up its eastward march, leaving Montbrehain for Brancourt and then from Brancourt to Premont. The troops spent quick, cold nights on the ground. It rained almost every day. K Company corporal Francis Duffy, in a letter to his parents in Malone, said, "We've been carrying on since Sept. 27th without a stop and it has been some hard pulling—over the top five times in the last three weeks. We had Jerry on the run all the time and we didn't have much time to rest."[20] Leland, now in temporary command of I Company, explained to his family, "The easy days of soldiering are gone and it is march and fight sunshine or rain, day after day." He was proud of his men. "Tired, hungry, wet and miserable, they never hesitate—hoping to get this wretched business through as soon as possible—and back home to the old U.S.A."

Finally on 11 October, the regiment reached Vaux Andigny. At five the next morning, it moved back into the line in relief of the Thirtieth Division's 118th Infantry.

Sgt. Jerry Stanton remembered how dark it was moving into the line. "Mile after mile we plodded along in the dark; the night was what I call dark and I know dark nights! For an instant the distant sky is a blaze of red—result of a fire set by the Hun, and the incessant vivid flashes of our guns and his, light up the way; only for a second then all is black; and then you step in a shell hole or trip over a dead body." Mingled with the smell of bombs and guns, Stanton picked up the "sweet odor of a dead horse" or the "stench of rotting human flesh." Before morning, the artillery bombardment from both sides quieted down and, according to Stanton, the night became "filled with the clatter of horses hoofs, drawing heavily loaded ammunition casons up to the smaller 18's in front, the shouts of the drivers, as well as the heavy rumbling of the wheels and clank of harness chains, add to the chorus."

Cpl. Lauren Stout described how "at night away ahead of us we occasionally saw the sky turned red from towns being burned by the Germans."[21]

When the first rays of sunlight broke over the horizon, Leland beheld "German rifles, grenades, cowhide knapsacks, long strings of Maxim ammunition, trench helmets, little round gray-green fatigue caps with red bands, several perfectly good machine guns—everything but Iron Crosses—were strewn over the terrain." He noticed, too, that "many of the enemy dead had new uniforms and equipment as though recently brought up from the replacement depots. Their trenches were full of the plunder from the village, furniture, mattresses, bedding, and in one place, a fine silk dress and other feminine apparel lying in the mud." Poking around one of the trenches that had only been abandoned a few hours earlier, Cpl. Harry Burke "found a girl's head of beautiful blonde hair and all her clothes."[22]

Van Buren wrote home, "We keep moving East every other day and the further we go the deeper we get into the darkness of this dream."

CHAPTER 17

Hell Popped That Morning

T he Selle River is a puny stream, about fifteen to eighteen feet wide
and chest deep in most places. It runs past Le Cateau and the small
farming villages of St. Benin, Molain, and St. Souplet. Between
Molain and St. Souplet the river narrows even more. In the rainy autumn
of 1918, the terrain on the Selle's western bank was open and gently rolling, and close to the river it grew marshy and hard to cross. On the eastern
bank, the land abruptly rose. Orchards and thick hedges and tall grassy
fields stretched beyond the river. The steady rain that had accompanied
the division on its march eastward had swollen the river, making it more
treacherous to cross. To make matters worse, the fleeing Germans had
dammed the Selle below St. Souplet. After crossing the river, they blew up
all the bridges. On the eastern heights, they barricaded themselves behind a new line of defense, called the Hermann *Stellung.*

A fretting Gen. Sir Henry Rawlinson entered in his diary of 11 October: "The Boche is evidently going to make a stand on the Selle River. We
shall be up against an organized line, and shall have to get up our artillery
to break through satisfactorily. I am not at all satisfied with the progress
made by our railways, which are of vital importance." As far as the British

general knew, facing his Fourth Army, which was now encamped on the opposite bank, were at least four fresh German divisions, two exhausted divisions, and in reserve, twelve more worn-out divisions. Rawlinson realized that his own army was also exhausted. The Forty-sixth Division, which had spearheaded the breaking of the Hindenburg Line south of the St. Quentin Canal Tunnel, had been fighting steadily since early August. Rawlinson also worried about the strength of the American II Corps.[1] After its assault on the Hindenburg Line, it was weak in numbers. In Maj. Gen. John O'Ryan's division, whole battalions had dwindled to the size of companies. The average size of his companies was fewer than sixty infantrymen. The 107th Infantry was down to 648 rifles. The Machine Gun Company had only two Vickers guns left and was quickly learning how to operate the German Maxim guns it had recovered on the battlefield. No replacements were forthcoming for Ryan. He had to make do with what was left of his New Yorkers.

The task assigned to the much-weakened American II Corps, according to Rawlinson's chief of staff, was to "cross the headwaters of the Selle between Molain and St. Souplet and capture the important hamlet of Arbre Guernon and the villages of Mazinghein and Ribeauville." He emphasized, "The obstacle formed by the stream was made more formidable by the fact that the enemy held the hamlets of Molain and St. Martin Rivere and the eastern outskirts of St. Souplet, which lay astride the river; while the Le Cateau-Wassigny railway, which was admirably adapted for defense, barred the way to the high ground about Arbre Guernon."[2] The railway also concerned O'Ryan. The stone embankment holding the tracks rose thirty and forty feet above the ground, an ideal defensive barrier. Beyond the embankment was a low ridge of land that sloped away into a valley. Several farms dotted the undulating land that formed this valley. The Germans had strongly fortified the farms, the foremost being Bandival Farm. Eastward still, as the land rose up again, was Jonc de Mer Farm. There was another dip, another ridge, and then several more farms, known as the Val de Mer and La Rue farms. The valley finally ended at the St. Maurice River, a smaller stream than the Selle but whose eastern bank was just as steep.

Rawlinson seemed rather confident of success. In a letter dated 12 October to Sir Henry Wilson, his country's military representative to the

Supreme War Council, he provided assurances that by the end of the month his army would be on the move again, making eight to ten miles a day so that by the end of November it would be on the German frontier. "I have my eye on Malmédy for the Fourth Army, with my headquarters at Spa." He closed by telling Wilson of his present situation and his belief that if his army won the coming battle of the Selle River, then the Germans would be finished and the war all but officially over. "The Boche has brought up five new divisions on my front during the last two days, so I am making another deliberate attack on him in a few days' time. He is very anxious to prevent us from getting to the Valenciennes railway, which is only fourteen miles from Le Cateau, where I am now. If we succeed in cutting that before you agree to an armistice, I think a large part of his army may have to lay down its arms."[3]

Germany's Erich Ludendorff had no intentions of laying down his arms. On the eve of the battle, he informed the German cabinet that his armies would not lose the Selle. A captured order during the battle confirmed Ludendorff's belief that he would hold the line. "The Higher Command," the order read, "states that the possibility of an armistice being brought about depends on the battle brought to a standstill. . . . The English must not cross the Selle."[4]

Because the weather was constantly overcast, gray, and dreary, air reconnaissance had proven ineffective. O'Ryan sent a patrol across the Selle to obtain prisoners. The raid resulted in a number of captured Boche. From them, O'Ryan learned that fresh troops had been brought down from the Vosges Mountains with the orders to hold the new line at all costs.

While O'Ryan's troops were in the line awaiting orders, they had to tolerate continuous gas and artillery barrages. The gas attacks were particularly heavy. In the mist and rain, shells poured down on them. O'Ryan felt that this constant shelling and sniping "tested the endurance and morale" of his men because of their fatigued condition. He was especially concerned about the shelling that fell on the headquarters of the 107th Infantry's Second Battalion, commanded by Capt. Rowland Tompkins. Tompkins's headquarters was at Imberfayt Farm, which ran up to the river's edge. From 12 October, the time the 107th moved into the line along the banks of the Selle River, until 16 October, the Second Battalion took ninety-four casualties. Eighteen men were hit with gas.

Robert Waddell recalled, "For four days the boys lived like prairie dogs in bivvies dug along the side of the road embankment. The German snipers had an enfilading fire through the road, and their artillery harassed us constantly with gas and high explosive shells."[5] Cpl. Francis Miller remembered the rain and the cold and how it made holding the line a real hardship. "A dugout was a thing unknown in these trenches. One might be able to scratch a 'bivvie' with an entrenching tool but that was all. Lieutenant [Arthur] Brundage was gassed and had to leave the lines with other gas casuals."[6]

If the boys of the 107th thought they had it bad, the 108th Infantry had it worse. In the same four-day period, 216 men from the upstate regiment suffered gas wounds.

And worse yet, when the Americans entered the section of St. Souplet no longer held by the enemy, they found Germans dying by the score in the village churchyard and around the school, victims of their own gas attacks. In the cellars, terrified civilians, held in near slavery for almost four years, huddled in fear of the gas. Many of them died by the time the Americans entered the village. "Their pitiable condition brought a lump in my throat and a mist over my eyes," Kenneth Gow wrote to his father. Lt. Col. J. Leslie Kincaid reported, "Patrols from the Twenty-seventh began to percolate into the city. Deadly encounters between our patrols and those of the enemy occurred nightly in the deserted streets. Every rising sun saw dead Americans and Germans lying in the gutters beside corpses of non-combatants."[7]

A captain in the American Red Cross, Stephen N. Bobo, wearing his tin hat and gas mask, entered the village to aid the stricken civilians. When he saw their suffering, he ordered that the townspeople be evacuated to the rear. With volunteers, he combed the village in search of survivors, poking into dark corners, closets, and cellars. Guided by the civilians themselves, who tied rags and tablecloths and handkerchiefs on sticks and hung them out basement windows, he had them taken out of St. Souplet, using wheelbarrows as litters for those who could not walk. One of the volunteers was Gow, who brought out "three small children clinging to my coat-tails, with an old man and woman."

In the meantime, patrols continued to probe the enemy, and gas hovered over the valley of the Selle like a yellow blanket of death.

One of Gow's horses was wounded while he was bringing up supplies to the Machine Gun Company by horse and mule during the four days of artillery and gas attacks. "I have been continually running through Jerry's counter-barrages, machine gun fire and shells of every description and calibre, whizz-bangs, wooley-bears, Jack Johnsons, pound wonders, Tock Emmas, minnies, daisey-clippers, iron foundries and gas," he informed his father. "I haven't been scratched yet." A hunk of shrapnel did nick Gow's neck. "I have discovered that I have a very delicate nose and throat, which the slightest concentration of gas affects," he added. "So you see they cannot surprise me with the darned stuff. The gas-mask is a great thing, good against anything Jerry throws in the line of gas."

In the First Battalion, D Company 1st Lt. Arthur C. Lumley, a Seventh hand since 1909, was among the gas victims. His adventures, which he recorded in the January 1919 issue of the *Gazette,* began soon after the regiment arrived at the front and O'Ryan ordered out scouts to prod the enemy's defenses. Lumley and his squad had just come back from a night patrol across the river. They were making for the farmhouse where Tompkins's Second Battalion was holed up. He hoped to get directions to his own battalion at the village of Vaux Andigny. "We started single file across lots for the farmhouse; and just as we were strung out along the middle of a big field, 'Jerry' started to bombard the whole ridge. He got a direct hit on the barn of the farm we were making for and the barn went up in flames—a fine big bonfire which lighted up the whole ridge." Lumley got his men into a ditch, and there they crouched expecting to get hit at any moment. His patrol stayed put through the night without water or rations. When daylight came, they worked their way back to where they found the First Battalion and Capt. Clinton Fisk "sleeping comfortably in a cellar." The cellar looked inviting to a tired Lumley. He rolled up on the ground to sleep. At that moment, two German shells struck the farmhouse. The sleeping party scurried to safety, covered in brick dust. Undeterred, mostly because he was so exhausted, Lumley then dug a little bivvie in the sodden earth and climbed in. He slept for an hour. He awoke with a start because his eyes stung and he could hardly open them.

"The Bosche suddenly took it into his head to shoot gas at us, and he certainly plastered Vaux Andigny to the Queen's taste" he wrote. "He let everything he had fly at us. . . . I tell you the sky rained shells for an hour. When it was over you could cut the gas with a knife—mustard gas mostly, although there may have been other kinds mixed with it." Ordered back to a casualty clearing station, Lumley was taken by train to the hospital in Rouen, where he was placed in a ward with twenty officers. One of them was Lt. Ralph Polk Buell, who had taken a bullet in the chest on 29 September. Lumley reported that his eyes remained "closed right up for about a week, smarting like 'Sam Hill.' That mustard gas is certainly fine stuff."

On the morning of 13 October, the boys of I Company, peering over the crest of a sunken road, were amazed to see coming toward them across a field a young woman pushing a baby carriage that held all her worldly belongings and with a little boy of perhaps seven clutching her skirt. Claude Leland turned to Sgt. Harold B. Tuthill. "There must be some hokus about this," he whispered to him. "They wouldn't let a woman out in No Man's Land for her health at this season. Let her come on until she's within speaking distance and if she is aiming for our road we'll make her leave the carriage out there. Keep her covered."

Every eye in the battalion was glued on the woman as she steered the carriage closer. When she closed within two hundred yards of the sunken road, the roar of a machine gun broke the spell. Flecks of dirt kicked up at her heels where bullets spattered into the field. Grabbing the child in her arms, she bolted toward the New Yorkers. "I can still see her white face and hear the scream of the terrified little kid as they reached our end of the road and tumbled into the gun pit, safe and sound," Leland recalled. His men placed her and the boy in a hole on the bank of the sunken road. At that moment, British artillery began shelling the German line. The Boche answered with "the worst strafe imaginable," Leland noted in a letter home. "We took to our pits like ground hogs and stuck it out—but imagine what that woman and boy endured while shell and minewerfers were bursting a few feet away. Thank goodness they were'nt hurt and after I sent them back to safety. This is all in a day's work. We wonder every day how long it can last."

The next day, a trench mortar shell made a direct hit on I Company. Leland was thrown back against the wall of the sunken road, momentarily stunned. Someone called for the Red Cross. Lying next to Leland was Sgt. Stanley Brinckerhoff "with a very white face and his leg in a pool of blood." Further down the road, word came back that Pvt. Plato

Demetriou was killed. A hunk of hot steel from the mortar had pierced his heart. For the rest of the day, Demetriou's body lay out in the open. At dusk, he was wrapped in his blanket and buried behind a hedge. Leland located a box, fashioned it into a crude cross, and wrote on it, "Private Plato H. Demetriou, Co. I, 107th U.S. Infantry." He stuck it over the shallow grave. "He was a dark, slender Greek boy caught in the draft in New York and came to us at Spartanburg in April."

A day after Demetriou's death, Raeburn Van Buren and one of his bivvie mates from E Company were gathering wood for a fire to warm themselves. As usual, the evening was cold and wet. Both doughboys were hungry and down in the mouth. They found broken ammunition boxes scattered about and brought them to their clammy hole in the ground. They broke them up into small pieces. They then built a fire and cooked their mess. Continuing to stoke the fire to keep warm, Van Buren picked up a slab of wood and was ready to toss it on the crackling blaze when he noticed something scrawled in pencil on the board. "I took it over to the light," he wrote to his mother, "and this is what I saw. 'God is Love.' I can't describe to you the way those words hit me—the tragedy they pictured. Only a few days before we landed in this place the Huns had fought a terrible battle for it and lost. There were signs everywhere of the terrible battle that had taken place. Some of our men had won the ground and no doubt one of our men had placed that little sign upon that box to help make that rotten hole seem worth the effort it took to capture it."

The Battle of the Selle River had been delayed too long, because Rawlinson could not bring up his artillery fast enough. Thus, for five days both the British Fourth Army and the French First Army on its right flank had been stalled. Further south, Gen. John Pershing's First Army and now his new Second Army were still stuck in the Meuse Valley. The Germans in front of Rawlinson continued to dig in. When his artillery finally got into place, he called for the Allied forces to renew their attack on the morning of 17 October. Behind the American II Corps, he stationed eight brigades of heavy artillery, ten brigades of field artillery, four siege batteries, and two Australian army brigades. A refitted 301st Tank Battalion, which had been decimated in front of the Hindenburg Line, was once again assigned to the doughboys. The question now was not if there were any hidden land mines, but whether the tanks could successfully cross the river.

The 105th and 108th Infantries were given the honor of leading the attack, with the 106th and 107th to follow in the second wave. Their first objective was that section of St. Souplet on the east bank of the Selle still controlled by the Germans. Once all of St. Souplet had been secured, they were to fight eastward into the valley, capturing the villages of Arbre Guernon, Mazinghein, and Ribeauville and the fortified farms along the way. In the way were five Germans divisions—the Twenty-fourth, 204th, and 243d Infantry Divisions, the Fifteenth Rifle Division, and the Third Naval Division—well over fifty thousand Boche.

In a memorandum to brigade officers, O'Ryan reminded them, "The first obstacle to be met is Le Selle River. The leading battalions in order to keep up with the barrage will have to cross this river by wading it." He added that the following battalions must also keep to the time schedule. They were to be helped across the river by guide ropes to prevent them from falling into deep holes. As soon as possible, the engineers were to throw a footbridge across the Selle.

When O'Ryan was scratching out the memorandum on the 15th, he received orders recommending that he promote the commander of the 107th Infantry, Charles DeBevoise, to brigadier general. Also, that Roscoe Roys, first sergeant of K Company from Malone, be sent to officers' training. After his promotion, DeBevoise, the stockbroker, was to report to O'Ryan's Fifty-third Brigade as its new commander. DeBevoise had replaced Col. Willard Fisk soon after the 107th landed in France and had taken a liking to the silk stocking soldiers. Aware that the coming battle was important, he wanted to be with them. He requested to stay with his boys until after the fight. O'Ryan granted that request, although he appointed Maj. Mortimer Bryant of the 106th Machine Gun Battalion to succeed DeBevoise following the Battle of the Selle River. The grandnephew of the poet William Cullen Bryant, Bryant, like DeBevoise, was a Brooklyn native, where he had been publisher of the Brooklyn *Times*.

Sergeant Roys also requested permission to stay with his troops until the battle was over. Instead of staying well behind the lines on the night of 16 October, he moved into a farmhouse close to the front with a squad of

K Company men. He and 1st Lt. Griswold "Tot" Daniell decided to share a bed. At the last minute, "Tot" joined Leland for the night in his shack, which they called "Unterofficer Kasino" and said looked like the top of a salt shaker because of all the holes punched in the roof by German artillery. Roys then rounded up several of his boys to share the bed and the rest of the farmhouse. Except for Cpl. Harold Mills from New York City, most of them were from around his hometown of Malone, including acting 1st Sgt. Edward Langford; Cpl. Francis Duffy; Pfcs. Jack Stone, John Miebaum, and Stephen Finnigan; and Pvt. Floyd Malette. There wasn't enough elbow room on the bed for Duffy or Stone, so they bunked elsewhere.

In a letter to Malette's mother, Duffy explained how he was taking care of her boy, because it was his first time in battle. Malette had been in transport and thus spared front-line duty. Now with the shortage of men, he had been sent back to the company. He was one of the boys sharing Roys's bed that night. Before turning in, Duffy and Malette talked through the evening while getting their gear ready for the next day. "You can't imagine the feeling of tenseness with which we wait for 'zero' hour," Duffy wrote "No one knows what the morrow will bring for him. It may be your last day on earth."[8]

That same evening, Gow, who had just been brought up to command the Machine Gun Company because all its officers had either been killed or were in the hospital, got off a letter describing the situation. "Just think, old Jerry Boche but 500 yards from where I am writing. I am in a cellar, and wish I could enclose some of the noise going on above my head." He closed by saying, "I am commanding the company, Walter. Just think, I am the last officer that is left alive. It is an odd feeling to watch them go one by one until you are the last. It makes one feel as though his time is coming with the sureness of death."

In E Company, Corporal Miller noted that throughout the night "The necessary preparations were made for an 'over-the-top' stunt. The blankets carried in the trenches were turned in here, rifles were cleaned and petted bomb pins were straightened out, in order that the rings might be pulled speedily, and other essential preparations were attended to."[9] The doughboys were given extra ammunition belts and picks or shovels. Pfc. Harold Chasmar said they were also given one day's rations of cheese, canned beef, and bread. He said that he prayed after he had gotten his extra gear. "Not for myself alone, but for those back home that we love and love us." His simple prayer: "God be good to them, our loved ones, keep them safe from all harm and, if Thou will, spare me for them. Amen." He then wrote letters to his mother and father and "the dearest girl in all the world." He gave the letters to a guard who was not going forward, and turned in.[10]

About two in the morning, three hours before zero hour, a German shell struck the farmhouse in which K Company had bedded down. The start of the heavy bombardment had at first awakened Duffy. He lay in his blanket on the floor in a cold sweat, listening to the shells explode near him. "Then came a loud crash from the next room and the cries of the wounded. Everything was in darkness, and confusion." Jack Stone lit a candle and he and Duffy entered the room. It had been completely demolished. Plaster and brick had fallen on the men. Dust rose in a thick reddish cloud. Duffy and Stone clawed through rubble, yelling for help. They first freed Sergeant Langford. Even though his ears rang so loud from the explosion that had nearly killed him and now left him deaf, Langford took charge of getting the rest of his wounded bedmates pulled from the debris. Miebaum had been killed outright. The others were seriously maimed. They were carried down to a first-aid station. It was there that Malette and Finnigan died. Sergeant Roys hung on for two days. He died 19 October.[11]

Mills was also severely wounded and buried in the rubble. "I was just outside of door & piece of shell hit me on the head," he scrawled in his diary the next day from the hospital at Rouen. "Covered with bricks as house fell on me. Malette killed and probably more. Ran for help at Bat. Headquarters. Dig our men out. Had head dressed." The doctor at Rouen looked at Mills's head and "said I had some nasty wounds." Suffering from terrible headaches, Mills stayed in the hospital until the end of November.

Langford told Duffy that when the shells hit the farmhouse, the boys were writing letters home to their parents. Later that morning, when the 107th Infantry stormed across the Selle River, among K Company sergeants leading the charge was Langford—his ears still ringing.

Amid the noise of bursting bombs, the sound of the steady clatter of boots on the cobblestones, mingled with the jingle-jangle and creaking of cartridge belts, entrenching tools, canteens, gas masks, and the low commands of officers and the swearing of men, the 107th Infantry took up its position in a field south of the village of Escaufourt. The village was just west of St. Souplet. Chasmar remembered the "tramp, tramp of marching feet and an occasional spark of light as a hobbed shoe struck a stone. Then a muttered oath would be heard up the line—someone having slipped and received a mud bath."[12] Another noise assailed the ears of Leland—the pitiful wailing of a boy who sat by the roadside as the soldiers marched by. Before the men reached the field, they had to don their gas masks. Every time Leland took off his nose guard he smelt either mustard gas or phosgene. When the 107th finally reached its place in the field, the gas had cleared enough so that the masks were removed. The troops then lay down in the dewy meadow. "A thick clammy mist now lay over the countryside, shut out the view and went to your marrow bones," Leland noted. "The grass wet our shoes and leggins as thoroughly as though we had forded the Selle itself."

Miller remembered how the men "stretched themselves flat on the ground, giving their rifles and gas masks the final inspection. The fog and smoke were dense. One could just make out the man six feet away from him."

Ahead of them, the 108th Infantry was about to cross the Selle. The Allied artillery began to shell the enemy lines in earnest. The Germans countered. Long-range shells hit close to the waiting silk stocking soldiers. They knew that the 108th was now on the attack. Their moment would come soon.

"Hell popped that morning and with a vengeance," Miller stated.

Miller's new company commander, Lt. Richard Raven, afire with hate and anxious to avenge his brother's death, strode up and down the line holding aloft a Boche rifle while he bucked up his tired men with "cheery and peppy remarks."[13] Leland had recollected before the fight how he and several officers kidded Raven about the German rifle. He gave them a strange look and said he carried the weapon because he "wanted with his own hand to make the Boche pay dearly for Bob lying up there in Guillemont. We kept still."

The Machine Gun Company, now in command of Gow, hid behind hedges in small dugouts, awaiting the full fury of the barrage. "It was only a few minutes until it began in great style," recalled 2d Lt. Horace C. Johnson, who earned his commission on, coincidentally, 29 September and had then been assigned to the depleted 107th Infantry officers' corps on 9 October. "There were, it seemed to be, a million field pieces firing just over our heads and we knew that many machine guns were engaged in the same work." When the barrage died down, the machine gunners marched quickly to St. Souplet.[14]

Gow, wearing his heavy trench coat, had taken four men, among them 1st Sgt. Charles Veitch from New York Mills, who had just turned twenty, and moved out with Captain Fisk's First Battalion. Gow needed to locate the best fields of fire, where he could then place what few Vickers guns his diminished company had left. Once he found the right places, he planned to send the others back with orders to quickly bring up the machine guns. Before they left under the cover darkness, Gow turned to his first sergeant. "Veitch," he said, patting his trench coat, "if anything happens you will find the maps in this pocket and instructions here." It was about five-thirty A.M. Veitch recalled that the "Germans were pouring hell in the form of steel right at us; although I don't suppose it was especially meant for us." Gow ordered his squad, which also included Cpl. Arthur Kinkel from Brooklyn and Pfcs. Conrad Bastedenbach and Emil Hartert, both from Manhattan, to hit the ground. "I flattened out, obeying Lt. Gow's orders by doing so, and did not look up for a few seconds," Veitch later wrote. "Lt. Gow was standing when I lay down, and when I looked up he was lying also, in a most natural position. We thought that, after having seen the men all down, he got down himself; but he didn't; he had been knocked down."[15] Shrapnel struck Gow behind his left ear and killed him instantly.

Veitch and the boys carried their lieutenant back to the picket line and laid him next to his beloved horses and mules of the company transport. There Pfc. Thomas Janson, who had been one of Gow's favorite wagoners, wrapped the body in a canvas shelter half until after the battle. In a letter sent to Summit, he said, "Never have I felt worse than when the boys came back in the morning and said: 'Janson, your friend is gone.'"[16]

The railroad cut at St. Souplet. The Seventh Regiment Fund

Lieutenant Johnson took over command of the Machine Gun Company. Not knowing exactly what to do, the new lieutenant sought out Captain Fisk, now acting major. Fisk ordered Johnson and his men to follow the Third Battalion.

For the 108th Infantry and then the 107th, crossing the Selle River proved easier than expected. The Germans put up little resistance. It was not until the New Yorkers started working inland, beyond the east bank, that it got hot. In front of the steep railroad embankment, the Boche fought back with a frenzy that stopped the troops. The Americans dug in on the western side. Here an artillery shell hit the Machine Gun Company's First Platoon, effectively wiping it out. The survivors of the entire company were then placed with the 105th Machine Gun Battalion.

Not all the companies in the regiment were stopped. In Fisk's First Battalion, A Company easily passed through St. Souplet, forded the river, and by one P.M. had caught up with and passed through the 108th Infantry. Advancing behind a barrage, the men had by late afternoon taken Bandival Farm. One of its soldiers, Cpl. Theis Roberts, recorded that "By this time we had ten men left. Company B had nine. So the two companies were combined under the command of Lt. [Frederick] Conklin, the one remaining officer." In B Company, Sgt. Drew Hill remembered the dense fog and how on the way up the men got lost for a moment, but then found Captain Fisk and followed him. "We zigzagged our way cross-country, through barbed-wire entanglements, and then along the road to St. Souplet, and through the town itself. All day we kept up the advance. The Boche attempted several times to hold us up by means of a rear-guard machine-gun action, but it was a useless attempt on his part."

That night both A and B companies dug in. We "seized a lot of Jerry's rations," Hill wrote, "and made the best of a very dreary night."[17]

D Company also crossed the Selle and took up a position in front of the railroad embankment. Lt. Oscar E. Hellquist, who had been in the company before his assignment as Fisk's intelligence officer, had distinguished himself many times in exciting scouting sorties into no-man's-land. Two days before the attack, following one of his undercover missions, he had fought his way back across the Selle and through St. Souplet alone. He seemed to escape death at every turn. But this time, caught ahead of the men from D Company, he was hit by shell fire. He was found and brought back to a dressing station. There was nothing the surgeons could do. All day and most of the night, Hellquist sang softly to himself. A soldier confined to the cot next to him recollected that in the morning when he awoke "Oscar's bed was empty." Hellquist was yet another of the boys from Summit to fall in battle.[18]

D Company pressed on, breaching the railroad embankment and reaching La Rue Farm. There it dug in for the night.

During the first day of the battle, the division had advanced past the railroad barrier and moved up to the heavily fortified farms and past the village of Arbre Guernon. It then spent a cold, sleepless night. In a letter home, Leland described the 107th's situation. "Just at present we are holding a sunken road outside a little village. Five hundred yards away on a ridge is the Boche and his light guns and trench mortars. They make our stay very unpleasant but we are well dug into the bank and not many get hurt, but oh gee! It's a hot place at times."

On the morning of the 18th, the 107th shoved off again. This time its orders called for it to leapfrog the 108th and thus lead the attack against the entrenched Germans. Before dawn, Fisk stood in front of his men, pointing them eastward. His battalion was spread out along a sunken road that ran north from Arbre Guernon to Le Cateau. "Stick to the sun, boys," the son of the old regimental commander called to them. A shell exploded next to him. Shrapnel tore into his body. The battalion leader fell. His death stunned everyone, the highest-ranking officer in the 107th to be killed in the war. When Brig. Gen. Palmer Pierce, the brigade commander, found Fisk's body, he wrote to his father, "Your son's face was not at all disfigured, and his expression in death was very noble and without any of the signs of anguish that one so frequently sees." Corporal Roberts wrote, "One of the bravest and best loved officers in the regiment passed away."[19] A soldier from D Company remarked on the loss of Fisk and Hellquist, "I feel as though I had lost both a father and a brother."

At zero hour the saddened First Battalion advanced into the morning sun, as ordered. "At the first signs of daylight we were off again," stated Hill. "Now and then we would run across small detachments of British cavalrymen, and the universal question was 'Where's Jerry?'"[20] G Company sergeant Joe Clark noted, "Our advance patrols vainly search[ed] for the enemy, the only trace of him being his discarded equipment and ordnance."[21]

Yet Corporal Waddell recalled how F Company passed over several lines of German trenches, taking many prisoners. Leland described going down a slope over which hung the gray mists of morning. "It was barely light enough to distinguish trees against the skyline and groups of men flitting like ghosts through the smoke. Suddenly we were on the German trenches or their line of organized shell holes. We could see them begin to get up and run."

O'Ryan observed that although the enemy machine gunners were skillful and courageous, "Their supporting infantry detachments, however, were lacking in morale and frequently sought an opportunity to surrender." In comparison, his own men were "overfatigued." He believed that if he had the use of fresh troops, he would have "quickly overcome" the enemy. Instead, after seven days and nights of continuous fighting, his division's strength had been "depleted until companies of the infantry regiments had a rifle strength of twenty or thirty men each."

* * *

Cpl. Charles Stoll and Pfc. Frank Garvin from Manhattan and Pvt. Wasyl Kolonczyk from Cohoes, New York, all C Company soldiers, found a farmhouse filled with Germans. The enemy was putting up a terrific defense. Their machine-gun fire had the company pinned down in a field in front of the farmhouse. Stoll decided to attack. Garvin and Kolonczyk joined him. Garvin, whose family owned the Garvin Machine Company at Spring and Varick streets in New York City, was called "Spider" by his brothers because he was skinny. Kolonczyk was a Polish immigrant. He hated the Germans bitterly and had vowed to kill as many of them as humanly possible. His intense hatred worried Garvin. Just a youngster, Garvin had quit Rensselaer Polytechnic Institute in Troy in 1917 to enlist in the Seventh, where his brother, George, had been a member for several years. He did not want to take any unnecessary risks. The three men worked their way close to the farmhouse, keeping up a steady fire. They ran low and quickly, humped over, shooting from the hip. As they closed in on the enemy, the Germans threw down their weapons and quit. Thirty-six men and two officers walked out of the building with their hands up, while two others made a sprint for freedom. Stoll, Garvin, and Kolonczyk shot them down as they ran. Garvin expected Kolonczyk would then shoot all the prisoners, but the Polish-born private held his anger in check, and they rounded up the whole bunch and herded them back toward St. Souplet. Their action earned Stoll and Garvin the Distinguished Service Cross and the French Croix de Guerre. Kolonczyk, who had previously earned the Distinguished Service Cross at the Battle of the Hindenburg Line, received an Oak Leaf Cluster.[22]

In a similar action, three men from A Company attacked two machine-gun emplacements when heavy fire stopped them in their tracks. Sgt. Francis Bean from Utica and Pvts. Russell Brown from Morristown, New Jersey, and Isaac Rabinowitz from the Bronx charged the machine gunners. The Germans fled into a dugout. When the three doughboys closed in, firing their rifles, dozens of hands went up with the yell of "Kamerad." Thirty-five of the enemy emerged out of the darkness.

Germans were surrendering by the score now. At a farmhouse, Pvt. James Lee from Norwood, New York, forced the capture of thirty-five Boche at the point of his bayonet. He then rounded up more Germans hiding in an outhouse.

Not all of the doughboys were so fortunate. Pvt. Bernie Stegar, who came from Marlin, Texas, raced across open ground in front of a machine-gun nest to rescue a fallen comrade from F Company. A bullet knocked him down. Stegar scrambled up. The moment he reached his wounded friend, another bullet crashed into him, killing him.

Lieutenant Raven, who had lost a brother on patrol almost a month earlier, found his E Company stopped by another pesky but deadly machine-gun nest. He gave the order to rush the nest. As he ran forward, firing his German rifle, he was shot down and killed. Next to him, Cpl. George Schneider and Pfc. Arthur Conklin also lost their lives. In Leland's I Company, Cpl. Albert Usher took a bullet through his cheek that also tore off the tip of his nose. Leland saw that it had made a "bloody mess but by no means serious wound." On the way back to the clearing station, Usher contracted the flu and died ten days later. Second Lt. Carl Stock of H Company, who had been with the 107th only since July, had been shot through the stomach early in the morning and was unable to move. For the rest of the day he struggled to survive in a water-filled shell hole. By the time he was rescued, it was too late. He perished a day later. "His handsome boyish face with the blond hair brushed back from a white forehead haunts me still," Leland wrote.

But on went the 107th. As Corporal Roberts put it, "Once more to the east, for an advance of three miles to the west bank of the Canal de Sambre, where we dug in and established a new line which we held until midnight of the 20th."[23] When would it end? the New Yorkers wondered as they fought forward while the Germans retreated. "Well, only a few days more and we would all be gone, maybe only a few hours," Leland told himself. "Being dead, killed outright, couldn't be much worse than this going on and on. Not so good, though, to be shot through the stomach and left on the field all day like poor Stock. But suppose you didn't get killed but drew a nice blighty in the arm or leg and went back on one of those hospital trains in beds with white sheets on them, after a bath of hot water and an issue of clean clothes—oh boy!"

By the night of the 20th, the thinned-out regiment had advanced more than ten miles, reaching the banks of the St. Maurice River. For three days, it had fought beside the Thirtieth Division. The Germans were now retreating swiftly east along the length of this sector of the western front.

They had hurried across the Sambre and Oise Canal, three thousand yards from the St. Maurice River, and taken up yet another defensive position. During the chase, O'Ryan's division had captured fifteen hundred officers and men. The *Times of London* reported on 21 October: "Throughout the past three days the Two American Corps have again attacked daily, and on each occasion with complete success. Fighting their way forward from St. Souplet to the high ground west of the Sambre Canal, they have broken down the enemy's resistance at all points, beating off many counter-attacks and realising a further advance of nearly five miles."

But the cost had been high. In O'Ryan's division, twelve officers had been killed and thirty-three wounded. One hundred ninety-two men were either slain or died of wounds; another 866 had been wounded and 423 gassed. Sixty-five men of the 107th had laid down their lives in the advance.

Meanwhile, the British were massing for another attack, set for 23 October. It was to be launched without the aid of the American II Corps. On the banks of the St. Maurice River, what was left of the 107th Infantry received orders that its fighting days were over. The Twenty-seventh had no replacement troops to bolster its strength and was now too weak to be an effective fighting unit. The same fate had also struck the Thirtieth Division. Rawlinson ordered both units pulled from the line and sent back to a rest area. On the 20th and 21st, the British Seventy-first and Ninety-first Divisions moved in, relieving the silk stocking soldiers.

K Company sergeant Robert Peek never forgot that night of the 20th. The boys hung on "in the rain in a condition of utter exhaustion." The men were so spent that several of them died. Mess Sgt. Harmon Vedder, who had lost his brother James at the Hindenburg Line, was among those who succumbed to "the terrible physical strain."[24]

Pfc. Harold Chasmar wrote, "On October 20 we were relieved and God was good. We couldn't have stood it much longer. We didn't care . . . what happened and had given up all hopes, but just as the last straw was breaking our relief came. Gee, we were tired and wet, but indeed thankful."[25]

"We dragged ourselves back to St. Souplet, absolutely exhausted, but cheered at the prospects for food and a husky rum issue," reported Corporal Hill. "There were seven of us in Company B present, with the

'Hacksaw' [Clarence] Twaddle in charge."[26] When C Company was relieved, Pvt. Albert Ingalls counted fourteen officers and men. Left behind
for burial parties were thirty-eight men. The rest of the men in the company had either been wounded or gassed in the advance.[27] In E Company,
according to Sergeant Miller, eight men came out of the line, led by Cpl.
Albert Brown. "Played out to the point of exhaustion, affected by exposure to such an extent they could only speak in a whisper, dirty, badly in
need of a shave and wet, they expressed no regrets upon being relieved,
falling asleep immediately, not caring how, when or where they were as
long as there was room to stretch out."[28]

Cpl. Robert Waddell of F Company wrote, "On the 21st we were finally relieved by an English battalion, and the company whose fighting
strength at this time consisted of fifteen men, marched back through the
darkness across the open shell-swept area to St. Souplet. At St. Souplet we
received a welcomed ration and a good feed and then the boys scattered
and made their bunks in the shattered houses of the town."[29] Sgt. Joe
Clark added that in G Company "a mere handful, left the lines. We were
tired and dirty, but through it all happy in our victory."[30]

In St. Souplet, the division commander watched the Fifty-fourth Brigade march through the battle-scarred village. "Some of them were apparently asleep while they walked. They were covered with mud and
many of them bleeding. . . . At first glance they seemed to be in a semi-
stupor, but everywhere individual men upon seeing the inspecting party
made a supreme effort, if only by a glance, to indicate that their spirit
still survived."

After the Battle of the Selle River, the war was, indeed, effectively over.
Yet the role of the New Yorkers, as an essential part of this British triumph
known as the One Hundred Days' Campaign, has largely been ignored
or forgotten. From its first turn in the trenches up in Flanders to the
smashing of the Hindenburg Line to chasing the Germans to the banks
of the St. Maurice River, the Empire Division was in battle only fifty-
seven days. Of the twenty-nine American divisions that actually were in
battle in the Great War, sixteen were in the front lines for a longer time.
But only four of the twenty-nine divisions had casualty rates higher than
the Twenty-seventh. For every day O'Ryan's Roughnecks saw combat,

they suffered, on average, 32 men killed and 148 wounded.[31] There were more than eighteen hundred deaths and nearly 8,500 wounded.

The 107th Infantry bore the brunt of the division's casualties. Some 579 officers and men of the regiment died.[32]

On the dark side of statistics are the names of the fallen. Billy Leonard. Fancher Nicoll. Dick Raven and his brother Robert. Harmon Vedder and his brother James. Roscoe Roys. T. J. Oakley Rhinelander. Bert Lobdell. Oscar Hellquist and his hometown pals from Summit, Bill Drabble, Nick Kelly, John Mallay Jr., Edward Willis, Tommy O'Shea, winner of the Medal of Honor, and Kenneth Gow, who on the eve of the Battle of the Hindenburg Line wrote that "a big game can be played but once."

Only days after the silk stocking soldiers had marched off their last battlefield and with the Germans in full retreat, a weary Harold Chasmar simply stated to his parents in Port Chester: "We played the game!"[33]

It's Over and Now I Know
I'm Going to Live!

I just received some drawing material from Paris," Raeburn Van Buren happily proclaimed to his parents on the eve of the Battle of the Selle River. "It looks good enough to eat."

Now that the 107th Infantry had been pulled out of the line and was resting more than fifty miles west of St. Souplet near a place called Corbie, along with the rest of the division to await the outcome of the war and then orders for home, Van Buren was drawing up a storm. The redhead wasn't alone. The artists, writers and poets, ex-newspapermen, and advertising executives started working on a special edition of *The Gas Attack* magazine, written and produced within shouting distance of the front lines. Tristram Tupper was editor. Pvt. Leslie Rowland from L Company was assistant editor, but actually did most of the work. Van Buren acted as art editor. His gag drawings appeared on almost every page.

"I am working hard to make my end of it as good as possible," he boasted to his mother and father in a letter dated 31 October. "I have already turned out four large drawings and the 'rise' they got from the few who have seen them encourages me to do more." He also drew a portrait of the division commander. When Maj. Gen. John O'Ryan saw how tense

Van Buren was, he offered the private a shot of rum to settle his nerves. Later, Van Buren felt his portrait of the major general was every bit as good as the one Sargent had done a few months earlier in Flanders Field. "I have the job of collecting other work and it isn't as easy as doing it myself but I think variety makes a magazine more interesting. [Cpl. Lauren] Stout is going to do a couple of little sketches for me and a fellow by the name of Beal [Pfc. C. C. Beall of G Company] will be represented by some decorations. The magazine will be printed in Paris and will be sold to the boys for a franc a copy." As Van Buren sketched away, he discovered that his work had matured. As he related to his parents, "I seem to get into every picture I do and it shows up in the finished product."

After Christmas, when the issue finally appeared in New York, a reporter for the *Times* felt the same way about Van Buren's work. He compared it to that of the famous British illustrator Bruce Bairnsfather, and dubbed him the "American Bairnsfather."[1]

The Gas Attack wasn't the only project going on in the division. The Broadway Boys under the collaboration of Lt. William Halloran Jr., who had directed *You Know Me, Al,* and Pvt. Harry Gribble, worked on another musical, *Let's Beat It.* Bound for Broadway when the division returned

Private Van Buren, nicknamed the "American Bairnsfather" after the famed British illustrator, thought his sketch of Maj. Gen. John O'Ryan (right) compared favorably with that of famous portraitist John Singer Sargent (left). The Seventh Regiment Fund

home—whenever that might be—the new play was a "state secret," according to assistant editor Rowland. But when he got a chance to view a rehearsal, he reported that he "wanted to write to Dorothy Parker, she who makes it a business to disagree with everybody on everything, and travels via subway in order to reach every show late, but who juggles the words in her reviews so cleverly that one doesn't care whether she pans or praises a show.

"If Dorothy doesn't like this frothy, flippant importation of mirth and music we'll buy, and before July 1 next, too."

He then went on to give Parker the "meat" for her review. "Every line and note of the production was composed by men of the 27th Division, by boys who have been through the fiercest kind of warfare. And the chaps who will appear in the piece didn't lie in triple-mattressed French beds sipping tea while the Division was punching holes in Hindy's concrete line."[2]

While the doughboys waited—and waited some more—life far behind the lines was not all "mirth and music."

Perhaps the most somber moment came on 10 November, the day before the Armistice. Maj. Gen. George W. Read, commander of the American II Corps, reviewed what was left of the Empire Division in a field outside of Corbie. He and O'Ryan sat on their horses, their staffs arrayed behind them. The 102d Field Signal Battalion, escorted by a color guard of four mounted troopers, marched through the square of Corbie, past Read and O'Ryan and into the field. The Headquarters Troop came next. The regiments then marched out, led first by the 105th Infantry, then the 106th and 108th. Last was the 107th, with its new commander, Col. Mortimer Bryant. Trailing each regiment were packs of dogs that had wandered into the encampment and were adopted by the soldiers. O'Ryan was amazed at the collection of dogs, in their own way victims of the war. Maurice Swetland reported that "as the units passed in review, their dog mascots, some twenty of them, that had been befriended by the men, trudged along beside them, as if understanding the ceremony that was taking place."[3]

When the division halted and stood at attention, the division's bands gathered and played "Nearer My God to Thee." There was a moment of silence to honor the dead now buried in over fifty cemeteries in Flanders Field, along the Hindenburg Line, and near the banks of the Selle River. During the brief quiet of that Sunday morning, O'Ryan saw a little dog sitting near him. The dog squatted there for a second or two before looking at the other dogs to its right and left. The dog, "seeming to sense his unsoldierly action," O'Ryan later wrote, "promptly resumed a standing and attentive attitude."

Although the war was over, death still came calling. Almost every day, word trickled in that another veteran of the 107th Infantry had succumbed to his wounds in some faraway hospital. But now worse than the dying wounded was the influenza epidemic—more deadly in its own way than the war itself. In fact, more people would die from the flu in 1918 and 1919 than during the entire war. From the time the boys from New York quit the line on 21 October until they landed in New York City in mid-March, thirty-four of them would perish from either the flu or pneumonia. On 12 January, in Rochester, New York, where he had gone on leave to attend his sister's wedding, Cpl. James Throckmorton Vought of K Company, a few days before the ceremony, died of influenza.

The day after Read and O'Ryan reviewed their troops, Van Buren and Rowland arrived in Paris aboard a troop train. It was 11 November. Armistice Day. They were there to find a printer for the Christmas issue of *The Gas Attack*. They carried with them all the articles and sketches that would fill up thirty-six pages. Still wearing their cootie-infested uniforms, the two soldiers pushed through a massive throng now delirious with peace toward a hotel. "We had great difficulty getting there," Van Buren told his mother, "because the little French girls nearly smothered us with kisses, etc. During all my experiences at the front I never underwent more danger than I did on that 1/2 mile trip to the hotel. When we landed we were a funny looking sight. My overcoat pockets were full of flowers and my face was wet with French kisses."

Van Buren then went on to describe Paris and, of course, the girls. He had hoped to run into Neysa McMein, but because of the death of her father, she had recently left Paris for the States. Even so, Van Buren was exceedingly happy. "I love all the world now and soon I'll be with you!" he shouted from the pages of his letter. "It's over and now I know I'm going to live!"

Pfc. Dutch Wilbur, finally out of the hospital, and several of the boys from I Company went AWOL, making a beeline for Paris. Wilbur had always wanted to see the Folies Bergère. They got caught. But the mood of the 107th was upbeat, and the boys were confined to a guardhouse, where they took turns guarding each other until their punishment was over. To his family, Wilbur later said, "Oh, Paree! Oh, la, la!"[4]

Cpl. Albert Clark didn't make it to Paris. But he exclaimed to his parents back in Mount Vernon, "There were never such days as those—I gave up hope—and all and—hurray! Here I be. Look me over—alive and well."

There was more good news. A few days before Christmas, the mother of Pfc. William F. White, who had gotten a telegram after the Hindenburg Line fight that her son had been captured and was presumed dead, received another telegram.

YOUR SON WILLIAM FRANCIS WHITE REPORTED
RELEASED FROM GERMAN PRISON CAMP DULMEN
AND ARRIVED IN HULL ENGLAND IN GOOD HEALTH
    YOURS ADJUTANT GENERAL

White's health was good, except for his teeth. In England they were all pulled out. When he was released from the hospital, he rejoined E Company in time to sail home with the entire Twenty-seventh Division.[5]

What awaited them all was a welcome the likes of which had never before been seen in America.

Tuesday, 25 March 1919, turned out to be a perfect day for a welcome-home parade. The morning sky was as blue as the field of stars on the American flags that fluttered along New York's Fifth Avenue, from Washington Square north to 110th Street. The warm spring breeze had just enough patriotic force to unfurl the thousands of banners and pennants that hung from every street post and to ruffle the red, white, and blue bunting that covered almost every square inch of granite along the five-mile parade route.

The only thing that was not perfect was the crowd. It was too immense even for Manhattan with its population of two and a quarter million. Ever since the three troop ships, bringing the boys of the Twenty-seventh

Division home, had steamed into New York Harbor on March 6 and 9, first the *Leviathan,* then the *Mauretania,* and finally the *Nieuw Amsterdam,* men, women, and children began to pour into Gotham from nearly every city and hamlet in the state. On the day of the parade, Mount Vernon had turned into a ghost town. Many of them came from New Jersey, too, and Connecticut, Missouri, Pennsylvania, and Vermont—any state where a parent or friend or sweetheart lived or where an Empire Division soldier had called home before he enlisted. Even the South Carolina governor showed up.

Also, the English journalist Philip Gibbs, who had covered the British Fourth Army, arrived in New York for the first time in his life. For *Harper's* magazine, he wrote:

> The emotion of New York was visible in its streets. The city itself, mon-strous, yet dreamlike and mystical as one sees it first rising in fantastic shapes through the haze of dawn above the waters of the Hudson, seemed excited by its own historical significance. There was a vibration about it as sunlight splashed its gold upon the topmost stories of the sky-scrapers and sparkled in a thousand windows of the Woolworth tower and flung black bars of shadow across the lower blocks. Banners were flying everywhere in the streets that go straight and long between perpendicular cliffs of ma-sonry, and the wind that comes blowing up the two rivers ruffled them. They were banners of rejoicing, but reminders also of the service and sacri-fice of each house from which they were hanging with golden stars of death above the heads of the living crowd surging there below them. In these dec-orations of New York I saw the imagination of a people conscious of their own power, and with a dramatic instinct able to impress the multitudes with the glory and splendor of their achievement.[6]

The reported ten thousand regular and reserve policemen assigned for crowd control were too few to handle the three to five million people who had squeezed and shoved and spilled out onto Fifth Avenue. Van Buren's father, who had never been east of the Mississippi River until that day, had stuffed his hands into his pants pockets and was alarmed that the press of the crowd kept him from taking them out again. And so he had to watch the entire parade with his hands pinned to his sides. On the east side of Central Park a two-and-half-mile-long grandstand had been erected for, as one Poughkeepsie newspaper reporter claimed, "sixty thousand fathers and mothers, wives and sweethearts, sisters and little brothers, grandfathers and grandmothers, uncles and aunts of the men of the 27th."[7]

In front of St. Patrick's Cathedral, two hundred chairs were set up for wounded veterans who had come down from the Army Base Hospital 1 at Gun Hill in the Bronx. The police found the chairs violated parade regulations and had them taken down. The veterans were forced inside St. Patrick's, where they could not watch their comrades in arms march by. Joyce Kilmer's widow had been invited to sit with Mayor Hylan and Governor Al Smith but had showed up without a ticket and was not allowed in the mayoral grandstand in front of the Metropolitan Museum of Art. When Michael S. Hogan of the Knights of Columbus heard this, he gave up his front-row seat at his organization's grandstand to Mrs. Kilmer and her son.

"Every window on the whole line of march held a bevy of heads," wrote one reporter. "Roofs, fire escapes and balconies all jammed." Atop the lintel of St. Nicholas Church, three elderly women sat in folding chairs. Below them, the church's choir filled its own grandstand and "did some mighty effective singing," belting out "Onward Christian Soldiers" and "Mademoiselle Au Revoir."

Women fainted. Fights broke out. One man beat another to death. A police officer dropped dead of a heart attack. Another law officer was beaten by an old lady with an umbrella. Brass buttons were yanked off police uniforms. An unfortunate spectator fell from his perch on the roof of a building and crashed through a skylight.

As the crowd began to build and tension gripped the soul of the city, thousands of soldiers started arriving below the Washington Square Arch. They lined up by brigade, regiment, battalion, company, and platoon as two airplanes roared up Fifth Avenue, flying low between the tall buildings. By ten thirty the soldiers moved out from beneath the arch and started uptown.

Leading the parade was a caisson escorted by eight coal black horses led by eight honor guards of the division. Four of the soldiers had won American Distinguished Service Crosses, including Pvt. Jonathan

Moore Jr. of the 107th Infantry. Behind the caisson, a ninth horse wore an empty saddle with reversed stirrups. The caisson was a float of floral wreaths honoring the dead. One of the wreaths measured twenty feet in circumference with the phrase: "In token to a loving and eternal comradeship with those more gloriously victorious—the fallen." Next came a huge service flag held aloft by fourteen soldiers. Stitched on to the flag were 1,972 gold stars. The crowd kept a grim silence as the caisson and service flag passed by them. Afterward rolled a motorcade of the latest Ford limousines—most of them driven by women. At first the crowd kept quiet. They stopped waving their small American flags. They wondered why the soldiers were riding in such luxury and not marching. Then protruding from the windows they spotted crutches and bandaged heads, and boys with no legs and no arms. When they realized what they were seeing, they cheered.

One soldier waved his crutch at a pretty girl. She yelled to him over the din of the crowd, "Oh, you boys, if we ain't glad to have you back!"[8]

Flowers, cigarettes, and cigars fell like rain on the motorcade. The wounded were soon buried in floral wreaths of their own.

Thirty-five minutes after the start of the parade, the New York City police band stepped out from under the arch, followed by Maj. Gen. John F. O'Ryan on a spirited sorrel mount named Red Check. O'Ryan and his steed had barely reached Washington Mews when the mount reared up and whirled around. It slipped on the pavement. The crowd gasped as the horse fell. One reporter described how calm the general stayed and how he "kept his seat as coolly as though he were straddling the German ditch." An aide gave his horse to O'Ryan to ride.

Following the division commander came his staff and a detachment of Australians with their broad-brimmed campaign hats turned jauntily up on one side.

Next strode the Fifty-fourth Brigade—the 107th and 108th Infantry Regiments. The 107th stood out more than any other regiment because its men had painted their helmets a darker green.

At Madison Square, where a great victory arch had been set up with a thick silken cord attached to a series of huge pillars, the crowd finally broke. It flooded Fifth Avenue, and the soldiers were pressed together, able now to march only four abreast. Police put their brawny backs against the men, women, and children, trying to push them back. Mounted police also tried to drive the surging crowd out of the way. Instead, they eased their mounts out into Fifth Avenue, afraid they were about to trample people. Girls took that moment to leap onto the running boards of the cars in the motorcade and kiss the wounded soldiers. Finally, Medal of Honor winner Sgt. Reider Waaler cut the silken cord and the parade moved on.

For three hours, the division pushed its way through the great crowd, past the Waldorf-Astoria, where the chefs and busboys stood outside and cheered; past the public library, where veterans of the Civil War and Spanish-American War laid a great wreath of purple orchids at the foot of the Court of Heroic Dead that listed in gold letters the battles in which the division had fought; past the mansions of the Astors, the Fricks, the Vanderbilts, and the Rhinelanders, with a gold star for T. J. Oakley that hung in the window; past St. Patrick's Cathedral, where inside two hundred wounded veterans were kept from the spectacle while outside Archbishop Patrick Cardinal Hayes blessed the soldiers and chimes rang; and on past Central Park.

Near Sixty-sixth Street, the 107th Infantry band leader Matt Lawrence and his regimental band stepped out in front of the parading silk stocking soldiers and struck up the old Seventh's tune, "Greyjackets!" New Yorkers immediately recognized the melody. The masses of civilians, standing within a block of the Park Avenue armory, already yelling at the tops of their voices, broke into yet a more deafening roar. Shouts of "Welcome Home, Seventh!" descended on the soldiers. The crowd moved closer to the men, brushing up against them, clasping them on the shoulders and backs, embracing them and their upstate comrades-in-arms, too—the "appleknockers"—back into the very heart of New York's silk stocking district.

Notes

Prologue

1. Capt. G. H. F. Nichols, *The 18th Division in the Great War* (London: William Blackwood & Sons, 1992), 394.

2. J. F. O'Ryan, *The Story of the 27th Division* (New York: Wynkoop, Hallenbeck, Crawford, 1921), 789–92.

3. R. Ernest Dupuy and Trevor N. Dupuy, *The Encyclopedia of Military History,* 2d ed. (New York: Harper & Row, 1986), 979.

4. Tristram Tupper, *New York Evening Post,* 25 March 1919. "Division Adjutant's Official Account of What the New York National Guard Division Accomplished in Belgium and France."

5. Kenneth Gow, *Letters of a Soldier* (New York: Herbert B. Grover, 1920), 387.

6. Claude G. Leland, *From Shell Hole to Chateau with Company I* (New York: 7th Regiment, New York National Guard, 1950), 176.

7. Sir Frederick Maurice, *The Last Four Months: How the War Was Won* (Boston: Little, Brown, & Co., 1919), 128.

8. George Clarke Musgrave, *Four Flags under France* (New York: D. Appleton, 1918), 281–90.

9. Sir John Monash, *The Australian Victories in France* (1920; reprint, Nashville: The Battery Press, 1993), 219.

10. Tupper, *New York Evening Post,* "Division Adjutant's Official Account."

11. Philip J. Haythornthwaite, *The World War One Source Book* (London: Arms & Armour, 1992), 282.

12. G. H. F. Nichols, *18th Division,* 420.

13. Musgrave, *Four Flags under France,* 286.

14. Maurice J. and Lilli Swetland, *These Men* (Harrisburg, Pa.: Military Service Publishing, 1940), 145.

15. Monash, *Australian Victories in France,* 217.

16. Joseph Hyde Pratt, "The St. Quentin-Cambrai Canal Tunnel," *The Military Engineer,* Vol. 19, no. 106 (July–August 1927): 324–29.

17. Monash, *Australian Victories in France,* 217.

18. Tupper, *New York Evening Post,* "Division Adjutant's Official Account."

19. Maurice, *Last Four Months,* 144.

20. George W. Ely II, diary, 25 September 1918.

CHAPTER I

1. *New York Times (NYT),* 16 August 1917, 4.

2. Ibid., 1 and 4.

3. *The Seventh Regiment Gazette (Gazette),* August 1917.

4. George P. Nichols, *The First Hundred Years: Records and Reminiscences of a Century of Company I, 1838–1938* (New York: Seventh Regiment, New York National Guard, 1938), 204.

5. *NYT,* 27 May 1898.

6. Ibid., 31 May 1899.

7. Ibid., 1 June 1899.

8. Dewitt Clinton Falls, *History of the Seventh Regiment, 1889–1922* (New York: Veterans of the Seventh Regiment, 1948), 37.

9. *Gazette,* September 1917.

10. Gerald F. Jacobson, ed., *History of the 107th Infantry, USA* (New York: Seventh Regiment Armory, 1920), 7.

11. Martin Green, *New York Evening World,* 1919. From the archives of Kenneth H. Powers, historian, Sixty-ninth Regiment of New York, no date.

12. Father Francis Patrick Duffy, *Father Duffy's Story* (New York: George H. Doran, 1919), 18.

13. Green, *Evening World.*

14. Falls, *History of the Seventh Regiment,* 197.

15. Albert M. Ettinger and A. Churchill Ettinger, *A Doughboy with the Fighting 69th* (Shippensberg, Pa.: White Mane Publishing, 1992), 5.

16. Joyce Kilmer Collection, Rutgers University, New Brunswick, N.J.

17. Duffy, *Father Duffy's Story,* 16, 17.

18. Anton Schefer, *Letters from André Chéronnet Champollion* (New York: The Cheltenham Press, 1915), 11.

19. Ibid., 43, 27, 63, 64, 94, and 102.

20. George P. Nichols, *First Hundred Years,* 345–46.

21. Ibid., 347.

22. Ibid., 348.

23. From New York newspaper accounts, 16 August 1917.

24. Ettinger, *A Doughboy,* 6.

25. Duffy, *Father Duffy's Story,* 18.

CHAPTER 2

1. *NYT,* 6 June 1917.

2. Ibid.

3. Falls, *History of the Seventh Regiment*, 187.

4. *Flushing* (N.Y.) *Daily Times*, 6 August 1918.

5. Ibid.

6. Raeburn Van Buren letter to Fern Ringo, 17 June 1915.

7. Brian Gallagher, *Anything Goes: The Jazz Age Adventures of Neysa McMein and Her Extravagant Circle of Friends* (New York: New York Times Books, 1987), 38.

8. Author's interview with Van Buren, July 1979.

9. *NYT*, 27 March 1910, 11.

10. Rhinelander Family scrapbooks, personal papers.

11. Emmons Clark, *History of the Seventh Regiment of New York, 1806–1889* (New York: Seventh Regiment, 1890), 240.

12. Van Rensselaer Family scrapbooks, personal papers.

13. Gow, *Letters of a Soldier*, 443.

14. Bryant Library Local History Collection, Roslyn, N.Y.

15. Richard Ridgeley Lytle, *Scott Harrison Lytle Memory Book, 1889–1918* (privately printed, no date).

16. *New York Sun*, March 1912.

17. *New York Post*, from Van Rensselaer Family scrapbook.

18. Ettinger, *A Doughboy*, 4.

19. Annie Kilburn Kilmer, *Memories of My Son, Sergeant Joyce Kilmer* (New York: Frye Publishing, 1921), 120.

20. Annie Kilburn Kilmer, *Leaves from My Life* (New York: Frye Publishing, 1925), 121.

21. "Heroic Performance of Duty," *Home News*, 22 August 1918.

22. *NYT*, 12 September 1917.

23. Ibid.

24. *New York Sun*, 12 September 1917.

CHAPTER 3

1. Edwin P. Hoyt, *The Vanderbilts and Their Fortunes* (New York: Doubleday & Co., 1962), 331.

2. Cornelius Vanderbilt Jr., *Man of the World* (New York: Crown, 1959), 17.

3. *NYT*, 10 February 1918, sect. 2, p. 3.

4. O'Ryan, *Story of the 27th Division*, 64–65.

5. Bert Lobdell, letter to his father, 12 September 1917.

6. Summit, N.J., Historical Society.

7. Twenty-seventh Division's *The Gas Attack* magazine.

8. Robert Stewart Sutcliffe, ed., *Seventy-first New York in the World War* (New York: no publisher listed, 1922), 63.

9. Alexander T. M. Van Rensselaer letter, dated 25 February 1918.

10. Edward P. Dunphey, ed., *Newburgh in the World War* (Newburgh, N.Y.: Newburgh World War Publishing Co., 1924), 30.

11. Interviews with Robert V. Kissam Sr., 26 November 1999 and 8 December 1999.

12. Dunphey, *Newburgh in the World War,* 30.

13. Ibid., 31.

14. Ibid., 82.

15. Interview with Pat Egan Procak, daughter of Raphael Egan, 15 October 1998.

16. George P. Nichols, *First Hundred Years,* 367.

17. Letter to Raphael Egan from his mother, 6 April 1918.

18. George P. Nichols, *First Hundred Years,* 356–57.

19. Interview with August Engler, son of August Engler, 6 September 1999.

20. Interview with John W. Fetherolf, son of George Fetherolf, 11 September 1999.

21. Interview with Ellsworth Mills, nephew of Harold and Van Strycker Mills, 28 July 2000.

22. Interview with Kenyon FitzGerald, president, the Seventh Regiment Fund, 24 March 2000.

Chapter 4

1. Arthur W. Little, *From Harlem to the Rhine* (New York: Covici-Friede, 1936), 49–50.

2. *NYT,* 24 August 1917, 1.

3. Little, *From Harlem to the Rhine,* 52–70.

4. M. A. DeWolfe Howe and others, *Memoirs of the Harvard War Dead in the War against Germany* (Cambridge, Mass.: Harvard University Press, 1923), 370.

5. Jacobson, *History of the 107th,* 366.

6. *Flushing Daily Times,* 6 February 1918.

7. Letter from Pvt. John Donnelly to his sister, 5 December 1917.

8. Private Charles Divine, *City Ways and Company Streets* (New York: Moffat, Yard & Company, 1918), preface.

9. From Bryant Library Local History Collection, Roslyn, N.Y.

10. Gow, *Letters of a Soldier,* 423.

11. Howe, *Memoirs of the Harvard War Dead,* 384–85.

12. Nicholas H. Krayer, ed., *History of Company "E," 107th Infantry, 1917–1919* (New York: War Veterans Association, Co. E, 7th, New York National Guard, 1920), 20.

13. *Cornwall* (New York) *Press,* 6 December 1917.

Chapter 5

1. Jacobson, *History of the 107th,* 387.

2. Ibid., 338.

3. Ibid., 345.

4. Claude Leland letter home, dated 24 May 1918.

5. Jacobson, *History of the 107th*, 345.

6. Krayer, *History of Company "E,"* 81.

7. Jacobson, *History of the 107th*, 345.

8. Ibid., 367.

9. Will Hayward letter, 30 June 1918, published in *Mount Vernon Argus.*

10. Howe, *Memoirs of the Harvard War Dead*, 370.

11. From K Company scrapbook, New York State Military Museum and Veterans Research Center.

12. From the scrapbook of Pat Egan Procak.

13. Jacobson, *History of the 107th*, 425.

14. Ibid., 367.

15. Ettinger, *A Doughboy*, 58.

16. General John J. Pershing, *My Experiences in the First World War*, Vol. 1 (1931; reprint, New York: Da Capo Press, 1995), 79.

17. Ibid., 288.

18. John Keegan, *The First World War* (New York: Alfred A. Knopf, 1999), 357–58.

19. Pershing, *My Experiences*, Vol. 2, 28.

20. O'Ryan, *Story of the 27th Division*, 170–173.

21. From the diary of Harold Mills.

22. Jacobson, *History of the 107th*, 368.

23. Krayer, *History of Company "E,"* 82–83.

24. *Gazette*, September 1918.

25. James W. Evans, *Entertaining the American Army* (New York: Association Press, 1921), 4–5.

26. Ibid., 96.

27. Gallagher, *Anything Goes*, 46.

28. O'Ryan, *Story of the 27th Division*, 174–75.

29. Ibid., 178.

30. Jacobson, *History of the 107th*, 30.

CHAPTER 6

1. Hayward letter to parents, 10 July 1918, published in the *Mount Vernon Argus.*

2. Letter from Angelo Mustico to his family, 13 August 1918.

3. William F. Clarke, *Over There with O'Ryan's Roughnecks* (Seattle, Wash.: Superior Publishing Company, no date), 36.

4. Frederick Maurice, *The Life of General Lord Rawlinson of Trent* (London: Cassel Plc., 1928), 220.

5. Robert Blake, ed., *The Private Papers of Douglas Haig, 1914–1919* (London: Eyre & Spottiswoode, 1952), 313.

6. From the diary of Albert Breunig, New York State Military History Museum, Watervliet, N.Y.

7. Clarke, *Over There with Ryan's Roughnecks,* 38.

8. Ibid., 37.

9. Maurice, *Rawlinson,* 222.

10. Pershing, *My Experiences,* Vol. 2, 137.

11. C. E. W. Bean, *The Official History of Australia in the War, 1914–1918,* Vol. 6 (St. Lucia: University of Queensland Press, 1942), 279.

12. Maurice, *Rawlinson,* 222.

13. C. R. M. F. Cruttwell, *A History of the Great War, 1914–1918,* 2d ed. (Chicago: Academy Chicago Publishers, 1991), 532.

14. From "The Reminiscences of John F. O'Ryan," in the Oral History Collection of Columbia University, New York City, N.Y.

15. Monash, *Australian Victories in France,* 59.

16. Bean, *Official History of Australia in the War,* 330.

17. Pershing, *My Experiences,* Vol. 2, 138.

18. Krayer, *History of Company "E,"* 100.

19. Stanton Whitney, *Squadron A in the Great War, 1917–1918* (New York: Squadron Association, 1923), 29.

20. *NYT,* 23 March 1919.

21. Krayer, *History of Company "E,"* 86.

22. Jacobson, *History of the 107th,* 369.

23. *Flushing Daily Times,* June 1918.

24. Jacobson, *History of the 107th,* 369.

25. *Flushing Daily Times,* June 1918.

26. Jacobson, *History of the 107th,* 369.

27. Letter published in the *Flushing Daily Times,* 6 August 1918.

28. Letter by Claude Leland published in the *Flushing Daily Times,* no date.

CHAPTER 7

1. Excerpts from the letters of Finn and Ward were published in *NYT,* 27 February 1919, 3; 15 September 1918, 8, respectively.

2. Howe, *Memoirs of the Harvard War Dead,* 598–99.

3. From letters published in the *Mount Vernon Argus.*

4. Franklin W. Ward, *Between the Big Parades* (New York: Frederick M. Waterbury, 1932), 63.

5. Krayer, *History of Company "E,"* 86.

6. Howe, *Memoirs of the Harvard War Dead,* 373.

7. From Hayward letter to parents, 17 July 1918, published in the *Mount Vernon Argus.*

8. Krayer, *History of Company "E,"* 87.

9. Interviews with William F. White Jr., 12 November 1999 and 23 December 1999.

10. Capt. Harry W. Hayward letter to H. C. Larkin, courtesy Harvard University.

11. Sutcliffe, *Seventy-first New York*, 37.

12. Walter G. Andrews, compiler, *The Story of a Machine Gun Company, 1918–1919* (Buffalo, N.Y.: The Matthews-Northrup Works, 1924), 37.

13. Ibid., 31.

14. Ibid., 37.

15. Jacobson, *History of the 107th*, 323.

16. Harold Chasmar letter.

17. Howe, *Memoirs of the Harvard War Dead*, 498.

18. Hayward letter to parents, 18 July 1918, published in the *Mount Vernon Argus*.

19. Jacobson, *History of the 107th*, 323.

20. Howe, *Memoirs of the Harvard War Dead*, 498.

21. From the Hellquist family archives.

22. Bob Helstern letter to his mother, no date, published in the *Orange County Press*.

23. Accounts published in various New York City newspapers.

24. From the *Mount Vernon Argus*.

25. Jacobson, *History of the 107th*, 294.

26. Ibid., 294–95.

27. From the Hellquist family archives.

28. Richard Greene Holbrook, *A Handbook of Company K, 107th Infantry* (New York: Vail-Ballou Press, Inc., 1940), 113.

29. Maj. Tristram Tupper, "Sargent's Studio of Shellfire," *NYT*, 23 March 1919, 5.

30. Ibid.

31. Krayer, *History of Company "E,"* 96.

32. Capt. Hayward letters to H. C. and Mary Larkin, courtesy Harvard University, August 1918 (no day listed).

33. Krayer, *History of Company "E,"* 99.

34. Ibid.

35. Letter published in the *Newburgh Daily News*.

36. Interview with William F. White Jr., 12 November 1999.

37. Tupper, "Sargent's Studio of Shellfire," 5.

CHAPTER 8

1. Interview with Jeffrey Nicoll, grandson of Fancher Nicoll, 24 April 2000.

2. Fancher Nicoll letter to his sister Emily, 1 August 1918.

3. Letter from Harold Mills to his family, no date.

4. From letter published in the *Newburgh Daily News*.

5. Jacobson, *History of the 107th*, 371.

6. Ibid.

7. *Gazette*, November 1918.

8. *Flushing Daily Times.*

9. From the diary of Albert Breunig.

10. Interview with Nancy Hawley Wilsea, niece of Bronson Hawley, 19 January 1998.

CHAPTER 9

1. Blake, *Private Papers of Douglas Haig*, 323.

2. Pershing, *My Experiences*, Vol. 2, 218.

3. Ibid., Vol. 2, 219.

4. Ibid., Vol. 2, 229.

5. Marshal F. Foch, *The Memoirs of Marshal Foch* (Garden City, N.Y.: Doubleday, Doran, & Company, 1931), 346.

6. Pershing, *My Experiences*, Vol. 2, 230.

7. Foch, *Memoirs*, 398.

8. Blake, *Private Papers of Douglas Haig*, 325.

9. Keegan, *First World War*, 365.

10. Blake, *Private Papers of Douglas Haig*, 326.

11. Dupuy and Dupuy, *Encyclopedia of Military History*, 982.

12. Howe, *Memoirs of the Harvard War Dead*, 499.

13. From "The Reminiscences of John F. O'Ryan," in the Oral History Collection of Columbia University.

14. William Edwin Hall, ed., *History of the Class of 1900* (New Haven, Conn.: Sheffield Scientific School, Yale University, Tuttle, Morehouse & Taylor, 1922).

CHAPTER 10

1. Sutcliffe, *Seventy-first New York*, 80.

2. Jacobson, *History of the 107th*, 323.

3. Ibid., 340.

4. Krayer, *History of Company "E,"* 102–103.

5. Ibid., 103.

6. Jack Lydecker letter to his parents, 12 September 1918, published in the *Mount Vernon Argus*.

7. Maurice, *Rawlinson*, 232–33.

8. Maj. Gen. Sir Archibald Montgomery, *The Story of the Fourth Army in the Battles of the Hundred Days* (London: Hodder & Stoughton, 1919), 115.

9. Ibid., 118.

10. *Mount Vernon Argus*.

11. Jacobson, *History of the 107th*, 330.

12. Howe, *Memoirs of the Harvard War Dead*, 449.

13. Jacobson, *History of the 107th*, 323.

14. Paddy Griffith, *Battle Tactics of the Western Front* (New Haven: Yale University Press, 1994), 162.

15. Krayer, *History of Company "E,"* 102.

16. Jacobson, *History of the 107th*, 426.

17. Montgomery, *Story of the Fourth Army,* 122–24.

18. Tupper, "Sargent's Studio of Shellfire."

19. Lt. Col. William T. Starr, "As General Staff Saw Big 'Show,'" *New York Evening Post,* 25 March 1919.

20. Ward, *Between the Big Parades,* 118–19.

21. Sutcliffe, *Seventy-first New York,* 80.

22. Dupuy and Dupuy, *Encyclopedia of Military History,* 982.

23. Ralph Polk Buell letter to his wife, 14 September 1918.

24. Howe, *Memoirs of the Harvard War Dead,* 373–74.

25. Bean, *Official History of Australia in the War,* 915.

26. Montgomery, *Story of the Fourth Army,* 137.

27. Monash, *Australian Victories in France,* 235.

28. Ibid., 235–36.

29. Krayer, *History of Company "E,"* 103.

30. Jacobson, *History of the 107th,* 340–41.

31. Raymond Blauvelt letter published in Nyack, N.Y., newspaper, 21 November 1918.

32. Jacobson, *History of the 107th,* 426.

Chapter 11

1. Summit, N.J., Historical Society.

2. Lydecker letter to parents, 26 September 1918, published in the *Mount Vernon Argus.*

3. Maj. Tristram Tupper, "Thrilling Fights of New York's Heroes," *NYT,* 15 December 1918, sec. 4, p. 1.

4. Lydecker letter, 26 September 1918, *Mount Vernon Argus.*

5. Howe, *Memoirs of the Harvard War Dead,* 449.

6. Jacobson, *History of the 107th,* 350.

7. Krayer, *History of Company "E,"* 104.

8. Lydecker letter, 26 September 1918, Mount Vernon *Argus.*

9. Monash, *Australian Victories in France,* 246–48.

10. Lt. Col. J. Leslie Kincaid, "The 27th New York's Guard Division That Broke German Line," *New York Times Magazine,* 9 March 1919, 3.

11. Hall, *History of the Class of 1900.*

12. Ward, *Between the Big Parades,* 123.

13. Ibid.

14. Jacobson, *History of the 107th,* 50.

15. Ibid., 388–89.

16. Krayer, *History of Company "E,"* 104.

17. List is from Nicoll Family scrapbook.

18. Jacobson, *History of the 107th,* 305.

19. Ibid.

20. Sutcliffe, *Seventy-first New York,* 84.

21. Herbert Barry, compiler, *Squadron A: A History of Its First Fifty Years, 1889–1939* (New York: Association of Ex-Members of Squadron A, 1939), 223.

22. Ward, *Between the Big Parades,* 125.

23. Hall, *History of the Class of 1900.*

24. Sutcliffe, *Seventy-first New York,* 84.

25. Monash, *Australian Victories in France,* 251.

26. Ibid., 245.

27. G. H. F. Nichols, *18th Division,* 421.

28. Bean, *Official History of Australia in the War,* 946.

CHAPTER 12

1. Montgomery, *Story of the Fourth Army,* 154.

2. Howe, *Memoirs of Harvard War Dead,* 374.

3. Jacobson, *History of the 107th,* 318.

4. K Company scrapbook, New York State Military Museum.

5. Howe, *Memoirs of Harvard War Dead,* 499–500.

6. Jacobson, *History of the 107th,* 373.

7. Krayer, *History of Company "E,"* 105.

8. *Gazette,* December 1918.

9. Letter in the *Cornwall Press,* 26 December 1918, 1.

10. Ibid.

11. *Gazette,* November 1918.

12. O'Ryan, *Story of the 27th Division,* 295–96.

13. W. E. Berry, "A Visit to the Australians," *Times of London,* 6 October 1918.

14. Denis Winter, *Making the Legend: The War Writings of C. E. W. Bean* (St. Lucia: University of Queensland Press, 1992), 213.

15. Berry, "A Visit to the Australians."

CHAPTER 13

1. Interviews with Kenyon FitzGerald, president, Seventh Regiment Fund, 22 August 2000.

2. Weston Barclay, "Path of the Brave," New York *World-Telegram,* 1943, sect. 2, p. 1.

3. Ben Franklin, *Carry On.*

4. Barclay, "Path of the Brave," 1.

5. Father Hoey's letter was published in numerous New York State newspapers.

6. George P. Nichols, *First Hundred Years,* 411.

7. From the *Poughkeepsie* (New York) *Journal.*

8. *Mount Vernon Argus.*

9. Summit Historical Society.

10. Jacobson, *History of the 107th,* 318.

11. Gadebusch's first-person account appeared in several publications, including the *Gazette* and Andrews's history of the Machine Gun Company.

12. Andrews, *Story of a Machine Gun Company*, 120.

13. Ibid., 50.

14. Franklin, *Carry On*.

15. Ward, *Between the Big Parades*, 135.

16. Andrews, *Story of a Machine Gun Company*, 51.

17. Franklin, *Carry On*.

18. Jacobson, *History of the 107th*, 330.

19. Montgomery, *Story of the Fourth Army*, 157.

20. *Gazette*, December 1918.

21. From K Company scrapbook.

22. Summit, New Jersey, Historical Society.

23. Ibid.

24. Carl Rosenhagen, "A Day in the Life of a Tanker—September 1918," *Armor: The Magazine of Mobile Warfare* 82, no. 5 (September–October 1973): 34–35.

25. From Maj. Gen. John O'Ryan's written recommendation for Buell's Medal of Honor, 8 January 1920.

26. From the *Newburgh Daily News*.

27. Franklin, *Carry On*.

28. Andrews, *Story of a Machine Gun Company*, 51.

29. Montgomery, *Story of the Fourth Army*, 167.

30. G. H. F. Nichols, *18th Division*, 417.

31. *Mount Vernon Argus*.

32. Summit Historical Society.

33. *Gazette*, December 1918.

34. Summit Historical Society.

35. *Gazette*, December 1918.

36. Gadebusch's personal account, *Gazette*, December 1918.

37. Barclay, "Path of the Brave."

38. Summit Historical Society.

39. Ibid.

40. Barclay, "Path of the Brave."

41. From Egan interview published in various New York State newspapers, including the *Newburgh Daily News*, 16 April 1919.

42. Howe, *Memoirs of the Harvard War Dead*, 500–502.

43. K Company scrapbook.

44. The City of White Plains, New York, Archives.

45. *Newburgh Daily News*.

46. Interview with Kissam, 8 December 1999.

47. Jacobson, *History of the 107th*, 306.

48. Irving Savage letter to his mother, 2 October 1918, *Mount Vernon Argus*.

49. Nichols, *First Hundred Years,* 447.

50. Orange County *Press.*

51. Krayer, *History of Company "E,"* 106–107.

52. Ibid., 51.

53. Michael Houlahan to his mother, 2 October 1918, *Mount Vernon Argus.*

54. Richard McIntyre letter to his wife, 20 October 1918.

Chapter 14

1. Monash, *Australian Victories in France,* 260–61.

2. Berry, "A Visit to the Australians."

3. Sir Arthur Conan Doyle, "The Rent in the Line: A Picture of the Great Battle From the Roof of A Tank," *Times of London,* 3 October 1918, 9.

4. Berry, "A Visit to the Australians."

5. Conan Doyle, "Rent in the Line," 9.

6. Monash, *Australian Victories in France,* 249.

7. Tupper, "Sargent's Studio of Shellfire."

8. "New York's 27th First to Smash The Hindenburg Line, Comes Home," *Literary Digest,* 29 March 1919, 68–78.

9. Kincaid, "Division That Broke German Line."

10. Ward, *Between the Big Parades,* 136.

11. Monash, *Australian Victories in France,* 262 and 261.

12. Sir James E. Edmonds, ed. *History of the Great War: Military Operations France and Belgium, 1918,* vol. 5 (1947; reprint, Nashville: The Battery Press, 1993), 108.

13. F. M. Cutlack, *The Australian Flying Corps in the Eastern and Western Theatres of War, 1914–1918* (Sydney: Angus & Robertson, 1938), 331.

14. M. Paul Maze, *A Frenchman in Khaki* (London: William Heinemann, Ltd., 1934), 347–50.

15. Ward, *Between the Big Parades,* 138.

16. O'Ryan in the Oral History Collection of Columbia University.

17. Bean, *Official History of Australia in the War,* 962.

18. "27th First to Smash Hindenburg Line."

19. *Newburgh Daily News,* no date.

20. Ibid.

21. Interview with Virginia Cairns, daughter of Dutch Wilbur, 15 May 2000.

22. Tupper, "Division Adjutant's Official Account."

23. Starr, "As General Staff Saw Big 'Show.' "

Chapter 15

1. Bean, *Official History of Australia in the War,* 962.

2. Monash, *Australian Victories in France,* 261.

3. Ibid.

4. Bean, *Official History of Australia in the War,* 969.

5. Ibid.

6. Ibid., 976.

7. Sir Arthur Conan Doyle, *A History of the Great War,* Vol. 6 (New York: George H. Doran Co., 1918), 156–58.

8. Bean, *Official History of Australia in the War,* 976.

9. K Company scrapbook.

10. Bean, *Official History of Australia in the War,* 976–77.

11. Ibid., 977.

12. Monash, *Australian Victories in France,* 265.

13. Ward, *Between the Big Parades,* 139.

14. Conan Doyle, *A History of the Great War,* 156.

15. Kincaid, "Division That Broke German Line."

16. Montgomery, *Story of the Fourth Army,* 168.

17. *Times of London,* "Advance into the Blue," 3 October 1918.

18. Monash, *Australian Victories in France,* 266.

19. Wade Hampton Hayes's letter to George W. Chauncey, published in numerous newspapers, including the special section of the *New York Evening Post,* 25 March 1919.

20. Wade Hampton Hayes report to Gen. John Pershing, dated 15 October 1918, reprinted in Jacobson's *History of the 107th,* 113–22.

21. Hayes's letter to Chauncey, 18 October 1918.

22. Letter to author from Peter J. Linder, 22 April 1998. An expert on World War I casualties, Mr. Linder's number of those killed or died of wounds within several days of the battle lists 349 officers and men, although Major General O'Ryan listed 365 such casualties. The Seventh Regiment contends that it is the worst one-day slaughter ever of a U.S. regiment while in combat.

Chapter 16

1. Gregor Dallas, *At the Heart of a Tiger, Clemenceau and His World, 1841–1929* (New York: Carroll & Graf, 1993), 544–45.

2. Gadebusch's account (written in the third person) was published in the *Gazette,* 33, no. 2 (December 1918): 157–59.

3. Interview with Arnold "Dutch" Wilbur's family, 25 May 2000.

4. Interview with August Engler's son, 27 July 2000.

5. Franklin, *Carry On.*

6. *NYT,* 22 November 1918, 7.

7. Summit Historical Society.

8. Maj. Gen. John O'Ryan report to Gen. John Pershing submitted after the last action in which the Twenty-seventh Division participated, 18 December 1918.

9. Jacobson, *History of the 107th,* 261.

10. Father Hoey's letter was published in newspapers throughout New York State, including *Newburgh Daily News.*

11. Summit Historical Society.

12. Howe, *Memoirs of the Harvard Dead,* 502–504.

13. Letter to author from Dolores D. Capuani, George Delahay's niece, 19 December 1999.

14. Krayer, *History of Company "E,"* 25.

15. From the *Cornwall Press,* 19 December 1918, 3.

16. From dispatches to various newspapers.

17. Wilbur letter to his family, 7 October 1918.

18. Clinton Roosa letter to his family, no date.

19. Andrews, *Story of a Machine Gun Company,* 132.

20. Duffy's letter was found in K Company scrapbook.

21. Krayer, *History of Company "E,"* 343.

22. Burke's discovery of a girl's head in a trench was published in the *Gazette,* 33, no. 4 (January 1918): 234.

Chapter 17

1. Maurice, *Rawlinson,* 241.

2. Montgomery, *Story of the Fourth Army,* 216.

3. Maurice, *Rawlinson,* 241–42.

4. Edmonds, *History of the Great War,* 268.

5. Jacobson, *History of the 107th,* 351.

6. Krayer, *History of Company "E,"* 116.

7. Kincaid, "Division That Broke German Line."

8. From K Company scrapbook.

9. Krayer, *History of Company "E,"* 117.

10. Chasmar letter to his parents, 27 October 1918.

11. From K Company scrapbook.

12. Chasmar letter.

13. Krayer, *History of Company "E,"* 118–19.

14. Andrews, *Story of a Machine Gun Company,* 91

15. Gow, *Letters of a Soldier,* 419.

16. Ibid., 420–21.

17. Jacobson, *History of the 107th,* 326–27.

18. Thos. Baird of the Y. M. C. A. in a letter dated January 19, 1919, published in *The Summit New Jersey Herald.*

19. Jacobson, *History of the 107th,* 319.

20. Ibid., 326.

21. Ibid., 358.

22. Interview with Frank Garvin family, 15 July 1997.

23. Jacobson, *History of the 107th,* 319.

24. Ibid., 392.

25. Chasmar letter.

26. Jacobson, *History of the 107th,* 326–27.

27. Ibid., 331.

28. Krayer, *History of Company "E,"* 122.

29. Jacobson, *History of the 107th,* 352.

30. Ibid., 358.

31. "Battle Casualties in the World War," *Infantry Journal* 30, no. 1 (January 1927): 81–83.

32. Jacobson, *History of the 107th,* 146.

33. Chasmar letter.

EPILOGUE

1. *NYT,* 12 January 1919, sec. 7, p. 7.

2. Homecoming issue of *The Gas Attack,* March 1919.

3. Swetland and Swetland, *These Men,* 296.

4. Interview with Virginia Cairns, daughter of Arnold "Dutch" Wilbur, 25 May 2000.

5. Telegram from collection of William F. White Jr., 21 December 1918.

6. Philip Gibbs, "The Adventure of Life in New York." *Harper's,* August 1919, 326.

7. *Poughkeepsie Eagle News,* 26 March 1919, 1.

8. Accounts in numerous New York newspapers including the *Times, Sun, World, Tribune,* and *Herald,* 26 March 1919.

Selected Bibliography

BOOKS

Adams, Samuel Hopkins. *A. Woollcott: His Life and His World*. New York: Reynal & Hitchcock, 1945.

Adamson, Bruce C., George W. Ely, and William D. Hawkins. *The Life and Times of Captain George Ely (1840–1922)*. Santa Cruz, Calif.: Bruce Campbell Adamson, 1993.

Allen, Oliver E. *The Tiger: The Rise and Fall of Tammany Hall*. New York: Addison-Wesley Publishing, 1993.

Andrews, Walter G., comp. *The Story of a Machine Gun Company, 1918–1919*. Buffalo, N.Y.: The Matthews-Northrup Works, 1924.

Barry, Herbert, comp. *Squadron A: A History of Its First Fifty Years, 1889–1939*. New York: Association of Ex-Members of Squadron A, 1939.

Bean, C. E. W. *The Official History of Australia in the War, 1914–1918*. Vol. 6. St. Lucia: University of Queensland Press, 1942.

Blake, Robert, ed. *The Private Papers of Douglas Haig, 1914–1919*. London: Eyre & Spottiswoode, 1952.

Brook-Shepard, Gordon. *November 1918*. Boston: Little, Brown, & Co., 1981.

Chambers, John Whitelay, II. *To Raise an Army: The Draft Comes to Modern America*. New York: The Free Press, 1987.

Chernow, Ron. *The House of Morgan: An American Banking Dynasty and the Rise of Modern Finance*. New York: Touchstone, 1990.

Clark, Emmons. *History of the Seventh Regiment of New York, 1806–1889*. New York: Seventh Regiment, 1890.

Clarke, William F. *Over There with O'Ryan's Roughnecks*. Seattle, Wash.: Superior Publishing Company, no date.

Cruttwell, C. R. M. F. *A History of the Great War, 1914–1918*. 2d ed. Chicago: Academy Chicago Publishers, 1991.

Cutlack, F. M. *The Australian Flying Corps in the Eastern and Western Theatres of War, 1914–1918*. Sydney: Angus & Robertson, 1938.

Dallas, Gregor. *At the Heart of a Tiger: Clemenceau and His World, 1841–1929.* New York: Carroll & Graf, 1993.

Divine, Charles. *City Ways and Company Streets.* New York: Moffat, Yard, & Company, 1918.

Doyle, Sir Arthur Conan. *A History of the Great War.* Vol. 6. New York: George H. Doran Co., 1918.

Duffy, Father Francis Patrick. *Father Duffy's Story.* New York: George H. Doran, 1919.

Dunphey, Edward P., ed. *Newburgh in the World War.* Newburgh, N.Y.: Newburgh World War Publishing Co., 1924.

Dupuy, R. Ernest, and Trevor N. Dupuy. *The Encyclopedia of Military History.* 2d ed. New York: Harper & Row, 1986.

Edmonds, Sir James E., ed. *History of the Great War: Military Operations France and Belgium, 1918.* Vol. 5. 1949. Reprint, Nashville, Tenn.: The Battery Press, 1993.

Eggers, John H. *The 27th Division: The Story of Its Sacrifices and Achievements.* New York: Eggers Co., 1919.

Ellis, Edward Robb. *Echoes of Distant Thunder: Life in the United States, 1914–1918.* New York: Coward, McCann, & Geoghegan, 1975.

Ettinger, Albert M., and A. Churchill Ettinger. *A Doughboy with the Fighting 69th.* Shippensburg, Pa.: White Mane Publishing, 1992.

Evans, James W. *Entertaining the American Army.* New York: Association Press, 1921.

Falls, Dewitt Clinton. *History of the Seventh Regiment, 1889–1922.* New York: Veterans of the Seventh Regiment, New York, 1948.

Foch, Marshal F. *The Memoirs of Marshal Foch.* Garden City, N.Y.: Doubleday, Doran, & Company, 1931.

Gallagher, Brian. *Anything Goes: The Jazz Age Adventures of Neysa McMein and Her Extravagant Circle of Friends.* New York: New York Times Books, 1987.

Gibbs, Philip. *Now It Can Be Told.* New York: Harper & Brothers, 1920.

Gilbert, Martin. *The First World War: A Complete History.* New York: Henry Holt & Company, 1994.

Goldhurst, Richard. *Pipe and Clay Drill: John J. Pershing: The Classic American Soldier.* New York: The Reader's Digest Press, 1977.

Gow, Kenneth. *Letters of a Soldier.* New York: Herbert B. Covert, 1920.

Griffith, Paddy. *Battle Tactics of the Western Front.* New Haven: Yale University Press, 1994.

Hall, James N., and Charles B. Nordhoff. *The Lafayette Flying Corps.* Boston: Houghton Mifflin Company, 1920.

Harris, J. P. *Amiens to the Armistice.* Washington: Brassey's, Inc., 1998.

Hart, Capt. B. H. Liddell. *The Real War, 1914–1918.* Boston: Little, Brown, & Company, 1930.

Haythornthwaite, Philip J. *The World War One Source Book.* London: Arms and Armour, 1992.

Holbrook, Sgt. Richard Greene. *A Handbook of Company K, 107th Infantry.* New York, Seventh Regiment, 1940.

Howe, M. A. DeWolfe, and others. *Memoirs of the Harvard War Dead in the War against Germany.* Cambridge, Mass.: Harvard University Press, 1923.

Hoyt, Edwin P. *The Vanderbilts and Their Fortunes.* New York: Doubleday & Co., 1962.

Jackson, Kenneth T., ed. *The Encyclopedia of New York City.* New Haven, Conn.: Yale University Press, 1995.

Jacobson, Gerald, F., ed. *History of the 107th Infantry, USA.* New York: Seventh Regiment Armory, 1920.

Keegan, John. *The First World War.* New York: Alfred A. Knopf, 1999.

Kilmer, Annie Kilburn. *Leaves from My Life.* New York: Frye Publishing, 1925.

———. *Memories of My Son, Sergeant Joyce Kilmer.* New York: Frye Publishing, 1921.

Krayer, Nicholas H., ed. *History of Company "E," 107th Infantry, 1917–1919.* New York: War Veterans Association, Co., 7th New York National Guard, 1920.

Leland, Claude G. *From Shell Hole to Chateau with Company I.* New York: Seventh Regiment, New York National Guard, 1950.

Little, Arthur W. *From Harlem to the Rhine.* New York: Covici-Friede, 1936.

Lytle, Richard Ridgeley. *Scott Harrison Lytle Memory Book, 1889–1918.* Privately printed. No date.

Maurice, Sir Frederick. *The Last Four Months: How the War Was Won.* Boston: Little, Brown, & Co., 1919.

———. *The Life of General Lord Rawlinson of Trent.* London: Cassel Plc., 1928.

Maze, M. Paul. *A Frenchman in Khaki.* London: William Heinemann, Ltd., 1934.

Mitchell, Harry T. *Company L, 107th Infantry, 54th Infantry Brigade.* New York: War Veterans Association, 1920.

Monash, Sir John. *The Australian Victories in France.* 1920. Reprint, Nashville, Tenn.: The Battery Press, 1993.

Montgomery, Maj. Gen. Sir Archibald. *The Story of the Fourth Army in the Battles of the Hundred Days.* London: Hodder & Stoughton, 1919.

Musgrave, George Clarke. *Four Flags under France.* New York: D. Appleton, 1918.

Nichols, Capt. G. H. F. *The 18th Division in the Great War.* London: William Blackwood & Sons, 1992.

Nichols, George. *The First Hundred Years: Records and Reminiscences of a Century of Company I, Seventh Regiment, N.G.N.Y., 1838–1938.* New York: Seventh Regiment, 1938.

Oldman, Peter. *Battleground Europe: The Hindenburg Line.* London: Lee Cooper, 1997.

O'Ryan, Maj. Gen. John F. *The Story of the 27th Division.* 2 vols. New York: Wynkoop, Hallenbeck, Crawford, 1921.

Paschall, Col. Rod. *The Defeat of Imperial Germany, 1917–1918.* New York: Da Capo Press, 1994.

Pershing, General John J. *My Experiences in the First World War.* 2 vols. 1931. Reprint, New York: Da Capo Press, 1995.

Schefer, Anton. *Letters from André Chéronnet Champollion.* New York: The Cheltenham Press, 1915.

Starlight, Alexander. *The Pictorial Record of the 27th Division.* New York: Harper & Brothers, 1919.

Streeter, Lt. Edward. *Dere Mable: Love Letters of a Rookie.* Illustrated by Cpl. Bill Breck. New York: Frederick A. Stokes Co., 1918.

Sutcliffe, Robert Stewart, ed. *Seventy-first New York in the World War.* New York: no publisher listed, 1922.

Swetland, Maurice J., and Lilli Swetland. *These Men.* Harrisburg, Pa.: Military Service Publishing Company, 1940.

Thorne, Charles F., and Walter F. Austin. *Source Records of the Great War VI.* Indianapolis, Ind.: National Alumni, 1923.

Toland, John. *No Man's Land: 1918, The Last Year of the Great War.* New York: Konecky & Konecky, 1980.

Vanderbilt, Cornelius Jr. *Man of the World.* New York: Crown, 1959.

———. *The Vanderbilt Feud.* London: Hutchinson, 1957.

Ward, Franklin W. *Between the Big Parades.* New York: Frederick W. Waterbury, 1932.

Whitney, Stanton. *Squadron A in the Great War, 1917–1918.* New York: Squadron A Association, 1923.

Wilson, Dale E. *Treat 'Em Rough: The Birth of American Armor, 1917–1920.* San Francisco: Novato, 1989.

Winter, Denis. *Haig's Command: A Reassessment.* New York: Penguin Group, 1991.

———. *Making the Legend: The War Writings of C. E. W. Bean.* St. Lucia: University of Queensland Press, 1992.

ARTICLES, ORAL HISTORIES

"Acted as Guide for 'Moppers-up.'" *The Seventh Regiment Gazette* 33 (1919): 234–36.

Barclay, Weston. "Path of the Brave," *New York World-Telegram,* 1943.

"Battle Casualties in the World War." *Infantry Journal* 30, no. 1 (January 1927): 81–82.

Berry, W. E. "A Visit to the Australians." *Times of London,* 6 October 1918.

"The Broadway Boys Laugh 'Em Up in France." *The Gas Attack* (Christmas, 1918): 20.

Conan Doyle, Sir Arthur. "The Rent in the Line: A Picture of the Great Battle From the Roof of A Tank." *Times of London,* 3 October 1918.

Davenport, Pvt. Walter A. "Into the Valley of Breath." *The Gas Attack* (23 March 1918): 12–13.

Emery, Donald. "At the Sign of the Caduceus." *The Seventh Regiment Gazette* 32 (1918): 238–41.

Franklin, Ben. "This Corporal Swerved Tank by Waving His Leg." *Carry On* (1919).

"Gassed while Sleeping." *The Seventh Regiment Gazette* 33 (1919): 231–32.

Gibbs, Philip. "The Adventure of Life in New York." *Harper's*, August 1919, 326–36.

Hall, William Edwin, ed. *History of the Class of 1900.* New Haven, Conn.: Sheffield Scientific School, Yale University, Tuttle, Morehouse & Taylor, 1922.

"Heroic Performance of Duty." *Homes News*, 22 August 1918.

Kincaid, Lt. Col. J. Leslie. "The 27th New York's Guard Division That Broke German Line." *New York Times Magazine*, 9 March 1919.

Leonard, Bill. "Getting A New Uniform." *The Seventh Regiment Gazette* 32 (1918): 431.

———. "K.P." *The Seventh Regiment Gazette* 32 (1918): 233–35.

MacDonnell, Sgt. J. L. "The Seventh Departs for Spartanburg So. Car." *The Seventh Regiment Gazette* 32 (1917): 7–8.

———. "From the Backward Area to the Forward Area." *The Seventh Regiment Gazette* 33 (1918).

McIntyre, Lt. R. H. "Taken Prisoner in the Battle of Sept. 29th." *The Seventh Regiment Gazette* 33 (1919): 302–26.

"A Mix-up in the Dark." *The Seventh Regiment Gazette* 33 (1919): 236–37.

"New York Soldiers Joke with Pencil and Pen: Men of the Twenty-seventh Division Make Merry in Christmas Number of 'The Gas Attack'—An American Bairnsfather." *New York Times Magazine*, 12 January 1919.

"New York's 27th, First to Smash The Hindenburg Line, Comes Home." *Literary Digest*, 29 March 1919, 68–78.

O'Brien, Pvt. Eugene J. "First Grayjackets Leave for France." *The Seventh Regiment Gazette* 31 (1917): 235–38.

"The Old 'Greyjacket'—How He Fought and Died." *The Seventh Regiment Gazette* 33 (1919): 299–302.

"The 107th Infantry, U.S.A." *The Seventh Regiment Gazette* 33 (1918): 148–64.

O'Ryan, John F. The Reminiscences of John F. O'Ryan, in the Oral History Collection of Columbia University.

O'Ryan, Maj. Gen. John F. confidential report to commander in chief, American A.E. France, 18 December 1918.

Pancoast, Archer V. "Escort by Ex-Members of the Seventh on the Departure of the Regiment for Spartanburg, S.C., Sept. 11, 1917." *The Seventh Regiment Gazette* (1917): 8–18.

Pratt, Joseph Hyde. "The St. Quentin-Cambrai Canal Tunnel." *The Military Engineer* 19 (July–August 1927): 324–29.

"Reviews and Discussion." *Infantry Journal* 30 (1927): 81–83.

Rosenhagen, Carl. "A Day in the Life of a Tanker—September 1918." *Armor: The Magazine of Mobile Warfare* 82, no. 5 (September–October 1973): 34–35.

Rowland, Leslie W. "The Twenty-seventh Division Crashes Through." *The Gas Attack* (Christmas, 1918): 2–5.

———. "Let's Beat It." *The Gas Attack* (Home Again issue, 1919): 25–26.

"Spartanburg, South Carolina. The Temporary Home of the New York National Guard." *The Seventh Regiment Gazette* 32 (1917): 57–61.

Starr, Lt. Col. William T. "As General Staff Saw Big 'Show.'" *New York Evening Post,* 25 March 1919.

Streeter, Edward. "The Incinerator: Bill's Letter to Mable." *The Gas Attack* (9 February 1918): 5.

———. "The Incinerator." *The Gas Attack* (23 March 1918): 5.

———. "A Soldier's Letter to His Sweetheart." *The Gas Attack* (30 March 1918): 5.

———. "A Soldier's Letter to His Sweetheart." *The Gas Attack* (13 April 1918): 5.

"Three Narrow Escapes." *The Seventh Regiment Gazette* 33 (1919): 233–34.

"Through Hell without a Scratch." *The Seventh Regiment Gazette* 33 (1919): 232–33.

Tupper, Maj. Tristram. "Division's Adjutant's Official Account of What the New York National Guard Division Accomplished in Belgium and France." *New York Evening Post,* 25 March 1919.

———. "Sargent's Studio of Shellfire." *New York Times,* 23 March 1919.

———. "Thrilling Fights of New York Heroes." *New York Times,* 15 December 1918, sect. 4, p. 1.

"27th's Fighting Record." *New York Evening Post,* 25 March 1919.

"Victory!" *The Seventh Regiment Gazette* 33 (1918): 145–47.

"Welcome, 107th U.S. Infantry." *The Seventh Regiment Gazette* 33 (1919): 437–42.

Wynne, Capt. G. C. "The Hindenburg Line." *The Army Quarterly* 38 (1938–1939): 205–28.

Index

STEPHEN L. HARRIS is editor of the *Journal of Olympic History* and former editor of *Monogram,* the General Electric Company magazine. A native New Yorker, he now lives in Weybridge, Vermont, with his wife, Sue.